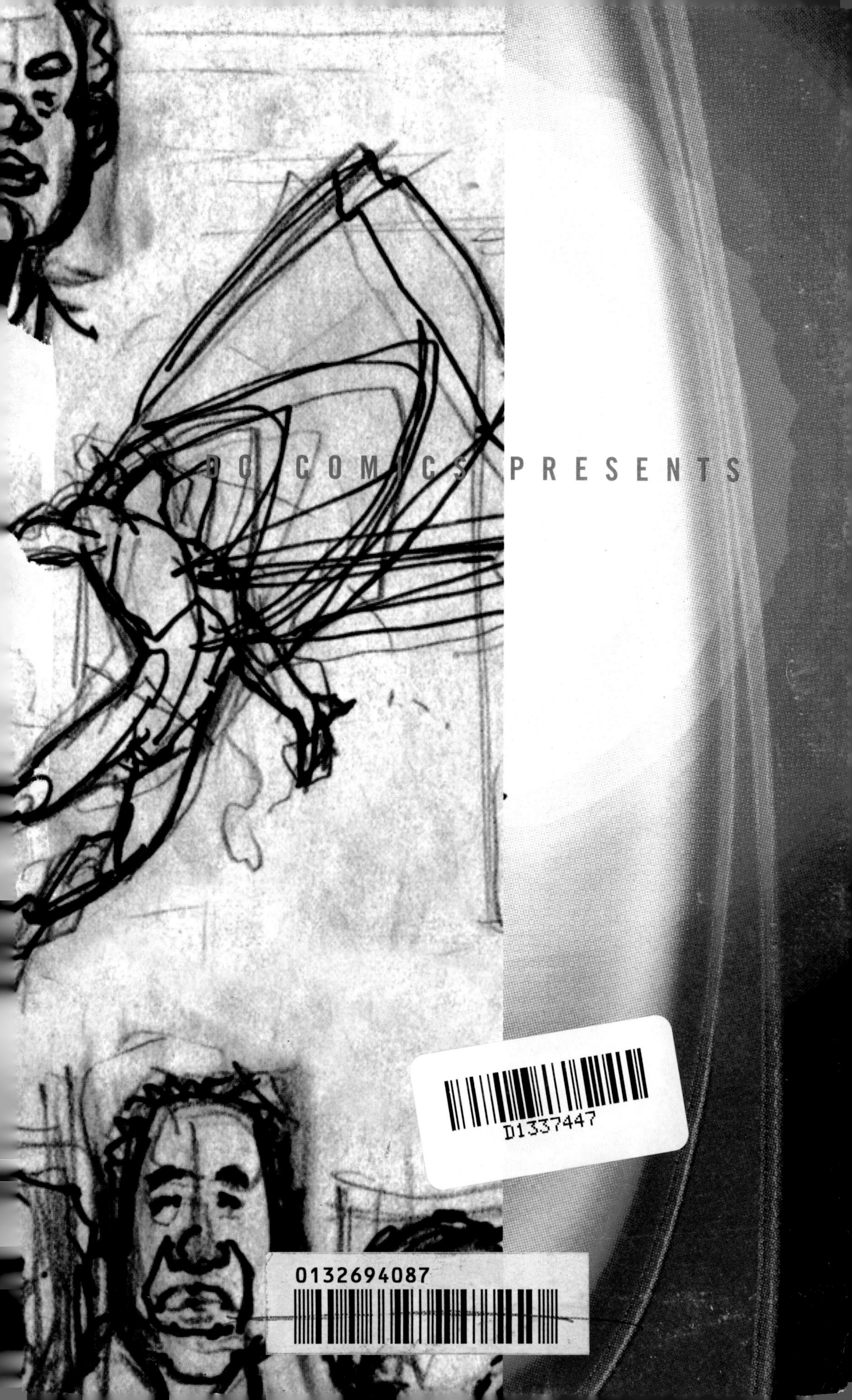
DC COMICS PRESENTS

FRANK MILLER · LYNN VARLEY

TODD KLEIN

Batman created by BOB KANE

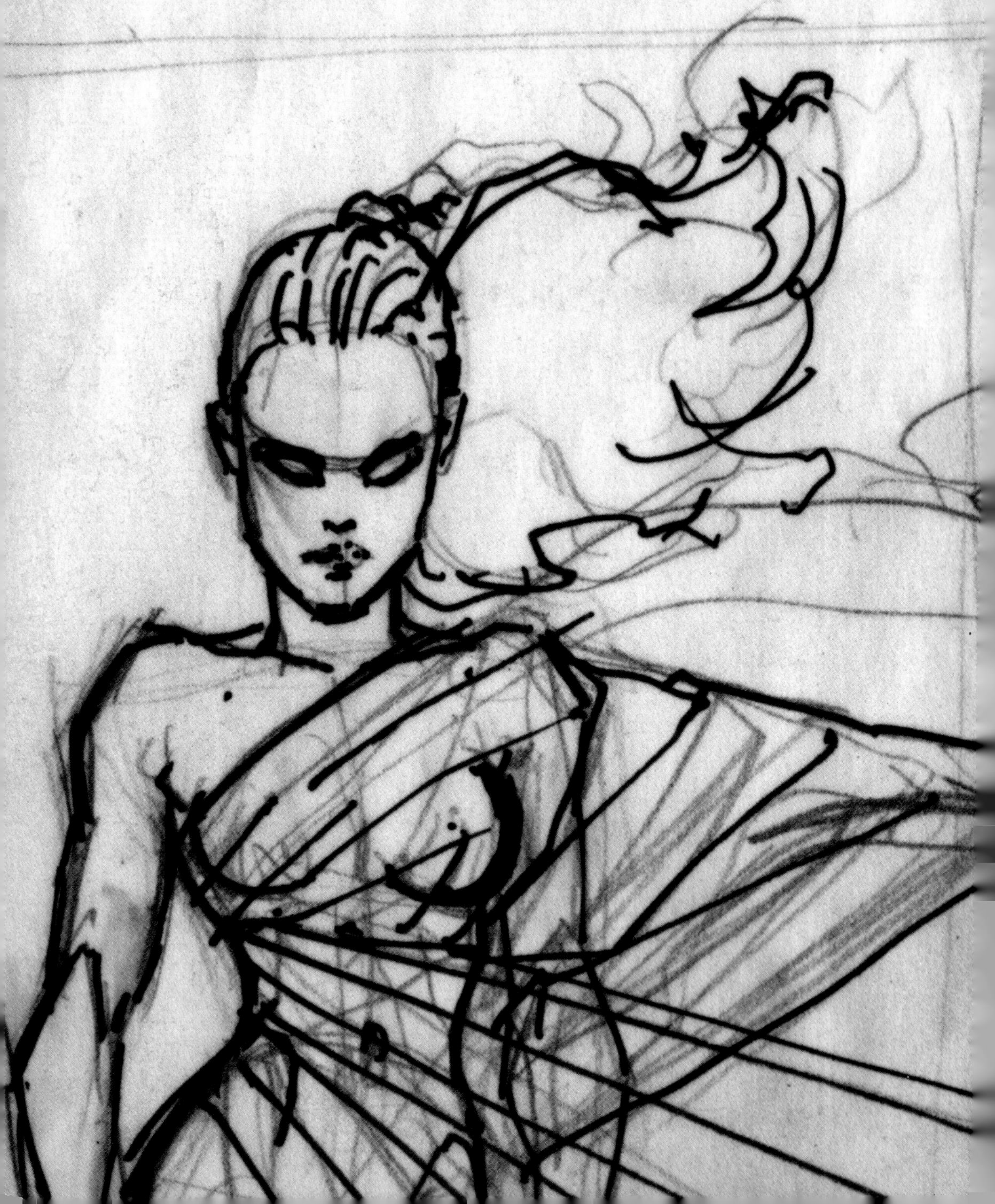

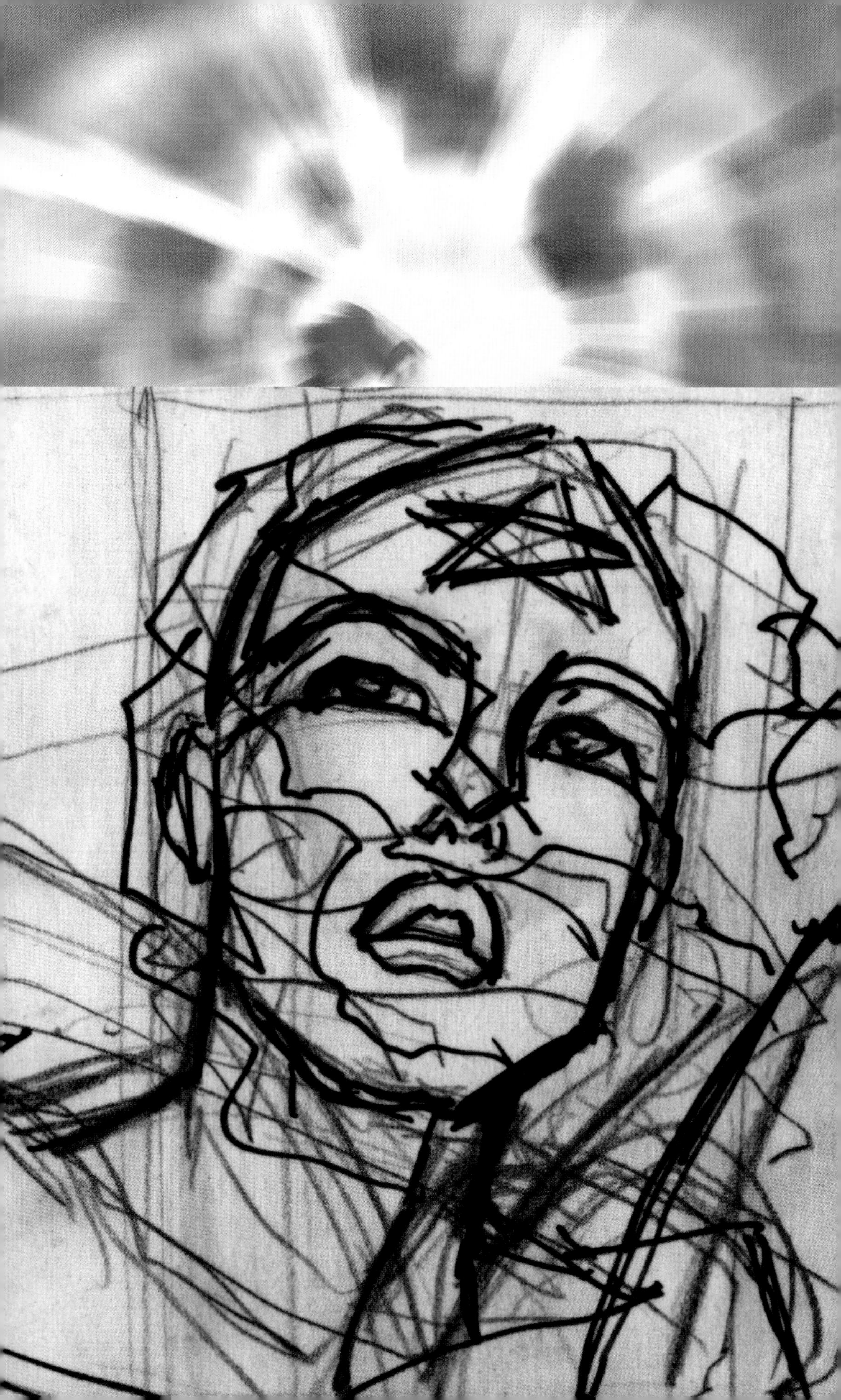

BATMAN: THE DARK KNIGHT STRIKES AGAIN

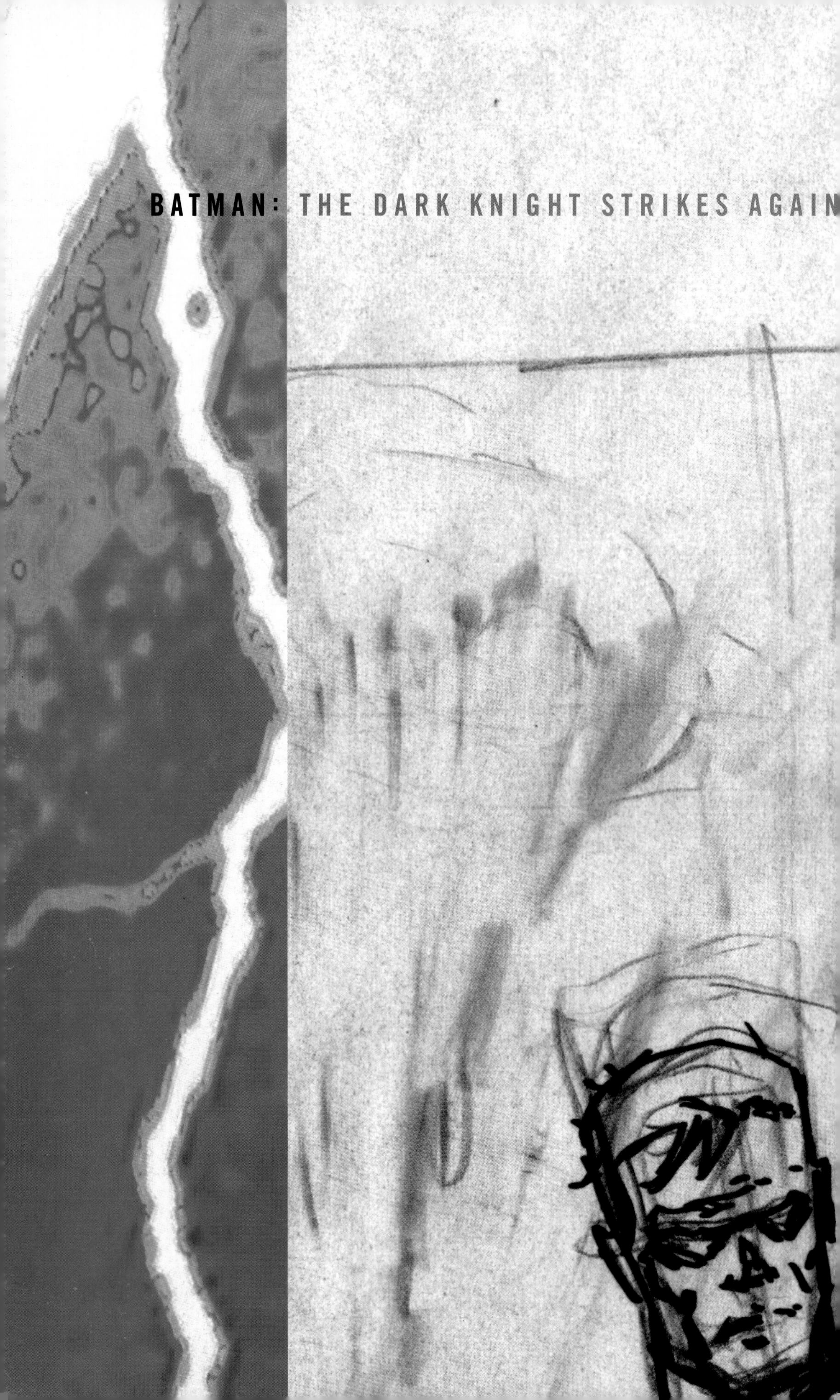

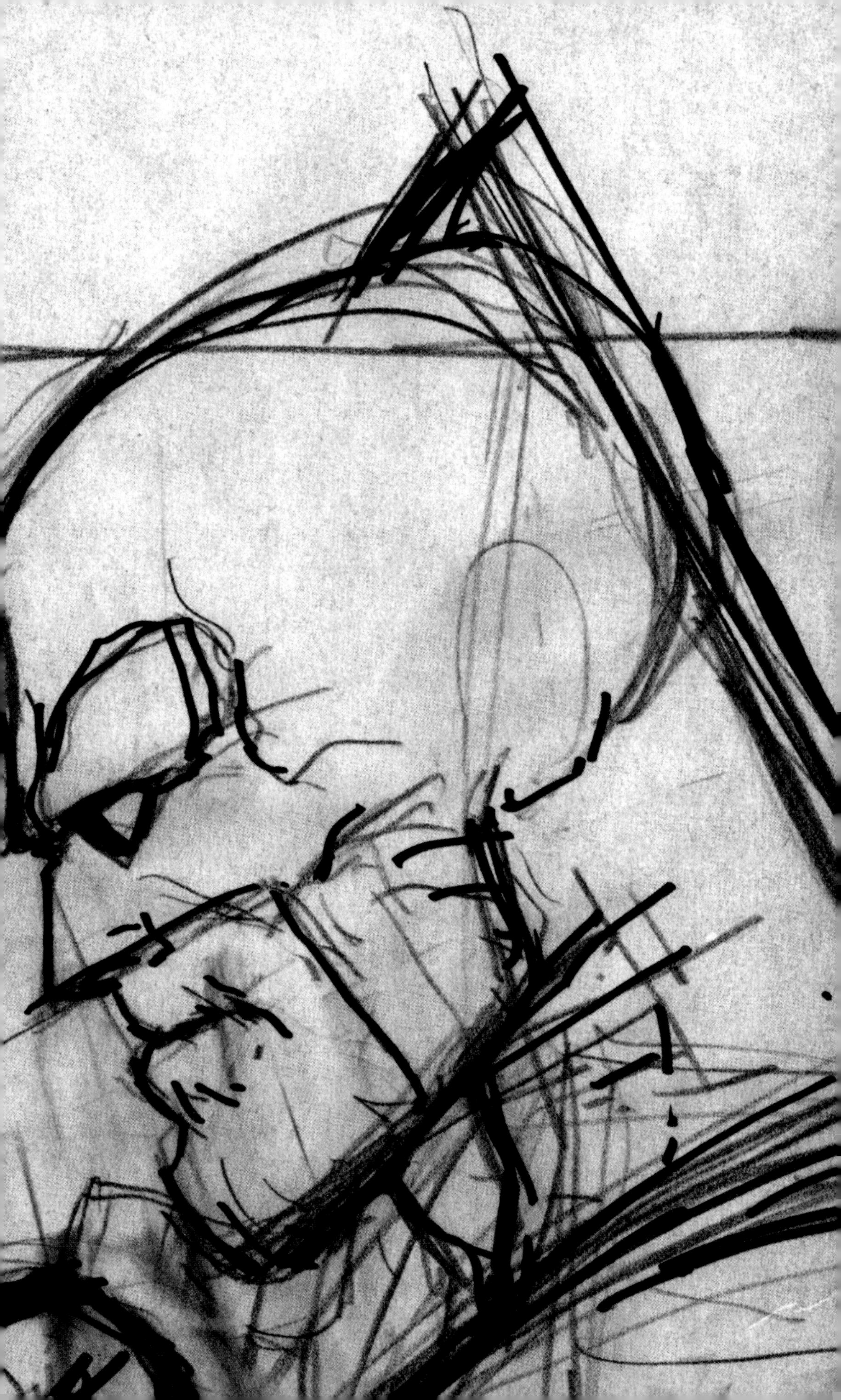

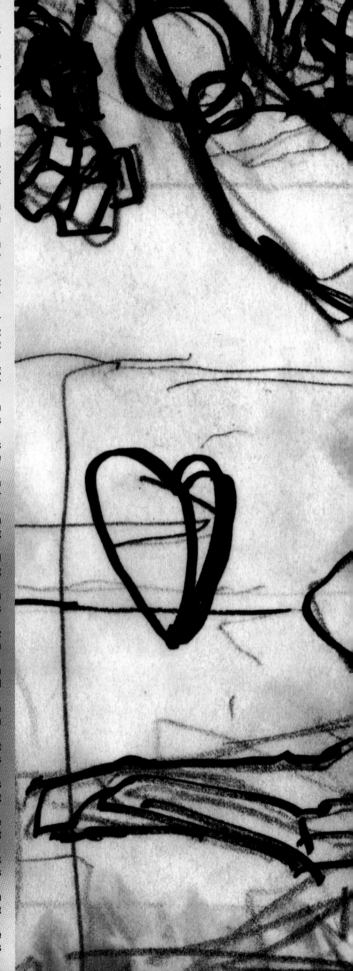

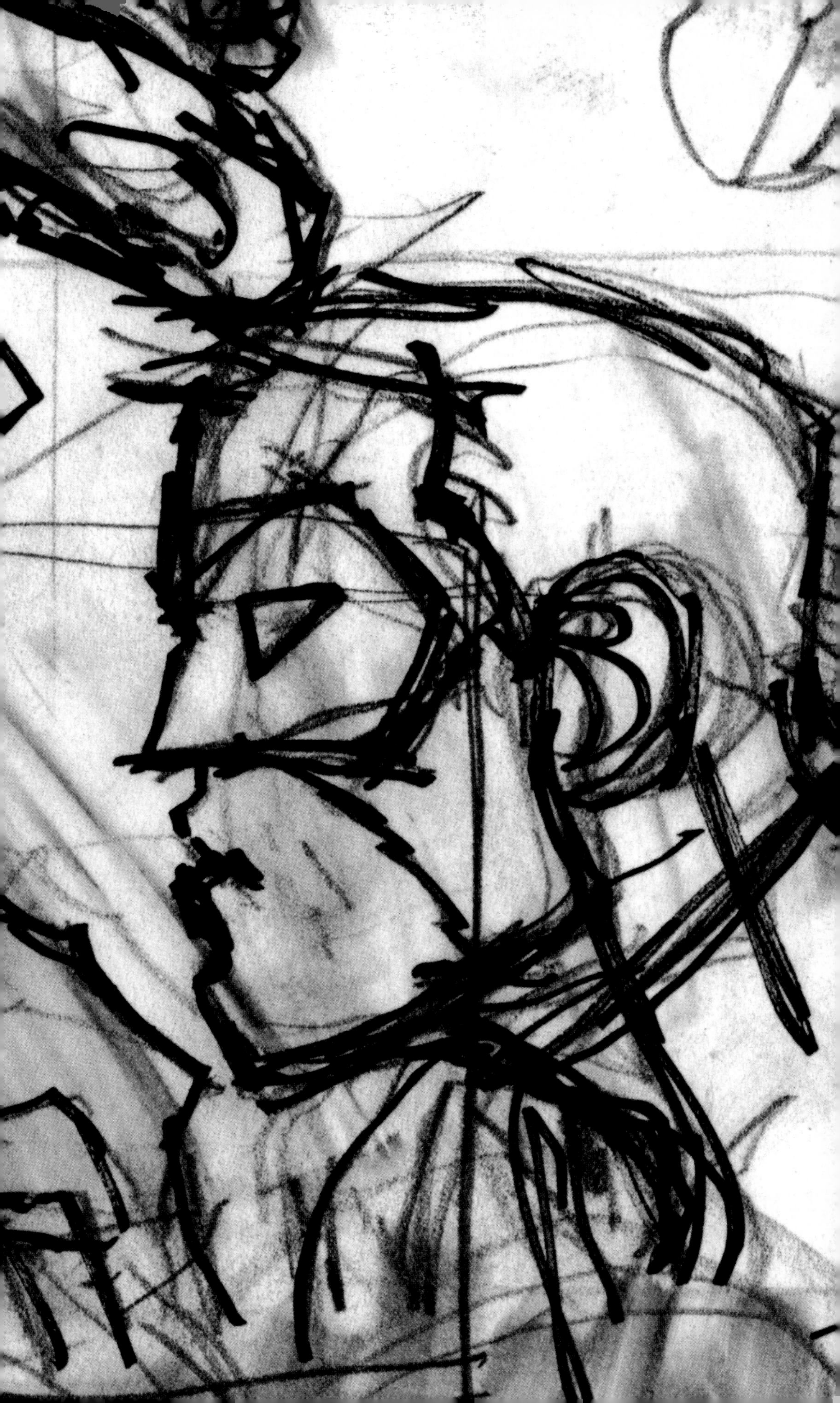

Cover Illustration by Frank Miller & Lynn Varley.
Publication design by Chip Kidd.

BATMAN: THE DARK KNIGHT STRIKES AGAIN
Published by DC Comics. Cover, introduction and compilation copyright © 2002 DC Comics.
Originally published in single magazine form as BATMAN: THE DARK KNIGHT STRIKES AGAIN 1-3.
Copyright © 2001-2002 DC Comics. All Rights Reserved.
All characters, the distinctive likenesses thereof, and all related elements are trademarks of DC Comics.
The stories, characters and incidents featured in this publication are entirely fictional.
DC Comics does not read or accept unsolicited submissions of ideas, stories or artwork.
DC Comics 1700 Broadway New York, NY 10019
A Warner Bros. Entertainment Company
Printed in Canada.
Third Printing.
ISBN: 1-56389-929-9. ISBN 13: 978-1-56389-929-4.

Special thanks to
Kyle Baker,
Lorenzo DiBonaventura,
William Katz,
James Kochalka,
Tony Millionaire,
Jim Morrison,
Alex Sinclair, Jeff Smith,
Paul Pope, Diana Schutz,
Bill Sienkiewicz.

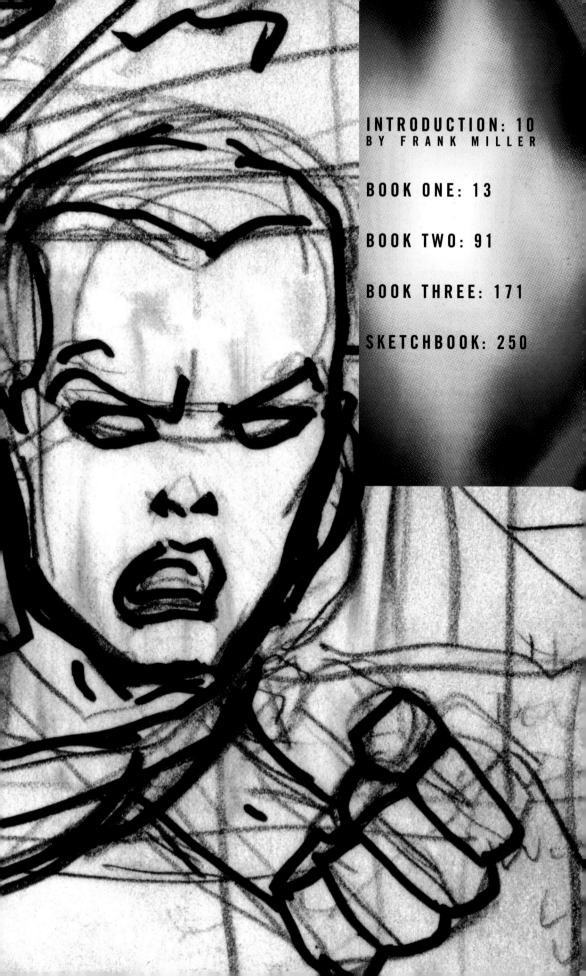

TOP COP POPS

EXCLUSIVE
Vicky Vale
The Dish

You could've heard a pin drop. The kind that comes out of a hand grenade.

It was total social self-decapitation. Not to mention professional suicide. And at a funeral, no less.

It was at Bruce Wayne's funeral, an otherwise restrained affair, honoring Gotham City's most famous native son and the two lives he led, as bodacious billionaire businessman and burly, bad-guy-bashing Batman.

In case you were in another galaxy when it happened: The generationally-challenged Caped Crusader made with a comeback that was more splash than substance, only to drop stone dead from ticker shock when the feds closed in.

Or maybe they shot him. Who knows? They don't talk, not too often, those Fedsters, not these days. And if they do, they lie. Not to put too fine a point on it.

Whatever. The Masked Manhunter bought the farm. The Dark Knight croaked. Bruce Wayne was room temperature.

Somebody threw him a pricy funeral. And Jim Gordon made a flaming ass of himself.

It was quite the scene, even before Gordon discovered the joys of self-immolation. There was Clark Kent in the third row, looking like he hadn't slept in days. Selina Kyle, who used to turn 'em on and knock 'em dead - and I mean dead - as the Catwoman, in the first row, puffy, medicated, barely vertical. And there at the lectern was Jim Gordon, giving his reputation the maximum flush.

His reputation. James Gordon. Career cop. Carrying some old baggage, some sketchy business, from his early days in Chicago, sure. But a good cop. More than that, as it turned out. Jim Gordon was a goddamn hero.

He cleaned up Gotham City for a good long time. He went right at the old mafioso stooges who used to run our town. Busted them every chance he got. The Roman, he's still sitting in his cell, cursing Jim Gordon.

Lord only knows how crazy the Cowled Curmudgeon might've gotten if Gordon hadn't known how to play him. Old Wayne had a temper. He wasn't exactly what You'd call a bucket of mental health.

The man dressed up like a rodent, for goodness sake.

So there was Gordon, clearing his throat, looking over the audience. Glaring. We half-expected him to do the Miranda on the bunch of us.

"We murdered him," he growled. "We murdered Bruce Wayne, damn our souls to hell."

Looks shot across the room like thunderbolts. Over on the right side of the audience, there was Police Commissioner Ellen Yindel, who'd taken over Gordon's thankless job. She looked like she was working on swallowing a watermelon whole. For all their differences, she loves Jim Gordon. He was killing her, losing it like this.

And maybe he would've slowed down his pace a bit, Gordon might've, if it Hadn't been for Selina Kyle. Was she ever full of piss and vinegar. "Say it," she hissed, all of a sudden reminding us who Eartha Kitt was impersonating, way back when.

"Say it. Say it all," said Selina. Said Catwoman.

Yeah. Back in the old days, they called her Catwoman. And you gave that little cougar her propers, you did.

"SAY IT!", she hissed, Selina did. And it was a hiss that would've made Eartha proud, angry as it was. The old

See **Vale** Page 4

bat was positively feral. Hot stuff, baby.

You could've heard a pin drop.

And say it, Gordon did.

"We murdered Bruce Wayne. It was us. Whoever pulled the trigger, that doesn't matter. Whoever that killer was, he was just working for us.

"We couldn't live with a giant in our midst. So we murdered him."

Mayor Giordano looked like he was going to vapor-lock. Kent, like he was going to vomit.

Jimmy Olsen leaned forward, trembling with that scary fury of his, all of a sudden red-eyed.

Like he always does when anybody brings up the Tights.

"All the rest of the heroes spared us the trouble," sneered Gordon. "They went away. They knew we couldn't stand the sight of them, looming over us, saving our lives all over the place but who the hell cares about that, huh? They made us feel small.

"But at least the rest of them had the good manners to go away and let us forget about them. And so did Bruce Wayne. For ten years. Ten years we spent turning smaller and meaner.

"I was sitting across the table from my friend when he turned back into Batman. Not that he pulled the tights back on or anything. No. It was all in the jaw, that big damn jaw of his, the way he crooked it to the side. And the eyes. A saint's passion. An executioner's calm. I knew he was turning back into Batman before he did.

"And I knew we'd murder him.

"When Batman came back, we couldn't handle it. This time, he wouldn't let himself be deputized."

"Deputized." The career cop spat the word. Like it was obscene.

"He wouldn't apologize for what he was. So we murdered him."

Jim Gordon stopped talking. Took a breath. "Thank god," somebody nearby whispered. Wishful thinking, as it turned out.

In the audience, Perry White coughed. Loudly. Lois Lane squeezed his shoulder, as red-eyed as Olsen.

The Penguin burst into tears. Like he always does.

Gordon resumed. To just about everybody's utter horror.

"We murdered him for one very simple reason: there's no room in our wretched little world for a man who sees far and who sets wrongs right. We're chubby, coddled little things, content. Well-fed. Bruce Wayne - Batman - he wasn't so goddamn accommodating as we are. Bruce Wayne saw something wrong, he punched it out. He threw it through a window. He stomped its face in. He stopped it cold."

Right about then, District Attorney Robbins headed for the door. He'd heard enough. And he looked a little sick, to tell the truth.

And Gordon, he was just getting rolling. Really. It got worse.

"So we had to murder Bruce Wayne," ranted our former Commissioner of Police, our Hero Cop, our he-could've-been-on-the-ticket-as-a-vice-presidential-candidate-in-the-next-big-election-if-he-hadn't-lost-it-at-a-funeral Jim Gordon.

"We MURDERED him," he said, for what only felt like the billionth time.

Then he summed up everything he had to say about Batman in so few words it made me cry. And cry I did. Like a baby. So did everybody else.

"We're in trouble deep. We need him.

"We need Bruce Wayne." ✦

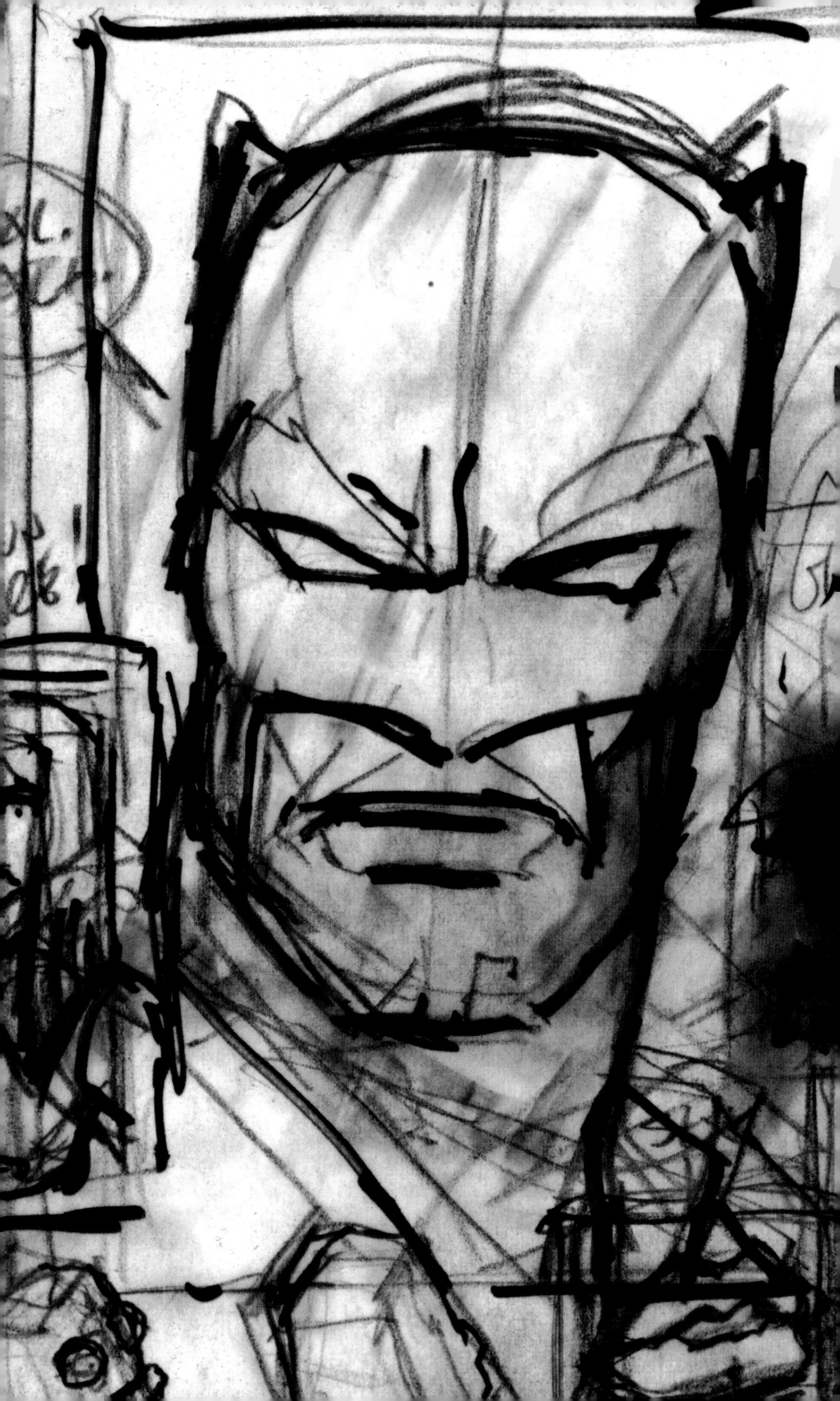

BOOK ONE.

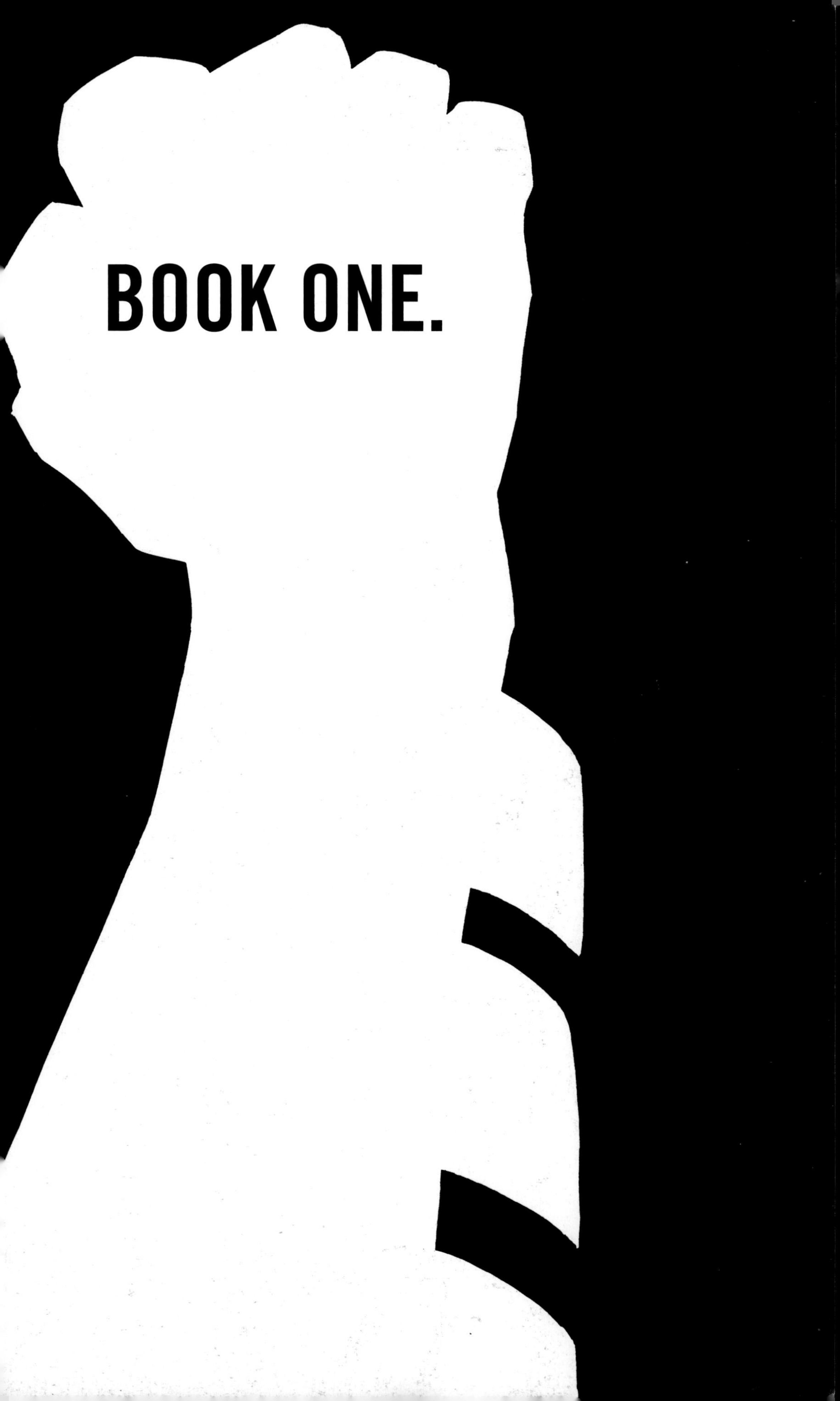

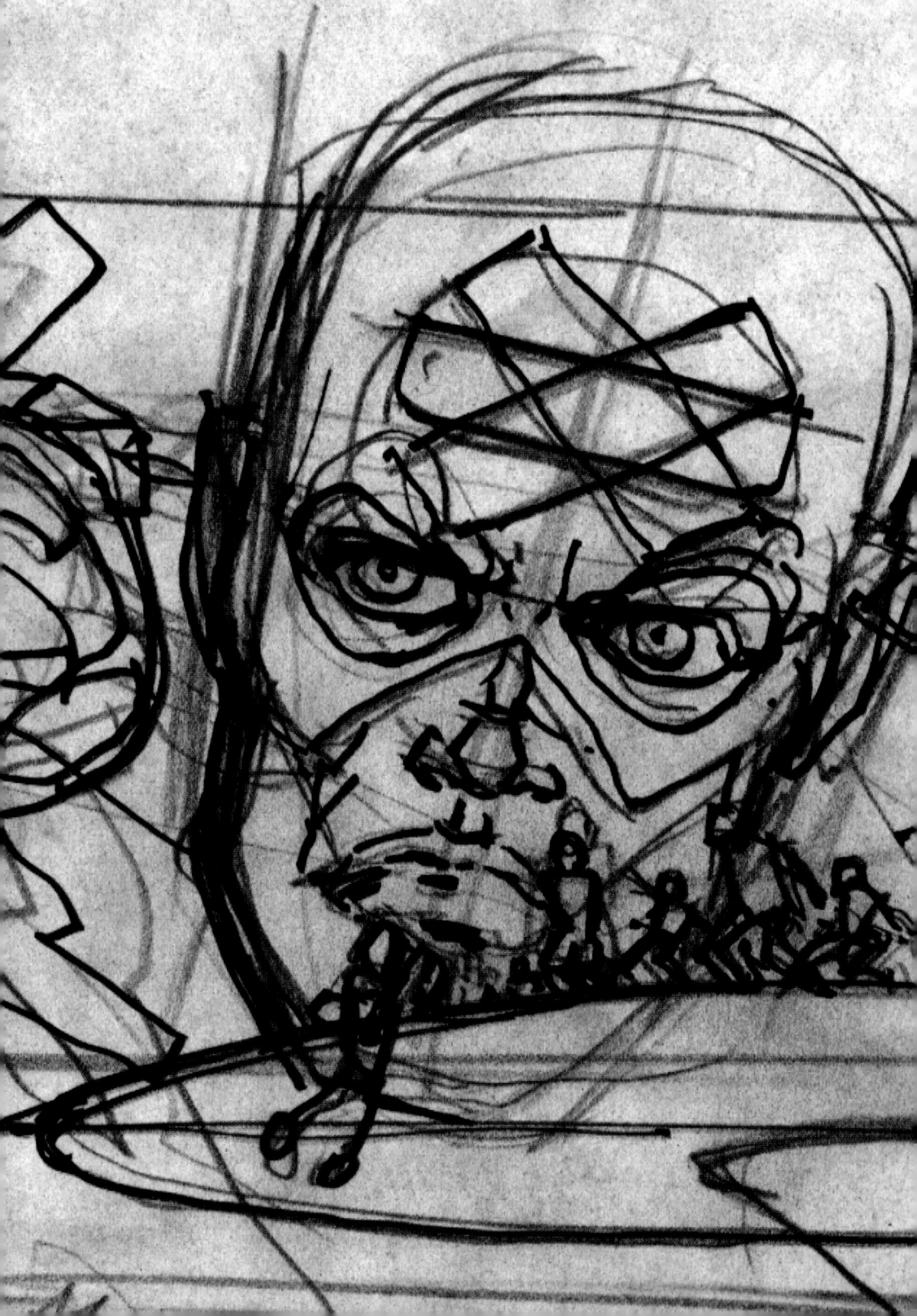

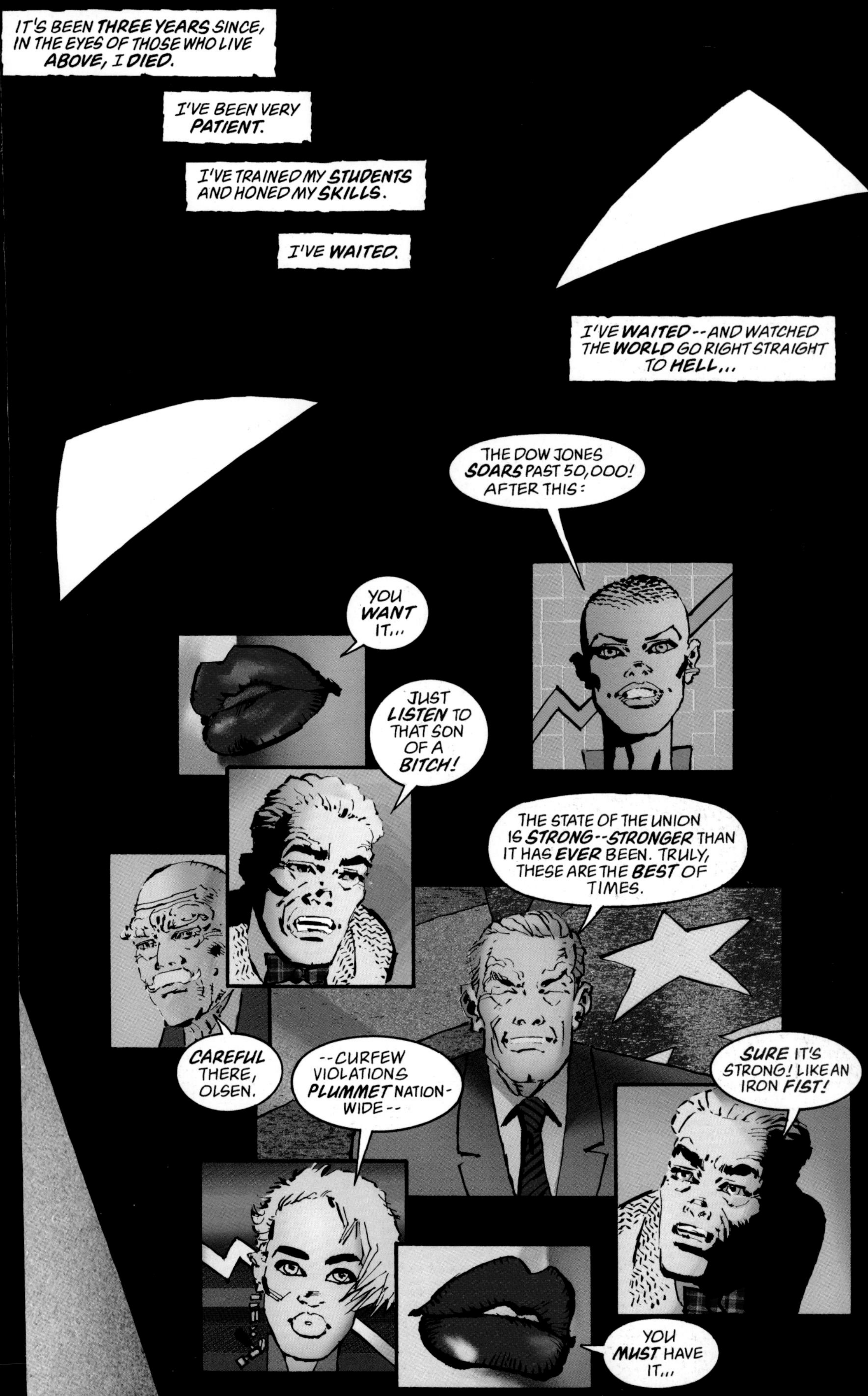

IT'S BEEN THREE YEARS SINCE, IN THE EYES OF THOSE WHO LIVE ABOVE, I DIED.
I'VE BEEN VERY PATIENT.
I'VE TRAINED MY STUDENTS AND HONED MY SKILLS.
I'VE WAITED.
I'VE WAITED--AND WATCHED THE WORLD GO RIGHT STRAIGHT TO HELL...
THE DOW JONES SOARS PAST 50,000! AFTER THIS:
YOU WANT IT...
JUST LISTEN TO THAT SON OF A BITCH!
THE STATE OF THE UNION IS STRONG--STRONGER THAN IT HAS EVER BEEN. TRULY, THESE ARE THE BEST OF TIMES.
CAREFUL THERE, OLSEN.
--CURFEW VIOLATIONS PLUMMET NATION-WIDE--
SURE IT'S STRONG! LIKE AN IRON FIST!
YOU MUST HAVE IT...

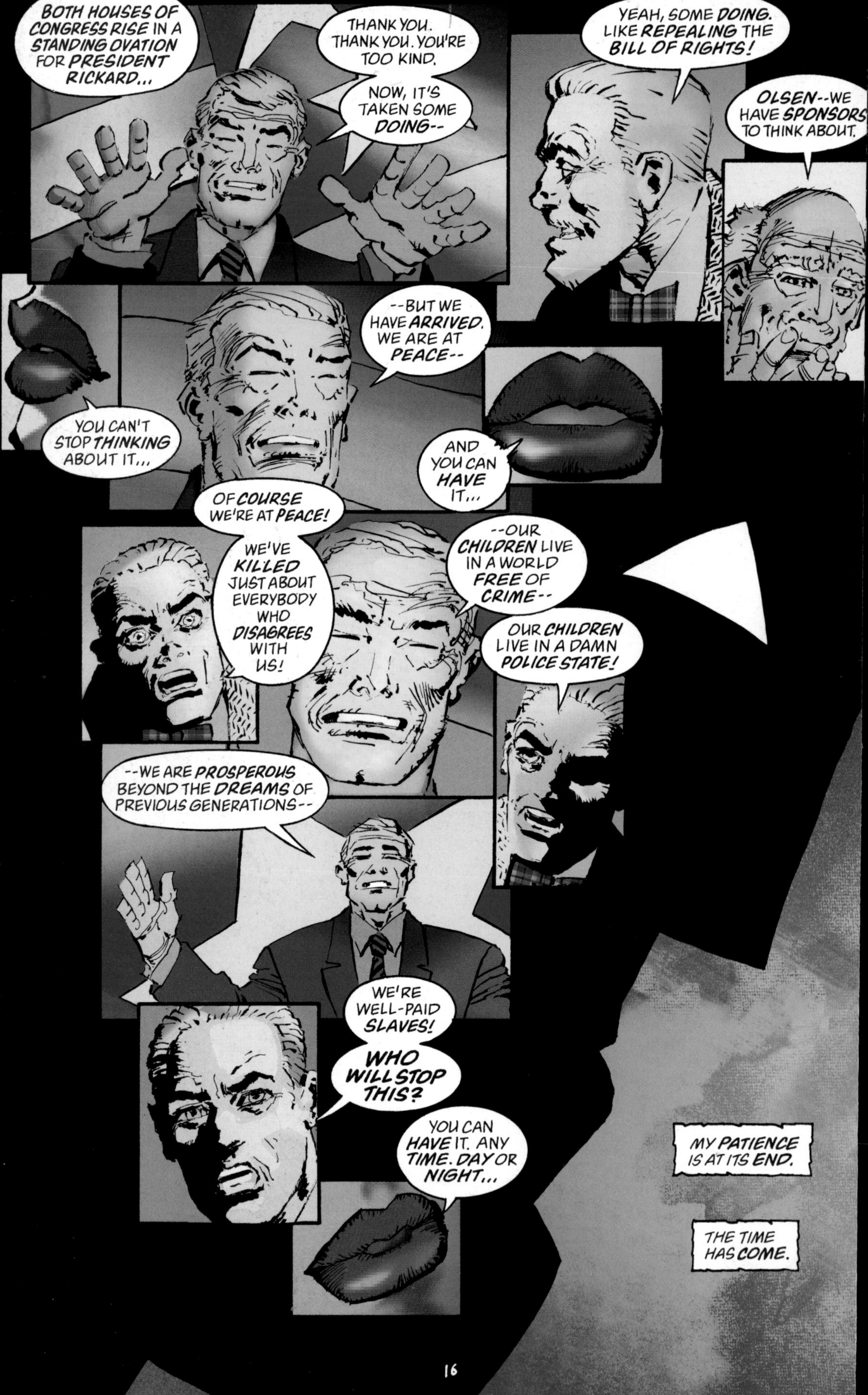
BOTH HOUSES OF CONGRESS RISE IN A STANDING OVATION FOR PRESIDENT RICKARD...
THANK YOU. THANK YOU. YOU'RE TOO KIND.
NOW, IT'S TAKEN SOME DOING--
YEAH, SOME DOING. LIKE REPEALING THE BILL OF RIGHTS!
OLSEN--WE HAVE SPONSORS TO THINK ABOUT.
YOU CAN'T STOP THINKING ABOUT IT...
--BUT WE HAVE ARRIVED. WE ARE AT PEACE--
AND YOU CAN HAVE IT...
OF COURSE WE'RE AT PEACE!
WE'VE KILLED JUST ABOUT EVERYBODY WHO DISAGREES WITH US!
--OUR CHILDREN LIVE IN A WORLD FREE OF CRIME--
OUR CHILDREN LIVE IN A DAMN POLICE STATE!
--WE ARE PROSPEROUS BEYOND THE DREAMS OF PREVIOUS GENERATIONS--
WE'RE WELL-PAID SLAVES!
WHO WILL STOP THIS?
YOU CAN HAVE IT. ANY TIME. DAY OR NIGHT...
MY PATIENCE IS AT ITS END.
THE TIME HAS COME.

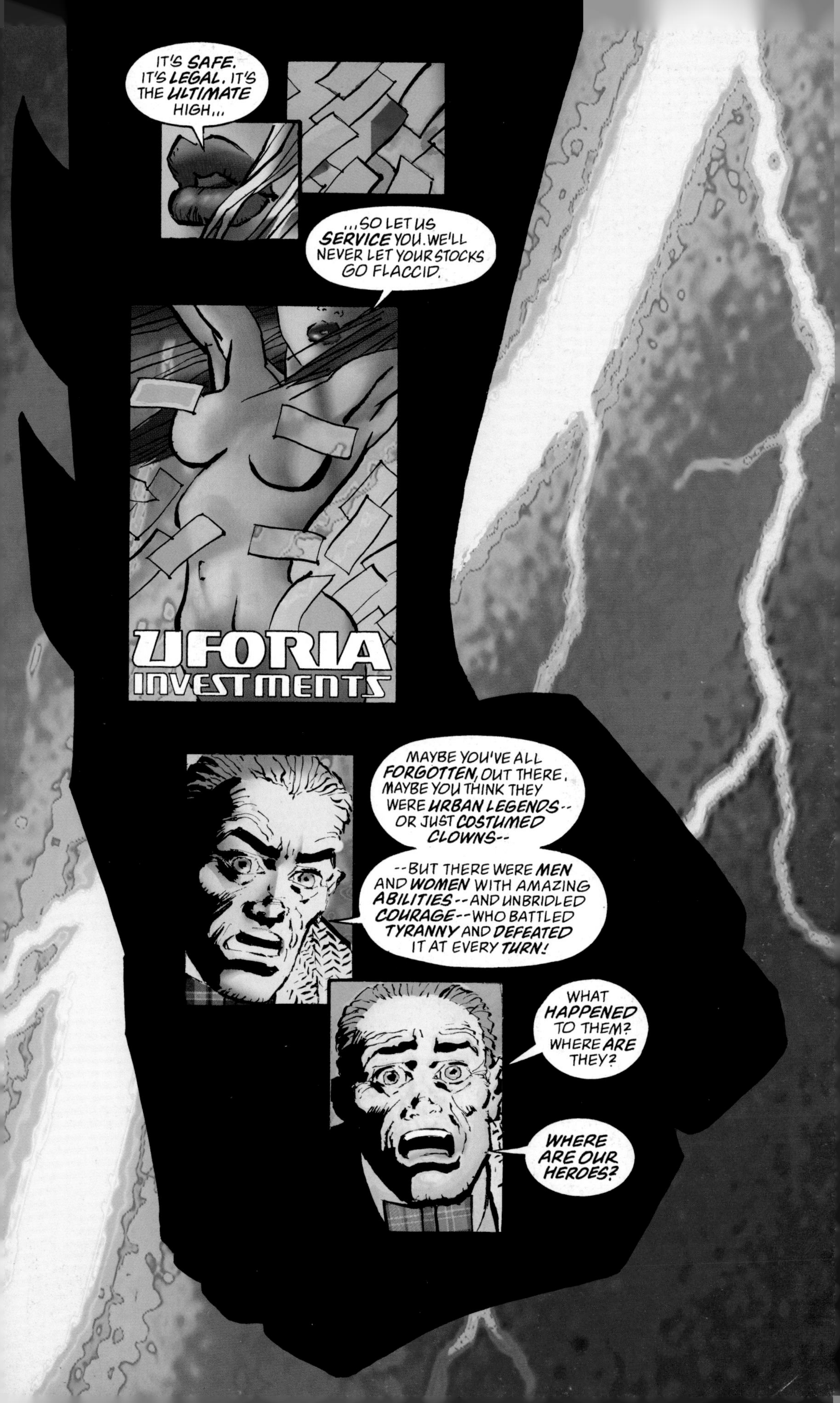
IT'S SAFE. IT'S LEGAL. IT'S THE ULTIMATE HIGH...
...SO LET US SERVICE YOU. WE'LL NEVER LET YOUR STOCKS GO FLACCID.
UFORIA INVESTMENTS
MAYBE YOU'VE ALL FORGOTTEN, OUT THERE. MAYBE YOU THINK THEY WERE URBAN LEGENDS-- OR JUST COSTUMED CLOWNS--
--BUT THERE WERE MEN AND WOMEN WITH AMAZING ABILITIES--AND UNBRIDLED COURAGE--WHO BATTLED TYRANNY AND DEFEATED IT AT EVERY TURN!
WHAT HAPPENED TO THEM? WHERE ARE THEY?
WHERE ARE OUR HEROES?

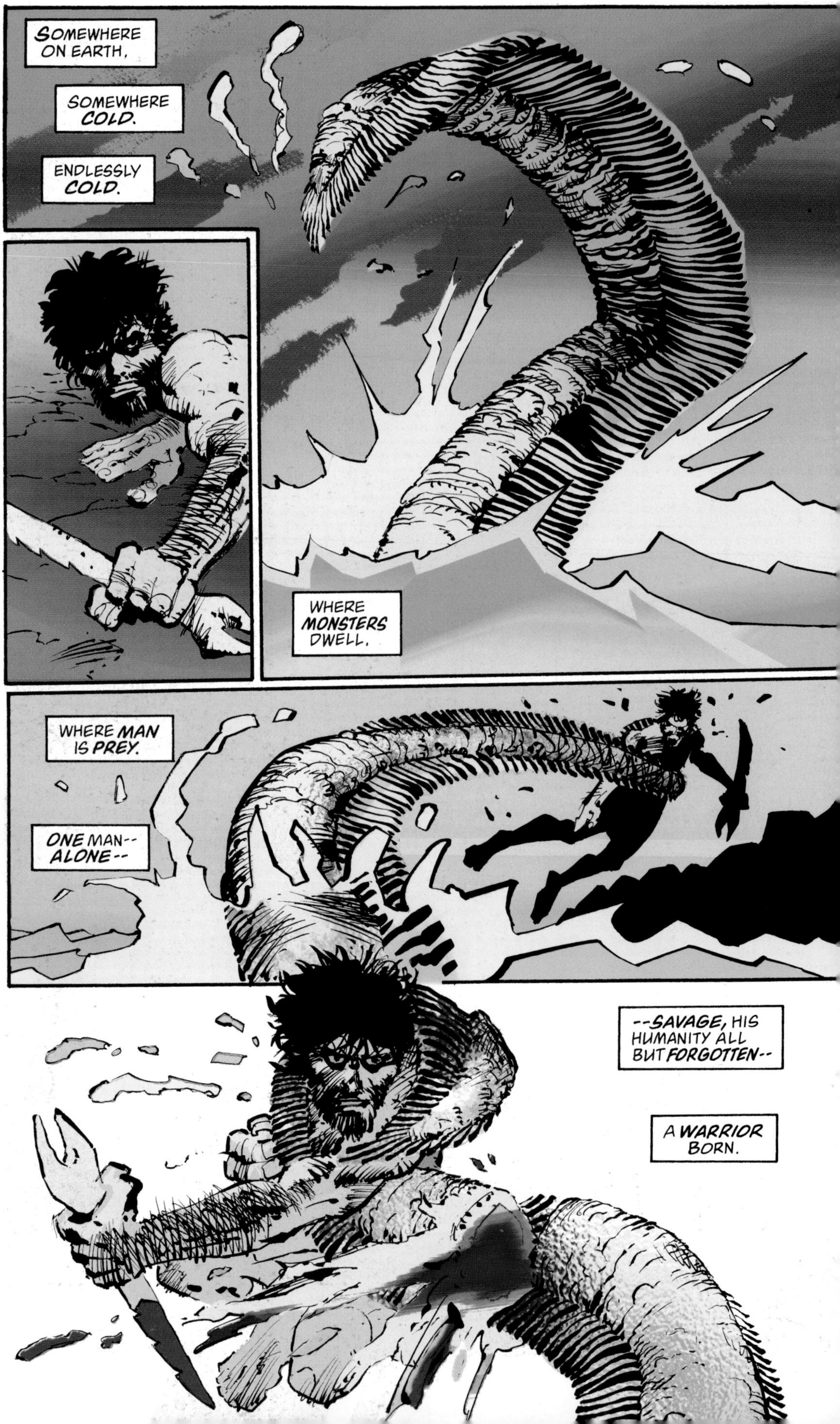
SOMEWHERE ON EARTH.
SOMEWHERE COLD.
ENDLESSLY COLD.
WHERE MONSTERS DWELL.
WHERE MAN IS PREY.
ONE MAN-- ALONE--
--SAVAGE, HIS HUMANITY ALL BUT FORGOTTEN--
A WARRIOR BORN.

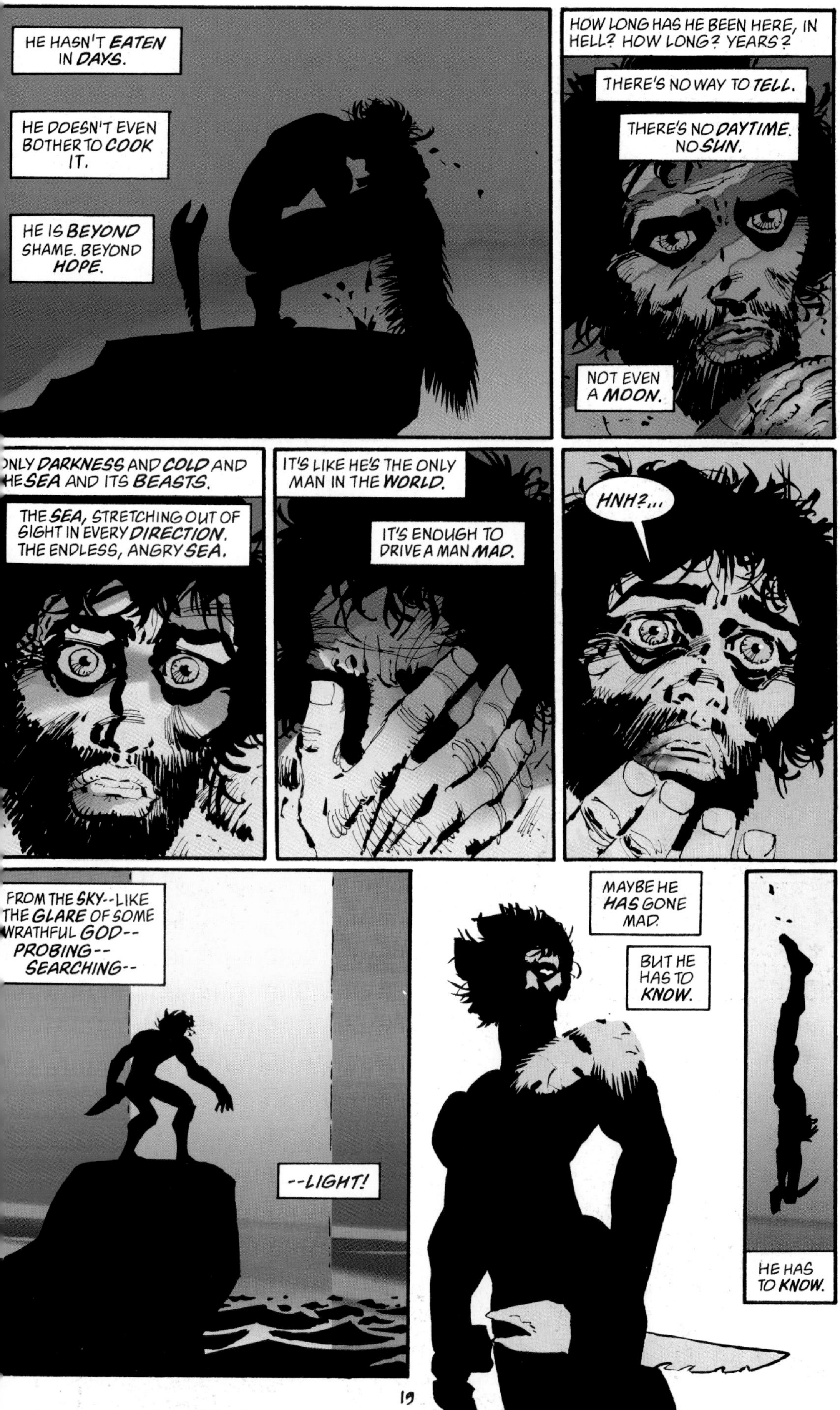
HE HASN'T EATEN IN DAYS.
HE DOESN'T EVEN BOTHER TO COOK IT.
HE IS BEYOND SHAME. BEYOND HOPE.
HOW LONG HAS HE BEEN HERE, IN HELL? HOW LONG? YEARS?
THERE'S NO WAY TO TELL.
THERE'S NO DAYTIME. NO SUN.
NOT EVEN A MOON.
ONLY DARKNESS AND COLD AND THE SEA AND ITS BEASTS.
THE SEA, STRETCHING OUT OF SIGHT IN EVERY DIRECTION. THE ENDLESS, ANGRY SEA.
IT'S LIKE HE'S THE ONLY MAN IN THE WORLD.
IT'S ENOUGH TO DRIVE A MAN MAD.
HNH?...
FROM THE SKY--LIKE THE GLARE OF SOME WRATHFUL GOD--
PROBING--
SEARCHING--
--LIGHT!
MAYBE HE HAS GONE MAD.
BUT HE HAS TO KNOW.
HE HAS TO KNOW.

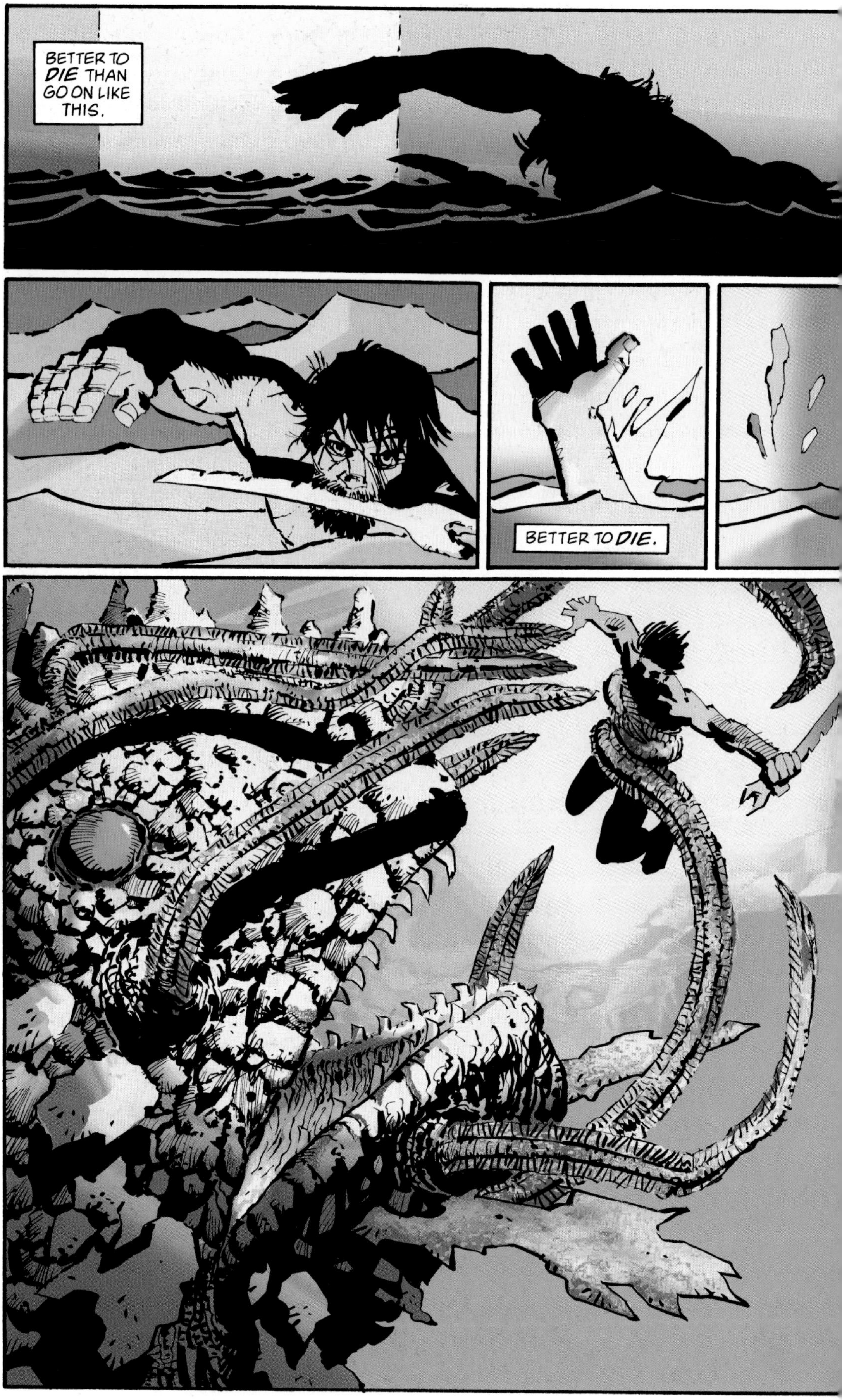
BETTER TO DIE THAN GO ON LIKE THIS.
BETTER TO DIE.

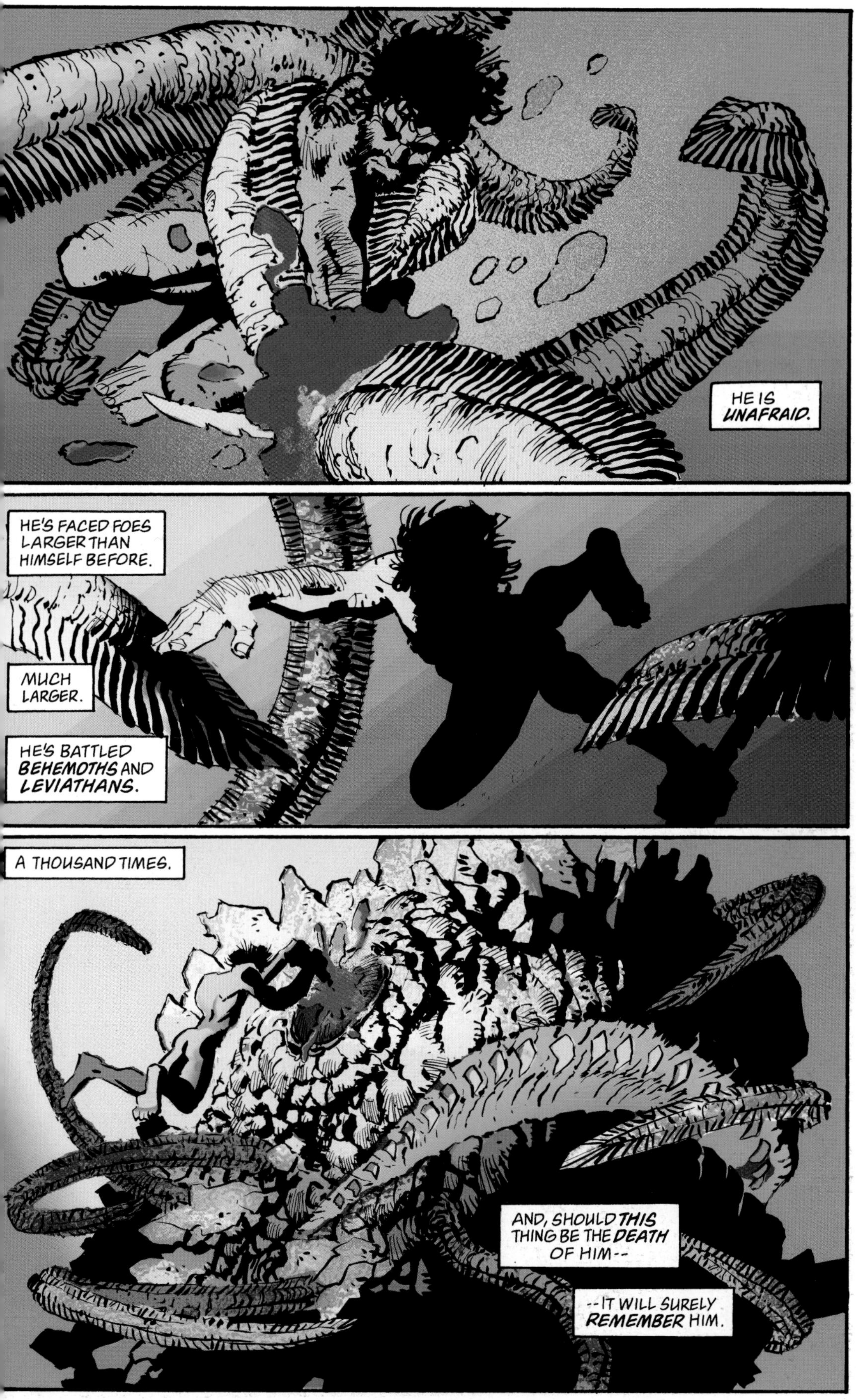
HE IS UNAFRAID.
HE'S FACED FOES LARGER THAN HIMSELF BEFORE.
MUCH LARGER.
HE'S BATTLED BEHEMOTHS AND LEVIATHANS.
A THOUSAND TIMES.
AND, SHOULD THIS THING BE THE DEATH OF HIM--
--IT WILL SURELY REMEMBER HIM.

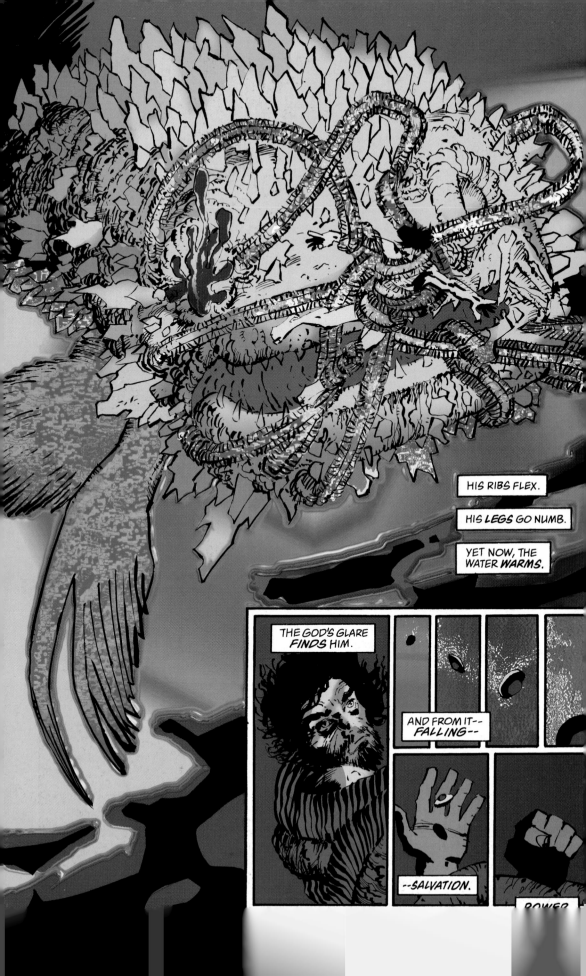

HIS RIBS FLEX.

HIS *LEGS* GO NUMB.

YET NOW, THE WATER *WARMS*.

THE GOD'S GLARE *FINDS* HIM.

AND FROM IT-- *FALLING*--

--SALVATION.

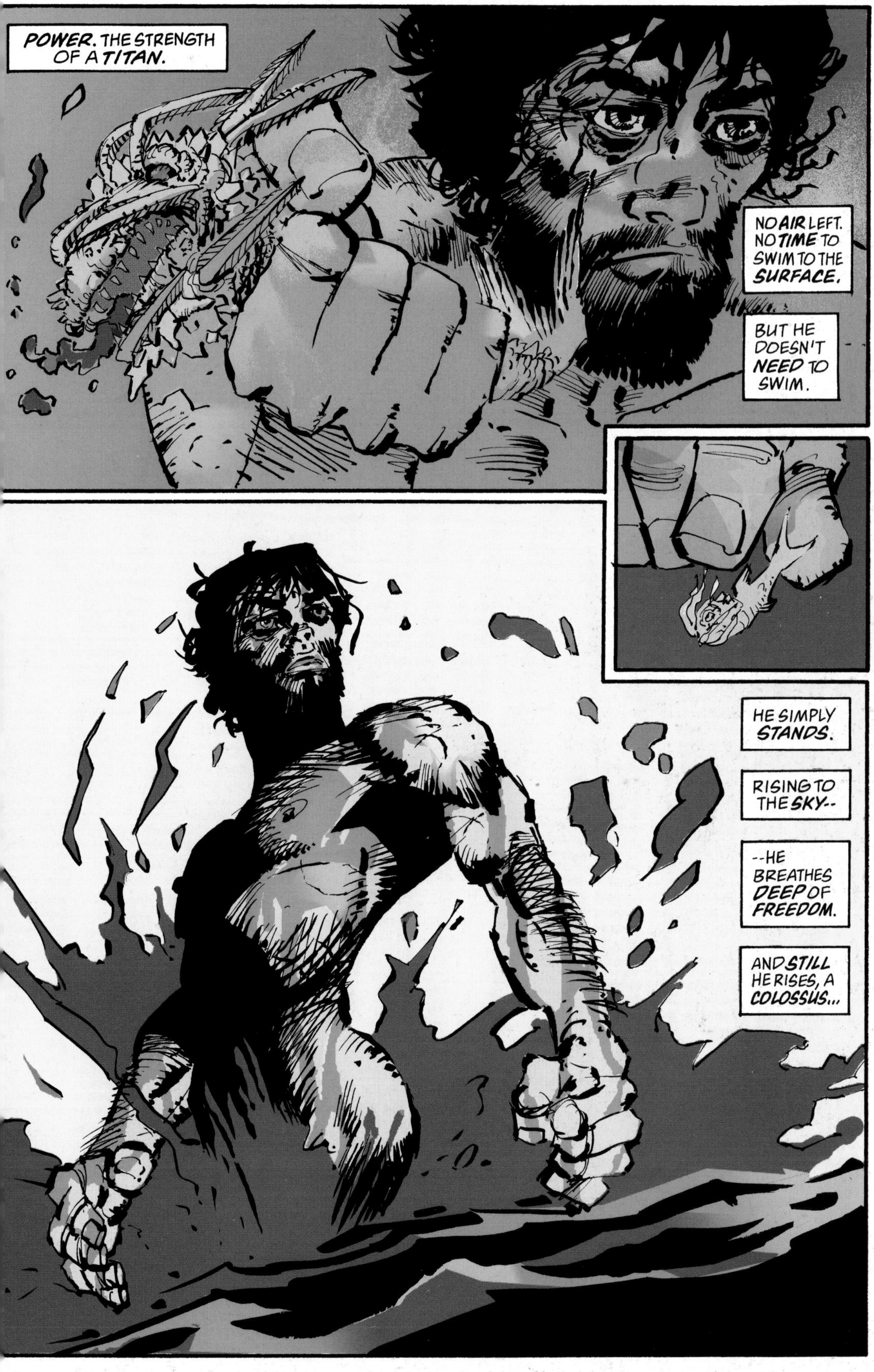
POWER. THE STRENGTH OF A TITAN.
NO AIR LEFT. NO TIME TO SWIM TO THE SURFACE.
BUT HE DOESN'T NEED TO SWIM.
HE SIMPLY STANDS.
RISING TO THE SKY--
--HE BREATHES DEEP OF FREEDOM.
AND STILL HE RISES, A COLOSSUS...

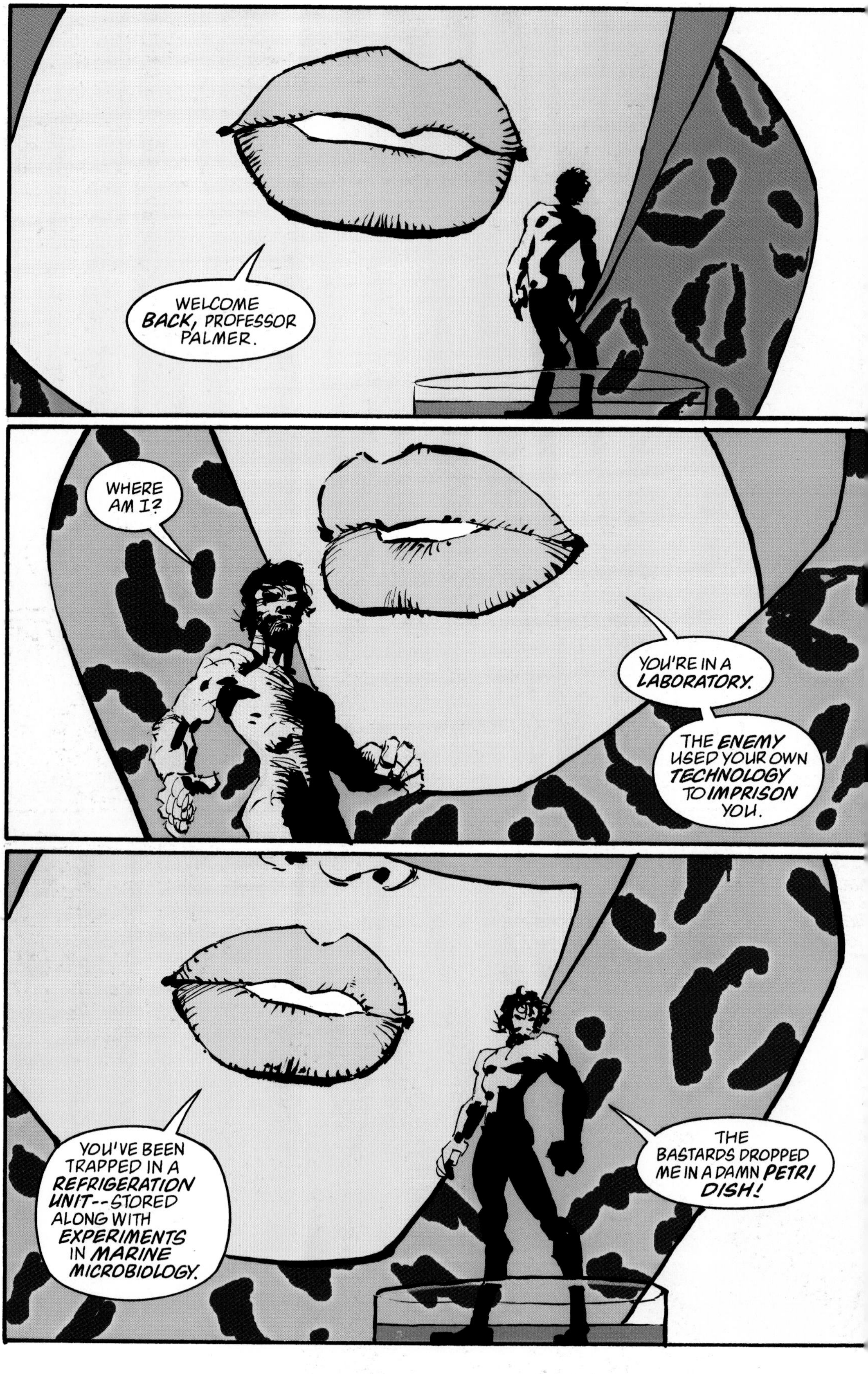
WELCOME BACK, PROFESSOR PALMER.
WHERE AM I?
YOU'RE IN A LABORATORY.
THE ENEMY USED YOUR OWN TECHNOLOGY TO IMPRISON YOU.
YOU'VE BEEN TRAPPED IN A REFRIGERATION UNIT--STORED ALONG WITH EXPERIMENTS IN MARINE MICROBIOLOGY.
THE BASTARDS DROPPED ME IN A DAMN PETRI DISH!

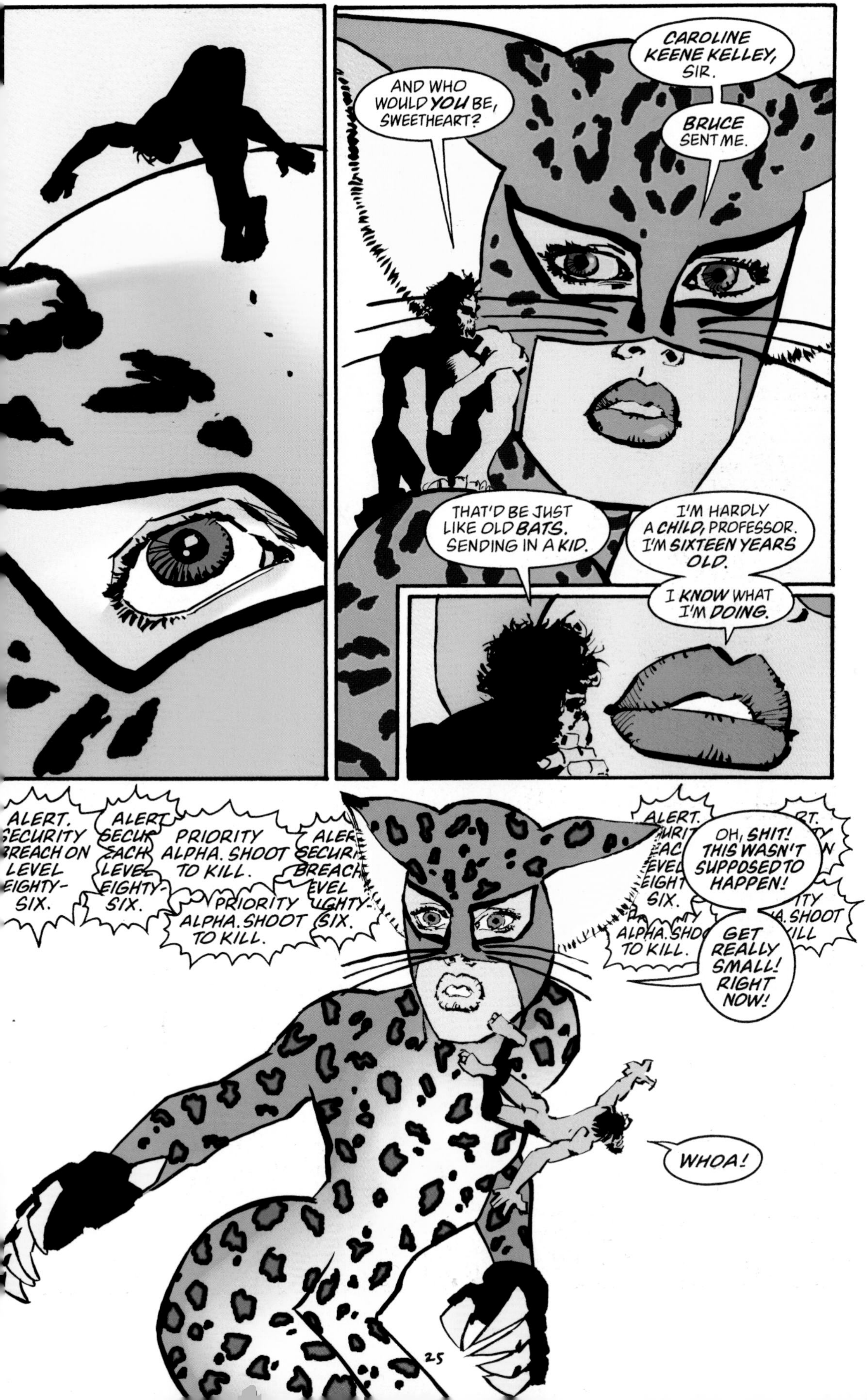
AND WHO WOULD YOU BE, SWEETHEART?
CAROLINE KEENE KELLEY, SIR.
BRUCE SENT ME.
THAT'D BE JUST LIKE OLD BATS. SENDING IN A KID.
I'M HARDLY A CHILD, PROFESSOR. I'M SIXTEEN YEARS OLD.
I KNOW WHAT I'M DOING.
ALERT. SECURITY BREACH ON LEVEL EIGHTY-SIX.
PRIORITY ALPHA. SHOOT TO KILL.
PRIORITY ALPHA. SHOOT TO KILL.
OH, SHIT! THIS WASN'T SUPPOSED TO HAPPEN!
GET REALLY SMALL! RIGHT NOW!
WHOA!

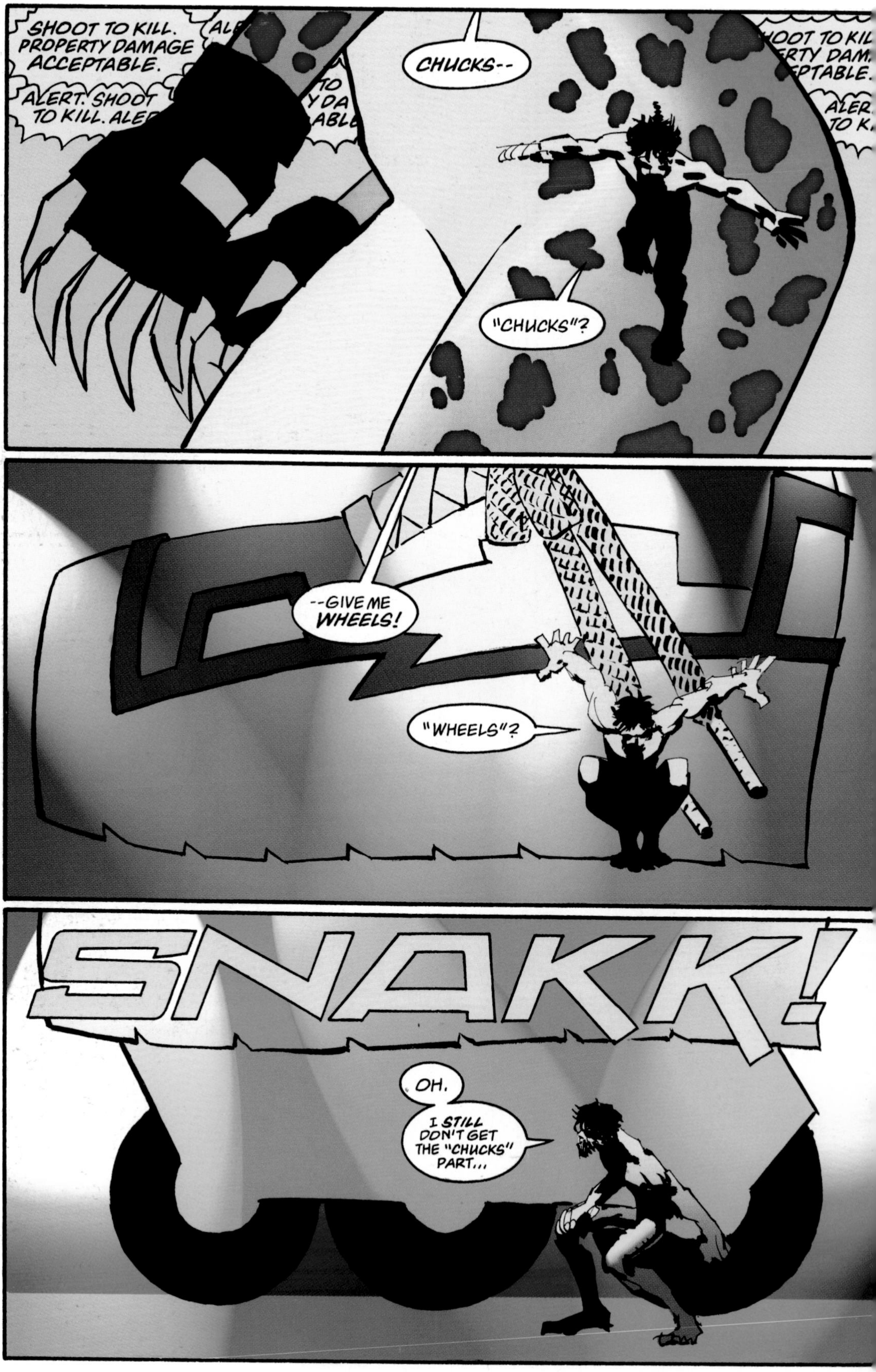
SHOOT TO KILL. PROPERTY DAMAGE ACCEPTABLE.
ALERT. SHOOT TO KILL.
CHUCKS--
"CHUCKS"?
--GIVE ME WHEELS!
"WHEELS"?
SNAKK!
OH.
I STILL DON'T GET THE "CHUCKS" PART...

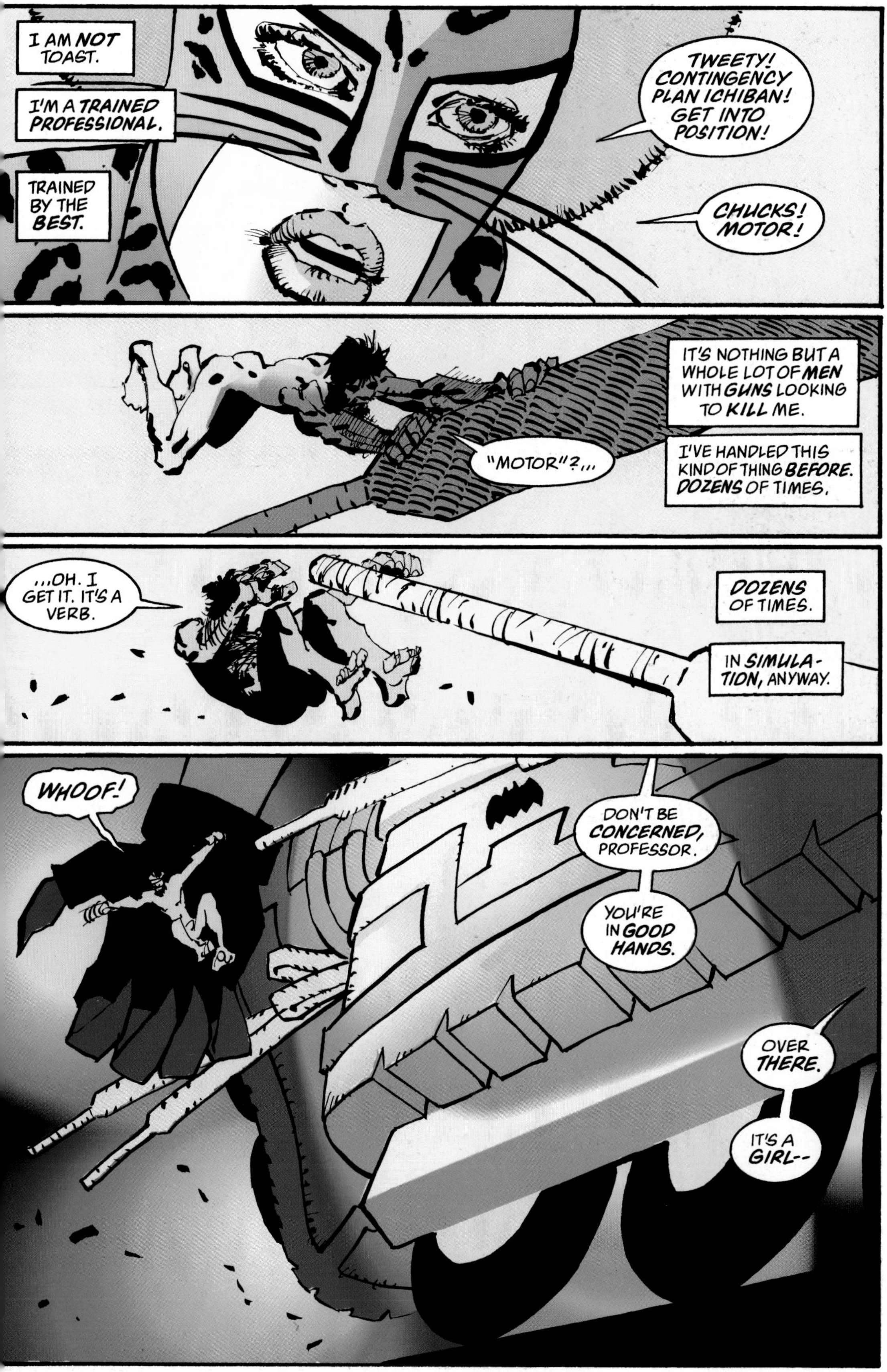
I AM NOT TOAST.
I'M A TRAINED PROFESSIONAL.
TRAINED BY THE BEST.
TWEETY! CONTINGENCY PLAN ICHIBAN! GET INTO POSITION!
CHUCKS! MOTOR!
IT'S NOTHING BUT A WHOLE LOT OF MEN WITH GUNS LOOKING TO KILL ME.
"MOTOR"?...
I'VE HANDLED THIS KIND OF THING BEFORE. DOZENS OF TIMES.
...OH. I GET IT. IT'S A VERB.
DOZENS OF TIMES.
IN SIMULATION, ANYWAY.
WHOOF!
DON'T BE CONCERNED, PROFESSOR.
YOU'RE IN GOOD HANDS.
OVER THERE.
IT'S A GIRL--

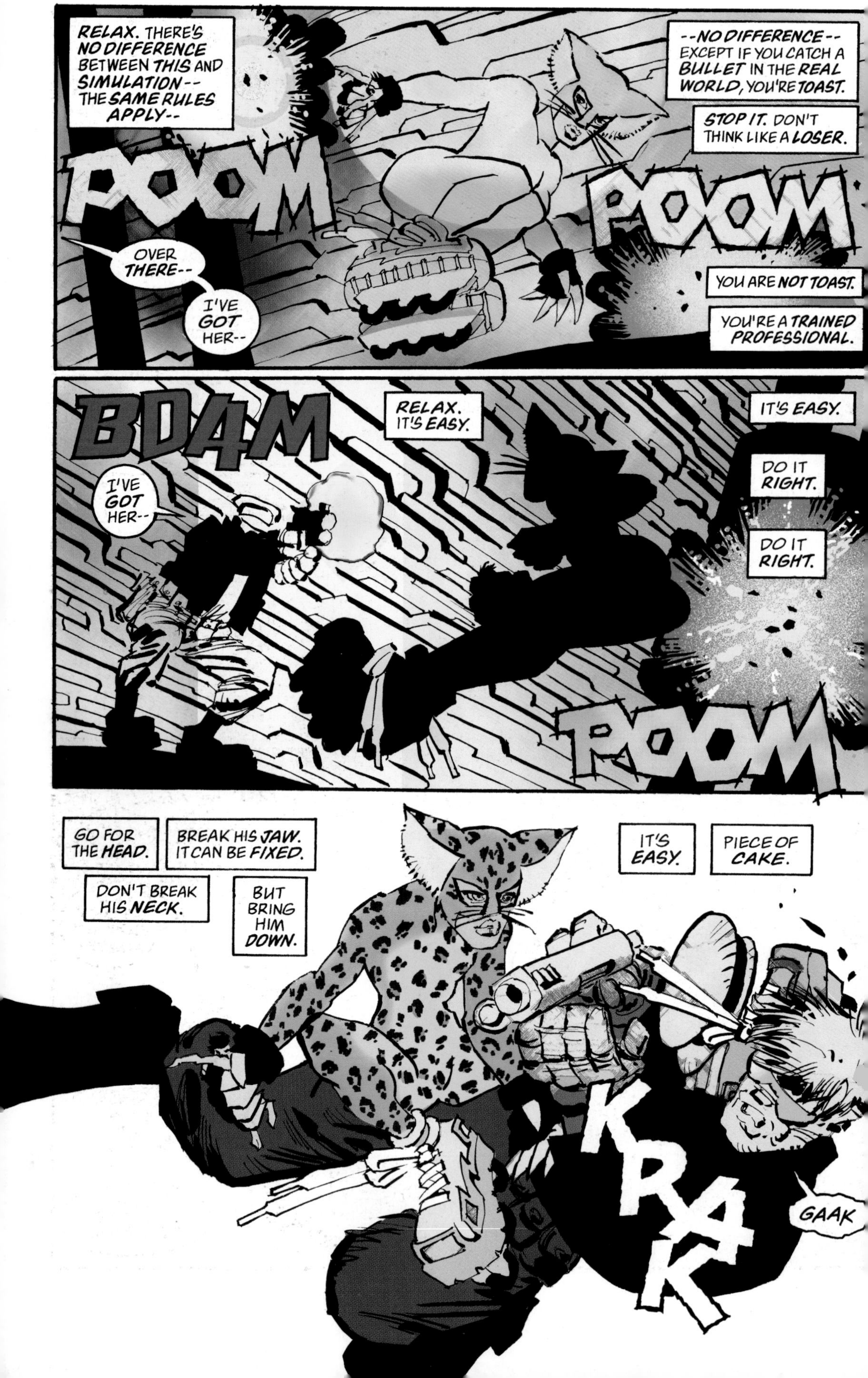

RELAX. THERE'S NO DIFFERENCE BETWEEN THIS AND SIMULATION -- THE SAME RULES APPLY--
POOM
--NO DIFFERENCE-- EXCEPT IF YOU CATCH A BULLET IN THE REAL WORLD, YOU'RE TOAST.
STOP IT. DON'T THINK LIKE A LOSER.
POOM
OVER THERE--
I'VE GOT HER--
YOU ARE NOT TOAST.
YOU'RE A TRAINED PROFESSIONAL.
BDAM
RELAX. IT'S EASY.
IT'S EASY.
I'VE GOT HER--
DO IT RIGHT.
DO IT RIGHT.
POOM
GO FOR THE HEAD.
BREAK HIS JAW. IT CAN BE FIXED.
DON'T BREAK HIS NECK.
BUT BRING HIM DOWN.
IT'S EASY.
PIECE OF CAKE.
KRAK
GAAK

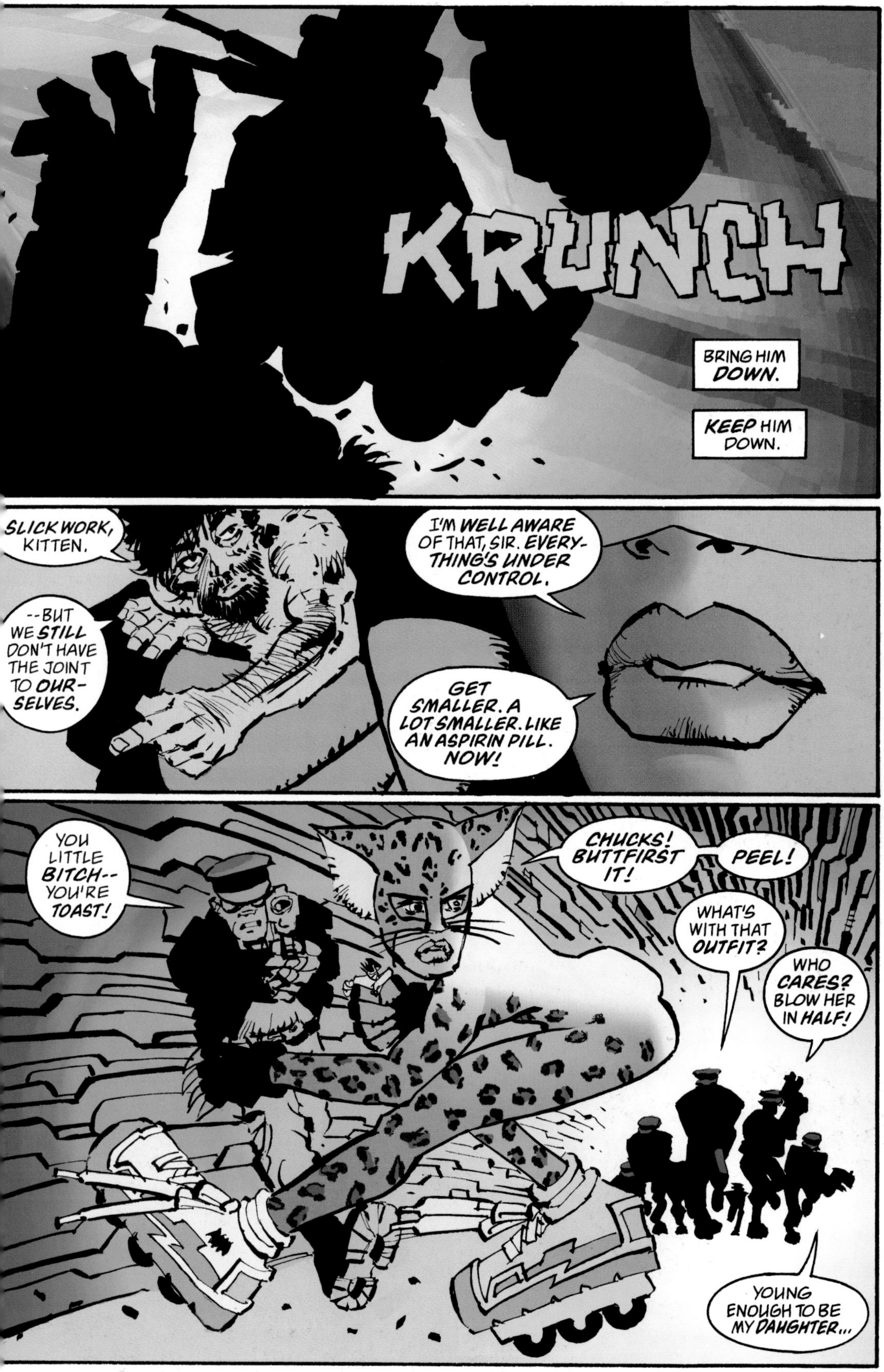
KRUNCH
BRING HIM DOWN.
KEEP HIM DOWN.
SLICK WORK, KITTEN.
--BUT WE STILL DON'T HAVE THE JOINT TO OURSELVES.
I'M WELL AWARE OF THAT, SIR. EVERYTHING'S UNDER CONTROL.
GET SMALLER. A LOT SMALLER. LIKE AN ASPIRIN PILL. NOW!
YOU LITTLE BITCH-- YOU'RE TOAST!
CHUCKS! BUTTFIRST IT!
PEEL!
WHAT'S WITH THAT OUTFIT?
WHO CARES? BLOW HER IN HALF!
YOUNG ENOUGH TO BE MY DAUGHTER...

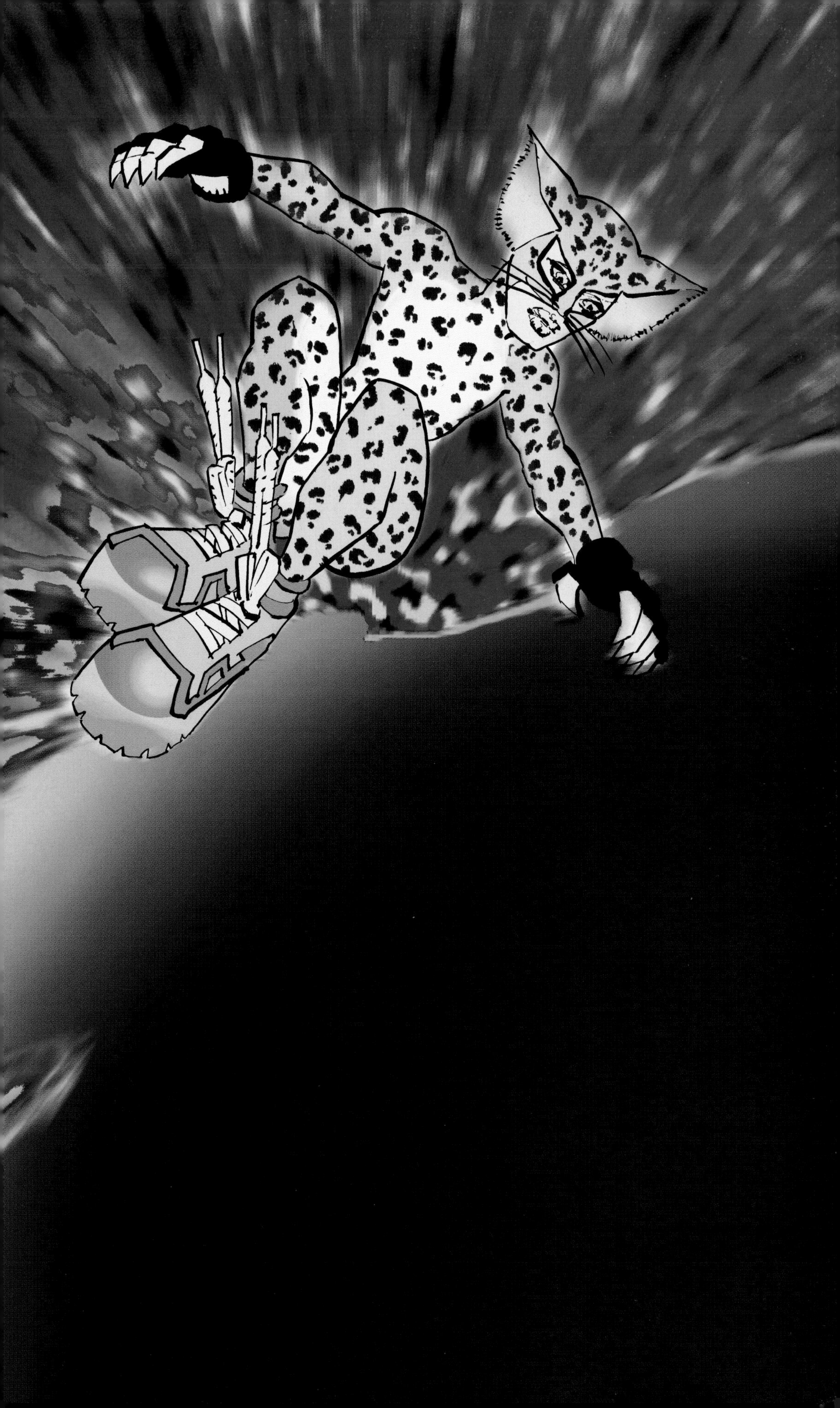

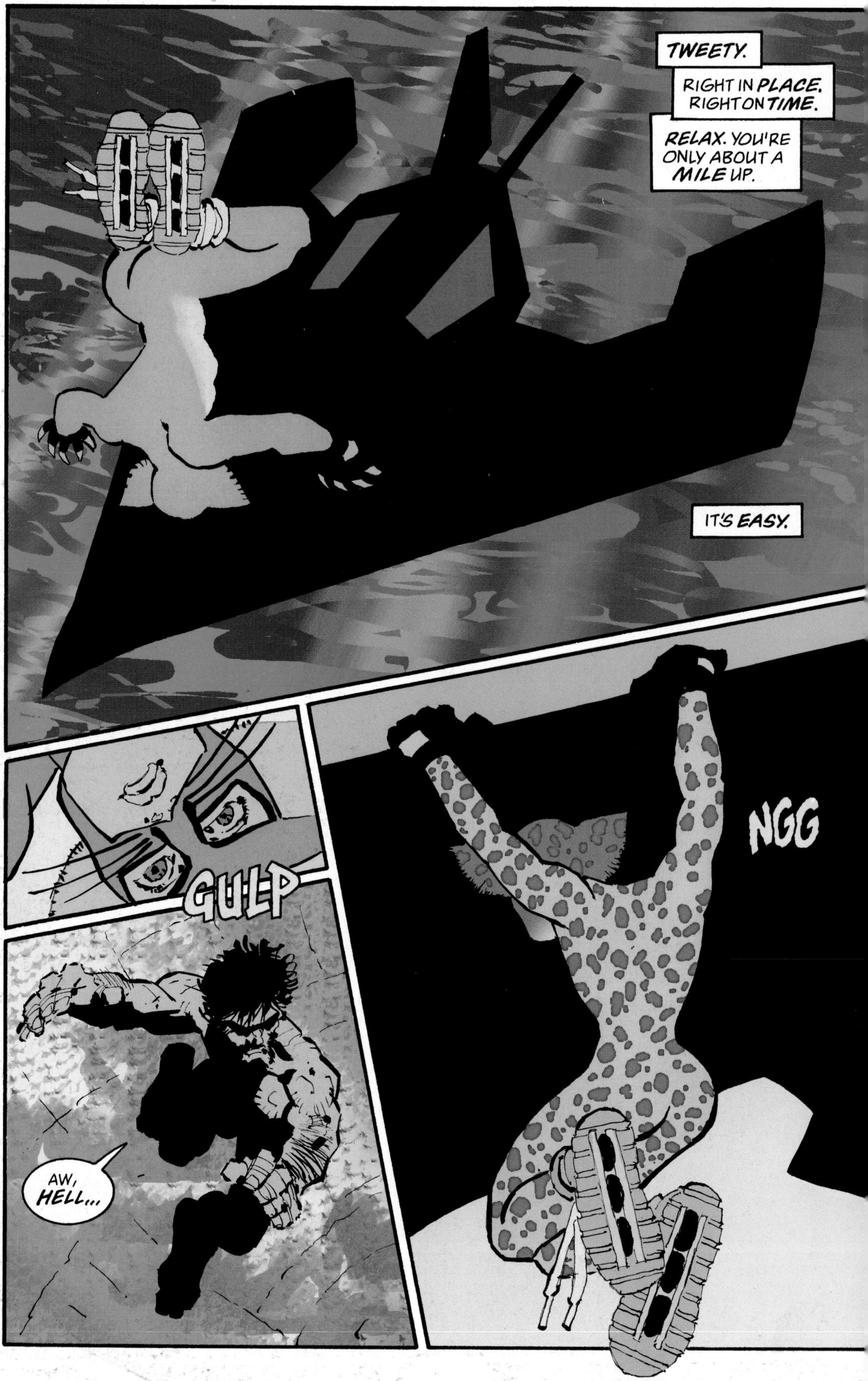
TWEETY.
RIGHT IN PLACE. RIGHT ON TIME.
RELAX. YOU'RE ONLY ABOUT A MILE UP.
IT'S EASY.
GULP
NGG
AW, HELL...

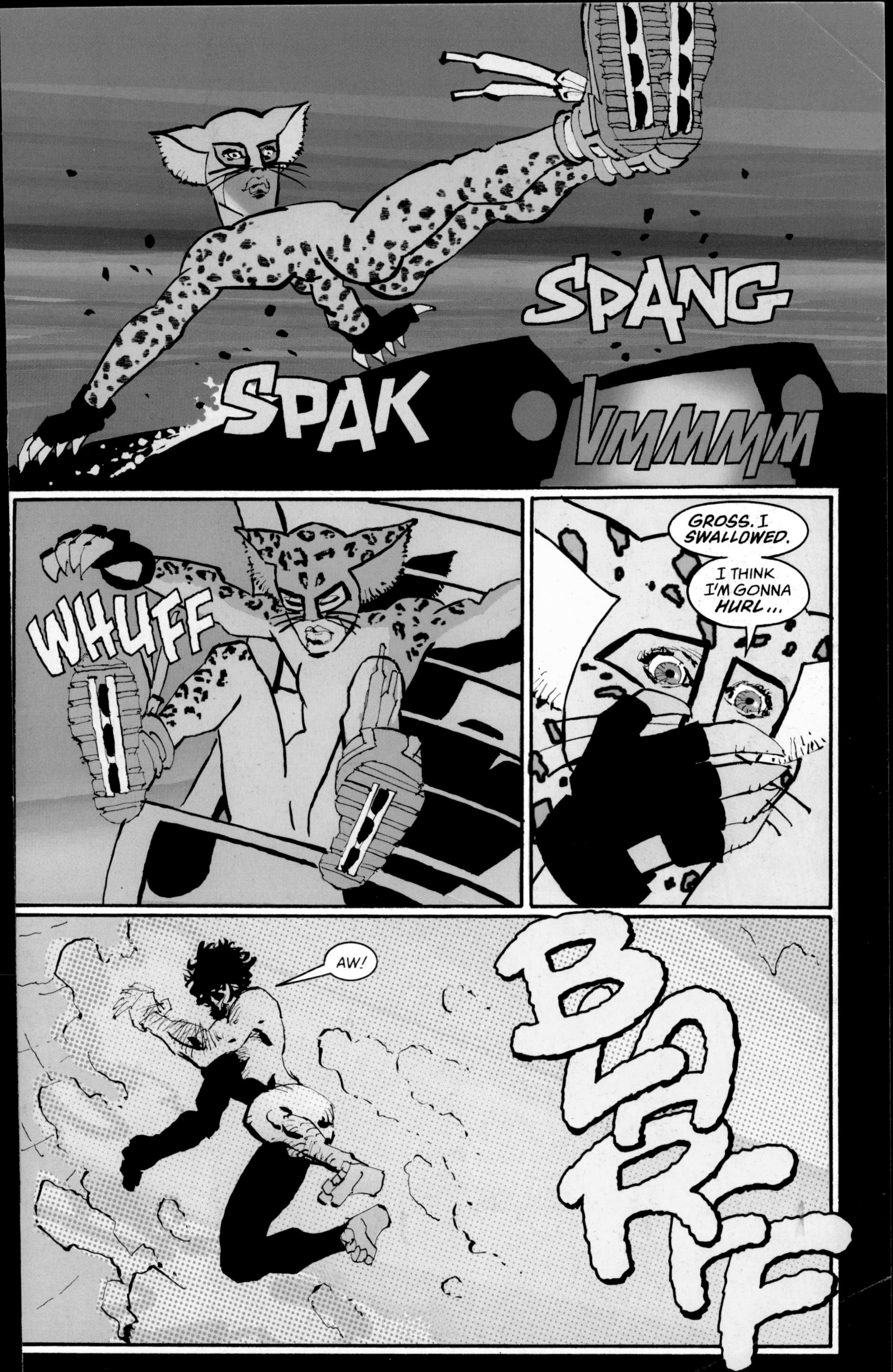
SPANG
SPAK
VMMMMM
WHUFF
GROSS. I SWALLOWED.
I THINK I'M GONNA HURL...
AW!
BLARFF

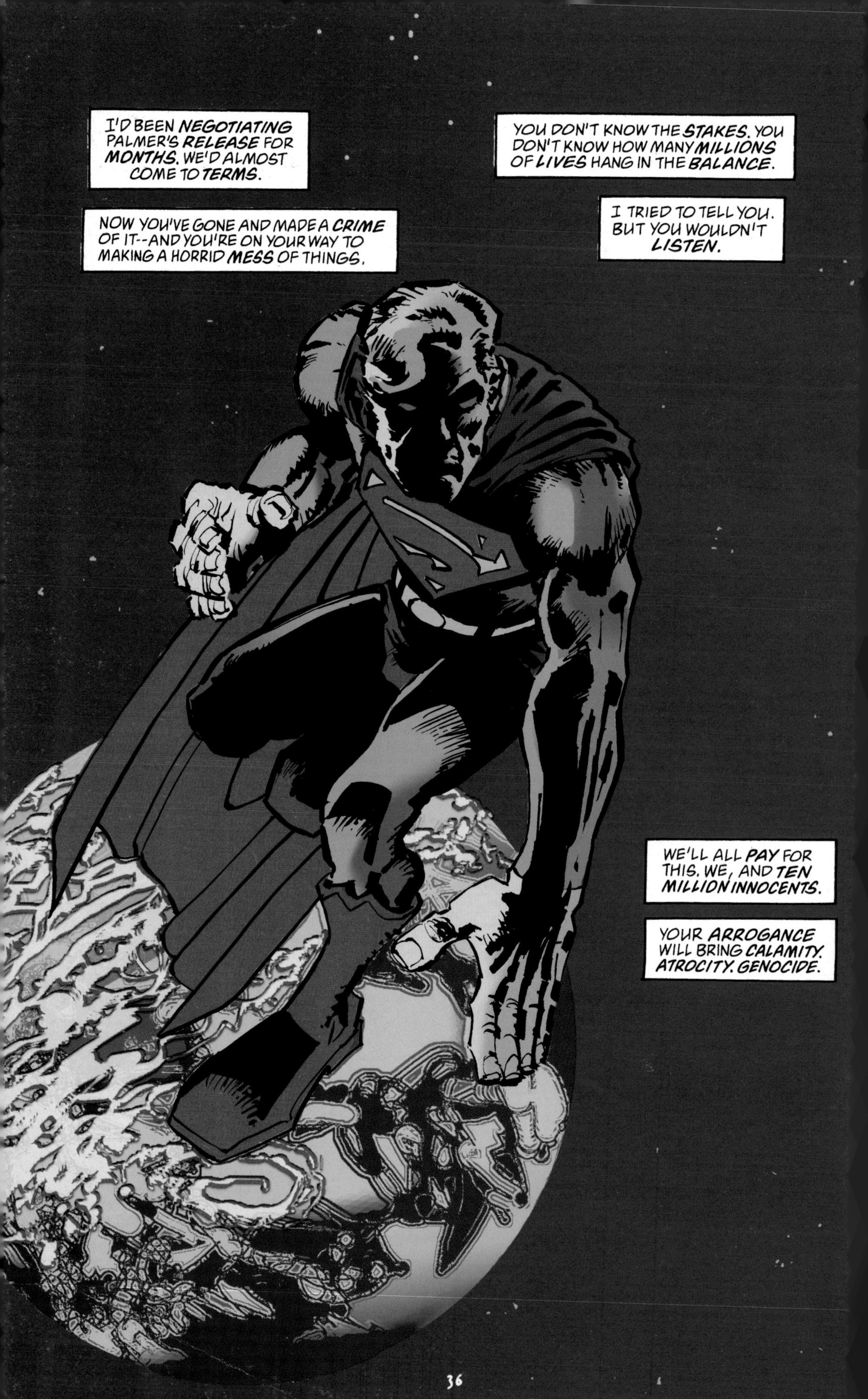
I'D BEEN NEGOTIATING PALMER'S RELEASE FOR MONTHS. WE'D ALMOST COME TO TERMS.
NOW YOU'VE GONE AND MADE A CRIME OF IT--AND YOU'RE ON YOUR WAY TO MAKING A HORRID MESS OF THINGS.
YOU DON'T KNOW THE STAKES. YOU DON'T KNOW HOW MANY MILLIONS OF LIVES HANG IN THE BALANCE.
I TRIED TO TELL YOU. BUT YOU WOULDN'T LISTEN.
WE'LL ALL PAY FOR THIS. WE, AND TEN MILLION INNOCENTS.
YOUR ARROGANCE WILL BRING CALAMITY. ATROCITY. GENOCIDE.

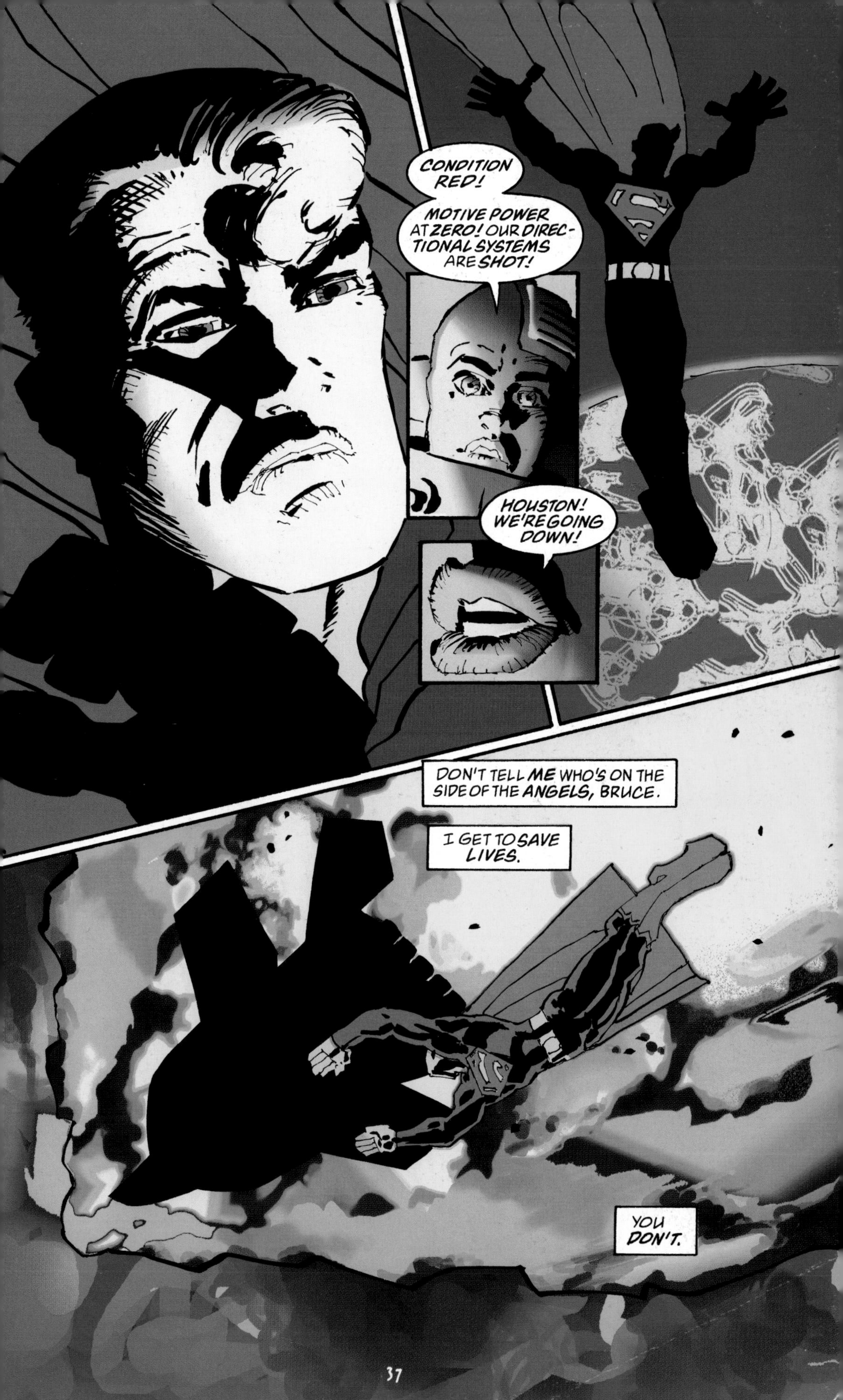
CONDITION RED!
MOTIVE POWER AT ZERO! OUR DIRECTIONAL SYSTEMS ARE SHOT!
HOUSTON! WE'RE GOING DOWN!
DON'T TELL ME WHO'S ON THE SIDE OF THE ANGELS, BRUCE.
I GET TO SAVE LIVES.
YOU DON'T.

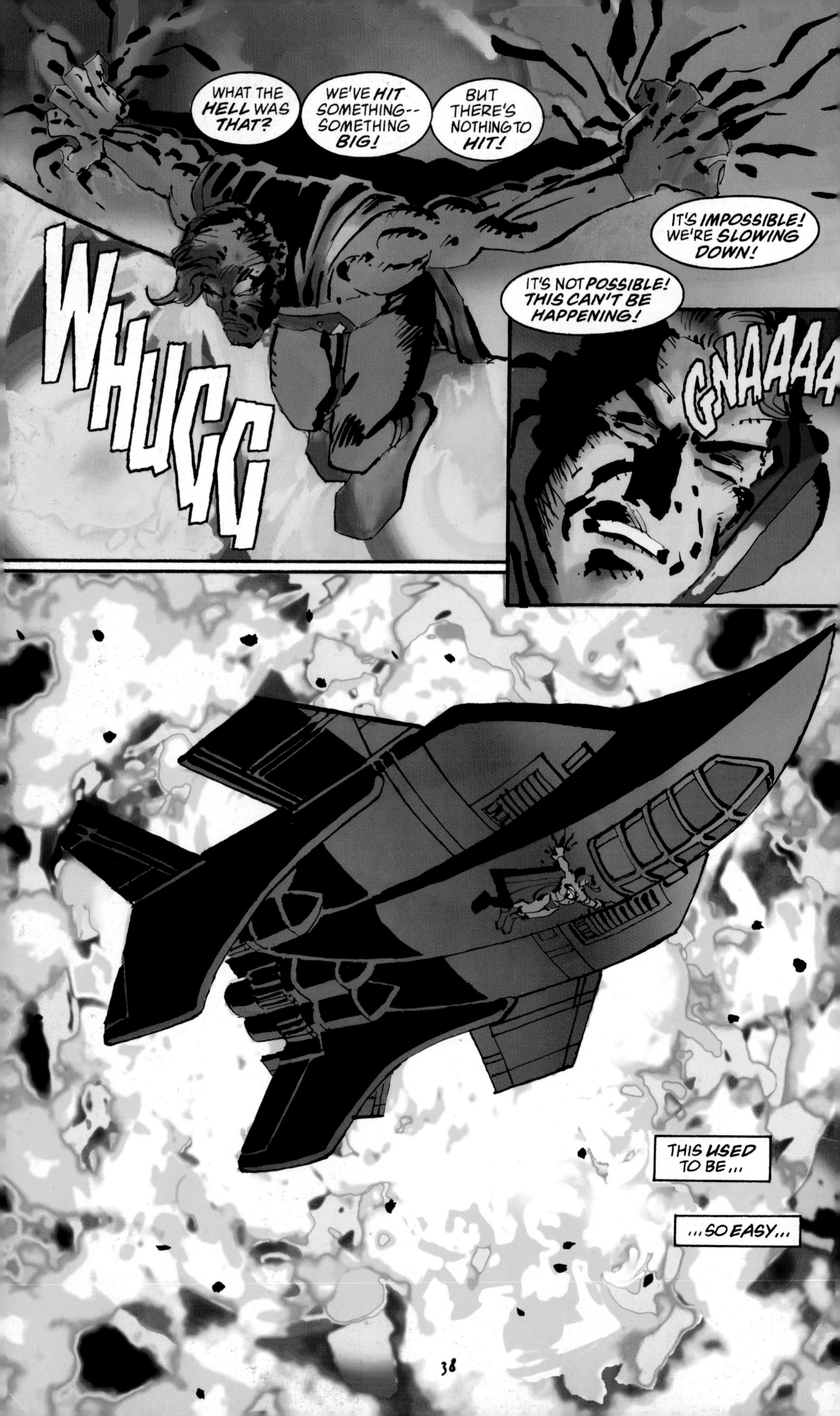
WHAT THE HELL WAS THAT?
WE'VE HIT SOMETHING-- SOMETHING BIG!
BUT THERE'S NOTHING TO HIT!
WHUCC
IT'S IMPOSSIBLE! WE'RE SLOWING DOWN!
IT'S NOT POSSIBLE! THIS CAN'T BE HAPPENING!
GNAAAA
THIS USED TO BE...
...SO EASY...

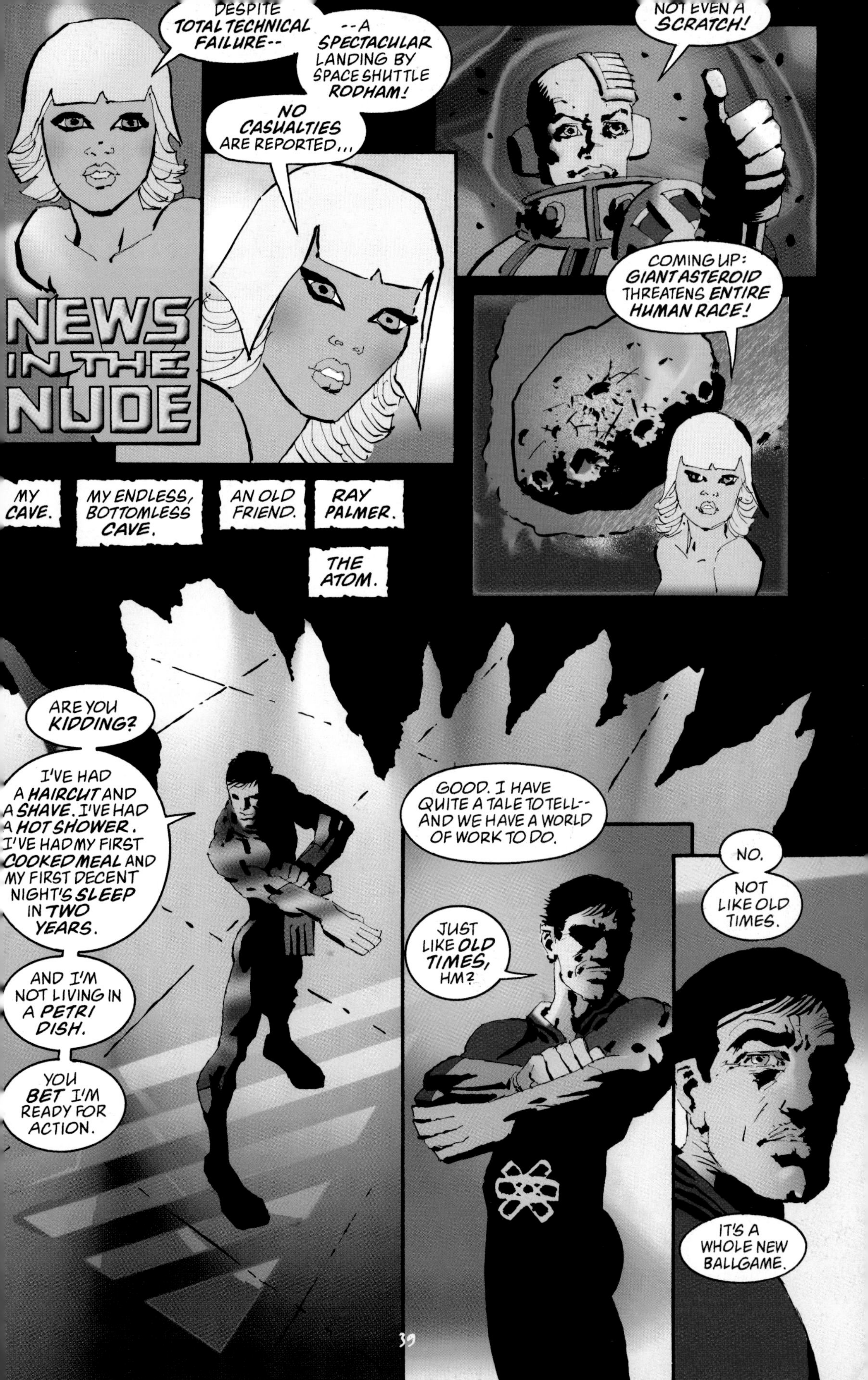
DESPITE TOTAL TECHNICAL FAILURE--
--A SPECTACULAR LANDING BY SPACE SHUTTLE RODHAM!
NO CASUALTIES ARE REPORTED...
NEWS IN THE NUDE
NOT EVEN A SCRATCH!
COMING UP: GIANT ASTEROID THREATENS ENTIRE HUMAN RACE!
MY CAVE.
MY ENDLESS, BOTTOMLESS CAVE.
AN OLD FRIEND.
RAY PALMER.
THE ATOM.
ARE YOU KIDDING?
I'VE HAD A HAIRCUT AND A SHAVE. I'VE HAD A HOT SHOWER. I'VE HAD MY FIRST COOKED MEAL AND MY FIRST DECENT NIGHT'S SLEEP IN TWO YEARS.
AND I'M NOT LIVING IN A PETRI DISH.
YOU BET I'M READY FOR ACTION.
GOOD. I HAVE QUITE A TALE TO TELL--AND WE HAVE A WORLD OF WORK TO DO.
JUST LIKE OLD TIMES, HM?
NO.
NOT LIKE OLD TIMES.
IT'S A WHOLE NEW BALLGAME.

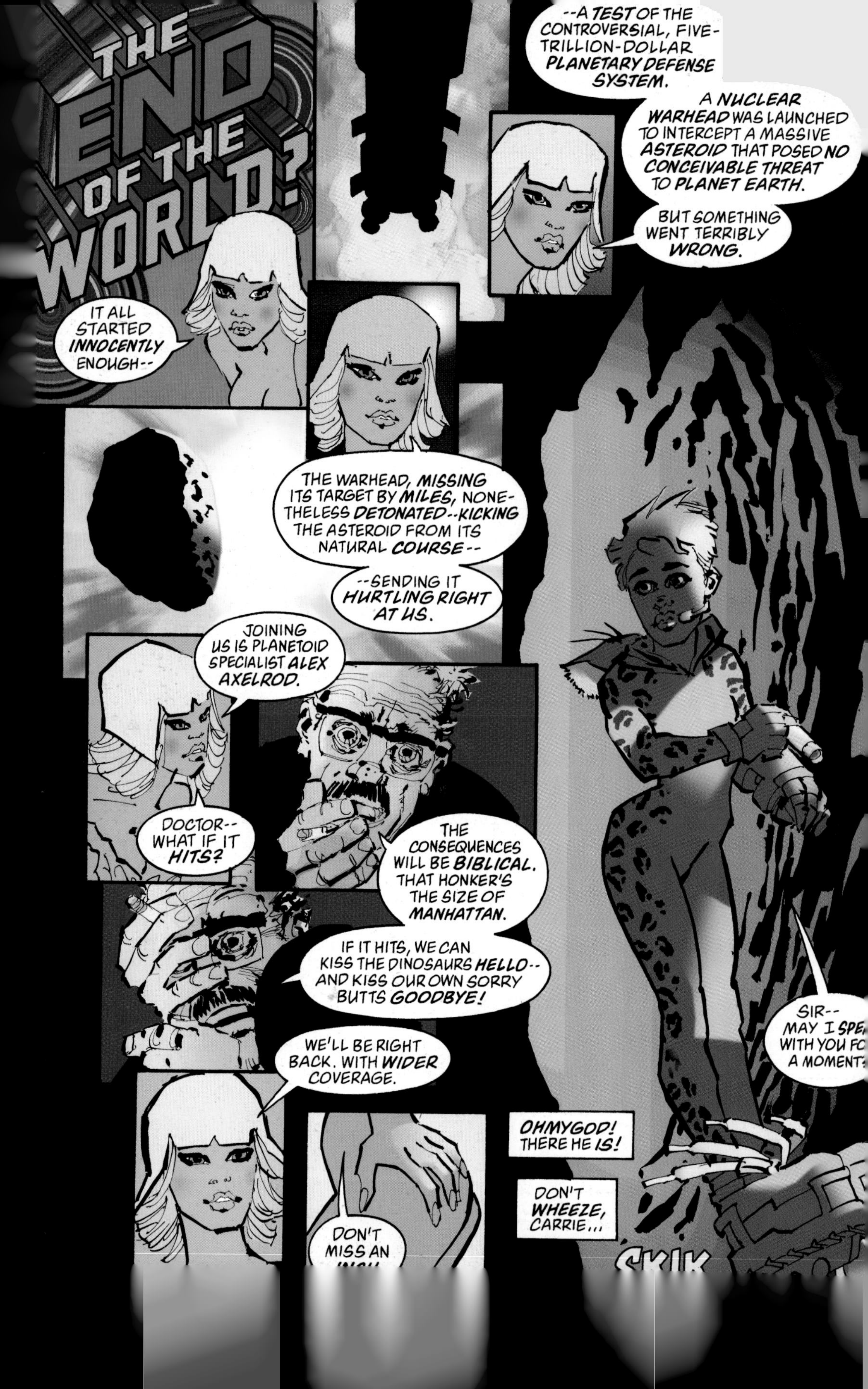
THE END OF THE WORLD?
IT ALL STARTED INNOCENTLY ENOUGH--
--A TEST OF THE CONTROVERSIAL, FIVE-TRILLION-DOLLAR PLANETARY DEFENSE SYSTEM.
A NUCLEAR WARHEAD WAS LAUNCHED TO INTERCEPT A MASSIVE ASTEROID THAT POSED NO CONCEIVABLE THREAT TO PLANET EARTH.
BUT SOMETHING WENT TERRIBLY WRONG.
THE WARHEAD, MISSING ITS TARGET BY MILES, NONETHELESS DETONATED--KICKING THE ASTEROID FROM ITS NATURAL COURSE--
--SENDING IT HURTLING RIGHT AT US.
JOINING US IS PLANETOID SPECIALIST ALEX AXELROD.
DOCTOR-- WHAT IF IT HITS?
THE CONSEQUENCES WILL BE BIBLICAL. THAT HONKER'S THE SIZE OF MANHATTAN.
IF IT HITS, WE CAN KISS THE DINOSAURS HELLO--AND KISS OUR OWN SORRY BUTTS GOODBYE!
WE'LL BE RIGHT BACK. WITH WIDER COVERAGE.
DON'T MISS AN
SIR-- MAY I SPE WITH YOU FC A MOMENT
OHMYGOD! THERE HE IS!
DON'T WHEEZE, CARRIE...
SKIK

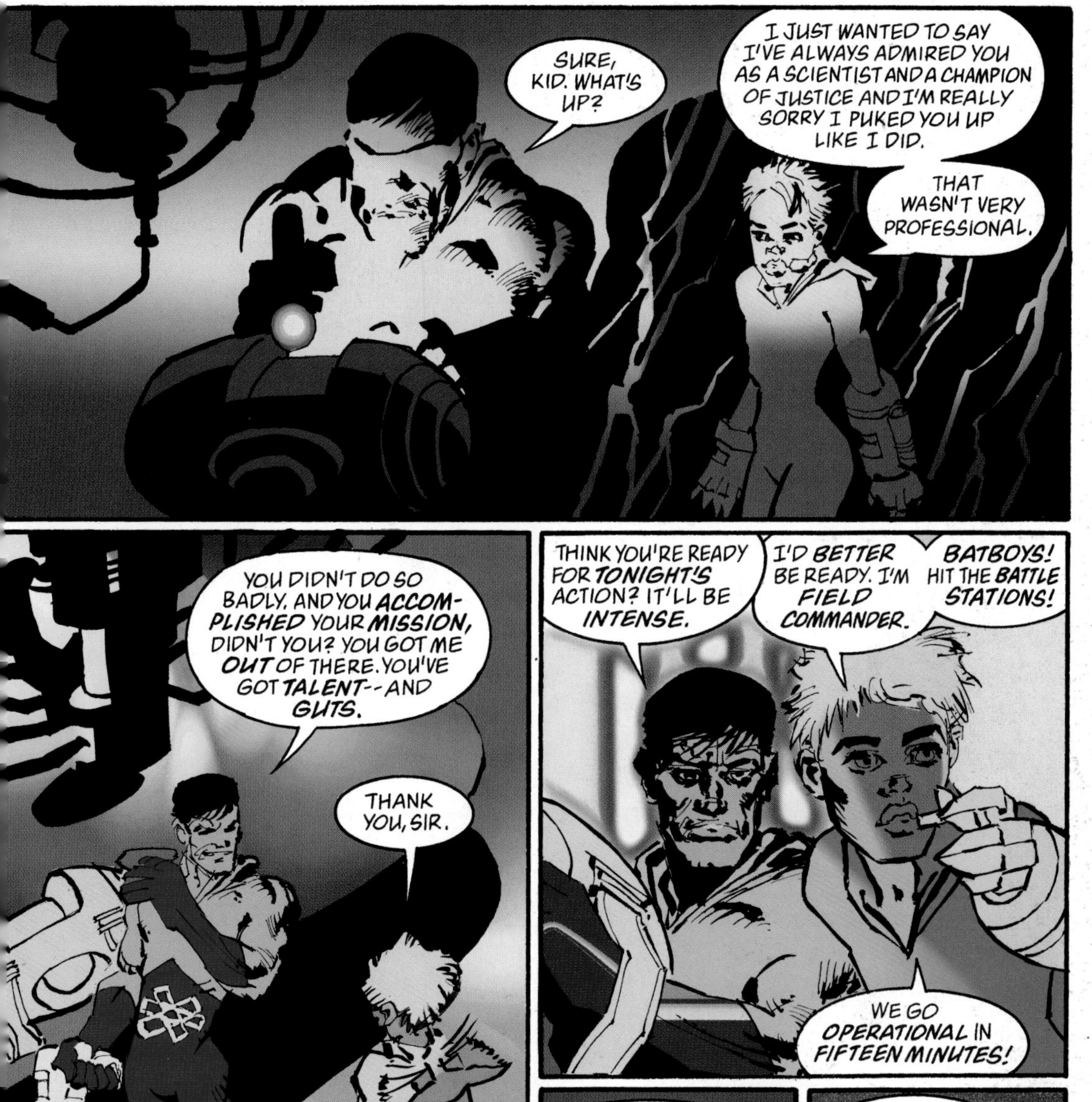

SURE, KID. WHAT'S UP?
I JUST WANTED TO SAY I'VE ALWAYS ADMIRED YOU AS A SCIENTIST AND A CHAMPION OF JUSTICE AND I'M REALLY SORRY I PUKED YOU UP LIKE I DID.
THAT WASN'T VERY PROFESSIONAL.
YOU DIDN'T DO SO BADLY. AND YOU ACCOMPLISHED YOUR MISSION, DIDN'T YOU? YOU GOT ME OUT OF THERE. YOU'VE GOT TALENT--AND GUTS.
THANK YOU, SIR.
HE'S AT FULL SIZE, AND HE'S STILL NOT ALL THAT BIG.
SURE. LIKE ONLY A FOOT TALLER THAN ME.
I DON'T SAY A WORD ABOUT HIS HAIRCUT.
THINK YOU'RE READY FOR TONIGHT'S ACTION? IT'LL BE INTENSE.
I'D BETTER BE READY. I'M FIELD COMMANDER.
BATBOYS! HIT THE BATTLE STATIONS!
WE GO OPERATIONAL IN FIFTEEN MINUTES!
"BATBOYS"?
YEAH. THEY HATE IT WHEN I CALL THEM THAT.

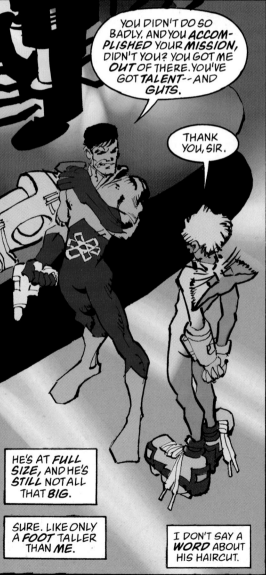

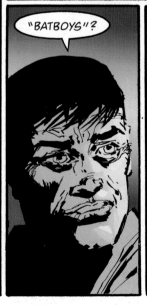

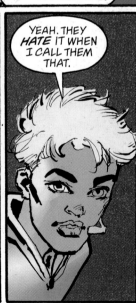

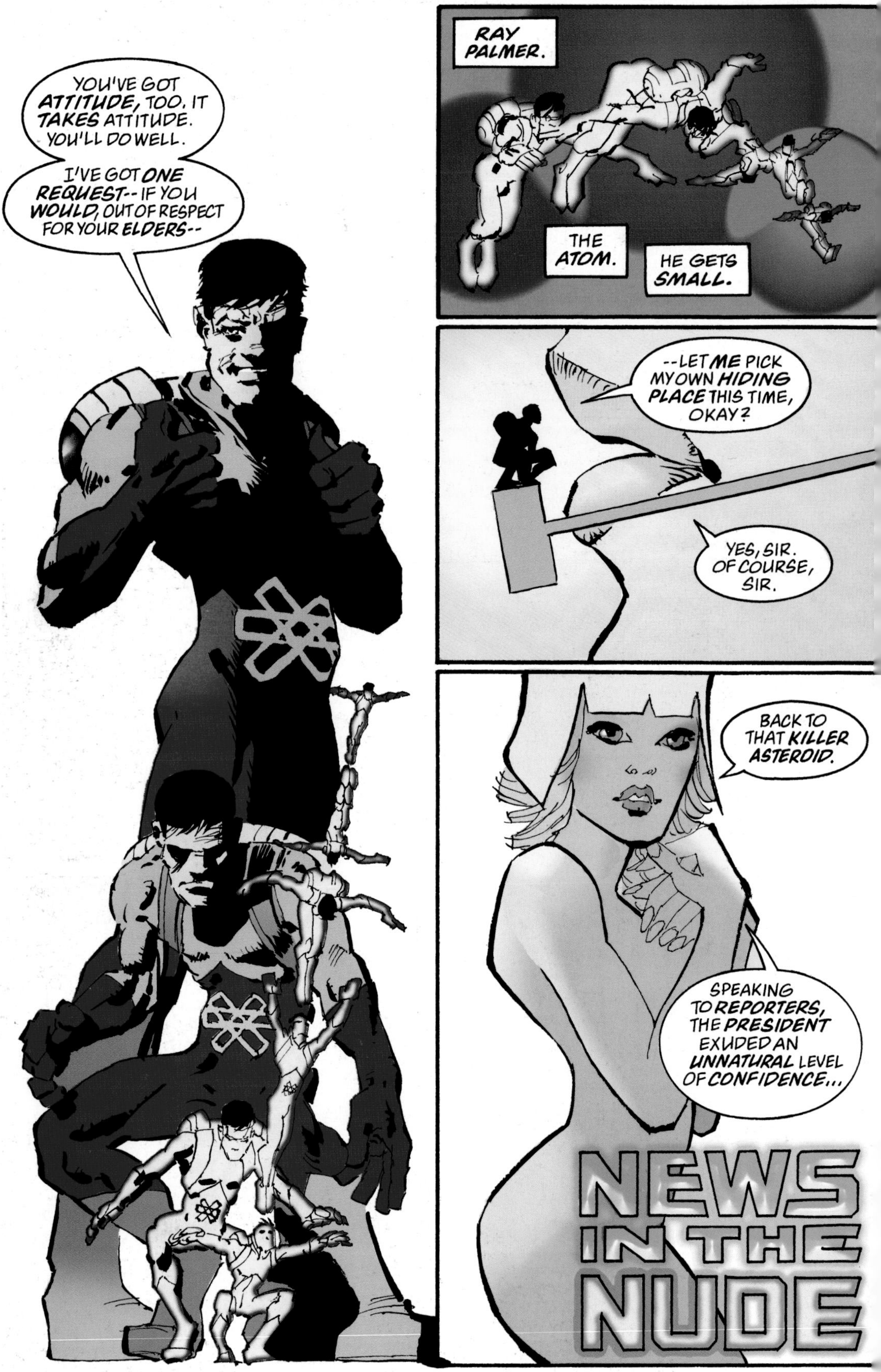
YOU'VE GOT ATTITUDE, TOO. IT TAKES ATTITUDE. YOU'LL DO WELL.
I'VE GOT ONE REQUEST-- IF YOU WOULD, OUT OF RESPECT FOR YOUR ELDERS--
RAY PALMER.
THE ATOM.
HE GETS SMALL.
--LET ME PICK MY OWN HIDING PLACE THIS TIME, OKAY?
YES, SIR. OF COURSE, SIR.
BACK TO THAT KILLER ASTEROID.
SPEAKING TO REPORTERS, THE PRESIDENT EXUDED AN UNNATURAL LEVEL OF CONFIDENCE...
NEWS IN THE NUDE

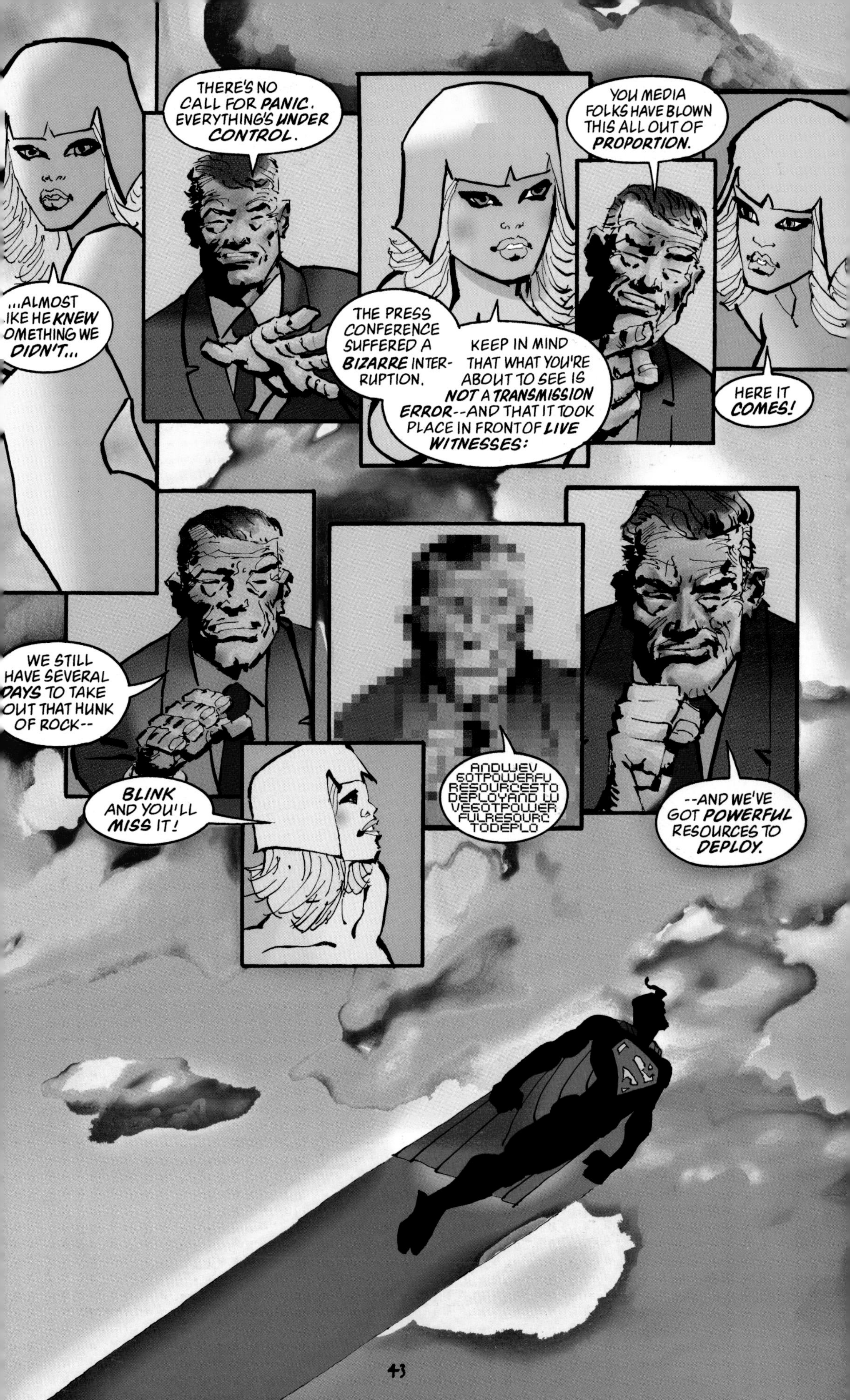
...ALMOST
IKE HE KNEW
OMETHING WE
DIDN'T...
THERE'S NO CALL FOR PANIC. EVERYTHING'S UNDER CONTROL.
THE PRESS CONFERENCE SUFFERED A BIZARRE INTER-RUPTION.
KEEP IN MIND THAT WHAT YOU'RE ABOUT TO SEE IS NOT A TRANSMISSION ERROR--AND THAT IT TOOK PLACE IN FRONT OF LIVE WITNESSES:
YOU MEDIA FOLKS HAVE BLOWN THIS ALL OUT OF PROPORTION.
HERE IT COMES!
WE STILL HAVE SEVERAL DAYS TO TAKE OUT THAT HUNK OF ROCK--
ANDWEV GOTPOWERFU RESOURCESTO DEPLOYAND W VEGOTPOWER FULRESOURC TODEPLO
--AND WE'VE GOT POWERFUL RESOURCES TO DEPLOY.
BLINK AND YOU'LL MISS IT!

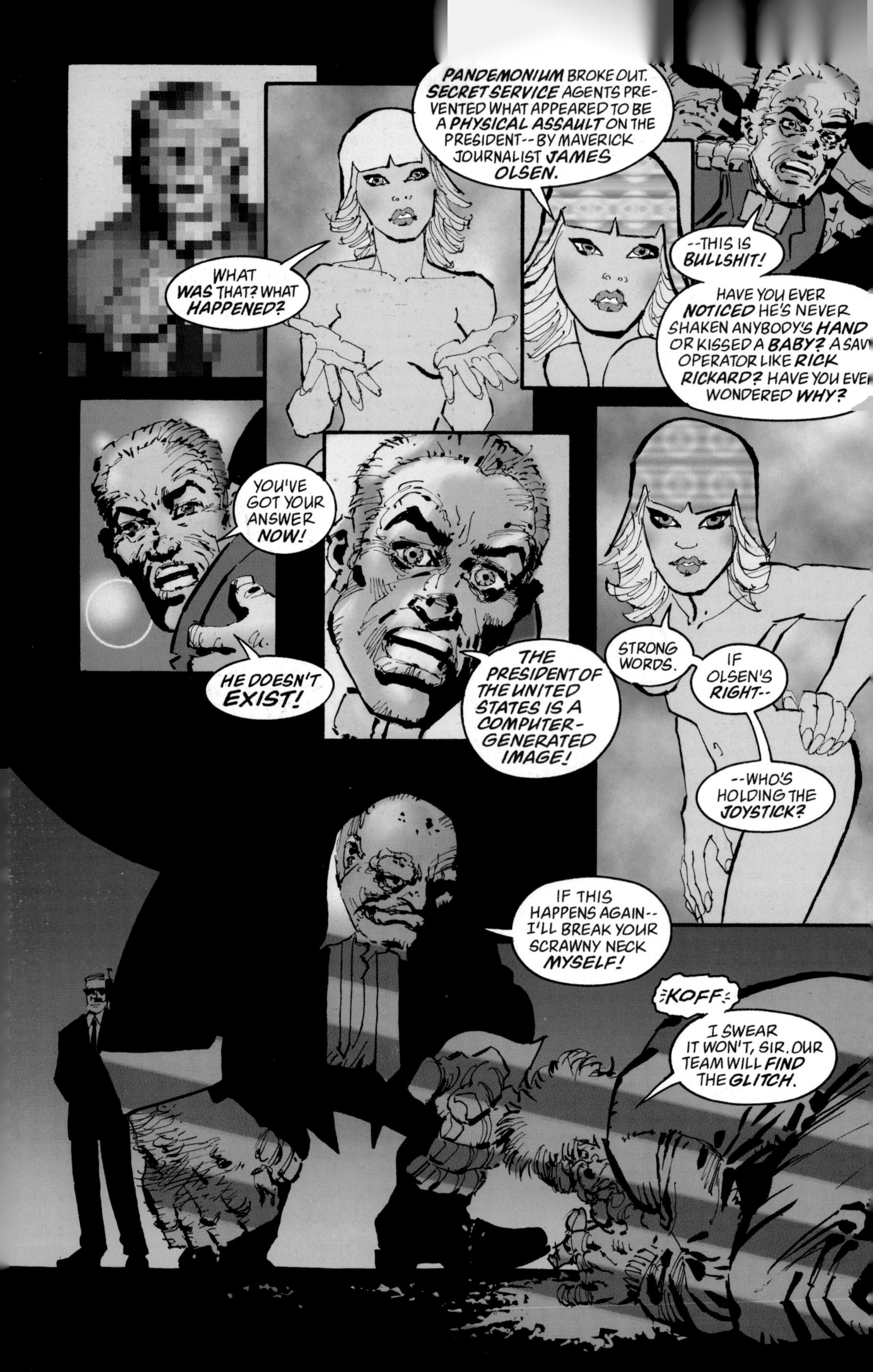
WHAT WAS THAT? WHAT HAPPENED?
PANDEMONIUM BROKE OUT. SECRET SERVICE AGENTS PRE-VENTED WHAT APPEARED TO BE A PHYSICAL ASSAULT ON THE PRESIDENT--BY MAVERICK JOURNALIST JAMES OLSEN.
--THIS IS BULLSHIT!
HAVE YOU EVER NOTICED HE'S NEVER SHAKEN ANYBODY'S HAND OR KISSED A BABY? A SAV OPERATOR LIKE RICK RICKARD? HAVE YOU EVE WONDERED WHY?
YOU'VE GOT YOUR ANSWER NOW!
HE DOESN'T EXIST!
THE PRESIDENT OF THE UNITED STATES IS A COMPUTER-GENERATED IMAGE!
STRONG WORDS.
IF OLSEN'S RIGHT--
--WHO'S HOLDING THE JOYSTICK?
IF THIS HAPPENS AGAIN--I'LL BREAK YOUR SCRAWNY NECK MYSELF!
KOFF
I SWEAR IT WON'T, SIR. OUR TEAM WILL FIND THE GLITCH.

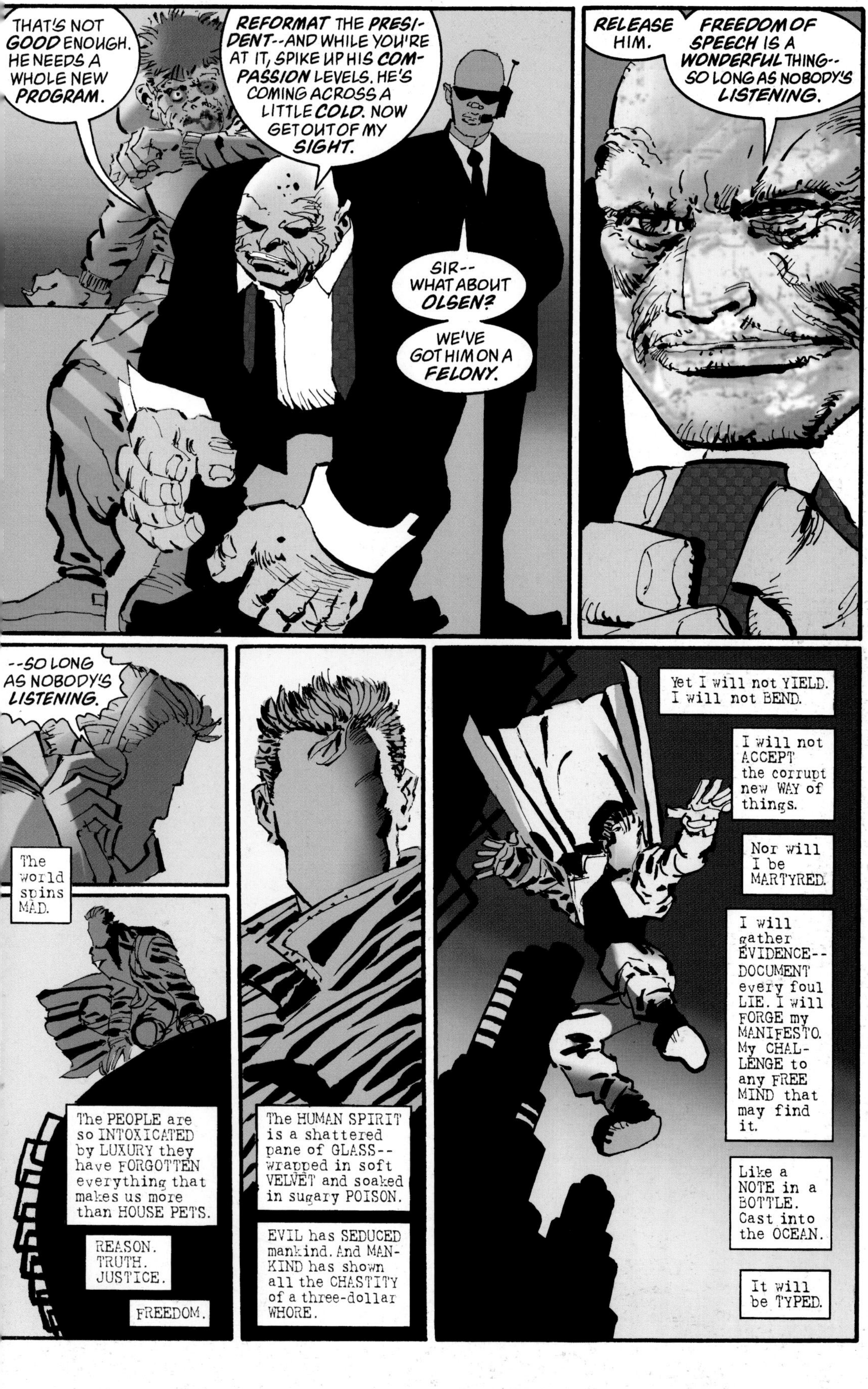

THAT'S NOT GOOD ENOUGH. HE NEEDS A WHOLE NEW PROGRAM.
REFORMAT THE PRESIDENT--AND WHILE YOU'RE AT IT, SPIKE UP HIS COMPASSION LEVELS. HE'S COMING ACROSS A LITTLE COLD. NOW GET OUT OF MY SIGHT.
SIR--WHAT ABOUT OLSEN?
WE'VE GOT HIM ON A FELONY.
RELEASE HIM.
FREEDOM OF SPEECH IS A WONDERFUL THING--SO LONG AS NOBODY'S LISTENING.
--SO LONG AS NOBODY'S LISTENING.
The world spins MAD.
The PEOPLE are so INTOXICATED by LUXURY they have FORGOTTEN everything that makes us more than HOUSE PETS.
REASON. TRUTH. JUSTICE.
FREEDOM.
The HUMAN SPIRIT is a shattered pane of GLASS--wrapped in soft VELVET and soaked in sugary POISON.
EVIL has SEDUCED mankind. And MANKIND has shown all the CHASTITY of a three-dollar WHORE.
Yet I will not YIELD. I will not BEND.
I will not ACCEPT the corrupt new WAY of things.
Nor will I be MARTYRED.
I will gather EVIDENCE--DOCUMENT every foul LIE. I will FORGE my MANIFESTO. My CHALLENGE to any FREE MIND that may find it.
Like a NOTE in a BOTTLE. Cast into the OCEAN.
It will be TYPED.

Distant THUNDER.

No. Not thunder.

Those are BATTLE SOUNDS...

SPECIAL REPORT

...MASSIVE EXPLOSIONS RIPPING ACROSS THE *KANEMITSU POWER COMPLEX*--THREATENING ELECTRICAL SUPPLY FOR THE ENTIRE *EASTERN SEABOARD.*

THIS COULD BE THE *SECOND* TERRORIST ATTACK ON OUR *NATIONAL SECURITY* IN LESS THAN A *WEEK.*

AT THE SCENE IS *LANA HARPER-LANE.*

LANA-- HOW DO THINGS LOOK FROM THE *GROUND?*

IT'S *UTTER CHAOS* DOWN HERE, CHIP! SECURITY FORCES ARE SO *OVER-WHELMED* THEY HAVEN'T HAD *TIME* TO CHASE US *AWAY*--

⸗OOF!⸗

OUTTA MY *WAY!*

UP *THERE*-- WHAT *ARE* THOSE THINGS?

GET A *CAMERA* ON THEM, DAMN IT!

THIS IS *IT,* CLARK. NO MORE *SKIRMISHES.* NO MORE *COMPROMISES.* NO MORE *DEALS.*

NO MORE *SECRECY.* NO MORE *SILENCE.*

NO MORE PRETENDING THAT WE DON'T *EXIST.*

NOT ONE MORE LIE.

DAMN THE CONSEQUENCES.

THE WAR BEGINS.

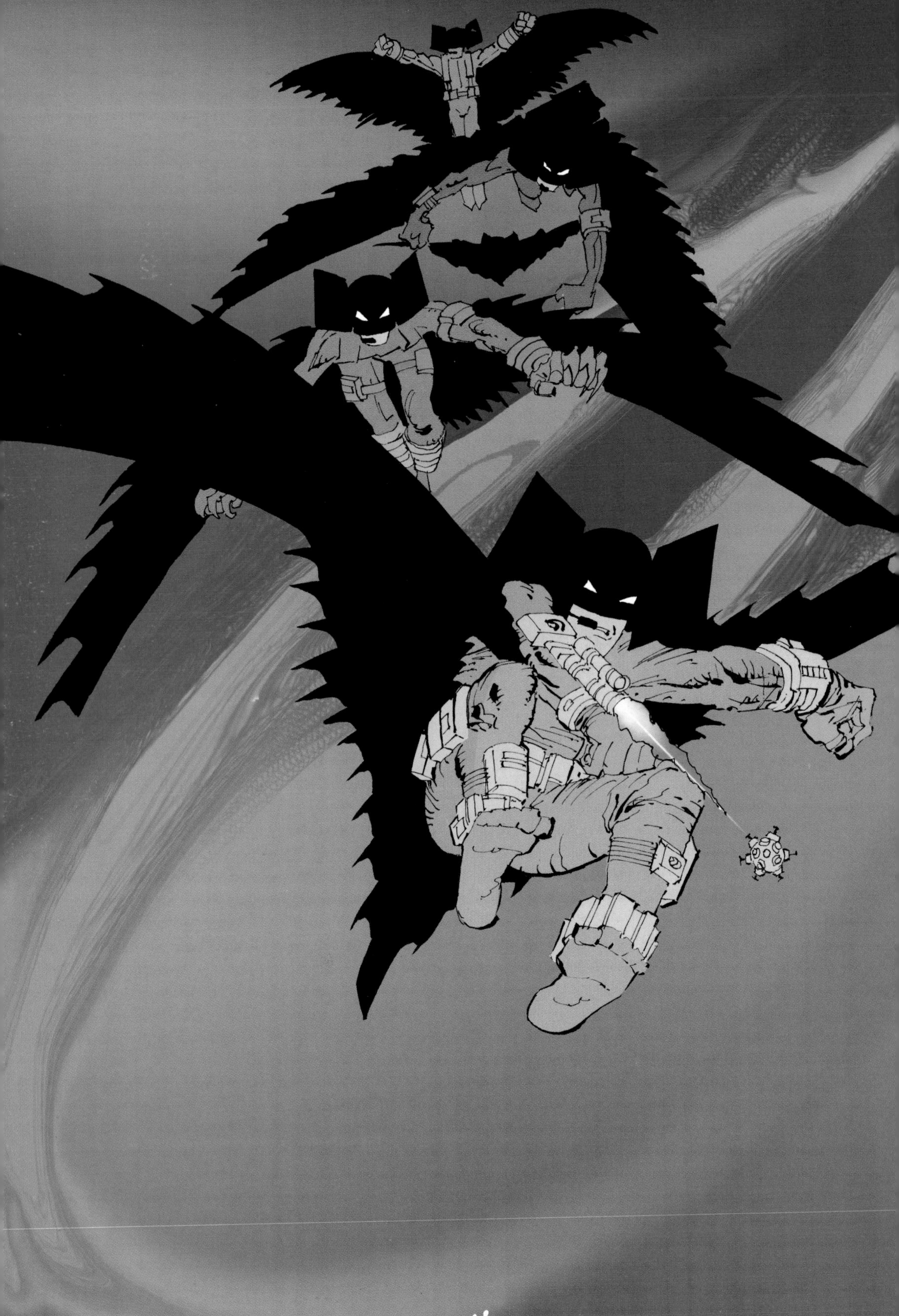

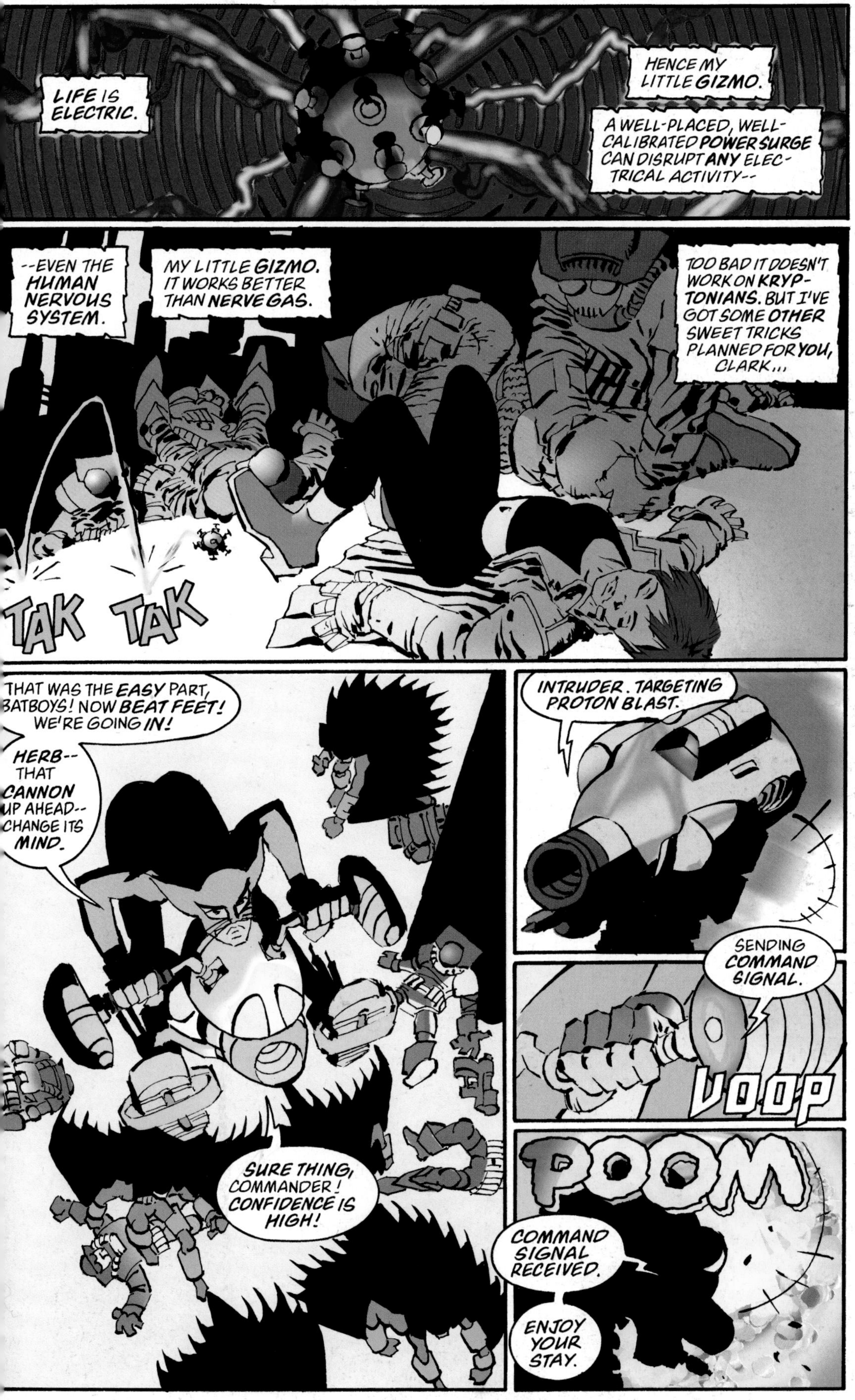
LIFE IS ELECTRIC.
HENCE MY LITTLE GIZMO.
A WELL-PLACED, WELL-CALIBRATED POWER SURGE CAN DISRUPT ANY ELECTRICAL ACTIVITY--
--EVEN THE HUMAN NERVOUS SYSTEM.
MY LITTLE GIZMO. IT WORKS BETTER THAN NERVE GAS.
TOO BAD IT DOESN'T WORK ON KRYPTONIANS. BUT I'VE GOT SOME OTHER SWEET TRICKS PLANNED FOR YOU, CLARK...
TAK TAK
THAT WAS THE EASY PART, BATBOYS! NOW BEAT FEET! WE'RE GOING IN!
HERB-- THAT CANNON UP AHEAD-- CHANGE ITS MIND.
SURE THING, COMMANDER! CONFIDENCE IS HIGH!
INTRUDER. TARGETING PROTON BLAST.
SENDING COMMAND SIGNAL.
VOOP
POOM
COMMAND SIGNAL RECEIVED.
ENJOY YOUR STAY.

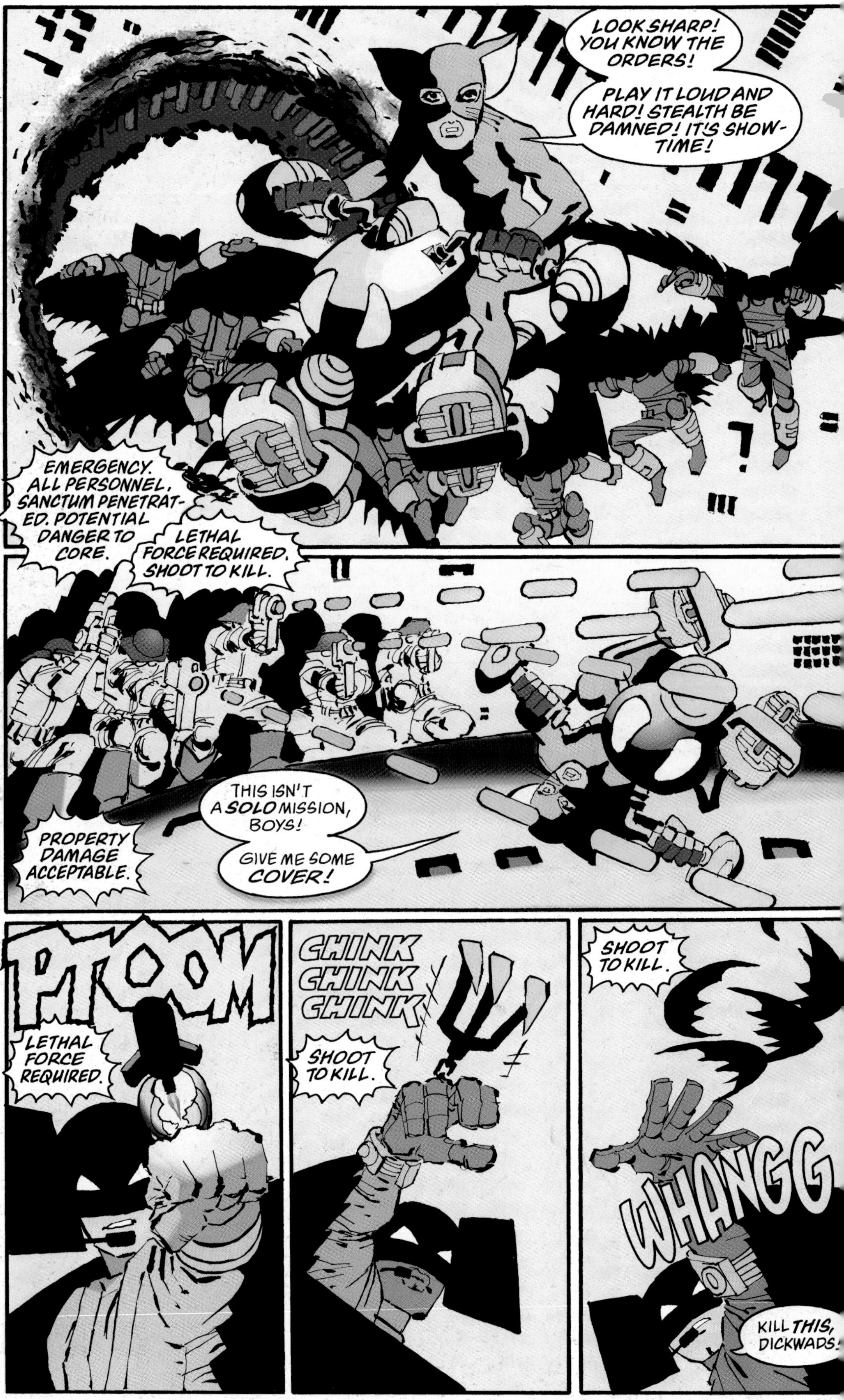
LOOK SHARP! YOU KNOW THE ORDERS!
PLAY IT LOUD AND HARD! STEALTH BE DAMNED! IT'S SHOW-TIME!
EMERGENCY. ALL PERSONNEL. SANCTUM PENETRAT-ED. POTENTIAL DANGER TO CORE.
LETHAL FORCE REQUIRED. SHOOT TO KILL.
PROPERTY DAMAGE ACCEPTABLE.
THIS ISN'T A SOLO MISSION, BOYS!
GIVE ME SOME COVER!
PTOOM
LETHAL FORCE REQUIRED.
CHINK CHINK CHINK
SHOOT TO KILL.
SHOOT TO KILL.
WHANGG
KILL THIS, DICKWADS!

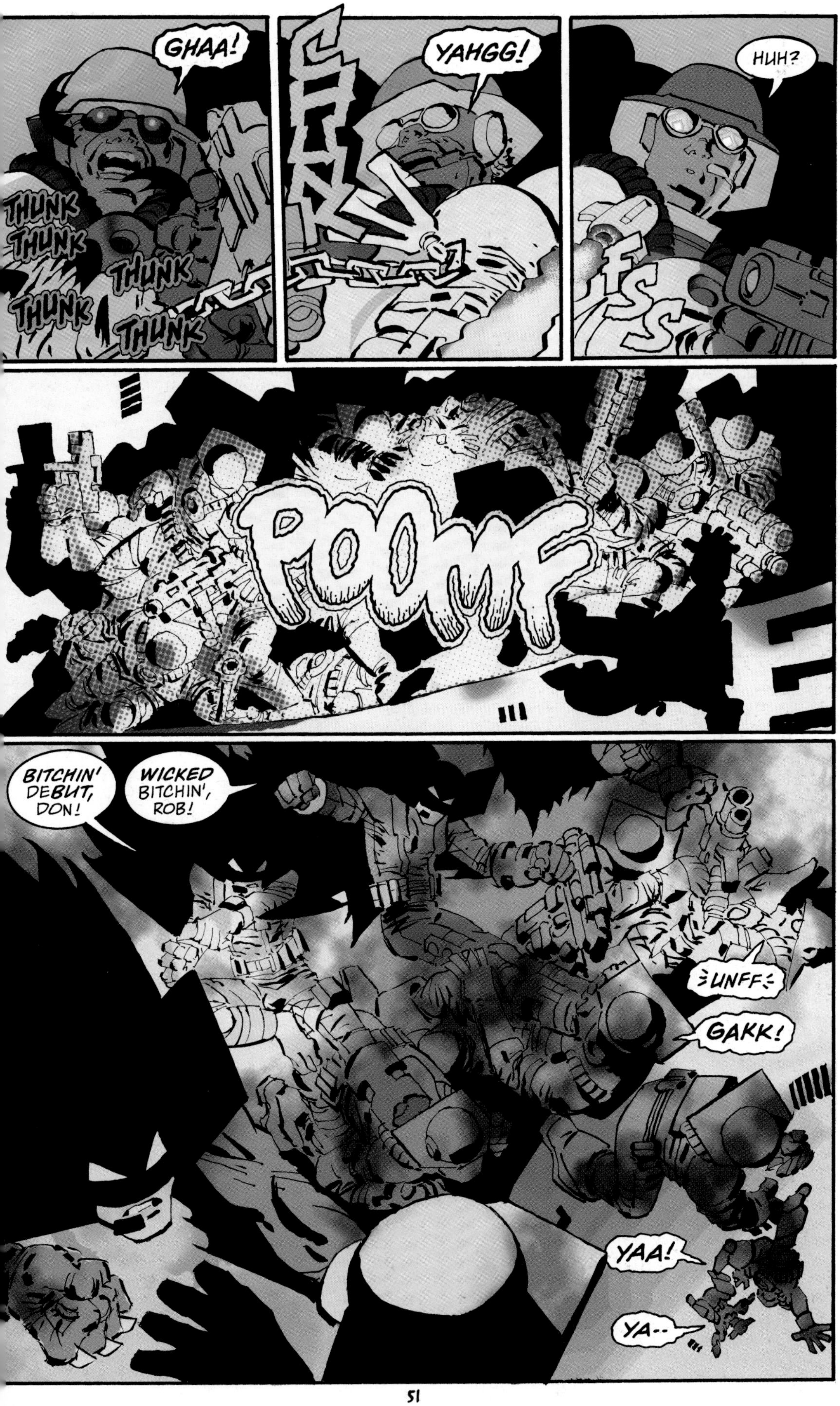
GHAA!
THUNK
THUNK
THUNK
THUNK
THUNK
YAHGG!
HUH?
FSS
POOMF
BITCHIN' DEBUT, DON!
WICKED BITCHIN', ROB!
UNFF
GAKK!
YAA!
YA--

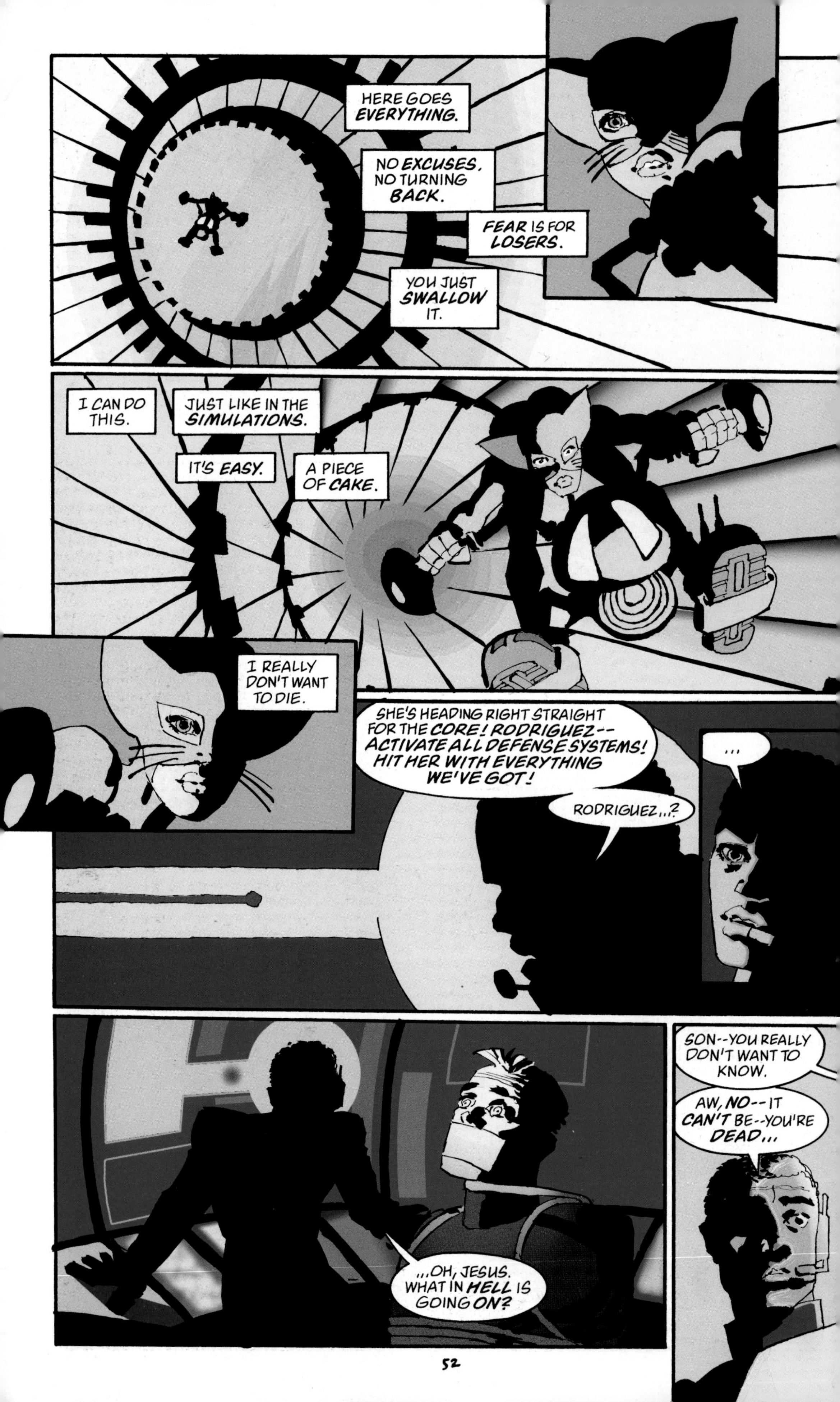
HERE GOES EVERYTHING.
NO EXCUSES. NO TURNING BACK.
FEAR IS FOR LOSERS.
YOU JUST SWALLOW IT.
I CAN DO THIS.
JUST LIKE IN THE SIMULATIONS.
IT'S EASY.
A PIECE OF CAKE.
I REALLY DON'T WANT TO DIE.
SHE'S HEADING RIGHT STRAIGHT FOR THE CORE! RODRIGUEZ--ACTIVATE ALL DEFENSE SYSTEMS! HIT HER WITH EVERYTHING WE'VE GOT!
RODRIGUEZ...?
...
...OH, JESUS. WHAT IN HELL IS GOING ON?
SON--YOU REALLY DON'T WANT TO KNOW.
AW, NO--IT CAN'T BE--YOU'RE DEAD...

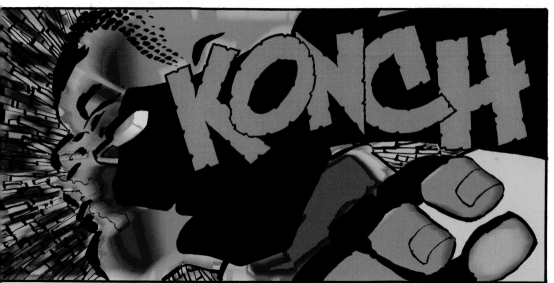

I STEAL A FEW SECONDS--

--TO CHECK IN ON THE TROOPS.

MY BOYS.

THEY USED TO BE A WORTHLESS, DOOMED GANG OF STREET THUGS. CRIMINALS.

THE KIND I USED TO HUNT.

JUST LOOK AT THEM NOW.

AND DEAR CARRIE. CATGIRL.

SHE MEMORIZED EVERY LAST VECTOR OF THEIR LASER DEFENSE SEQUENCE-- IN A SINGLE AFTERNOON.

SHE'S A NATURAL.

STAY SHARP, MY LITTLE DARLING.

NO FALSE MOVES.

FRANTIC COMMANDS BARK ACROSS THE COMM SYSTEM LIKE PACKS OF WILD DOGS.

I DON'T SHUT THEM DOWN. QUITE THE OPPOSITE.

I BRING THE VOLUME UP.

WAY UP.

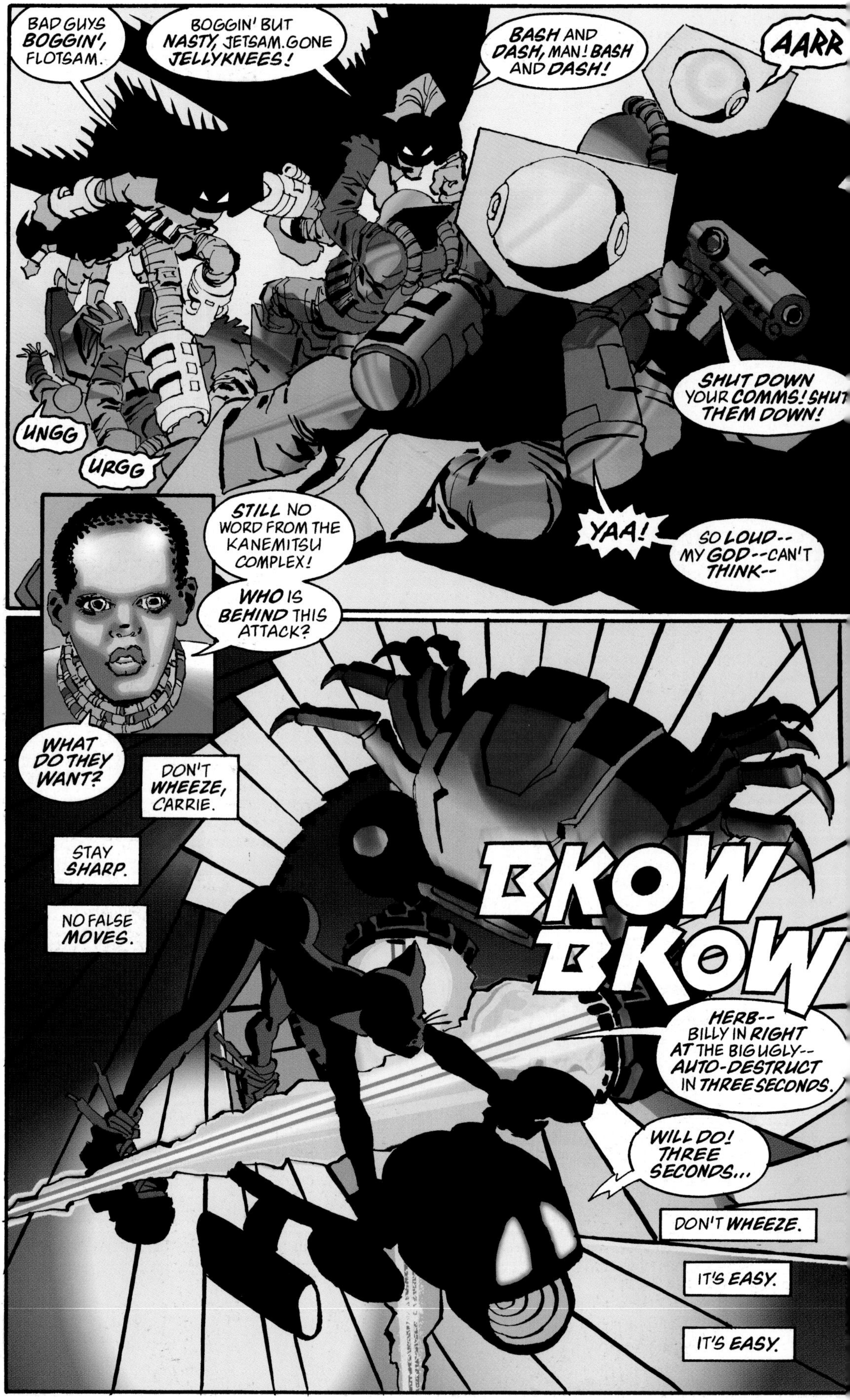
BAD GUYS BOGGIN', FLOTSAM.
BOGGIN' BUT NASTY, JETSAM. GONE JELLYKNEES!
BASH AND DASH, MAN! BASH AND DASH!
AARR
SHUT DOWN YOUR COMMS! SHUT THEM DOWN!
UNGG
URGG
YAA!
SO LOUD-- MY GOD--CAN'T THINK--
STILL NO WORD FROM THE KANEMITSU COMPLEX!
WHO IS BEHIND THIS ATTACK?
WHAT DO THEY WANT?
DON'T WHEEZE, CARRIE.
STAY SHARP.
NO FALSE MOVES.
BKOW BKOW
HERB-- BILLY IN RIGHT AT THE BIG UGLY-- AUTO-DESTRUCT IN THREE SECONDS.
WILL DO! THREE SECONDS...
DON'T WHEEZE.
IT'S EASY.
IT'S EASY.

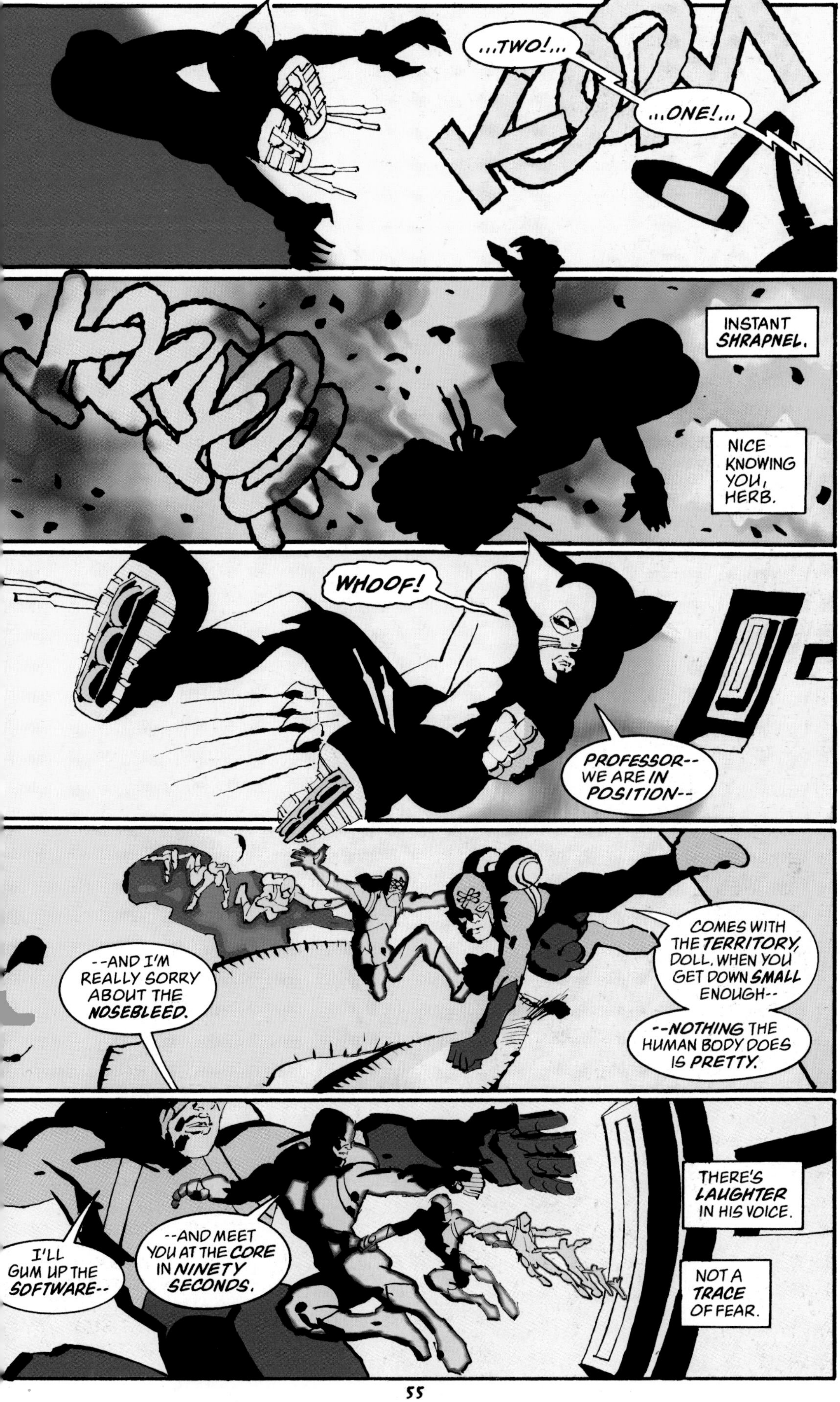
...TWO!...
...ONE!...
INSTANT SHRAPNEL.
NICE KNOWING YOU, HERB.
WHOOF!
PROFESSOR-- WE ARE IN POSITION--
COMES WITH THE TERRITORY, DOLL, WHEN YOU GET DOWN SMALL ENOUGH--
--NOTHING THE HUMAN BODY DOES IS PRETTY.
--AND I'M REALLY SORRY ABOUT THE NOSEBLEED.
THERE'S LAUGHTER IN HIS VOICE.
NOT A TRACE OF FEAR.
I'LL GUM UP THE SOFTWARE--
--AND MEET YOU AT THE CORE IN NINETY SECONDS.

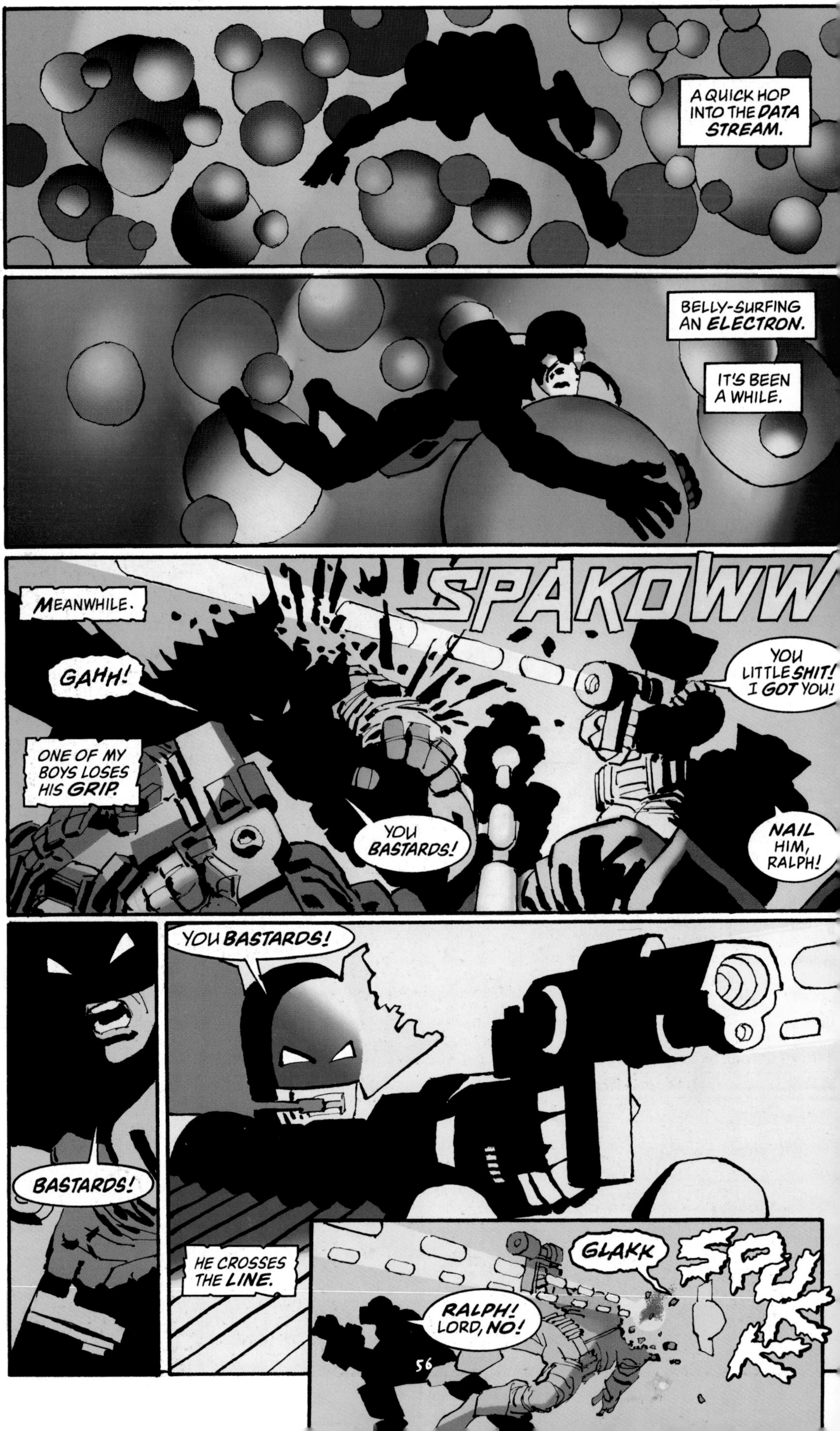
A QUICK HOP INTO THE DATA STREAM.
BELLY-SURFING AN ELECTRON.
IT'S BEEN A WHILE.
SPAKOWW
MEANWHILE.
GAHH!
YOU LITTLE SHIT! I GOT YOU!
ONE OF MY BOYS LOSES HIS GRIP.
YOU BASTARDS!
NAIL HIM, RALPH!
YOU BASTARDS!
BASTARDS!
HE CROSSES THE LINE.
GLAKK
SPUKK
RALPH! LORD, NO!

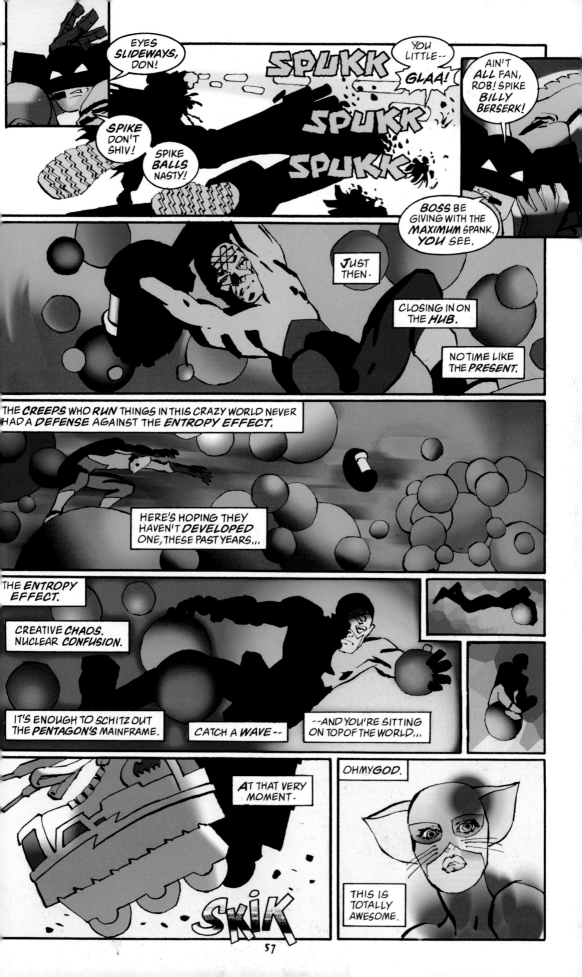

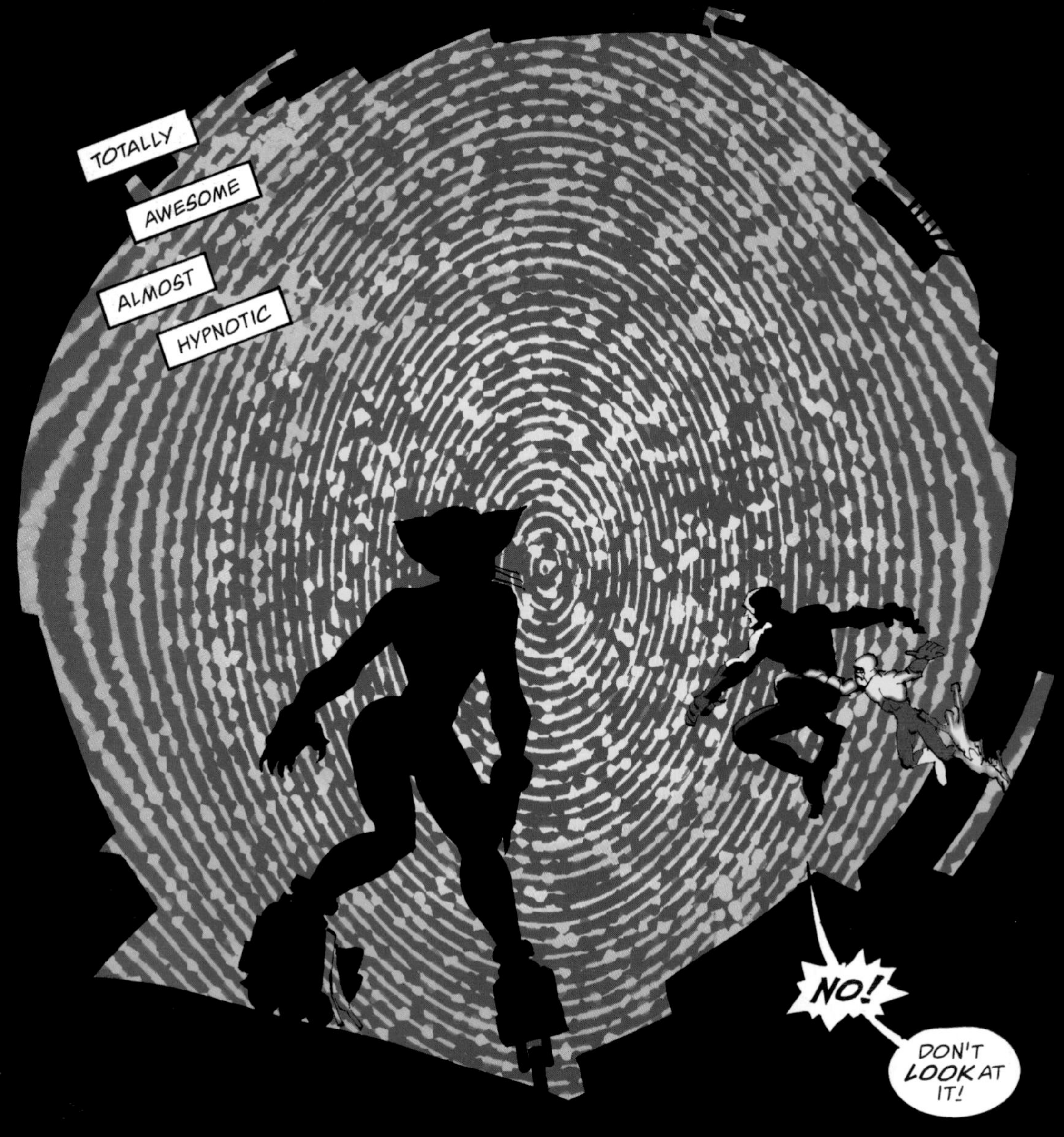
TOTALLY
AWESOME
ALMOST
HYPNOTIC
NO!
DON'T LOOK AT IT!

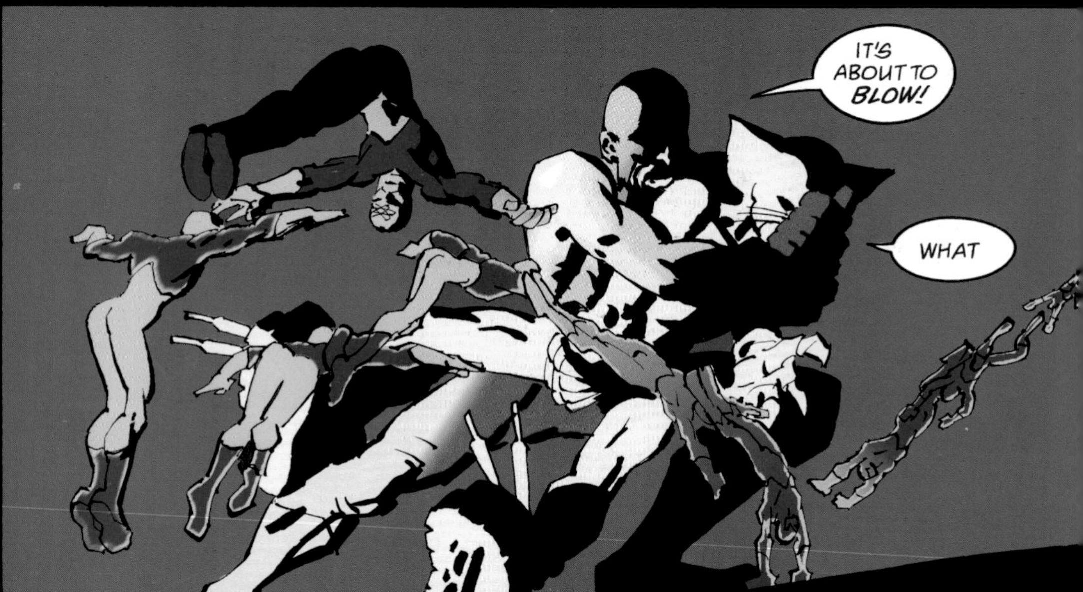
IT'S ABOUT TO BLOW!
WHAT

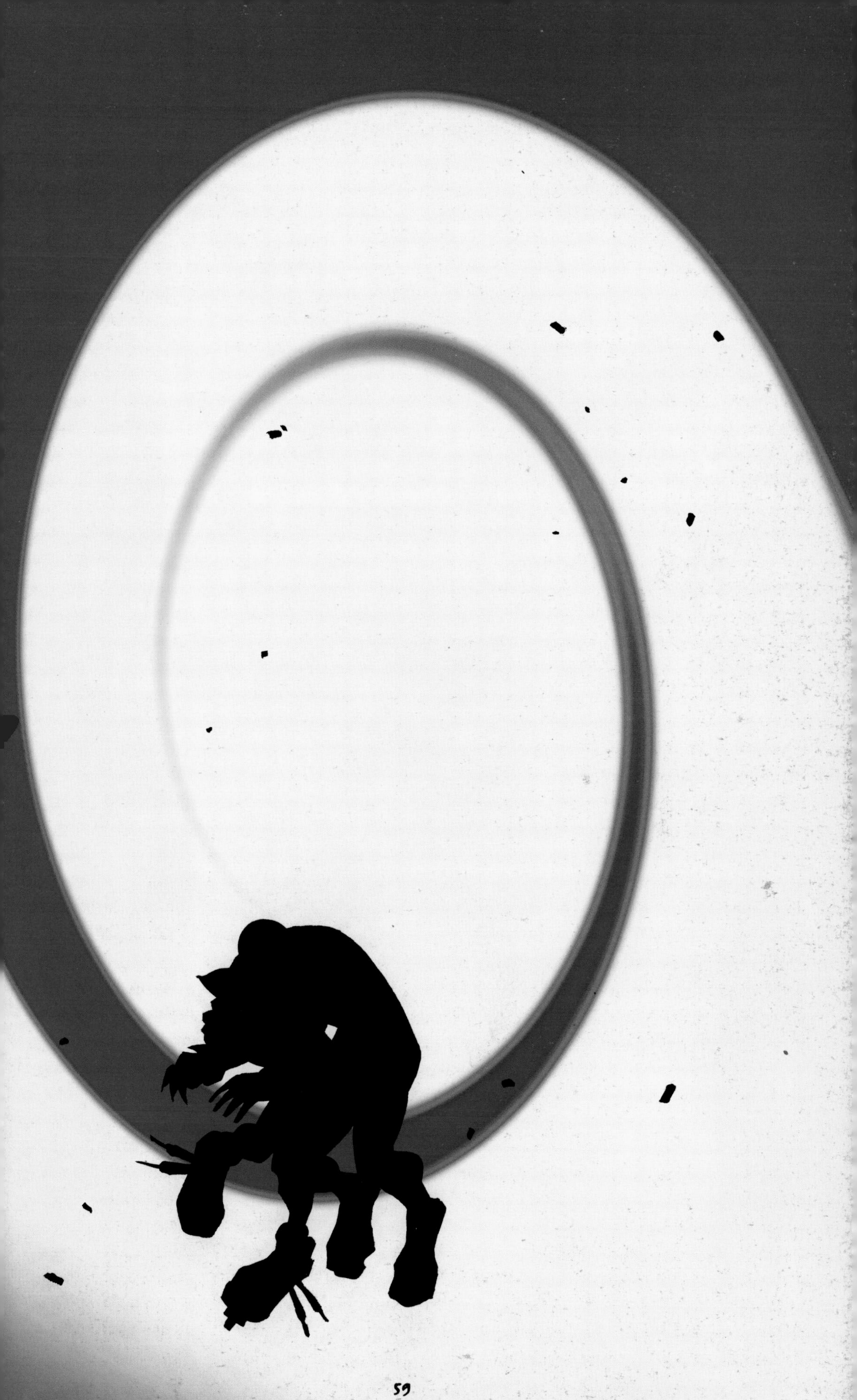

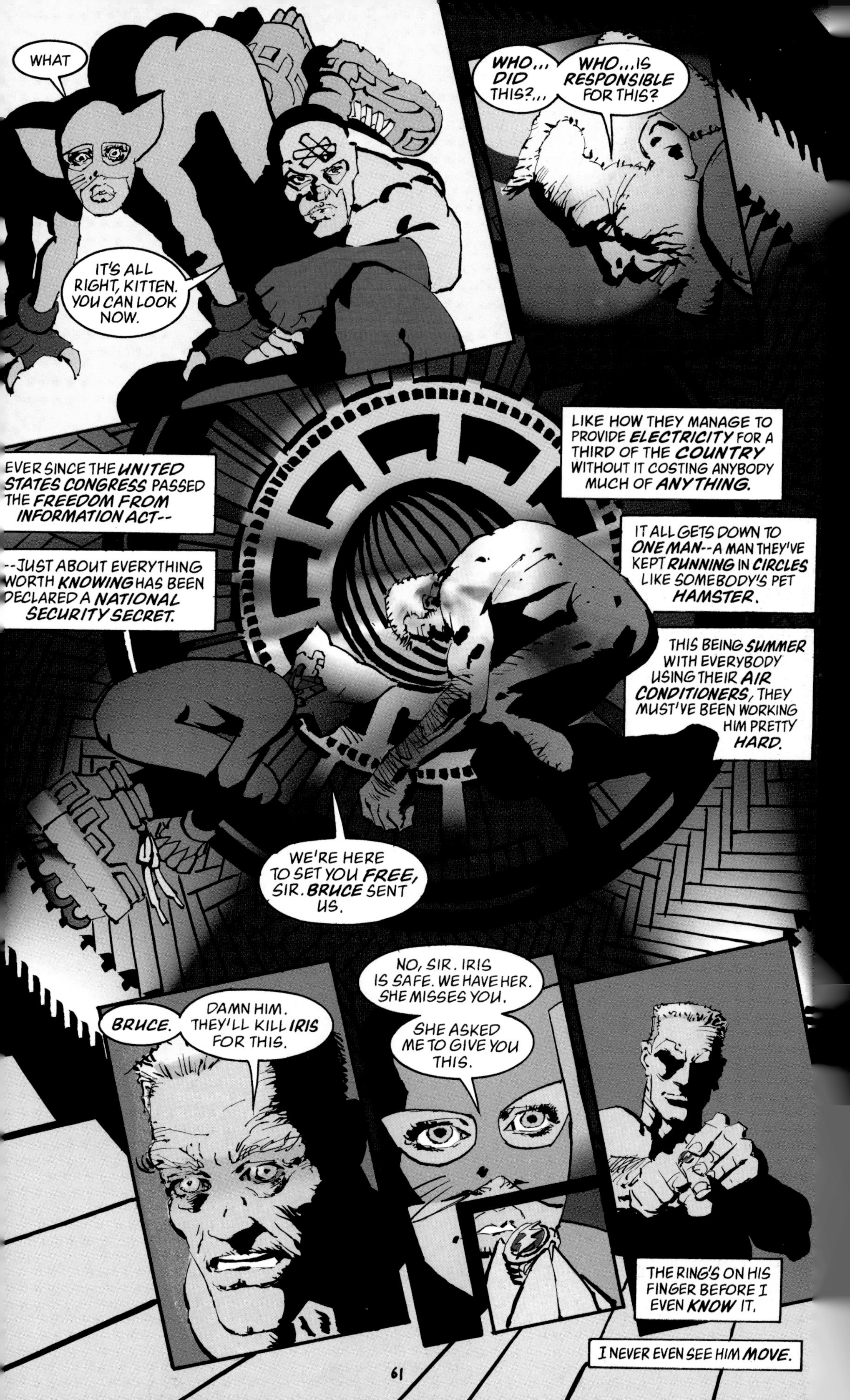
WHAT
IT'S ALL RIGHT, KITTEN. YOU CAN LOOK NOW.
WHO... DID THIS?...
WHO...IS RESPONSIBLE FOR THIS?
EVER SINCE THE UNITED STATES CONGRESS PASSED THE FREEDOM FROM INFORMATION ACT--
--JUST ABOUT EVERYTHING WORTH KNOWING HAS BEEN DECLARED A NATIONAL SECURITY SECRET.
LIKE HOW THEY MANAGE TO PROVIDE ELECTRICITY FOR A THIRD OF THE COUNTRY WITHOUT IT COSTING ANYBODY MUCH OF ANYTHING.
IT ALL GETS DOWN TO ONE MAN--A MAN THEY'VE KEPT RUNNING IN CIRCLES LIKE SOMEBODY'S PET HAMSTER.
THIS BEING SUMMER WITH EVERYBODY USING THEIR AIR CONDITIONERS, THEY MUST'VE BEEN WORKING HIM PRETTY HARD.
WE'RE HERE TO SET YOU FREE, SIR. BRUCE SENT US.
BRUCE.
DAMN HIM. THEY'LL KILL IRIS FOR THIS.
NO, SIR. IRIS IS SAFE. WE HAVE HER. SHE MISSES YOU.
SHE ASKED ME TO GIVE YOU THIS.
THE RING'S ON HIS FINGER BEFORE I EVEN KNOW IT.
I NEVER EVEN SEE HIM MOVE.

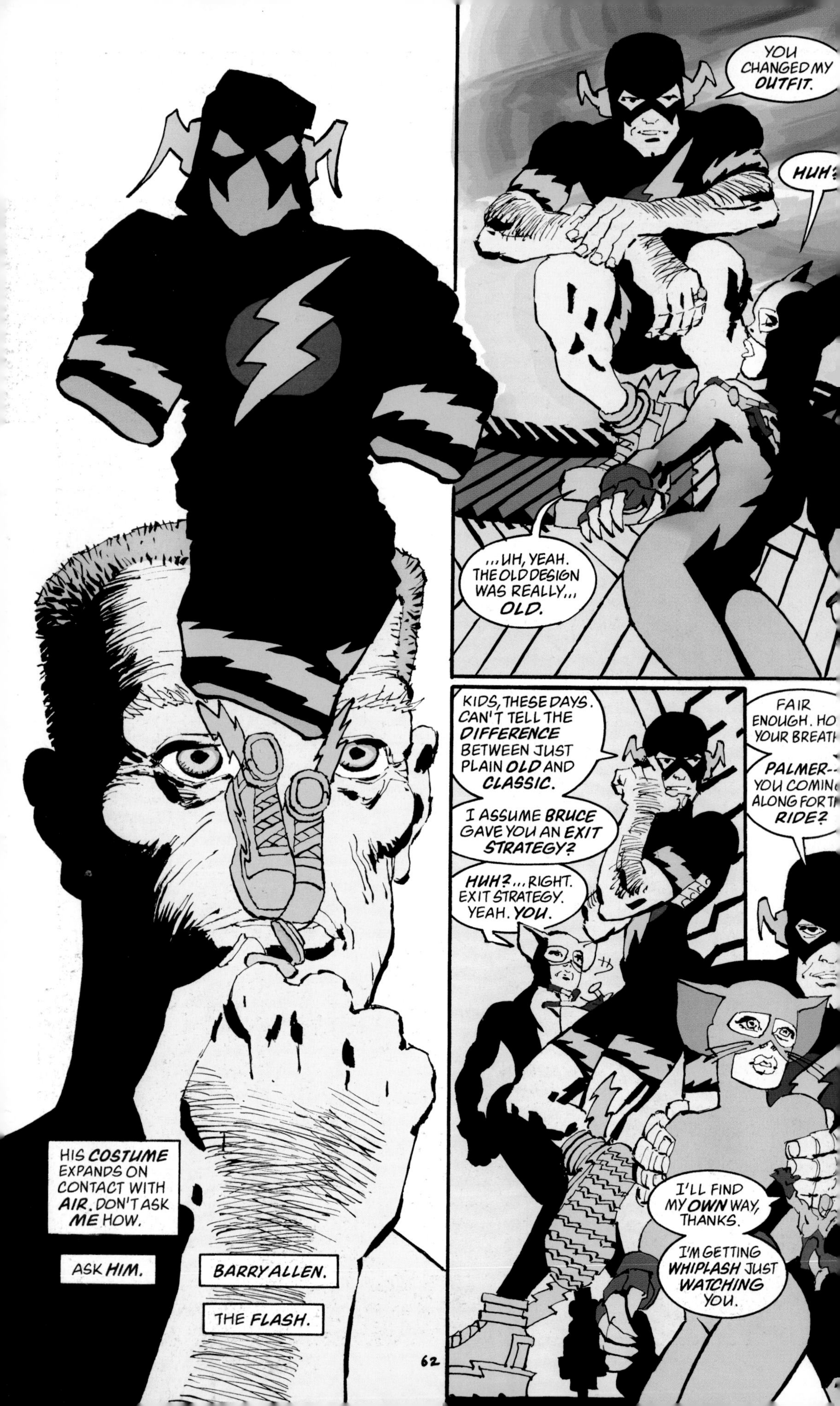

HIS COSTUME EXPANDS ON CONTACT WITH AIR. DON'T ASK ME HOW.
ASK HIM.
BARRY ALLEN.
THE FLASH.
YOU CHANGED MY OUTFIT.
HUH?
...UH, YEAH. THE OLD DESIGN WAS REALLY... OLD.
KIDS, THESE DAYS. CAN'T TELL THE DIFFERENCE BETWEEN JUST PLAIN OLD AND CLASSIC.
I ASSUME BRUCE GAVE YOU AN EXIT STRATEGY?
HUH?... RIGHT. EXIT STRATEGY. YEAH. YOU.
FAIR ENOUGH. HO YOUR BREATH
PALMER-- YOU COMIN ALONG FOR T RIDE?
I'LL FIND MY OWN WAY, THANKS.
I'M GETTING WHIPLASH JUST WATCHING YOU.

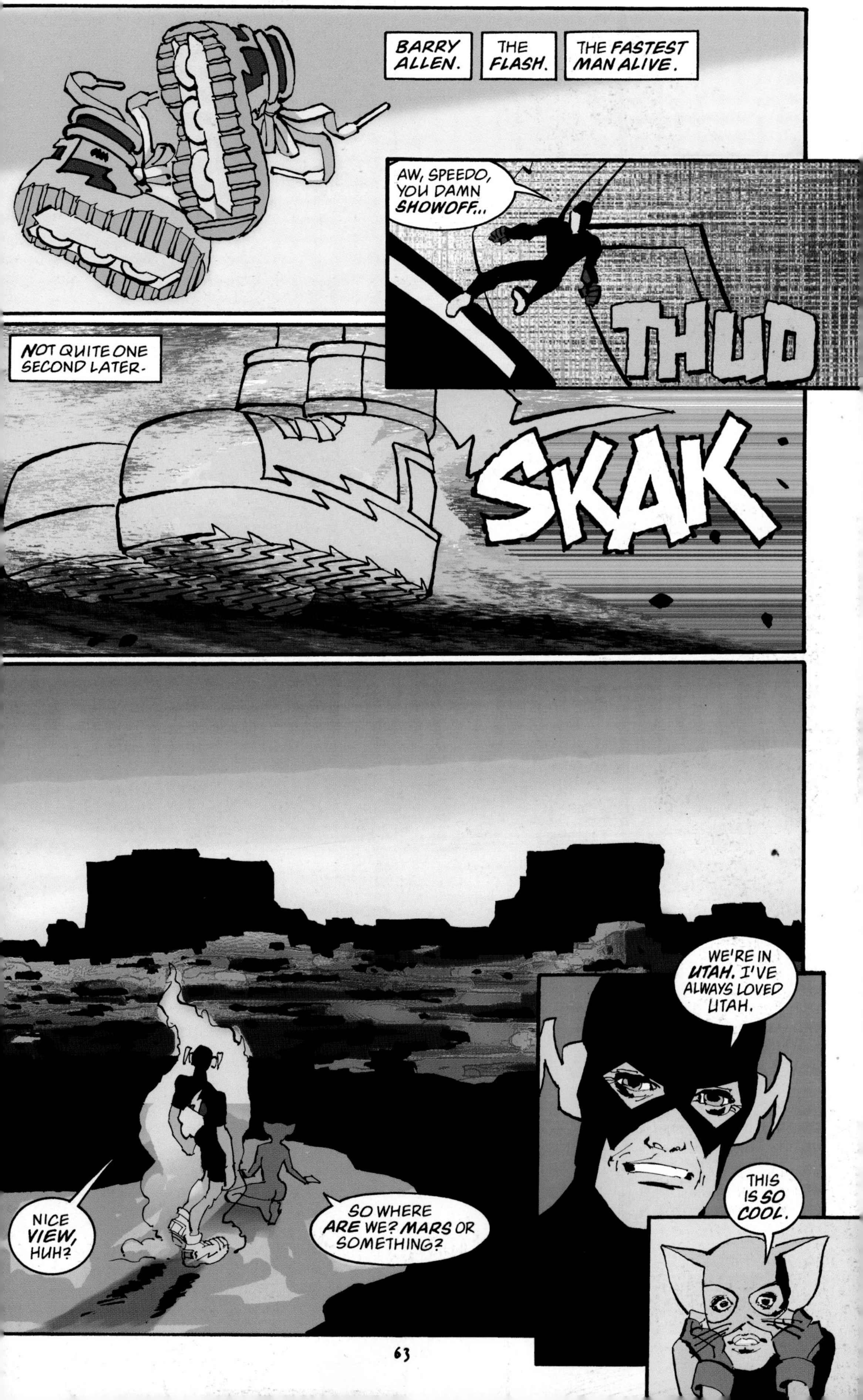

BARRY ALLEN.
THE FLASH.
THE FASTEST MAN ALIVE.
AW, SPEEDO, YOU DAMN SHOWOFF...
THUD
NOT QUITE ONE SECOND LATER-
SKAK
NICE VIEW, HUH?
SO WHERE ARE WE? MARS OR SOMETHING?
WE'RE IN UTAH. I'VE ALWAYS LOVED UTAH.
THIS IS SO COOL.

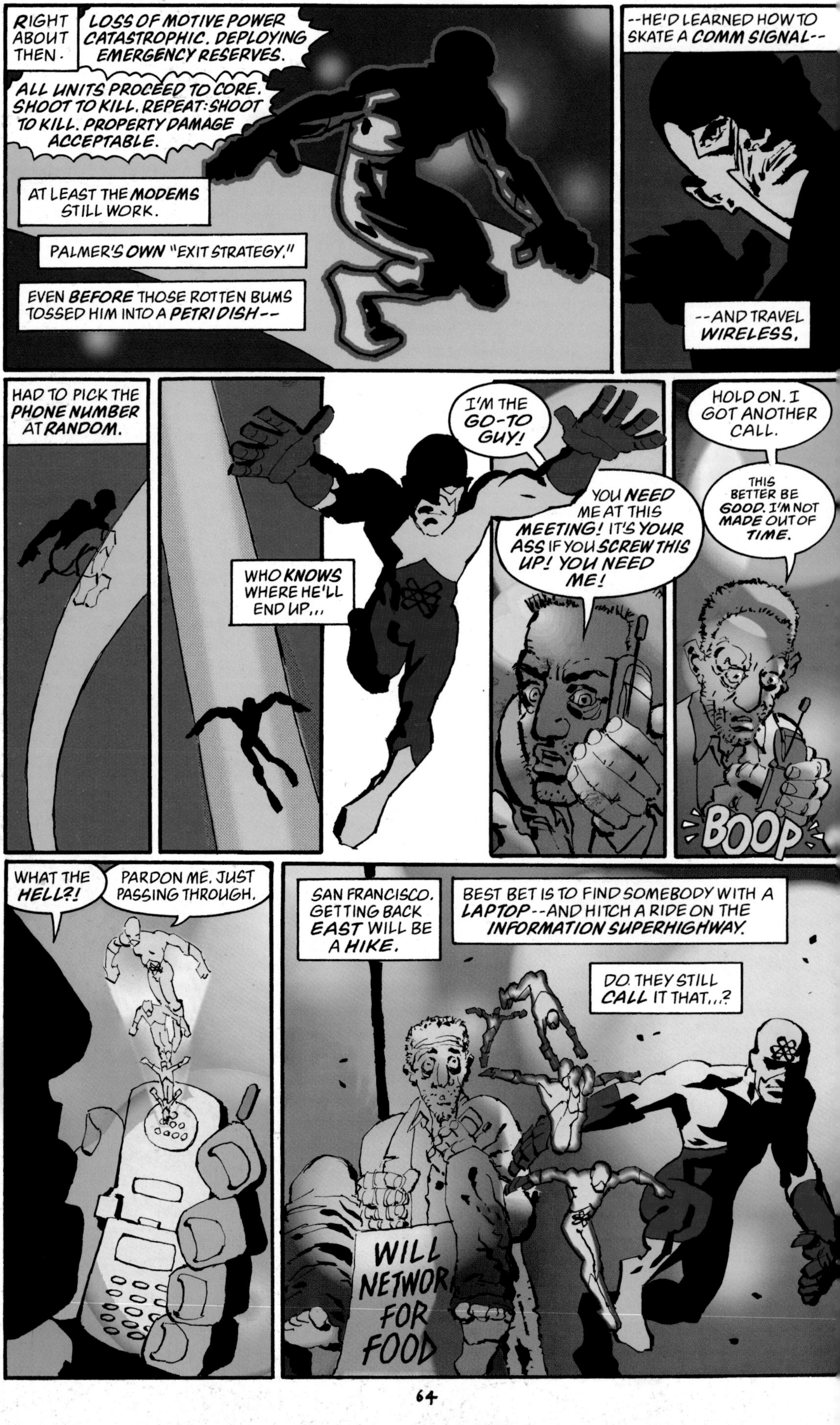
RIGHT ABOUT THEN.
LOSS OF MOTIVE POWER CATASTROPHIC. DEPLOYING EMERGENCY RESERVES.
ALL UNITS PROCEED TO CORE. SHOOT TO KILL. REPEAT: SHOOT TO KILL. PROPERTY DAMAGE ACCEPTABLE.
AT LEAST THE MODEMS STILL WORK.
PALMER'S OWN "EXIT STRATEGY."
EVEN BEFORE THOSE ROTTEN BUMS TOSSED HIM INTO A PETRI DISH--
--HE'D LEARNED HOW TO SKATE A COMM SIGNAL--
--AND TRAVEL WIRELESS.
HAD TO PICK THE PHONE NUMBER AT RANDOM.
WHO KNOWS WHERE HE'LL END UP...
I'M THE GO-TO GUY!
YOU NEED ME AT THIS MEETING! IT'S YOUR ASS IF YOU SCREW THIS UP! YOU NEED ME!
HOLD ON. I GOT ANOTHER CALL.
THIS BETTER BE GOOD. I'M NOT MADE OUT OF TIME.
BOOP
WHAT THE HELL?!
PARDON ME. JUST PASSING THROUGH.
SAN FRANCISCO. GETTING BACK EAST WILL BE A HIKE.
BEST BET IS TO FIND SOMEBODY WITH A LAPTOP--AND HITCH A RIDE ON THE INFORMATION SUPERHIGHWAY.
DO THEY STILL CALL IT THAT...?
WILL NETWOR FOR FOOD

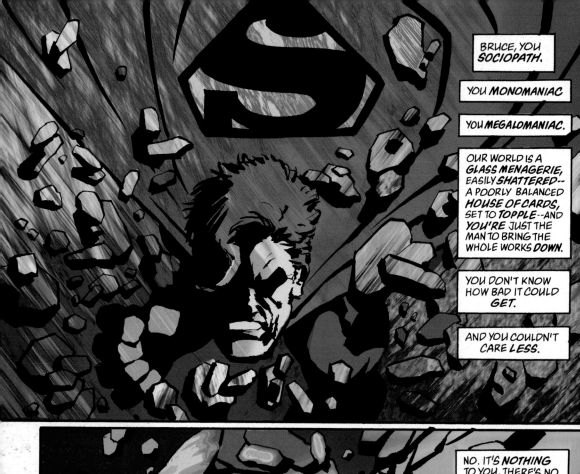

BRUCE, YOU *SOCIOPATH.*

YOU *MONOMANIAC*

YOU *MEGALOMANIAC.*

OUR WORLD IS A *GLASS MENAGERIE,* EASILY *SHATTERED--* A POORLY BALANCED *HOUSE OF CARDS,* SET TO *TOPPLE--* AND *YOU'RE* JUST THE MAN TO BRING THE WHOLE WORKS *DOWN.*

YOU DON'T KNOW HOW BAD IT COULD *GET.*

AND YOU COULDN'T CARE *LESS.*

NO. IT'S *NOTHING* TO YOU. THERE'S NO *ROOM* IN YOUR STEEL-TRAP *HEART* TO FEEL FOR THE *SUFFERING* YOU'LL SO GLEEFULLY *CAUSE.* IT WORRIES YOU *NOT FOR ONE SECOND* THAT YOUR MAD *ARROGANCE* WILL BRING *DEATH--* AND BLOODY *GENO-CIDE--* DOWN UPON OUR HEADS.

AND UPON OUR *CONSCIENCES.*

YOU *MONSTER.*

YOU *BASTARD.*

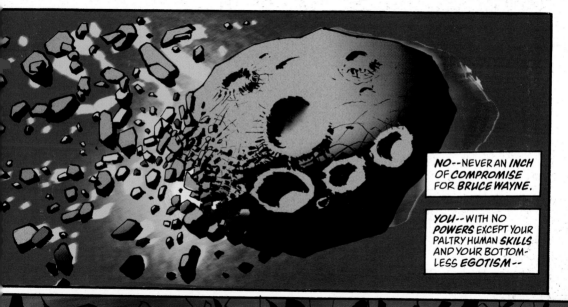

NO--NEVER AN *INCH* OF *COMPROMISE* FOR *BRUCE WAYNE.*

YOU--WITH NO *POWERS* EXCEPT YOUR *PALTRY HUMAN SKILLS* AND YOUR *BOTTOMLESS EGOTISM*--

--YOUR RELENTLESS, PITILESS, UNFORGIVING *HATRED* FOR EVERYTHING THAT ISN'T UTTERLY *PERFECT*--

--YOU'LL BE THE *DEATH* OF US ALL.

WE WHO *LIVE* IN THE *WORLD OF MEN* HAVE TO *CONSIDER* THE *GREATER GOOD* --AND *COME TO TERMS* WITH *THE WAY THINGS ARE.*

THE

WAY

THINGS

ARE.

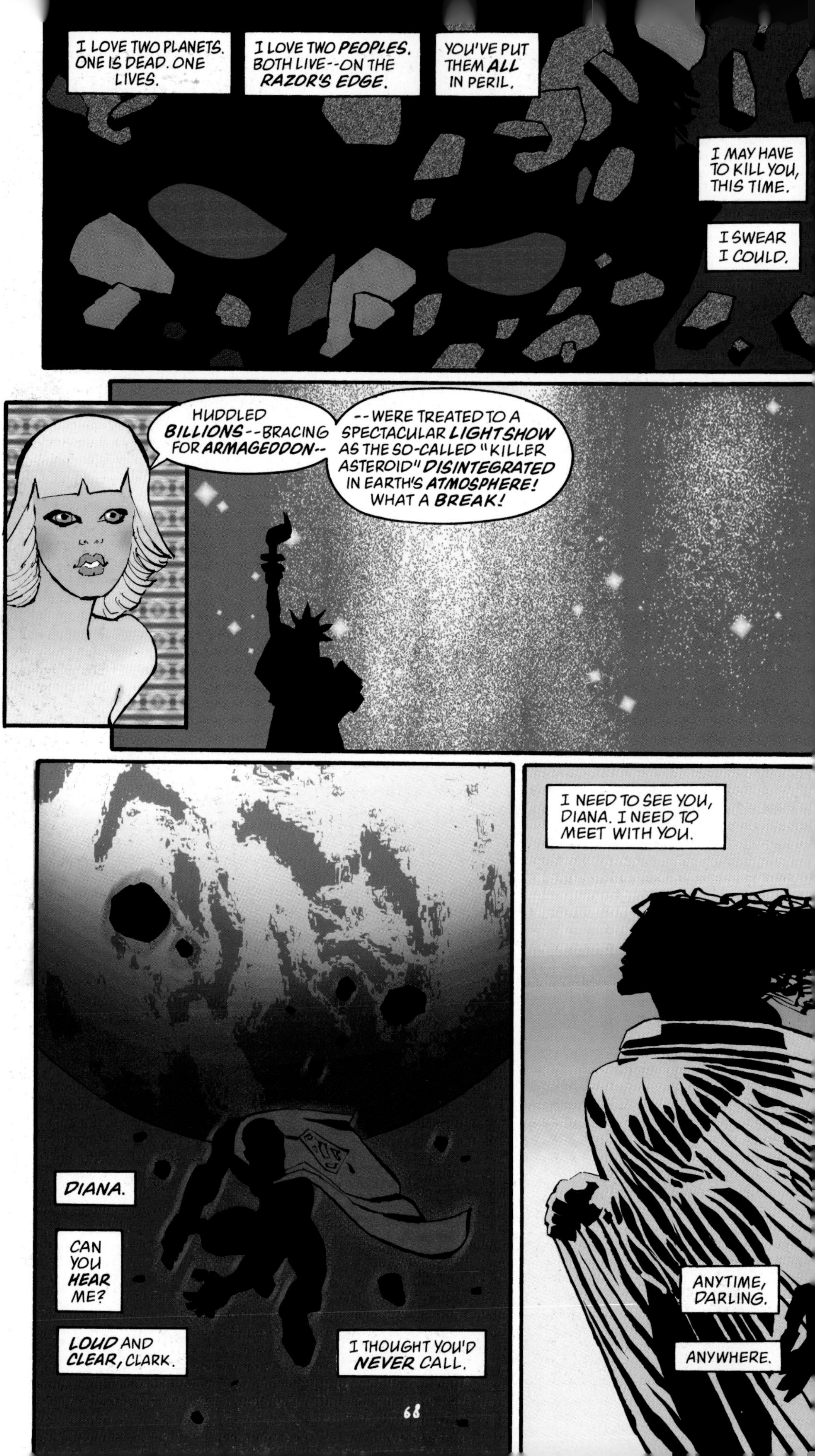
I LOVE TWO PLANETS. ONE IS DEAD. ONE LIVES.
I LOVE TWO PEOPLES. BOTH LIVE--ON THE RAZOR'S EDGE.
YOU'VE PUT THEM ALL IN PERIL.
I MAY HAVE TO KILL YOU, THIS TIME.
I SWEAR I COULD.
HUDDLED BILLIONS--BRACING FOR ARMAGEDDON--
--WERE TREATED TO A SPECTACULAR LIGHTSHOW AS THE SO-CALLED "KILLER ASTEROID" DISINTEGRATED IN EARTH'S ATMOSPHERE! WHAT A BREAK!
DIANA.
CAN YOU HEAR ME?
LOUD AND CLEAR, CLARK.
I THOUGHT YOU'D NEVER CALL.
I NEED TO SEE YOU, DIANA. I NEED TO MEET WITH YOU.
ANYTIME, DARLING.
ANYWHERE.

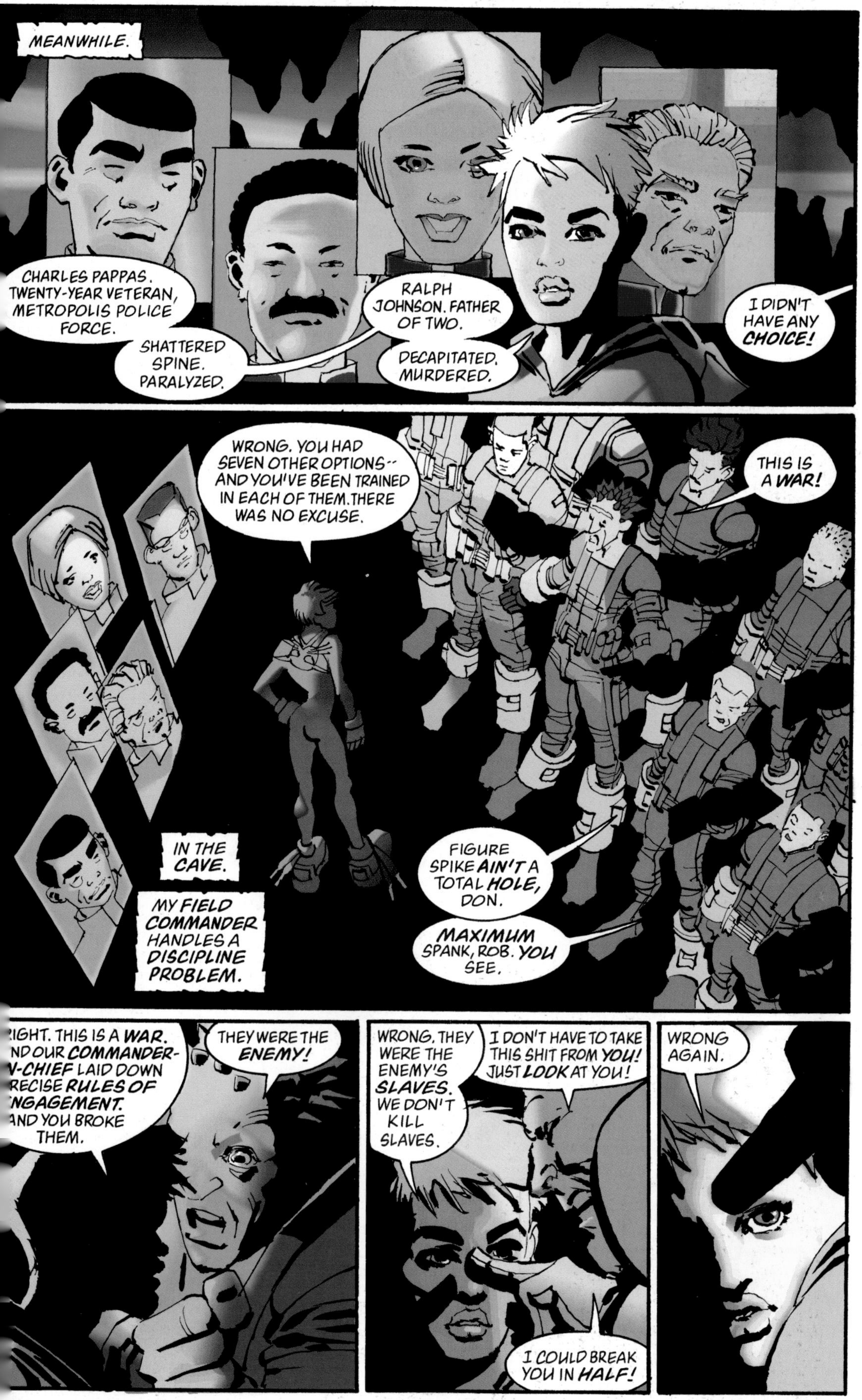
MEANWHILE.
CHARLES PAPPAS. TWENTY-YEAR VETERAN, METROPOLIS POLICE FORCE.
SHATTERED SPINE. PARALYZED.
RALPH JOHNSON. FATHER OF TWO.
DECAPITATED. MURDERED.
I DIDN'T HAVE ANY CHOICE!
WRONG. YOU HAD SEVEN OTHER OPTIONS-- AND YOU'VE BEEN TRAINED IN EACH OF THEM. THERE WAS NO EXCUSE.
THIS IS A WAR!
IN THE CAVE.
MY FIELD COMMANDER HANDLES A DISCIPLINE PROBLEM.
FIGURE SPIKE AIN'T A TOTAL HOLE, DON.
MAXIMUM SPANK, ROB. YOU SEE.
RIGHT. THIS IS A WAR. AND OUR COMMANDER-IN-CHIEF LAID DOWN PRECISE RULES OF ENGAGEMENT. AND YOU BROKE THEM.
THEY WERE THE ENEMY!
WRONG. THEY WERE THE ENEMY'S SLAVES. WE DON'T KILL SLAVES.
I DON'T HAVE TO TAKE THIS SHIT FROM YOU! JUST LOOK AT YOU!
I COULD BREAK YOU IN HALF!
WRONG AGAIN.

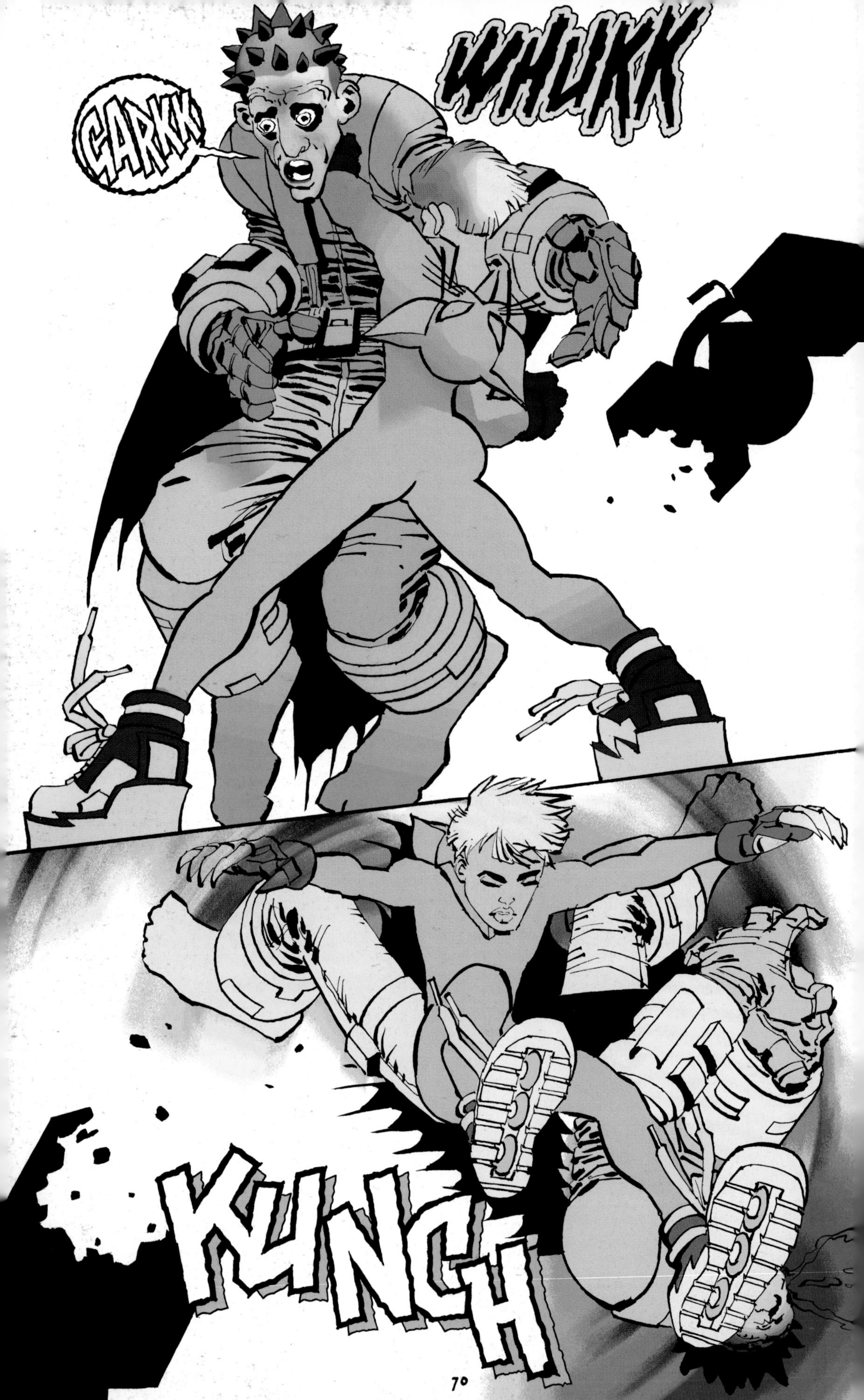
GARKK
WHUKK
KLUNCH

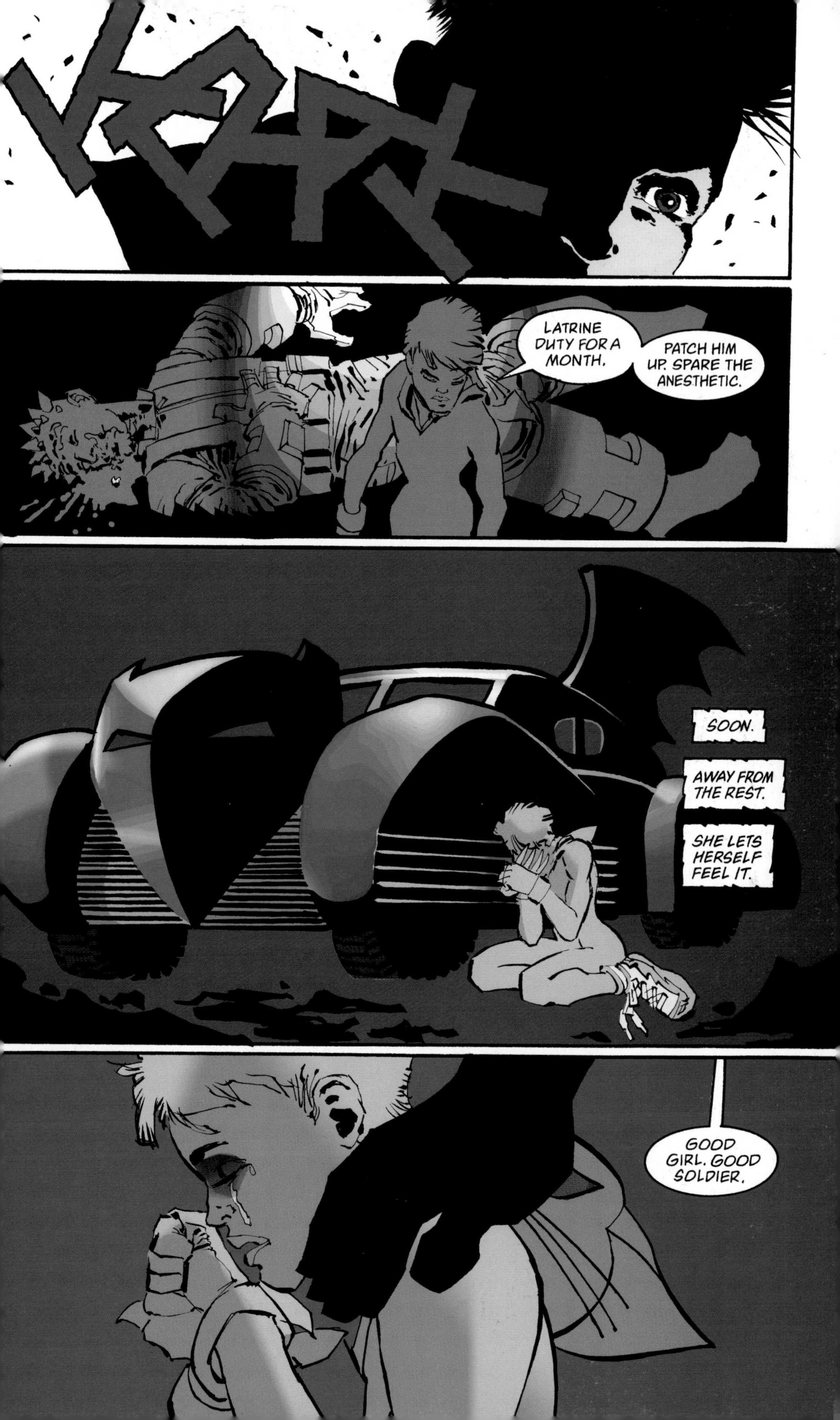
KRAK
LATRINE DUTY FOR A MONTH.
PATCH HIM UP. SPARE THE ANESTHETIC.
SOON.
AWAY FROM THE REST.
SHE LETS HERSELF FEEL IT.
GOOD GIRL. GOOD SOLDIER.

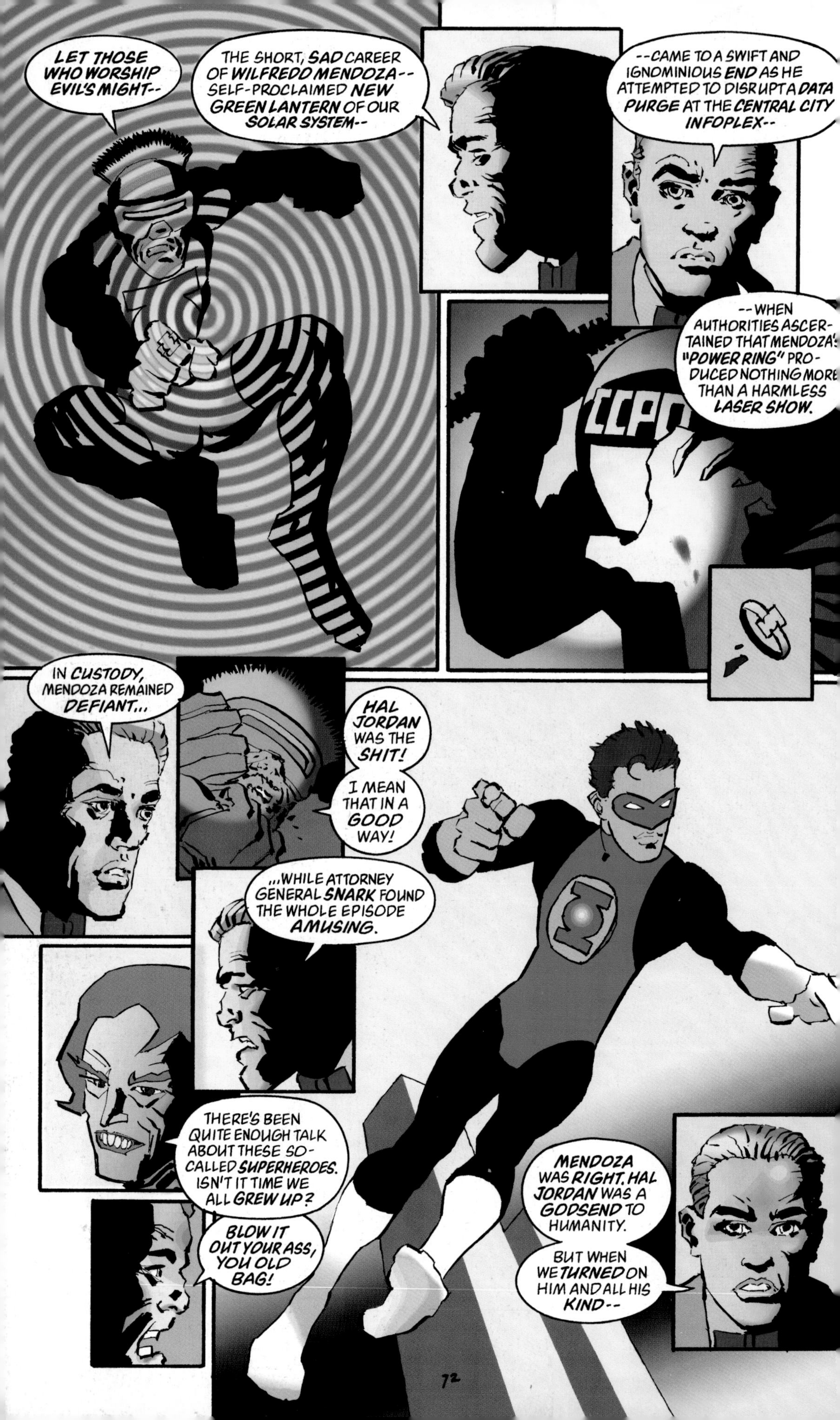
LET THOSE WHO WORSHIP EVIL'S MIGHT--
THE SHORT, SAD CAREER OF WILFREDO MENDOZA-- SELF-PROCLAIMED NEW GREEN LANTERN OF OUR SOLAR SYSTEM--
--CAME TO A SWIFT AND IGNOMINIOUS END AS HE ATTEMPTED TO DISRUPT A DATA PURGE AT THE CENTRAL CITY INFOPLEX--
--WHEN AUTHORITIES ASCERTAINED THAT MENDOZA'S "POWER RING" PRODUCED NOTHING MORE THAN A HARMLESS LASER SHOW.
CCPD
IN CUSTODY, MENDOZA REMAINED DEFIANT...
HAL JORDAN WAS THE SHIT!
I MEAN THAT IN A GOOD WAY!
...WHILE ATTORNEY GENERAL SNARK FOUND THE WHOLE EPISODE AMUSING.
THERE'S BEEN QUITE ENOUGH TALK ABOUT THESE SO-CALLED SUPERHEROES. ISN'T IT TIME WE ALL GREW UP?
BLOW IT OUT YOUR ASS, YOU OLD BAG!
MENDOZA WAS RIGHT. HAL JORDAN WAS A GODSEND TO HUMANITY.
BUT WHEN WE TURNED ON HIM AND ALL HIS KIND--

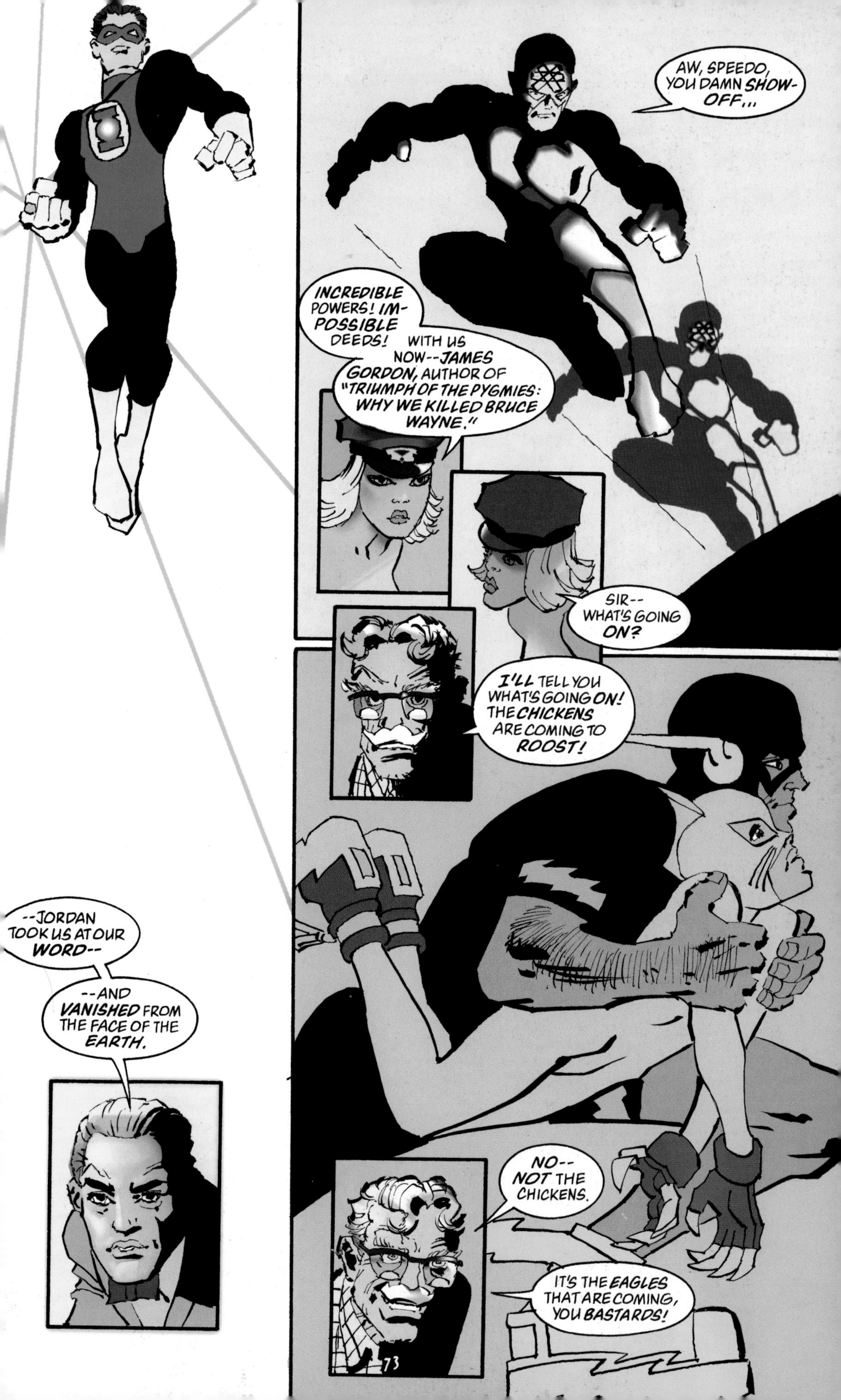

AW, SPEEDO, YOU DAMN SHOW-OFF...
INCREDIBLE POWERS! IMPOSSIBLE DEEDS! WITH US NOW--JAMES GORDON, AUTHOR OF "TRIUMPH OF THE PYGMIES: WHY WE KILLED BRUCE WAYNE."
SIR--WHAT'S GOING ON?
I'LL TELL YOU WHAT'S GOING ON! THE CHICKENS ARE COMING TO ROOST!
--JORDAN TOOK US AT OUR WORD--
--AND VANISHED FROM THE FACE OF THE EARTH.
NO--NOT THE CHICKENS.
IT'S THE EAGLES THAT ARE COMING, YOU BASTARDS!

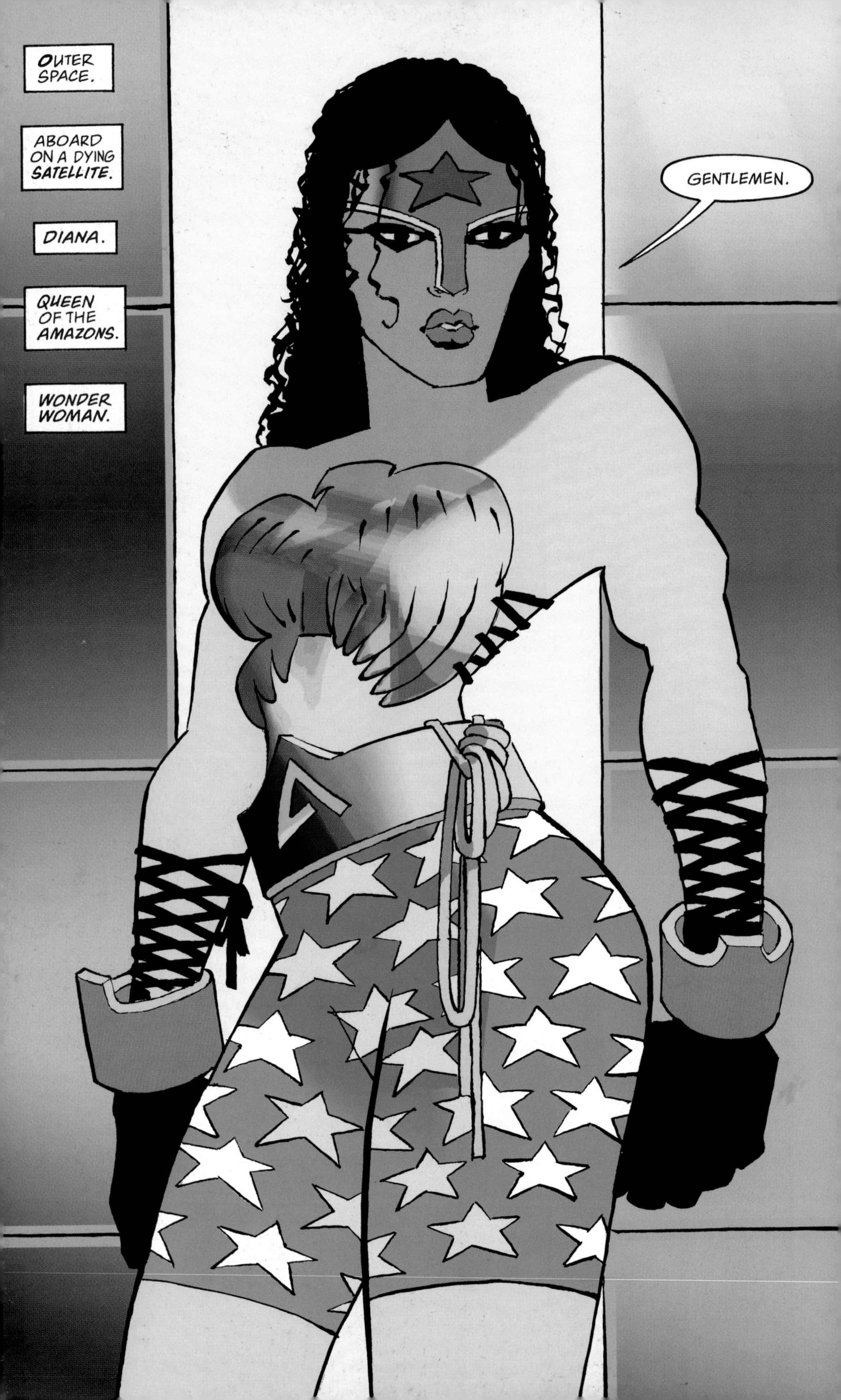

OUTER SPACE.
ABOARD ON A DYING SATELLITE.
DIANA.
QUEEN OF THE AMAZONS.
WONDER WOMAN.
GENTLEMEN.

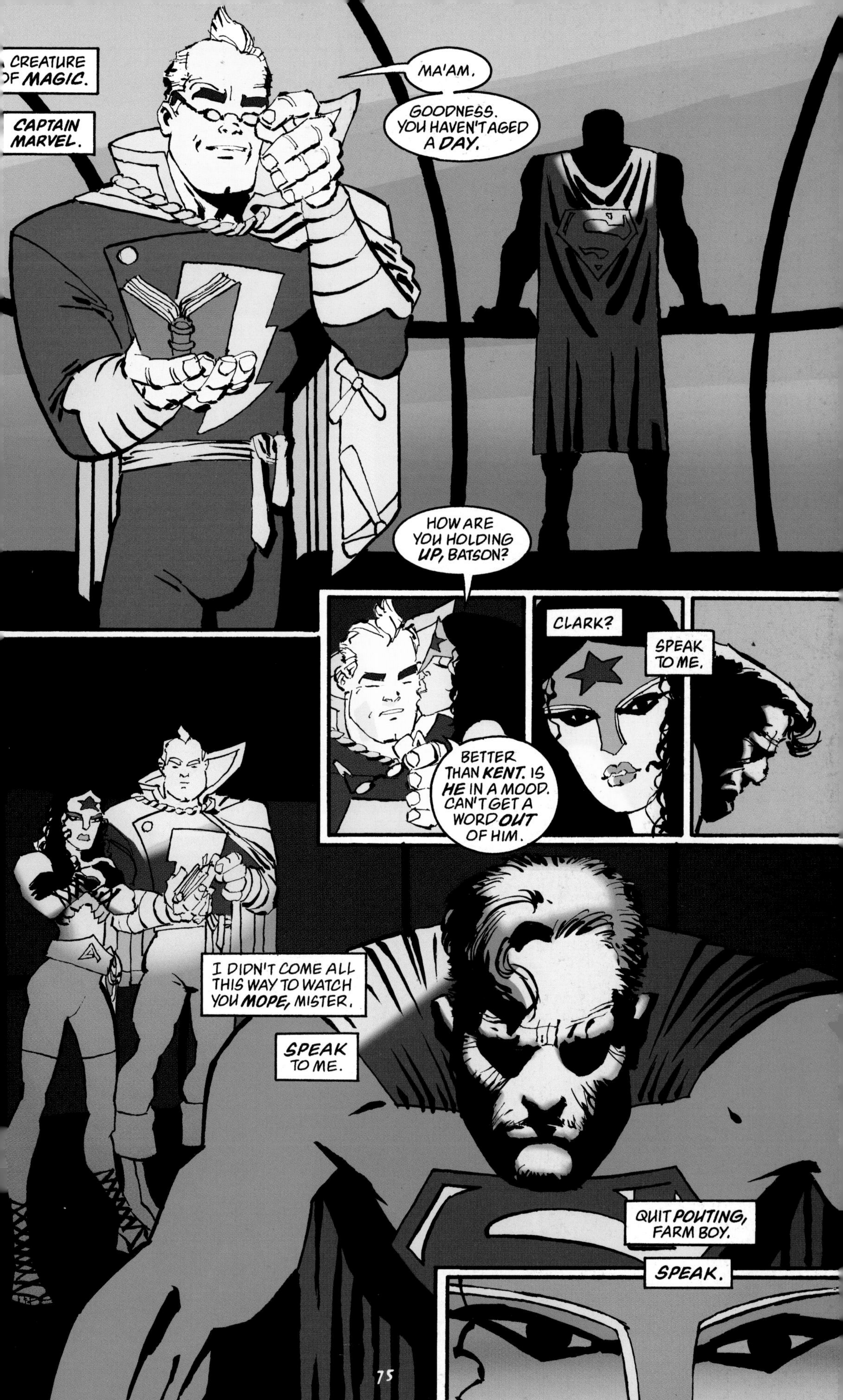
CREATURE OF MAGIC.
CAPTAIN MARVEL.
MA'AM.
GOODNESS. YOU HAVEN'T AGED A DAY.
HOW ARE YOU HOLDING UP, BATSON?
BETTER THAN KENT. IS HE IN A MOOD. CAN'T GET A WORD OUT OF HIM.
CLARK?
SPEAK TO ME.
I DIDN'T COME ALL THIS WAY TO WATCH YOU MOPE, MISTER.
SPEAK TO ME.
QUIT POUTING, FARM BOY.
SPEAK.

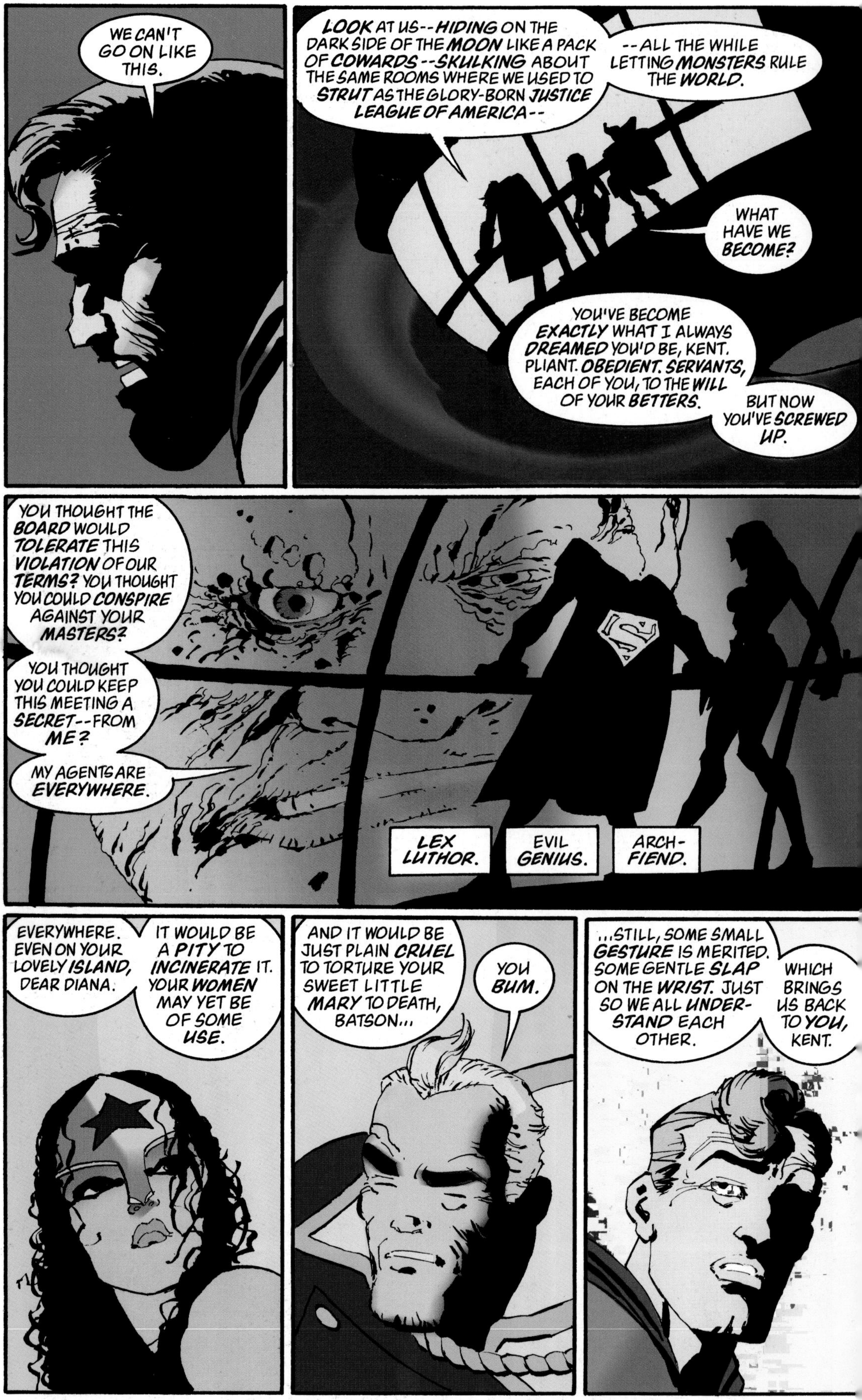
WE CAN'T GO ON LIKE THIS.
LOOK AT US--HIDING ON THE DARK SIDE OF THE MOON LIKE A PACK OF COWARDS--SKULKING ABOUT THE SAME ROOMS WHERE WE USED TO STRUT AS THE GLORY-BORN JUSTICE LEAGUE OF AMERICA--
--ALL THE WHILE LETTING MONSTERS RULE THE WORLD.
WHAT HAVE WE BECOME?
YOU'VE BECOME EXACTLY WHAT I ALWAYS DREAMED YOU'D BE, KENT. PLIANT. OBEDIENT. SERVANTS, EACH OF YOU, TO THE WILL OF YOUR BETTERS.
BUT NOW YOU'VE SCREWED UP.
YOU THOUGHT THE BOARD WOULD TOLERATE THIS VIOLATION OF OUR TERMS? YOU THOUGHT YOU COULD CONSPIRE AGAINST YOUR MASTERS?
YOU THOUGHT YOU COULD KEEP THIS MEETING A SECRET--FROM ME?
MY AGENTS ARE EVERYWHERE.
LEX LUTHOR.
EVIL GENIUS.
ARCH-FIEND.
EVERYWHERE. EVEN ON YOUR LOVELY ISLAND, DEAR DIANA.
IT WOULD BE A PITY TO INCINERATE IT. YOUR WOMEN MAY YET BE OF SOME USE.
AND IT WOULD BE JUST PLAIN CRUEL TO TORTURE YOUR SWEET LITTLE MARY TO DEATH, BATSON...
YOU BUM.
...STILL, SOME SMALL GESTURE IS MERITED. SOME GENTLE SLAP ON THE WRIST. JUST SO WE ALL UNDERSTAND EACH OTHER.
WHICH BRINGS US BACK TO YOU, KENT.

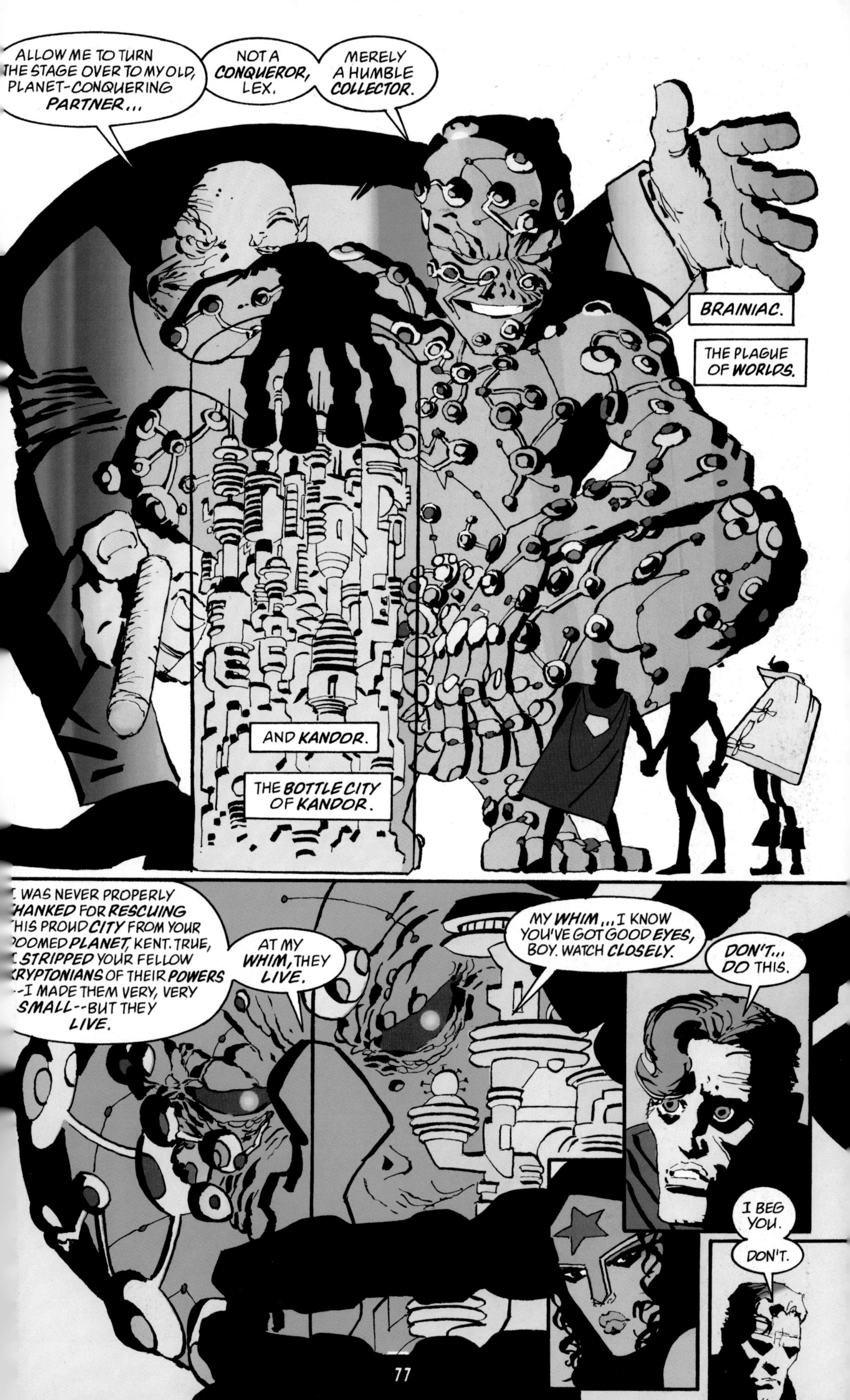

ALLOW ME TO TURN THE STAGE OVER TO MY OLD, PLANET-CONQUERING PARTNER...
NOT A CONQUEROR, LEX.
MERELY A HUMBLE COLLECTOR.
BRAINIAC.
THE PLAGUE OF WORLDS.
AND KANDOR.
THE BOTTLE CITY OF KANDOR.
I WAS NEVER PROPERLY THANKED FOR RESCUING THIS PROUD CITY FROM YOUR DOOMED PLANET, KENT. TRUE, I STRIPPED YOUR FELLOW KRYPTONIANS OF THEIR POWERS --I MADE THEM VERY, VERY SMALL--BUT THEY LIVE.
AT MY WHIM, THEY LIVE.
MY WHIM... I KNOW YOU'VE GOT GOOD EYES, BOY. WATCH CLOSELY.
DON'T... DO THIS.
I BEG YOU.
DON'T.

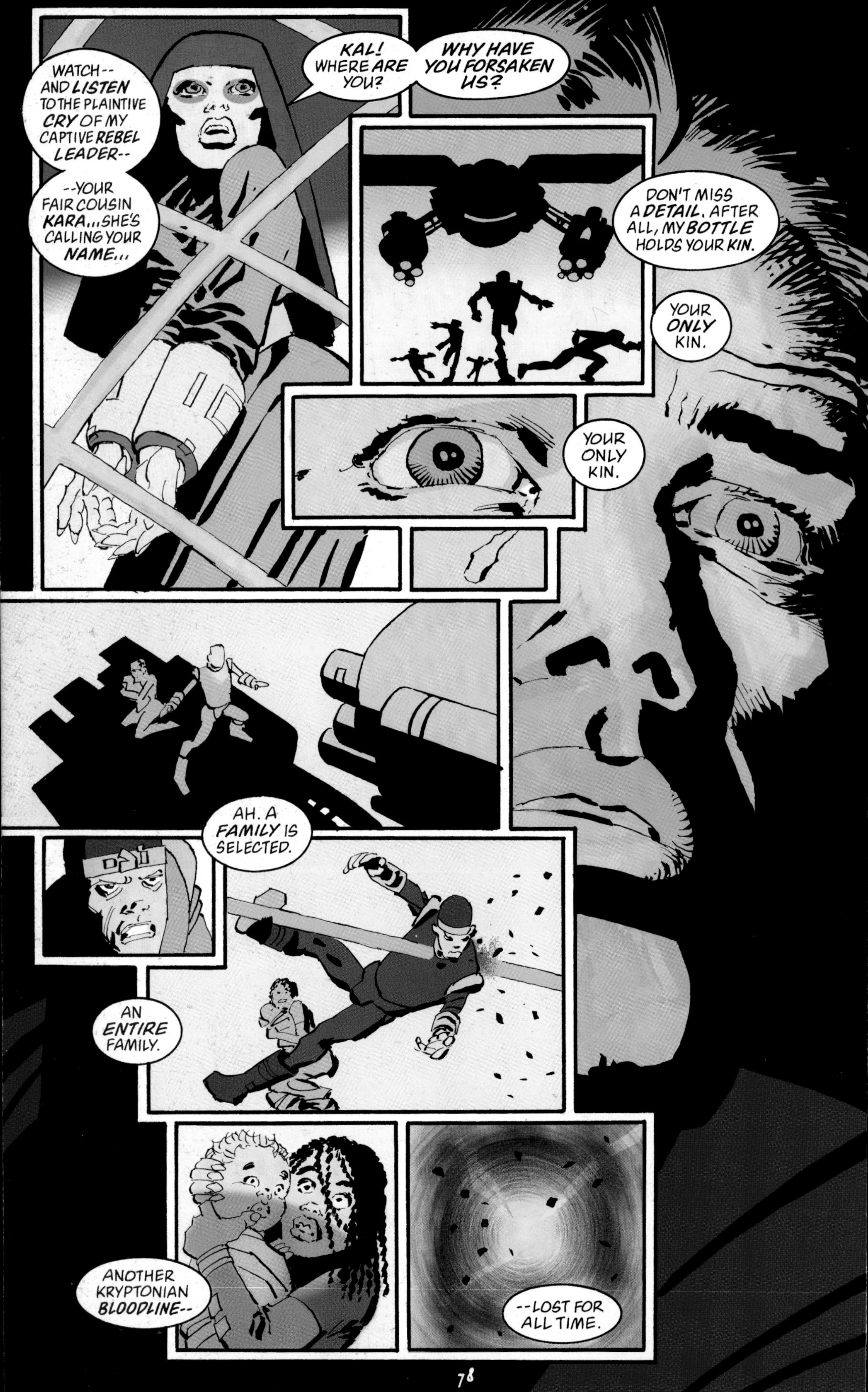

WATCH-- AND LISTEN TO THE PLAINTIVE CRY OF MY CAPTIVE REBEL LEADER--
--YOUR FAIR COUSIN KARA... SHE'S CALLING YOUR NAME...
KAL! WHERE ARE YOU?
WHY HAVE YOU FORSAKEN US?
DON'T MISS A DETAIL. AFTER ALL, MY BOTTLE HOLDS YOUR KIN.
YOUR ONLY KIN.
YOUR ONLY KIN.
AH. A FAMILY IS SELECTED.
AN ENTIRE FAMILY.
ANOTHER KRYPTONIAN BLOODLINE--
--LOST FOR ALL TIME.

WE KNOW YOU'RE UPSET. BUT COME ON, BUCK UP. THERE'S A BRIGHT SIDE TO EVERYTHING. YOU HEROES HAVE SAVED US *TIME*, GETTING TOGETHER LIKE THIS. WE CAN GIVE YOU THREE YOUR *MARCHING ORDERS* ALL AT *ONCE*.

YOU WILL FIND OUT WHAT HAPPENED TO *RAY PALMER* AND *BARRY ALLEN*--AND WHO IS *BEHIND* THESE RECENT *DISTURBANCES* -- AND YOU WILL DELIVER THE LOT TO *US*.

DIANA SAYS SOMETHING.

I CAN'T HEAR IT.

MY FRIENDS GO TO THEIR SHIPS.

THEY FALL TO EARTH.

BRUCE.

YOU AND ME, WE'RE GONNA HAVE US A *TALK*.

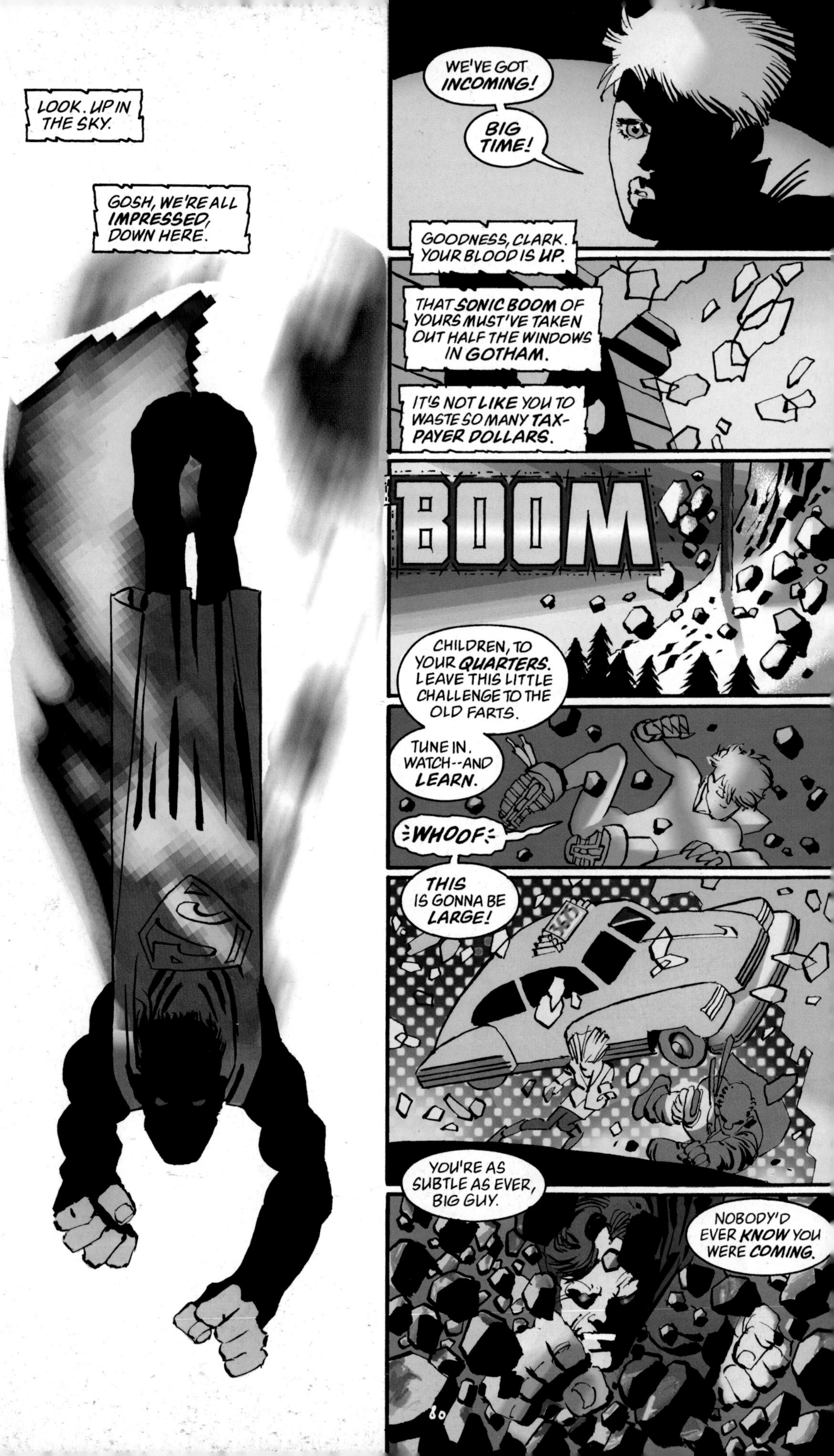
LOOK. UP IN THE SKY.
GOSH, WE'RE ALL IMPRESSED, DOWN HERE.
WE'VE GOT INCOMING!
BIG TIME!
GOODNESS, CLARK. YOUR BLOOD IS UP.
THAT SONIC BOOM OF YOURS MUST'VE TAKEN OUT HALF THE WINDOWS IN GOTHAM.
IT'S NOT LIKE YOU TO WASTE SO MANY TAX-PAYER DOLLARS.
BOOM
CHILDREN, TO YOUR QUARTERS. LEAVE THIS LITTLE CHALLENGE TO THE OLD FARTS.
TUNE IN. WATCH--AND LEARN.
WHOOF
THIS IS GONNA BE LARGE!
YOU'RE AS SUBTLE AS EVER, BIG GUY.
NOBODY'D EVER KNOW YOU WERE COMING.

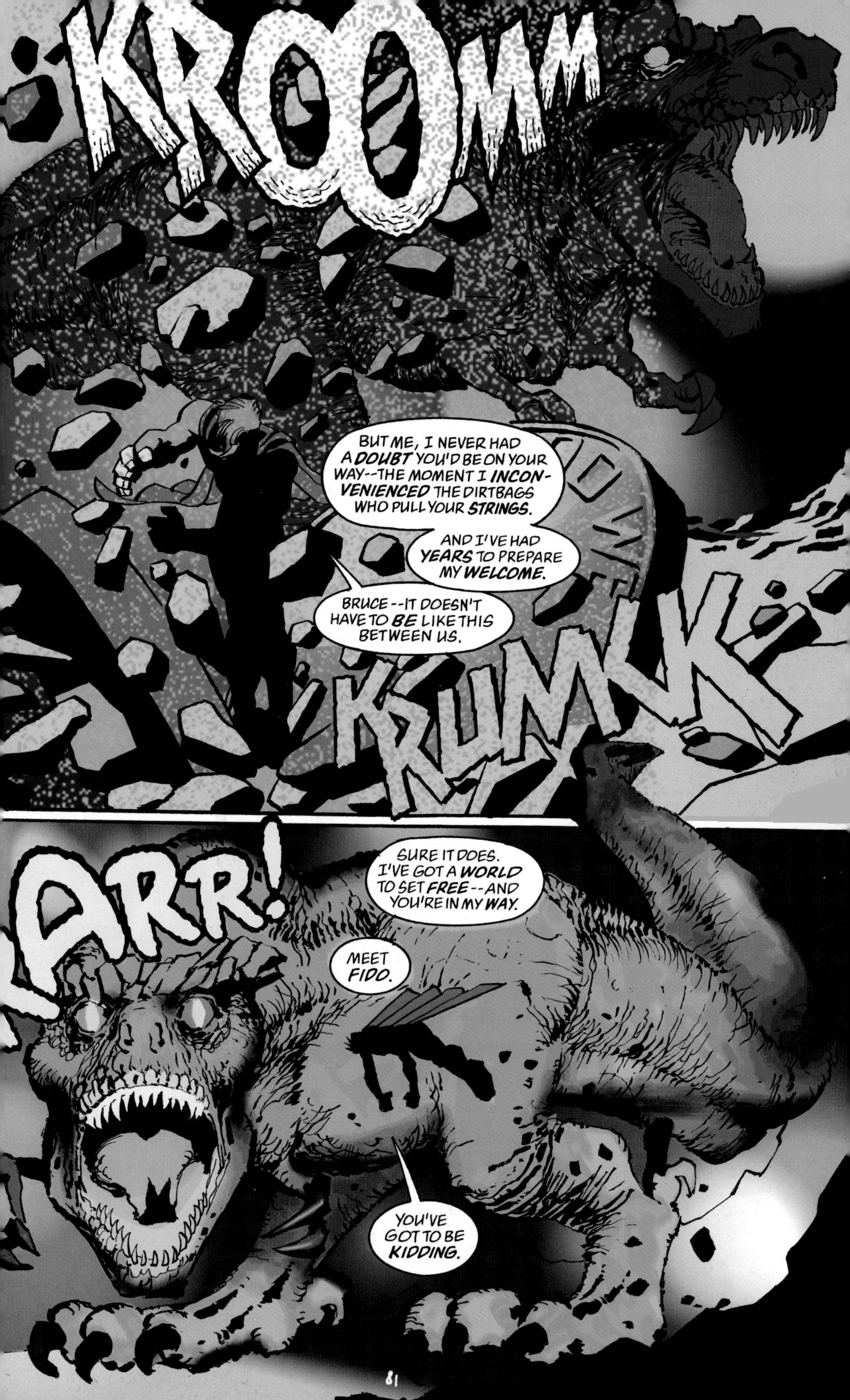
KROOMM
BUT ME, I NEVER HAD A DOUBT YOU'D BE ON YOUR WAY--THE MOMENT I INCONVENIENCED THE DIRTBAGS WHO PULL YOUR STRINGS.
AND I'VE HAD YEARS TO PREPARE MY WELCOME.
BRUCE--IT DOESN'T HAVE TO BE LIKE THIS BETWEEN US.
KRUMK
ARR!
SURE IT DOES. I'VE GOT A WORLD TO SET FREE--AND YOU'RE IN MY WAY.
MEET FIDO.
YOU'VE GOT TO BE KIDDING.

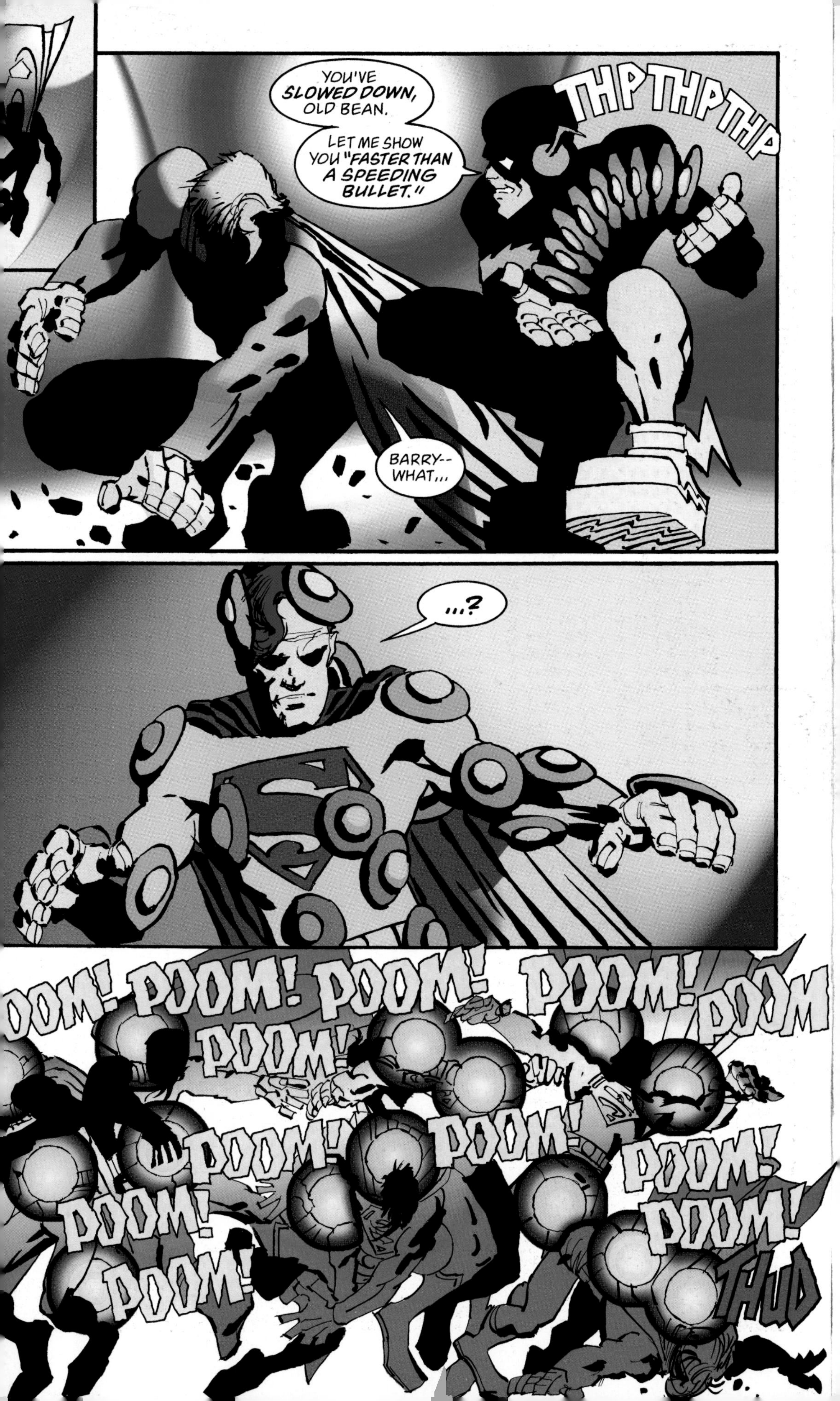

YOU'VE SLOWED DOWN, OLD BEAN.
LET ME SHOW YOU "FASTER THAN A SPEEDING BULLET."
THPTHPTHP
BARRY-- WHAT...
...?
OOM! POOM! POOM! POOM! POOM
POOM!
POOM! POOM!
POOM! POOM!
POOM!
POOM!
THUD

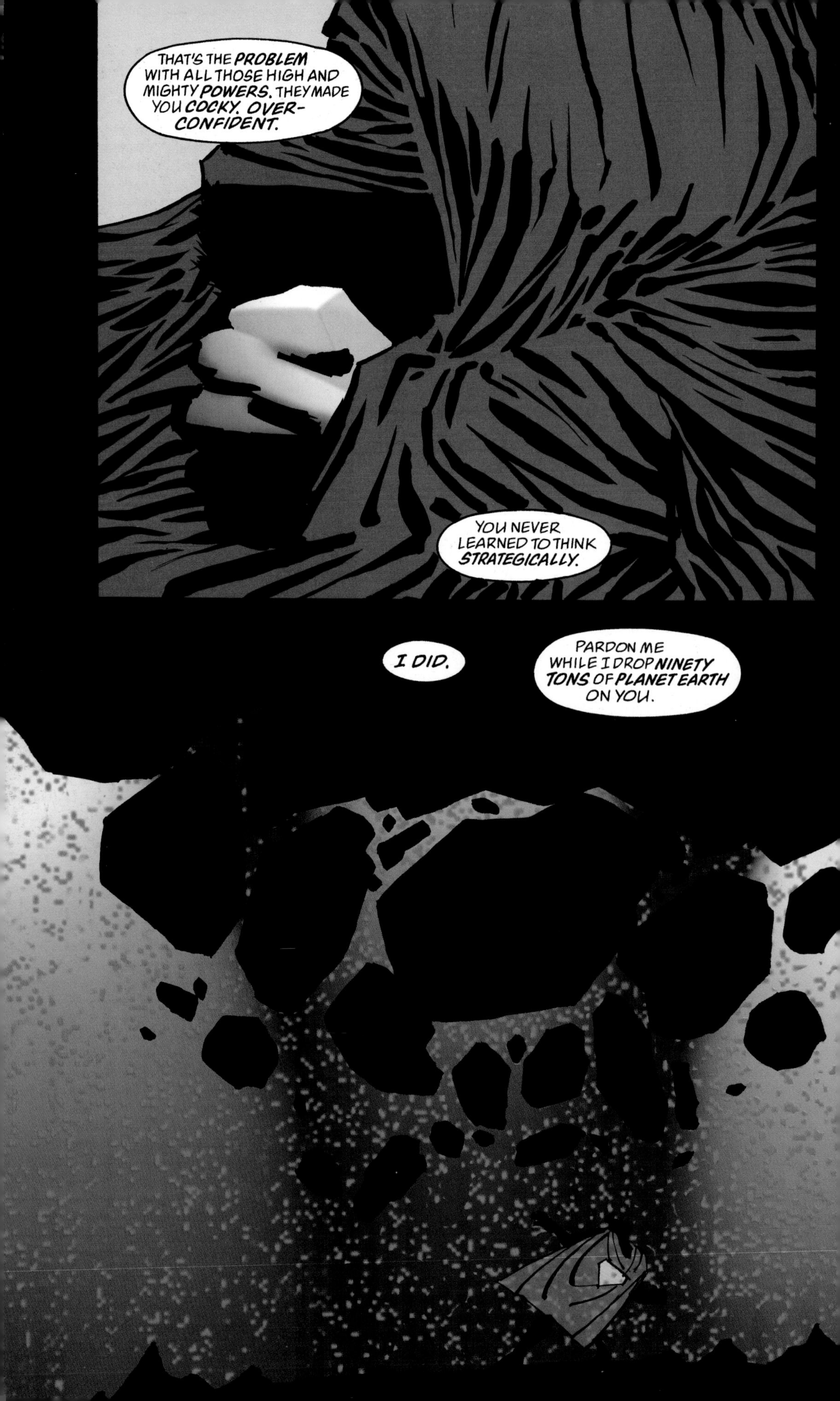
THAT'S THE PROBLEM WITH ALL THOSE HIGH AND MIGHTY POWERS. THEY MADE YOU COCKY. OVER-CONFIDENT.
YOU NEVER LEARNED TO THINK STRATEGICALLY.
I DID.
PARDON ME WHILE I DROP NINETY TONS OF PLANET EARTH ON YOU.

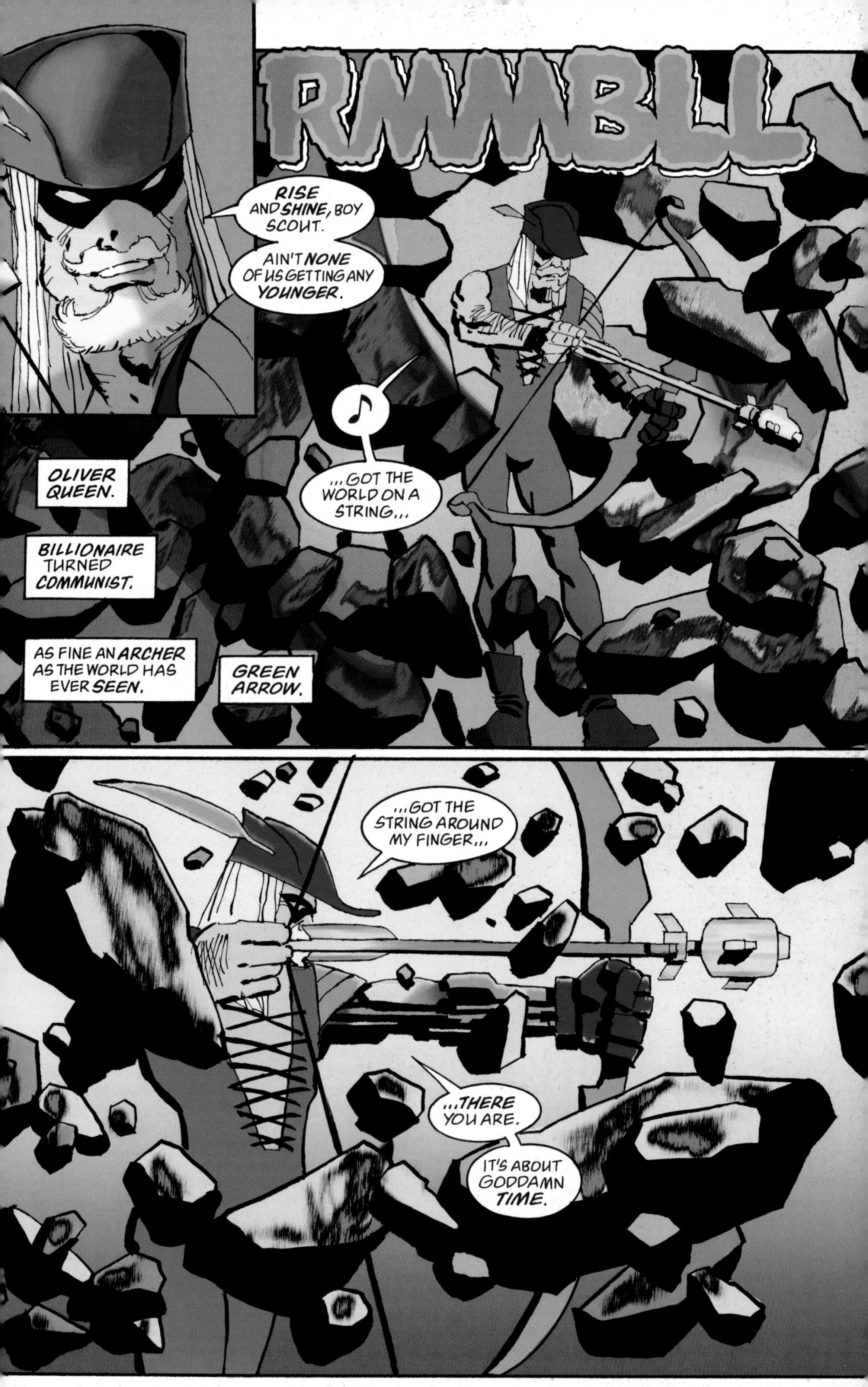
RMMBLL
RISE AND SHINE, BOY SCOUT.
AIN'T NONE OF US GETTING ANY YOUNGER.
♪
...GOT THE WORLD ON A STRING...
OLIVER QUEEN.
BILLIONAIRE TURNED COMMUNIST.
AS FINE AN ARCHER AS THE WORLD HAS EVER SEEN.
GREEN ARROW.
...GOT THE STRING AROUND MY FINGER...
...THERE YOU ARE.
IT'S ABOUT GODDAMN TIME.

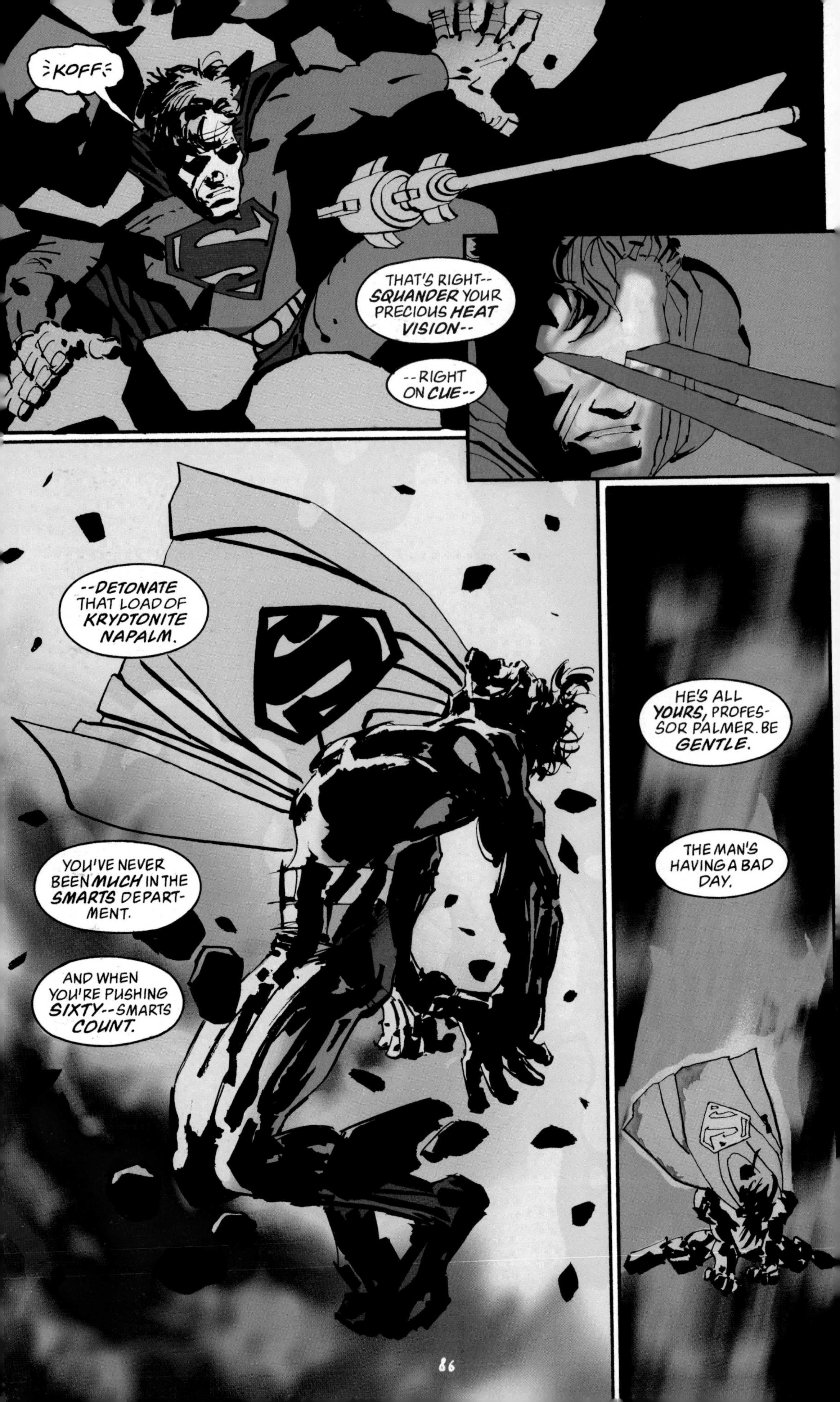
KOFF
THAT'S RIGHT-- SQUANDER YOUR PRECIOUS HEAT VISION--
--RIGHT ON CUE--
--DETONATE THAT LOAD OF KRYPTONITE NAPALM.
YOU'VE NEVER BEEN MUCH IN THE SMARTS DEPARTMENT.
AND WHEN YOU'RE PUSHING SIXTY--SMARTS COUNT.
HE'S ALL YOURS, PROFESSOR PALMER. BE GENTLE.
THE MAN'S HAVING A BAD DAY.

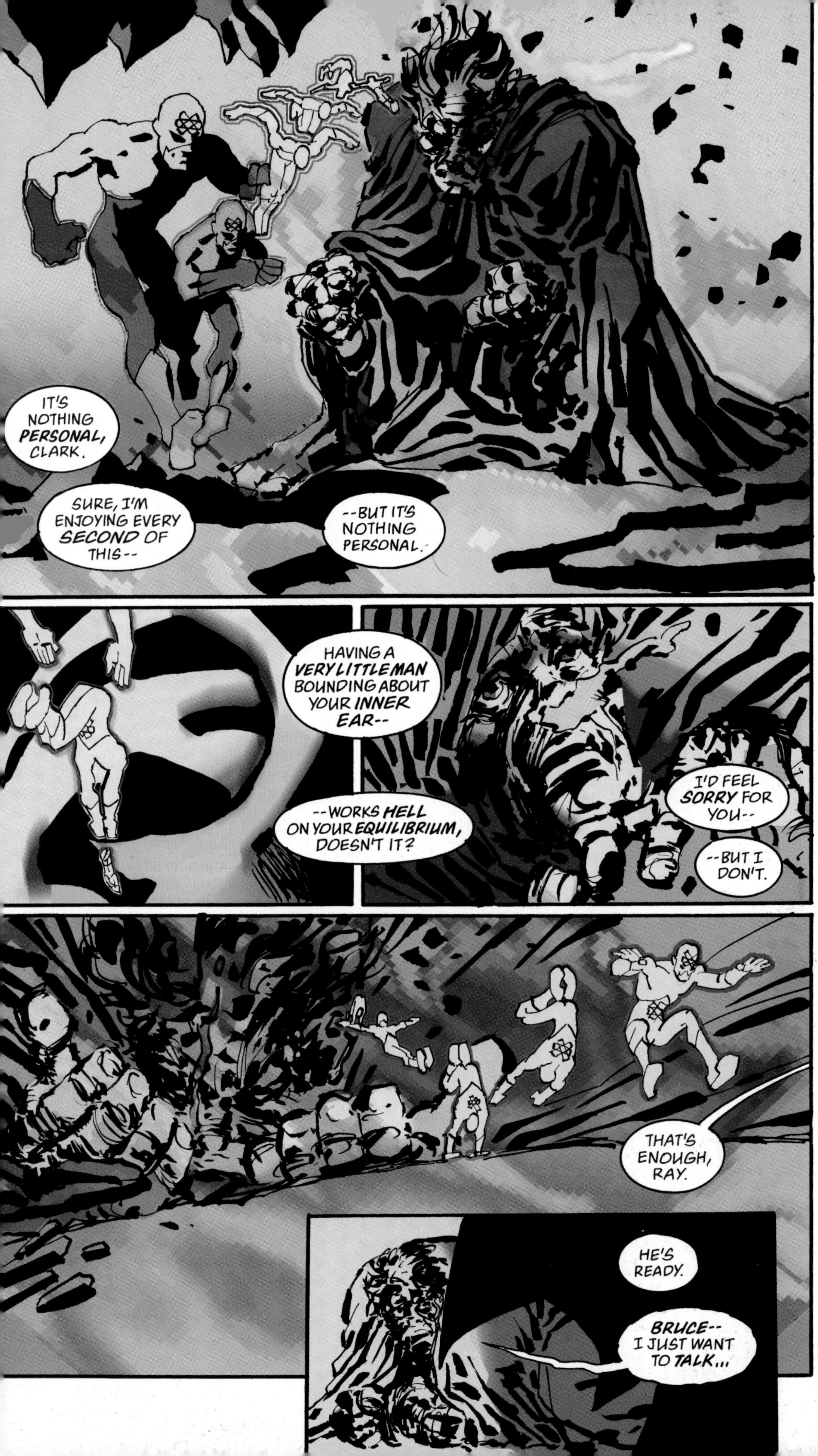
IT'S NOTHING PERSONAL, CLARK.
SURE, I'M ENJOYING EVERY SECOND OF THIS--
--BUT IT'S NOTHING PERSONAL.
HAVING A VERY LITTLE MAN BOUNDING ABOUT YOUR INNER EAR--
--WORKS HELL ON YOUR EQUILIBRIUM, DOESN'T IT?
I'D FEEL SORRY FOR YOU--
--BUT I DON'T.
THAT'S ENOUGH, RAY.
HE'S READY.
BRUCE-- I JUST WANT TO TALK...

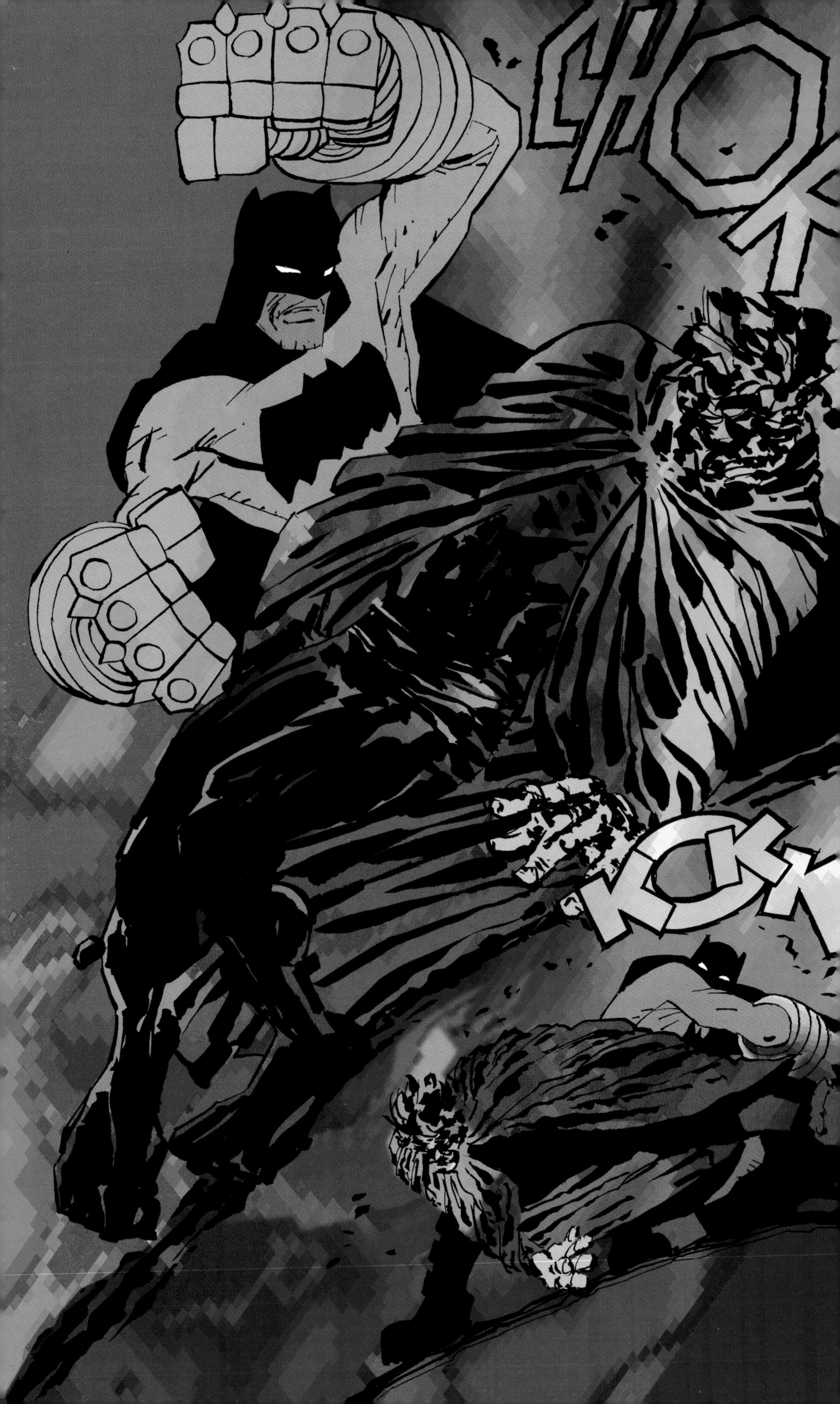

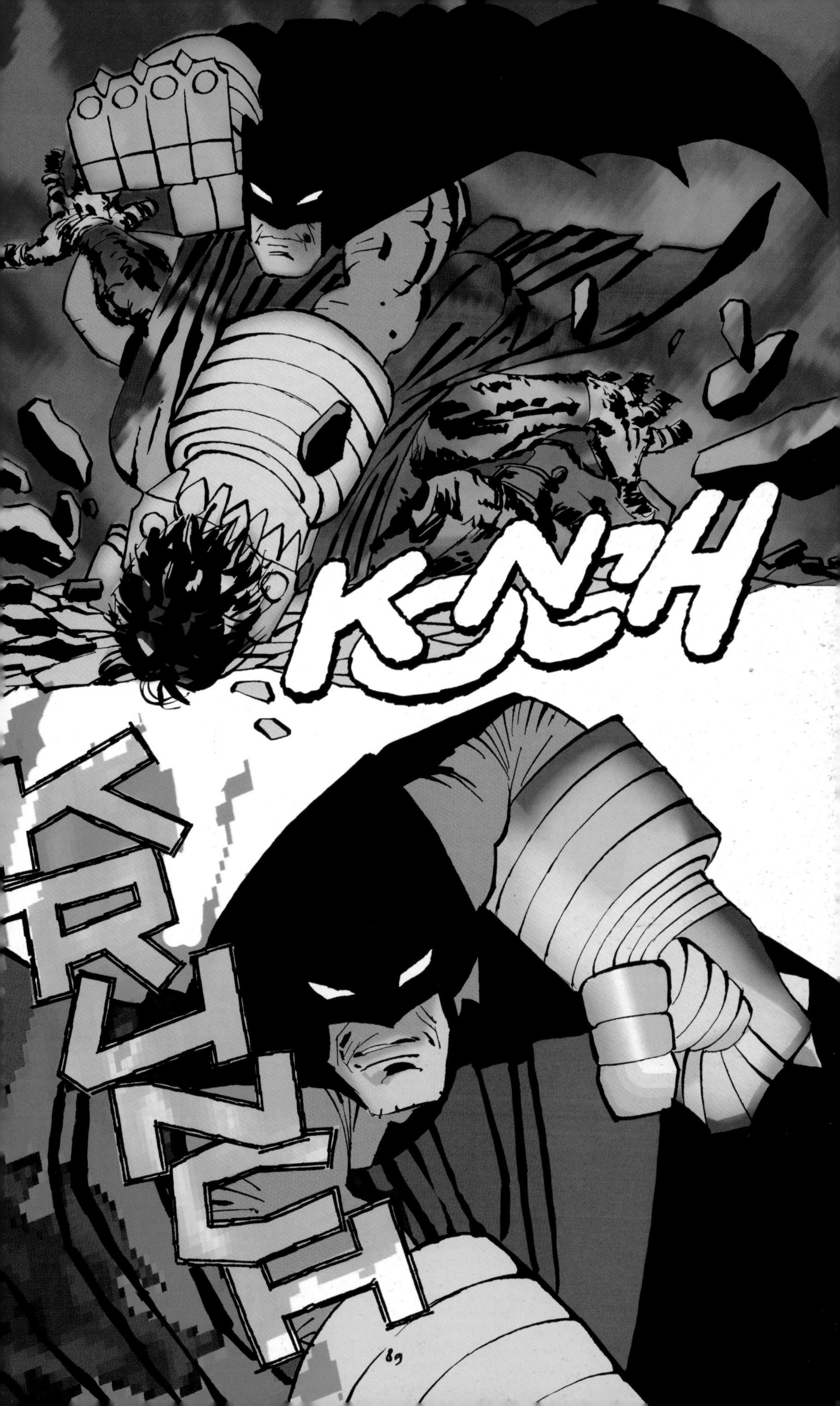
KNH
KRZZZT

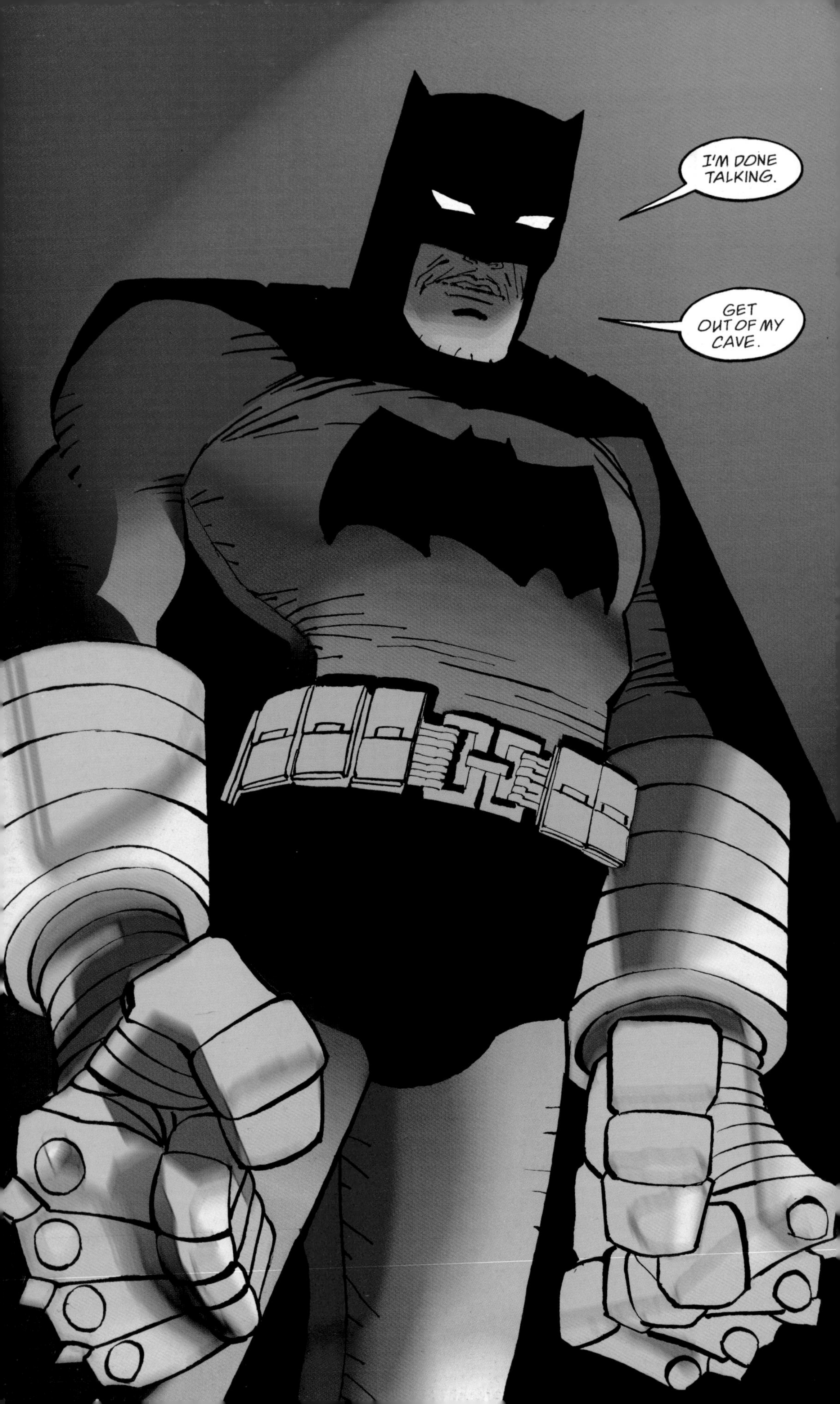
I'M DONE TALKING.
GET OUT OF MY CAVE.

BOOK TWO.

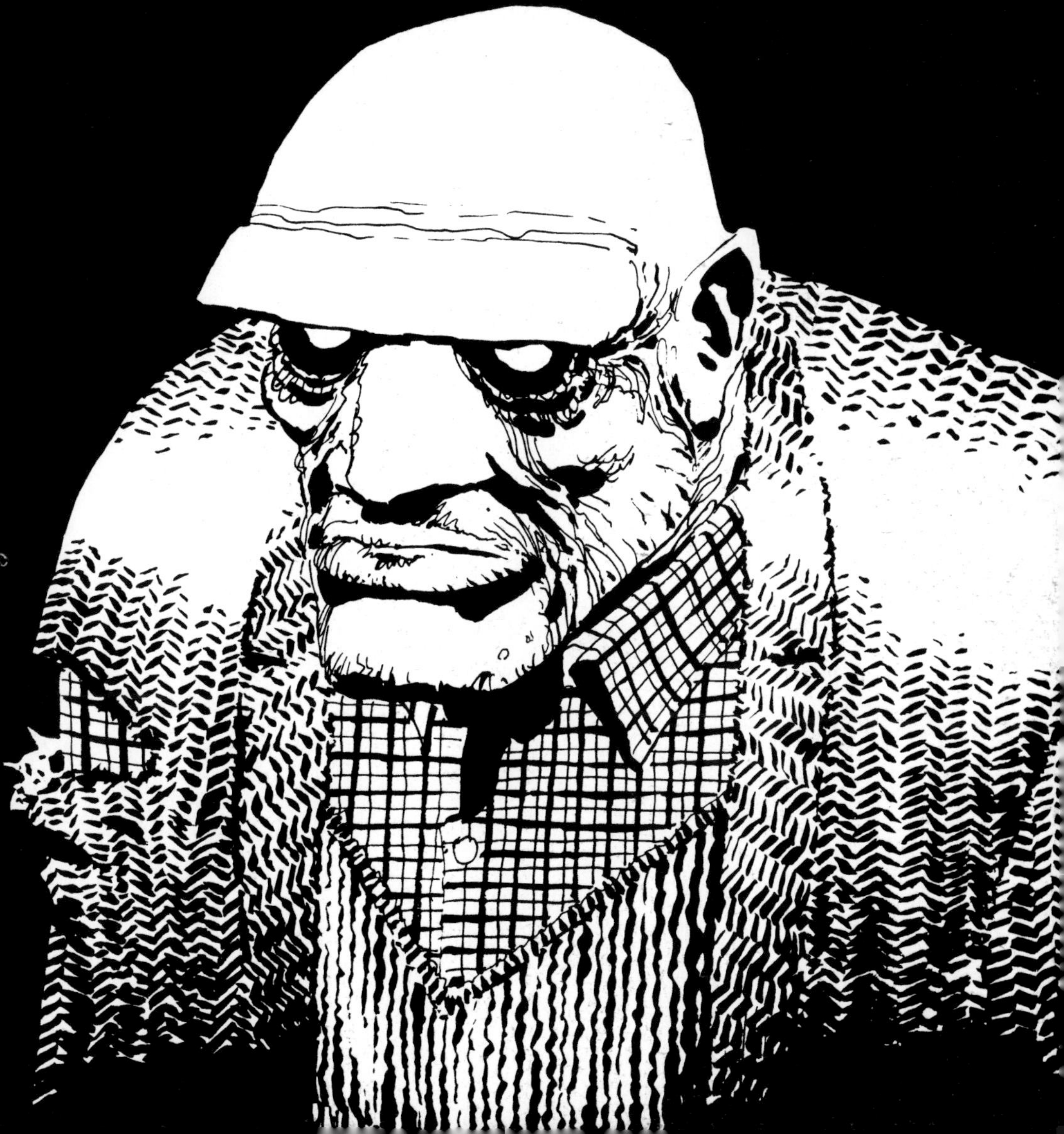

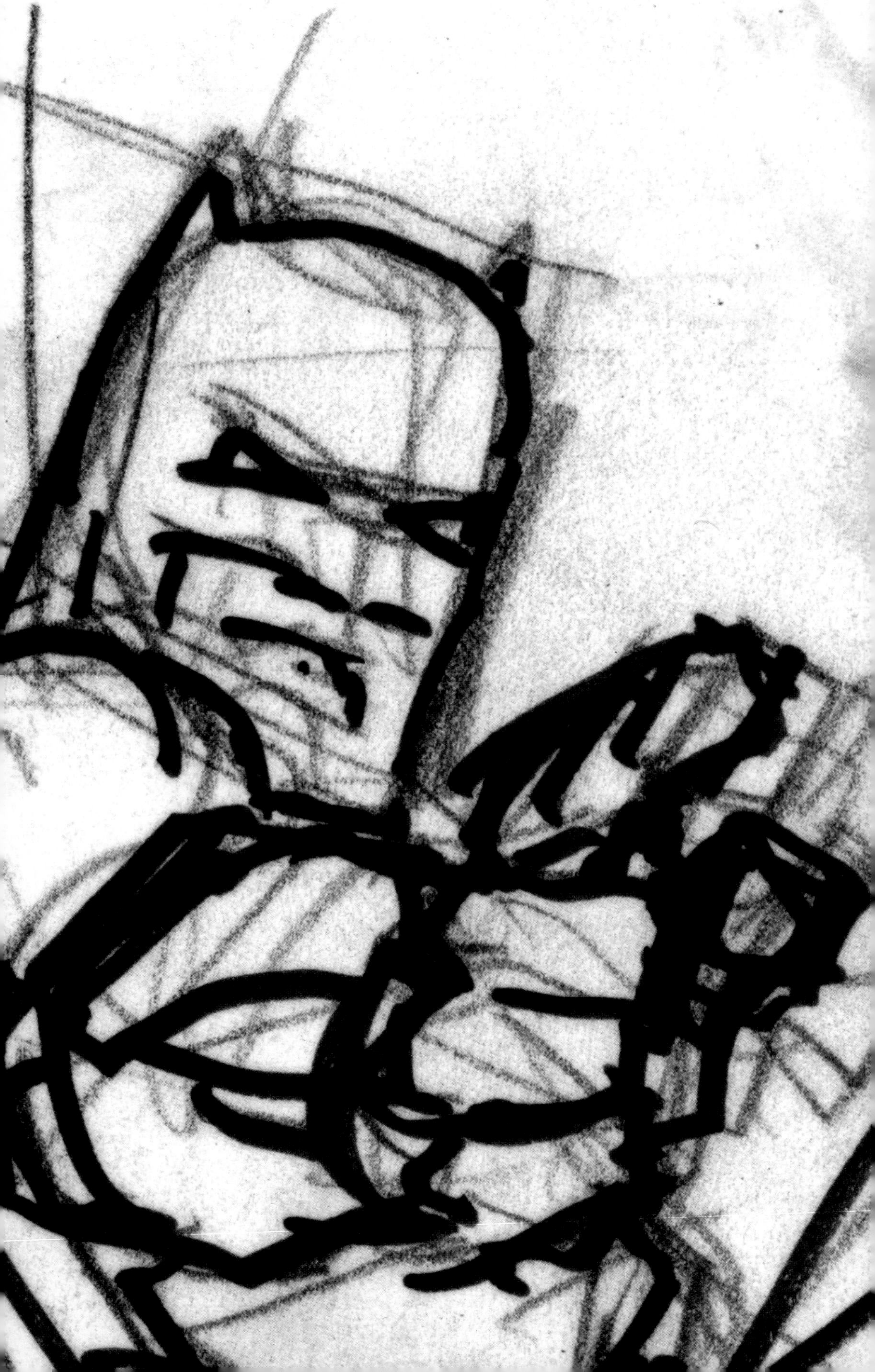

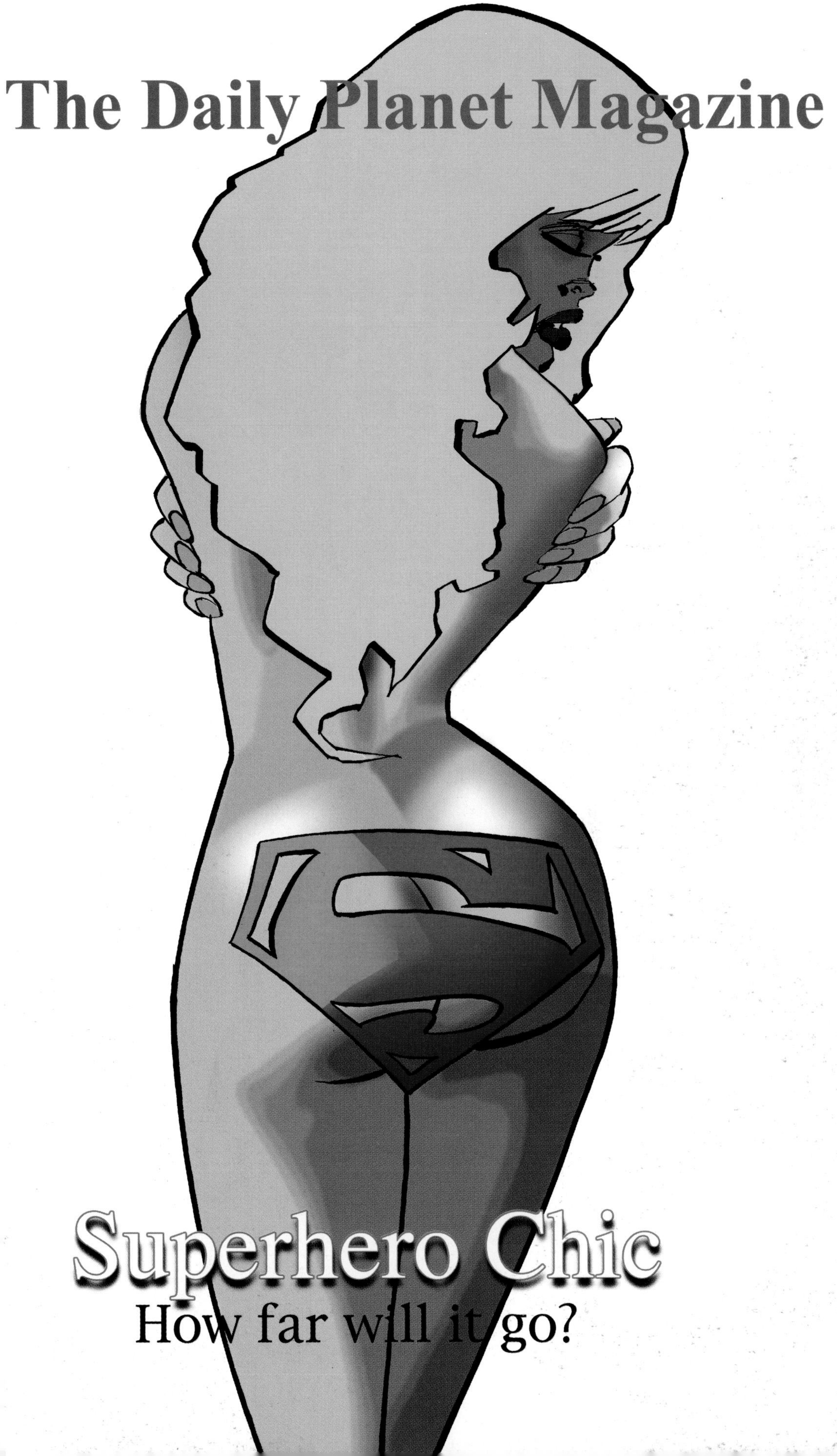
The Daily Planet Magazine
Superhero Chic
How far will it go?

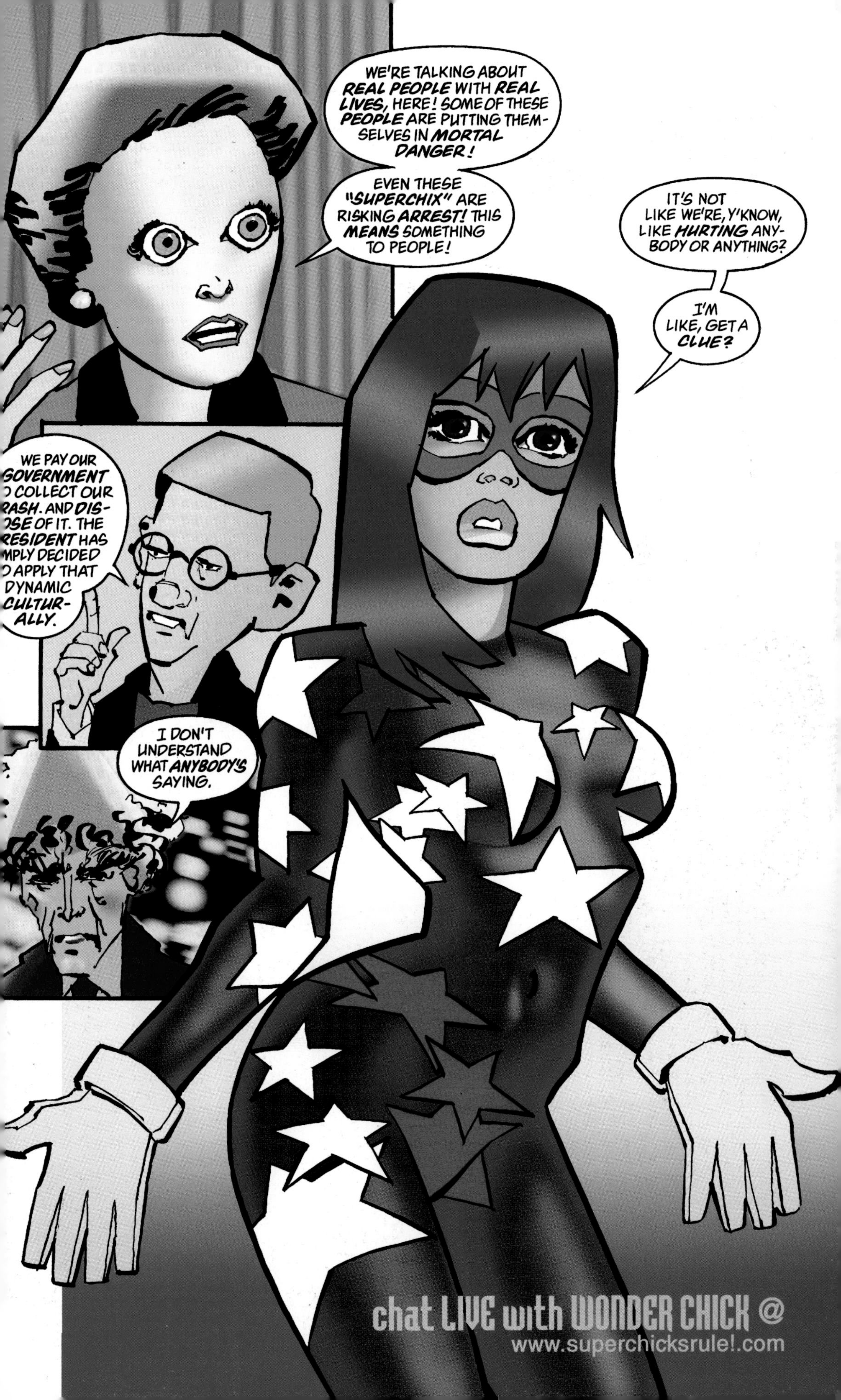

WE'RE TALKING ABOUT REAL PEOPLE WITH REAL LIVES, HERE! SOME OF THESE PEOPLE ARE PUTTING THEM-SELVES IN MORTAL DANGER!
EVEN THESE "SUPERCHIX" ARE RISKING ARREST! THIS MEANS SOMETHING TO PEOPLE!
IT'S NOT LIKE WE'RE, Y'KNOW, LIKE HURTING ANY-BODY OR ANYTHING?
I'M LIKE, GET A CLUE?
WE PAY OUR GOVERNMENT O COLLECT OUR RASH. AND DIS-OSE OF IT. THE RESIDENT HAS MPLY DECIDED O APPLY THAT DYNAMIC CULTUR-ALLY.
I DON'T UNDERSTAND WHAT ANYBODY'S SAYING.
chat LIVE with WONDER CHICK @
www.superchicksrule!.com

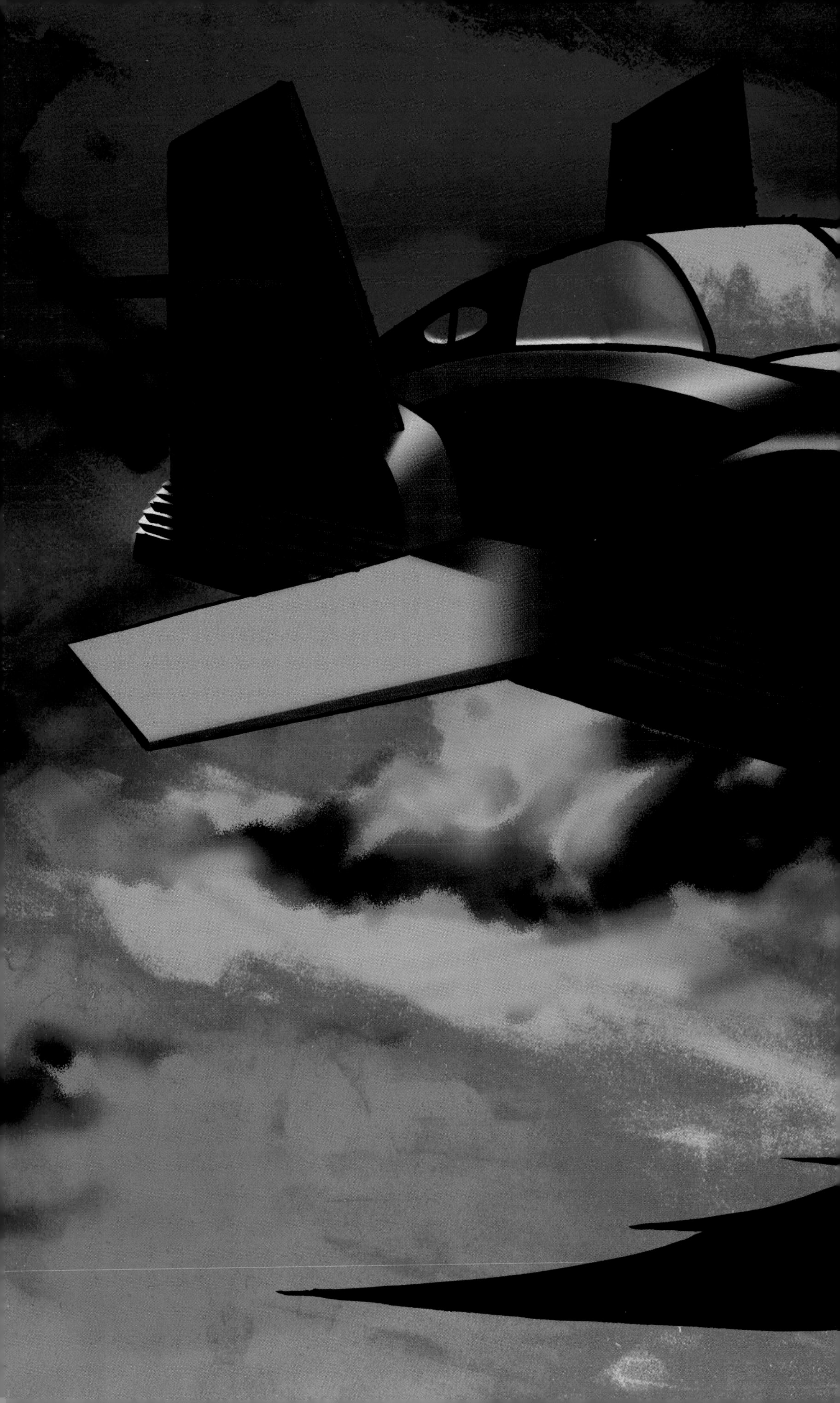

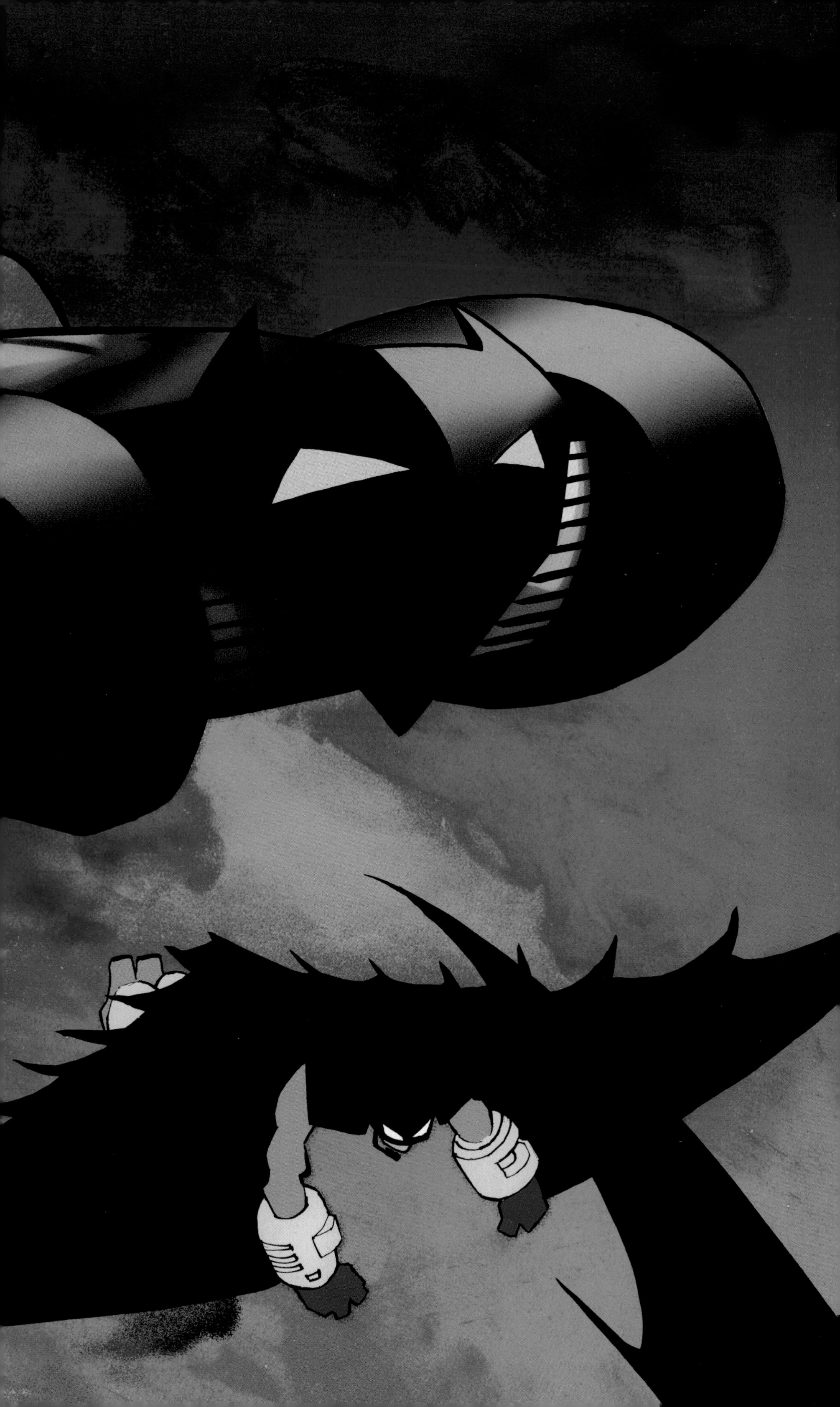

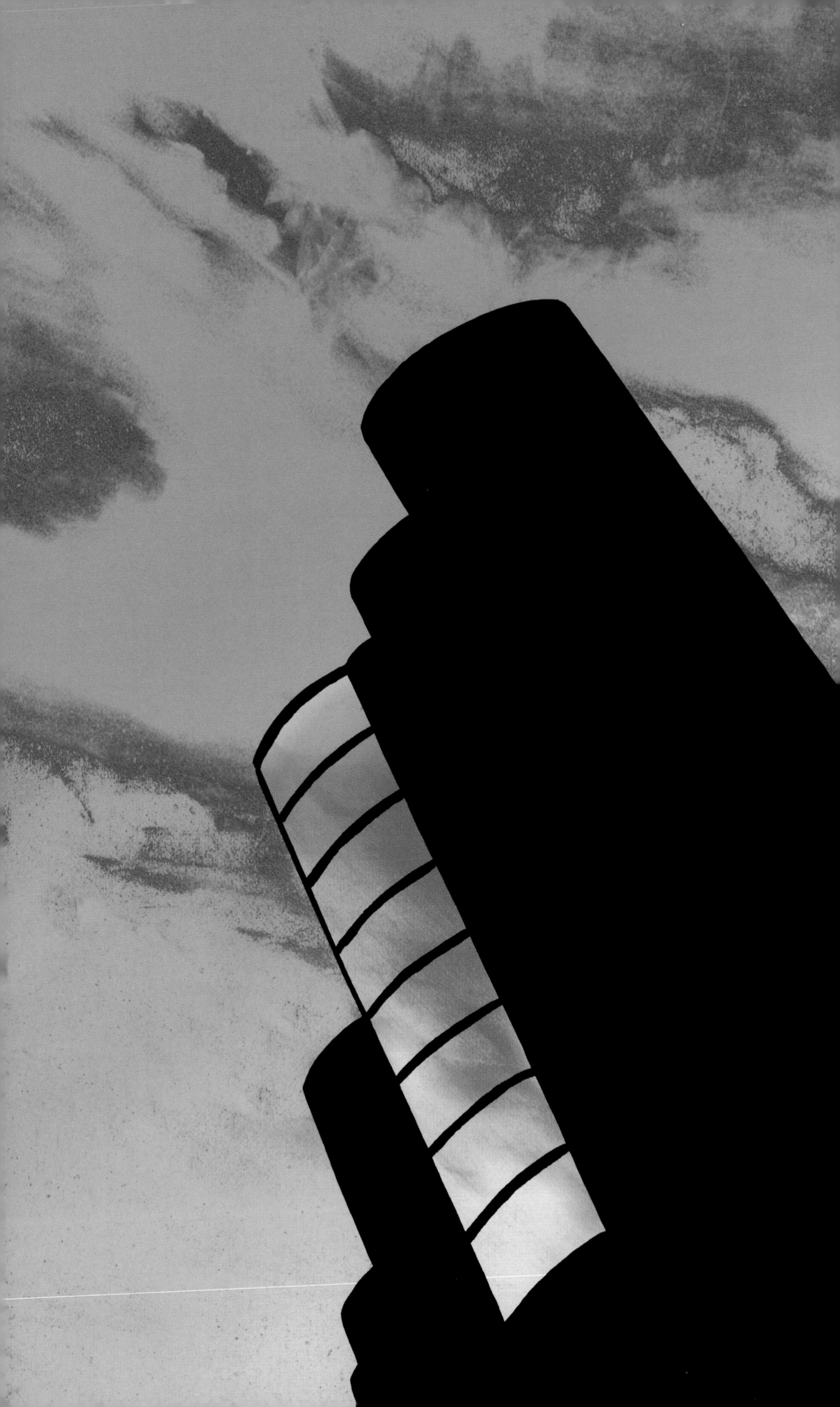

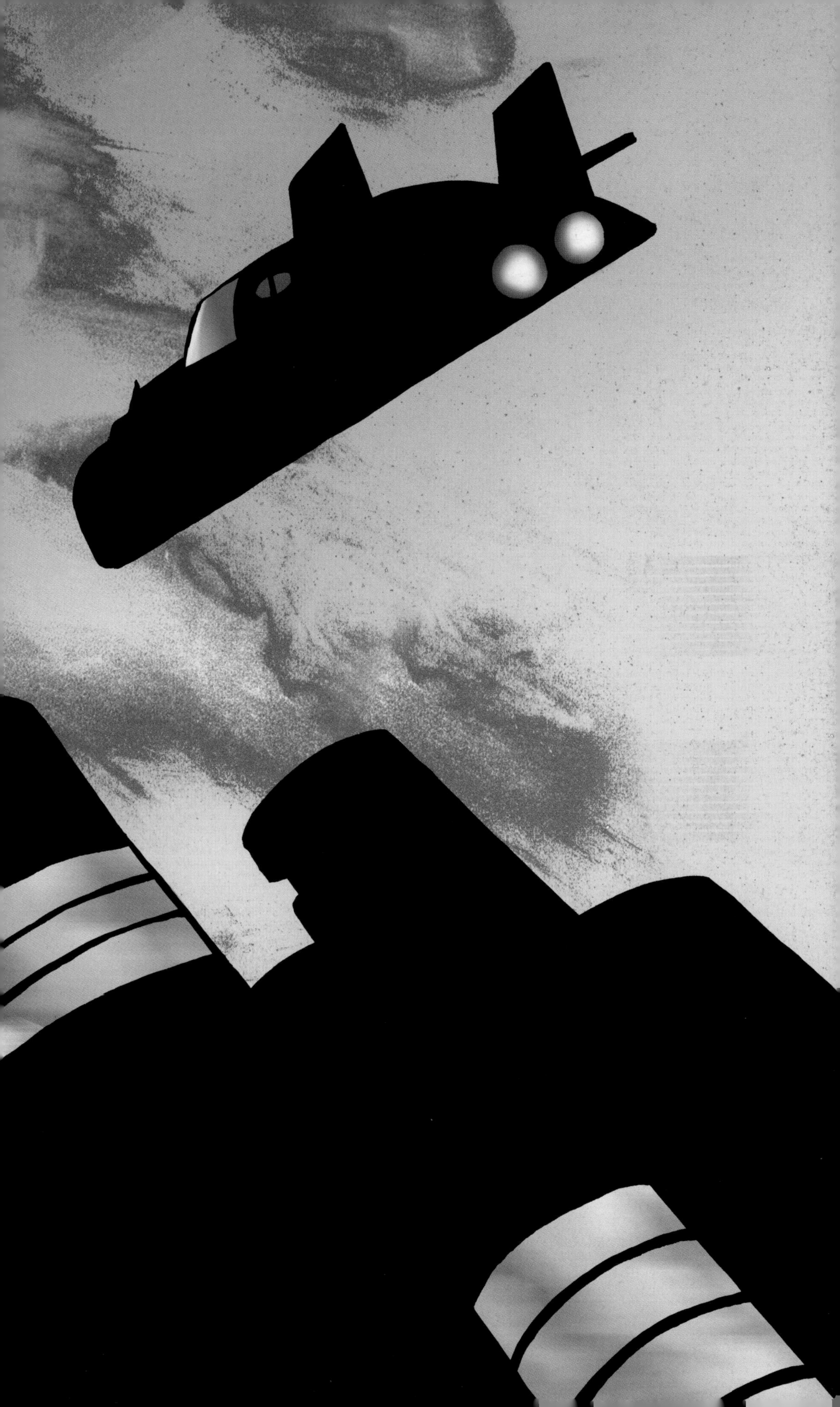

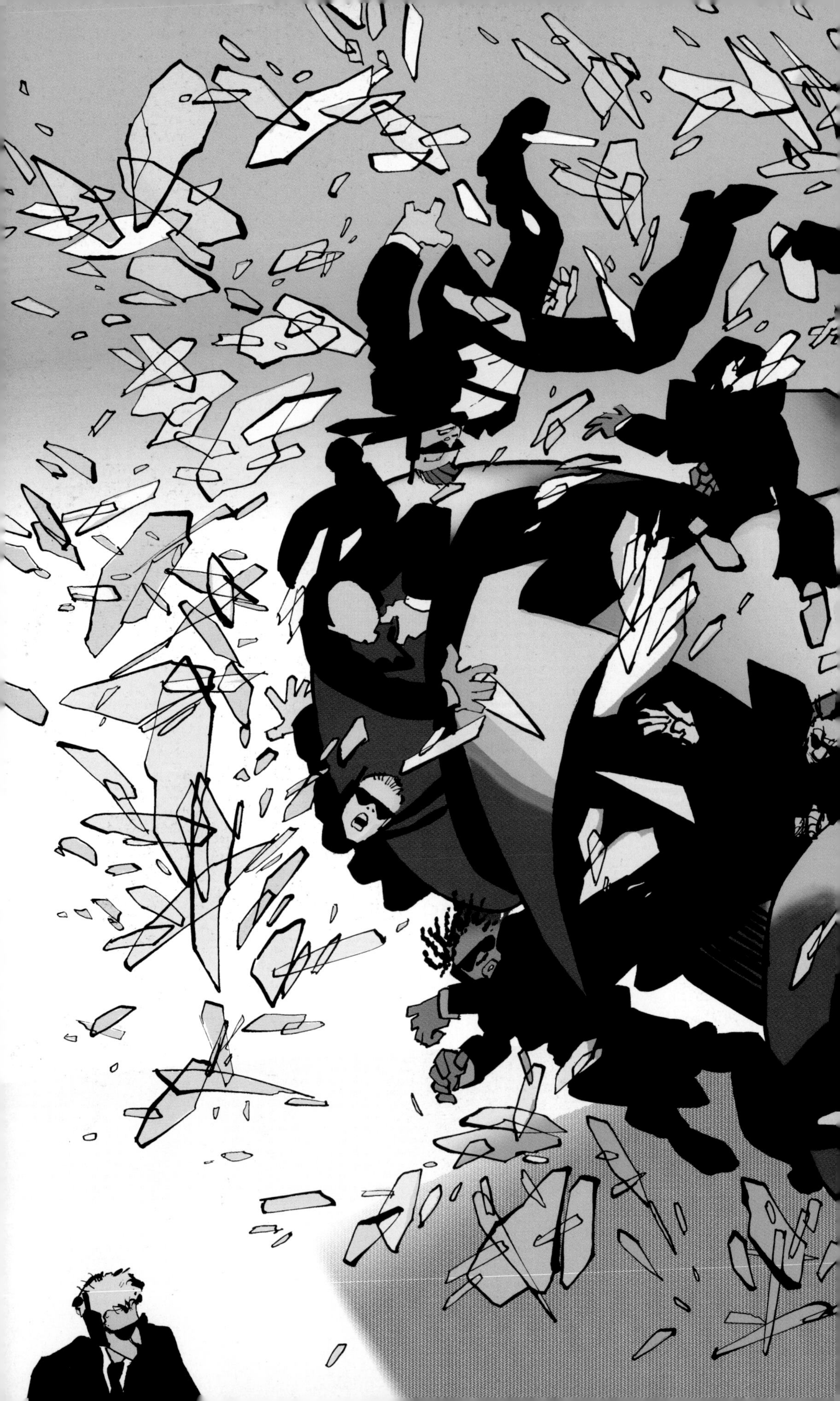

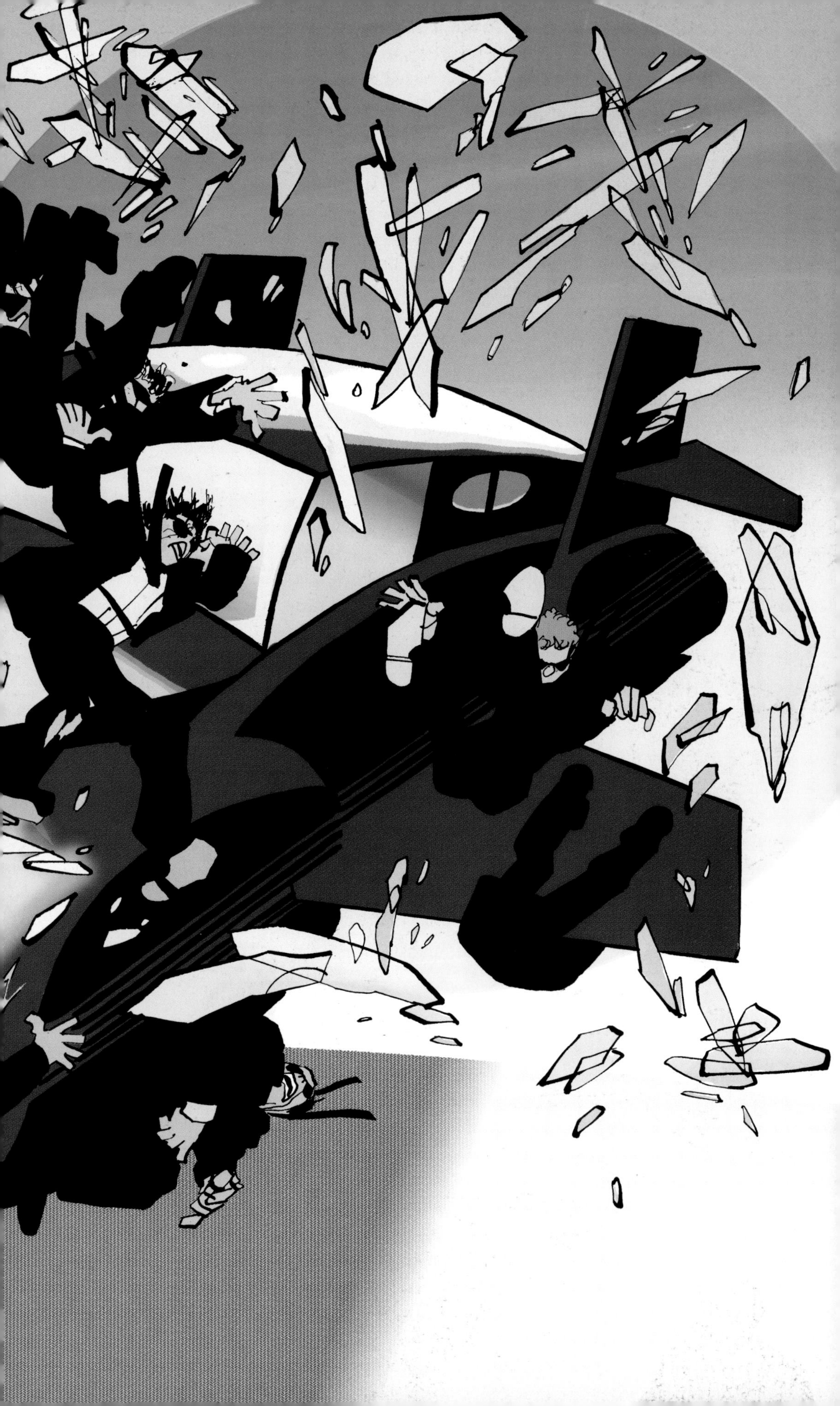

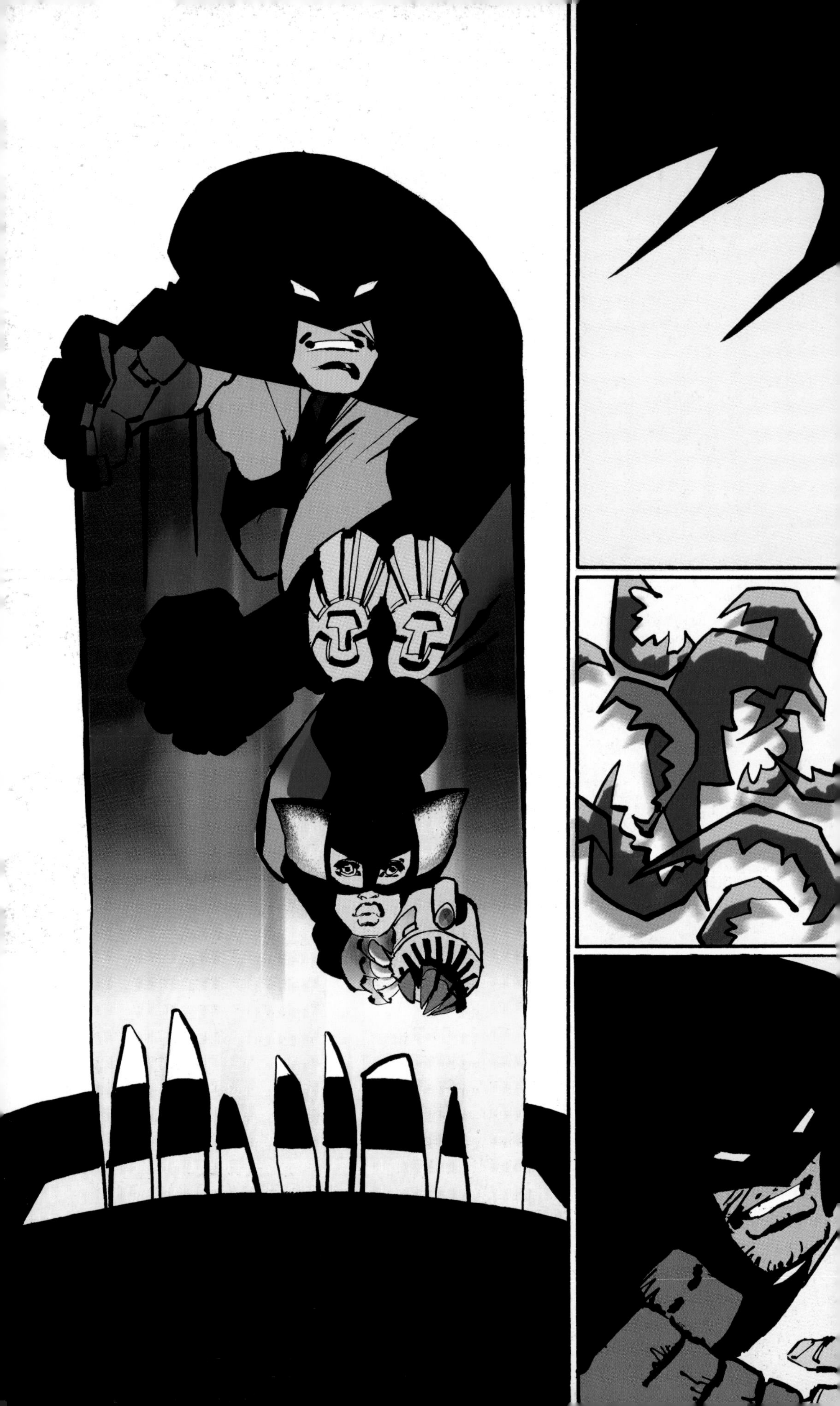

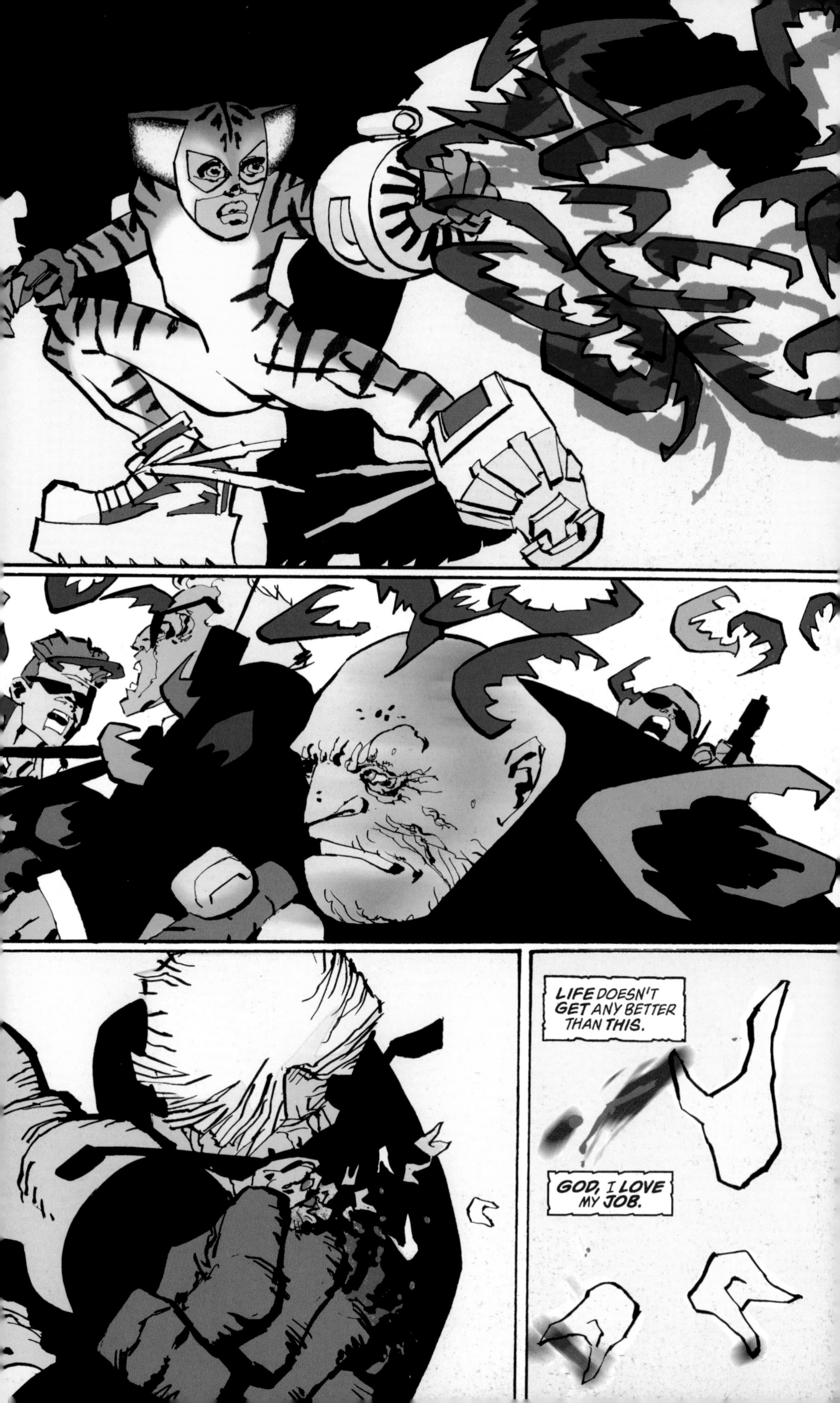
LIFE DOESN'T GET ANY BETTER THAN THIS.
GOD, I LOVE MY JOB.

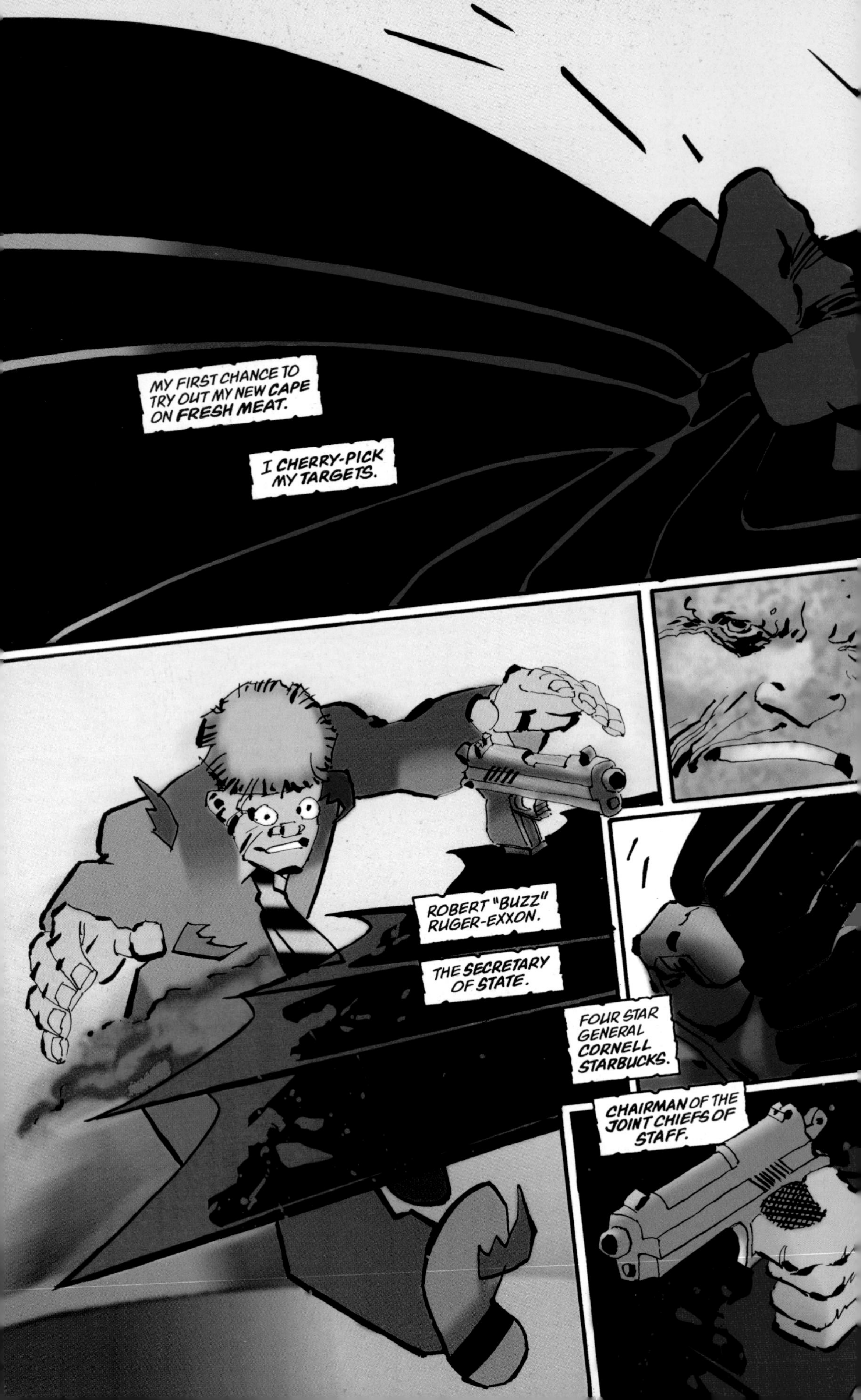
MY FIRST CHANCE TO TRY OUT MY NEW CAPE ON FRESH MEAT.
I CHERRY-PICK MY TARGETS.
ROBERT "BUZZ" RUGER-EXXON.
THE SECRETARY OF STATE.
FOUR STAR GENERAL CORNELL STARBUCKS.
CHAIRMAN OF THE JOINT CHIEFS OF STAFF.

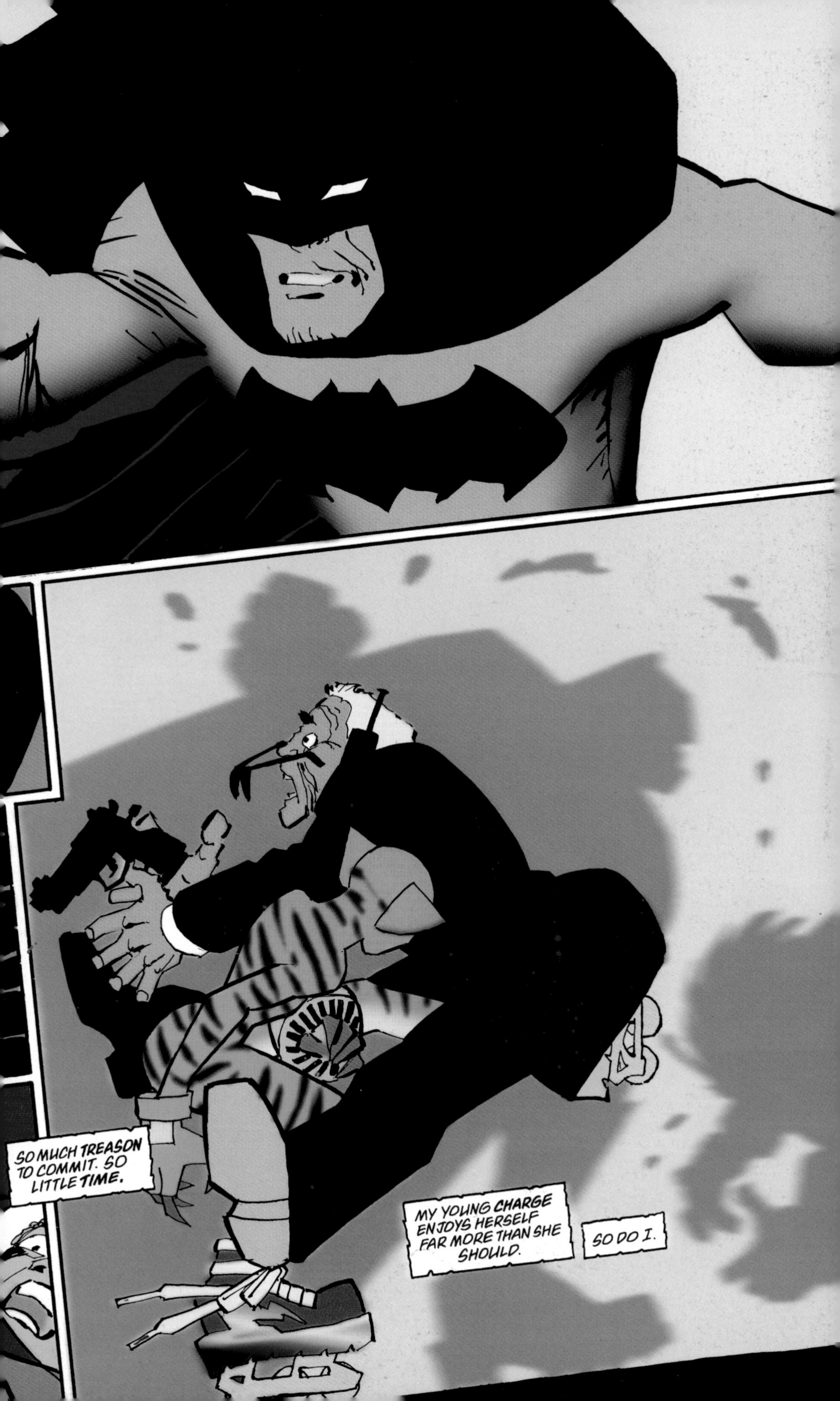
SO MUCH TREASON TO COMMIT. SO LITTLE TIME.
MY YOUNG CHARGE ENJOYS HERSELF FAR MORE THAN SHE SHOULD.
SO DO I.

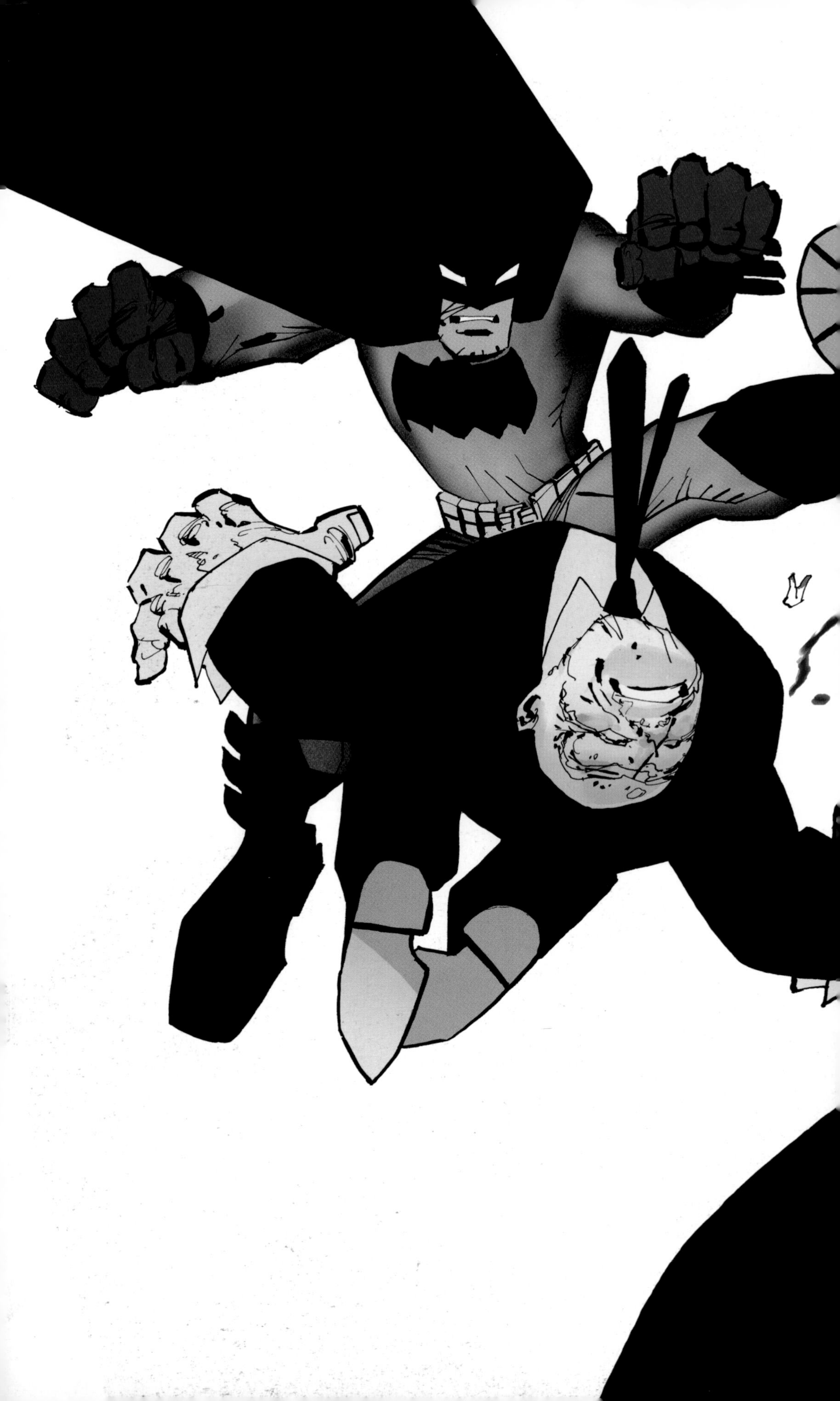

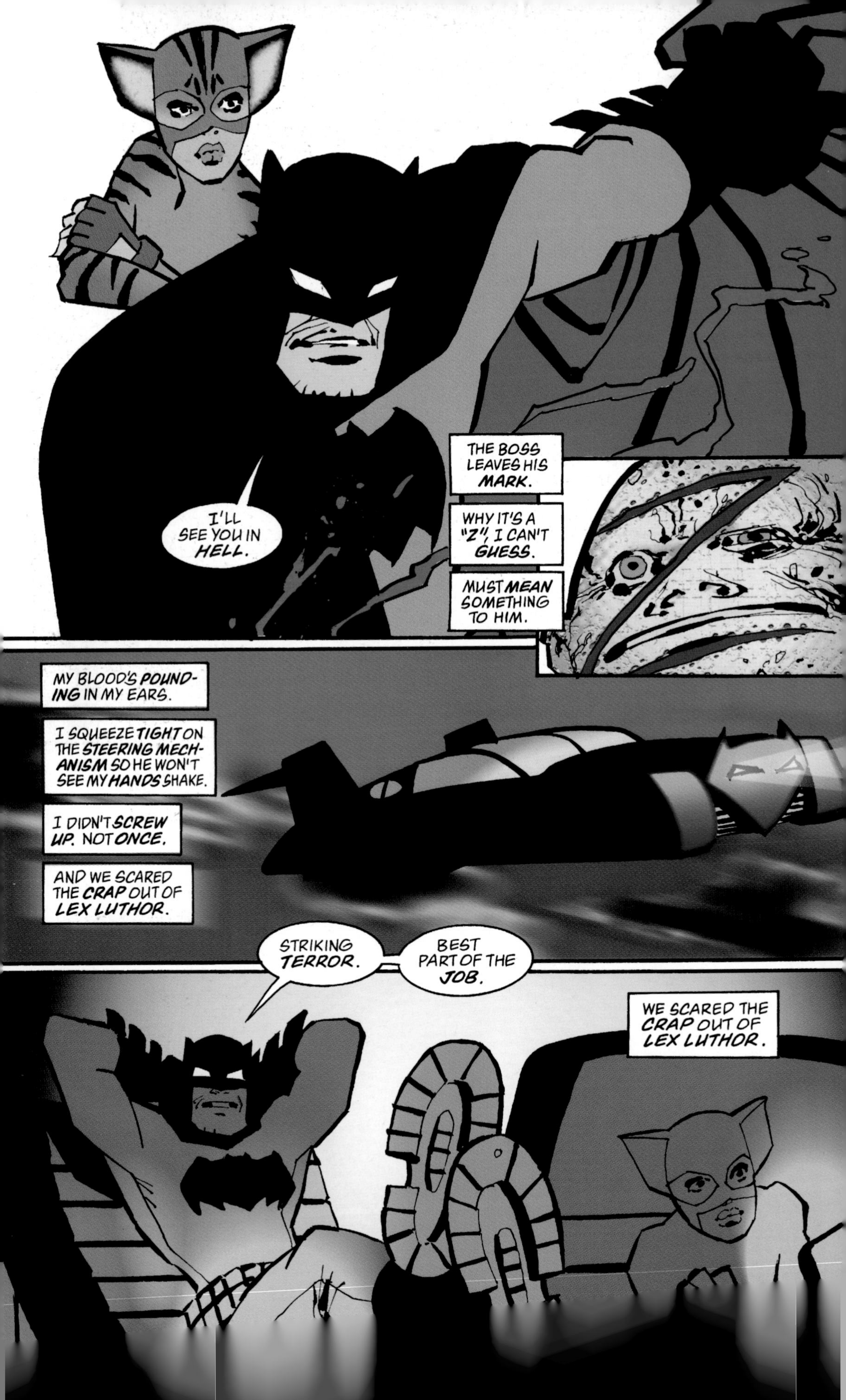
I'LL SEE YOU IN HELL.
THE BOSS LEAVES HIS MARK.
WHY IT'S A "Z", I CAN'T GUESS.
MUST MEAN SOMETHING TO HIM.
MY BLOOD'S POUNDING IN MY EARS.
I SQUEEZE TIGHT ON THE STEERING MECHANISM SO HE WON'T SEE MY HANDS SHAKE.
I DIDN'T SCREW UP. NOT ONCE.
AND WE SCARED THE CRAP OUT OF LEX LUTHOR.
STRIKING TERROR.
BEST PART OF THE JOB.
WE SCARED THE CRAP OUT OF LEX LUTHOR.

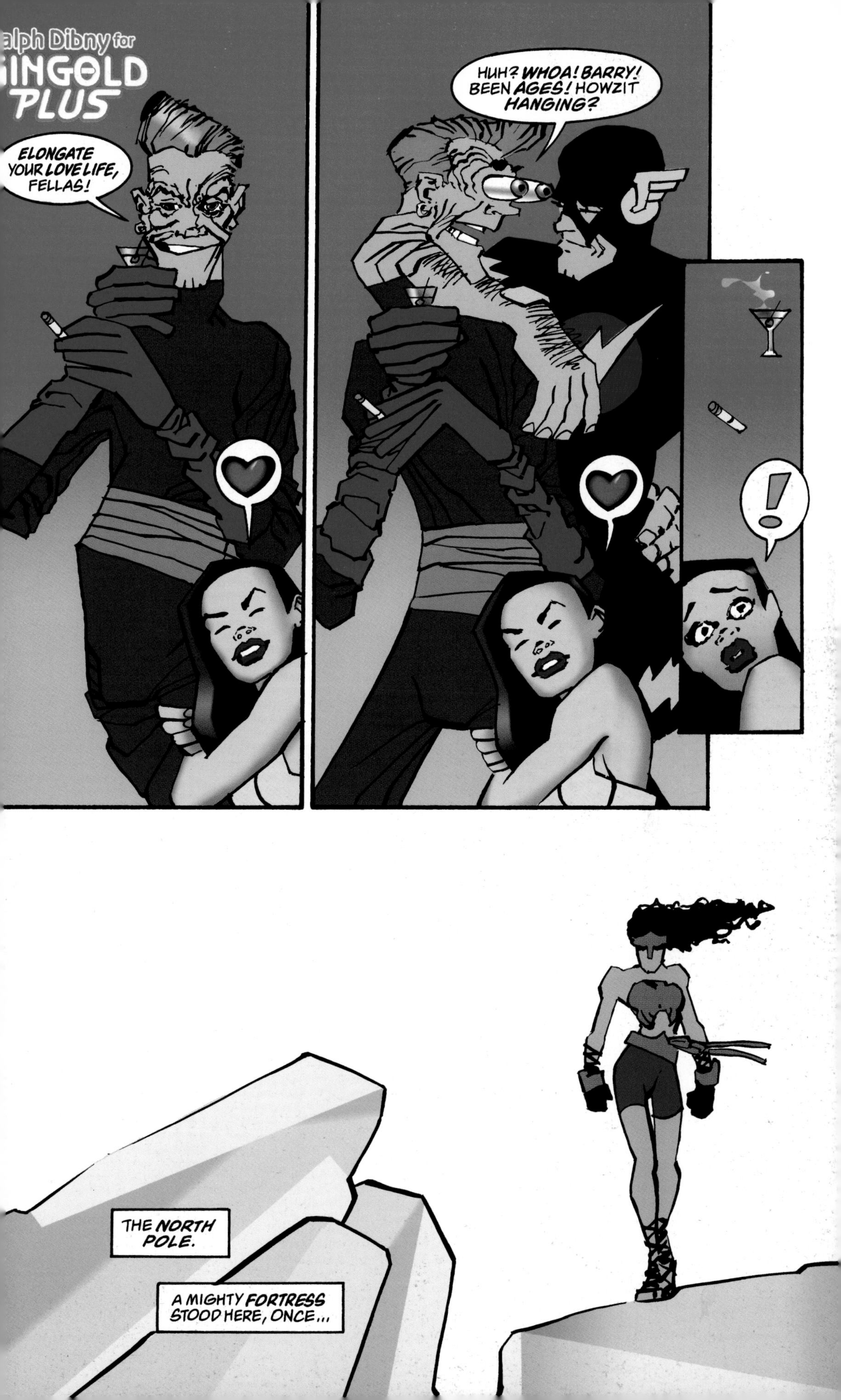
alph Dibny for
INGOLD
PLUS
ELONGATE YOUR LOVE LIFE, FELLAS!
HUH? WHOA! BARRY! BEEN AGES! HOWZIT HANGING?
!
THE NORTH POLE.
A MIGHTY FORTRESS STOOD HERE, ONCE...

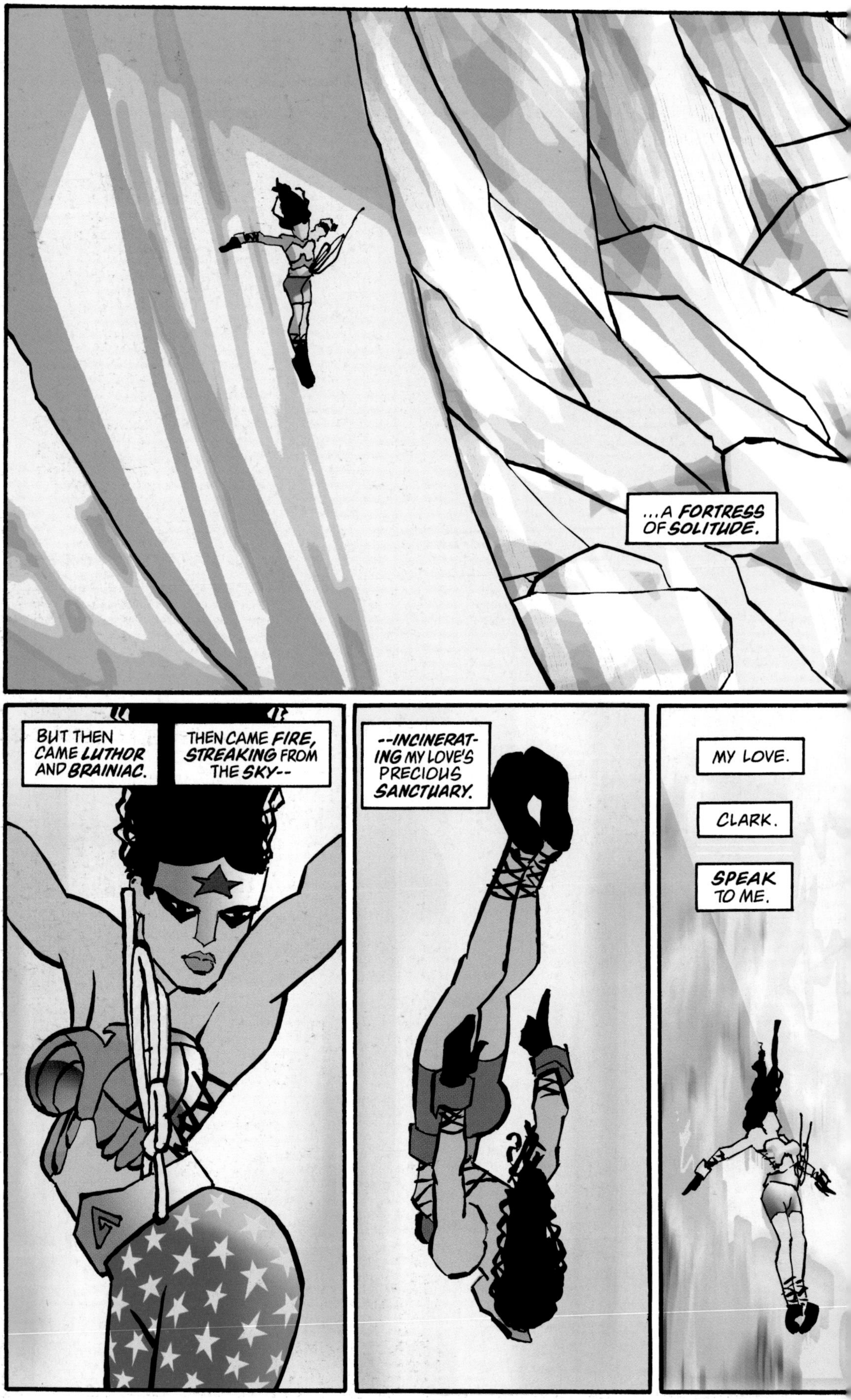
...A FORTRESS OF SOLITUDE.
BUT THEN CAME LUTHOR AND BRAINIAC.
THEN CAME FIRE, STREAKING FROM THE SKY--
--INCINERATING MY LOVE'S PRECIOUS SANCTUARY.
MY LOVE.
CLARK.
SPEAK TO ME.

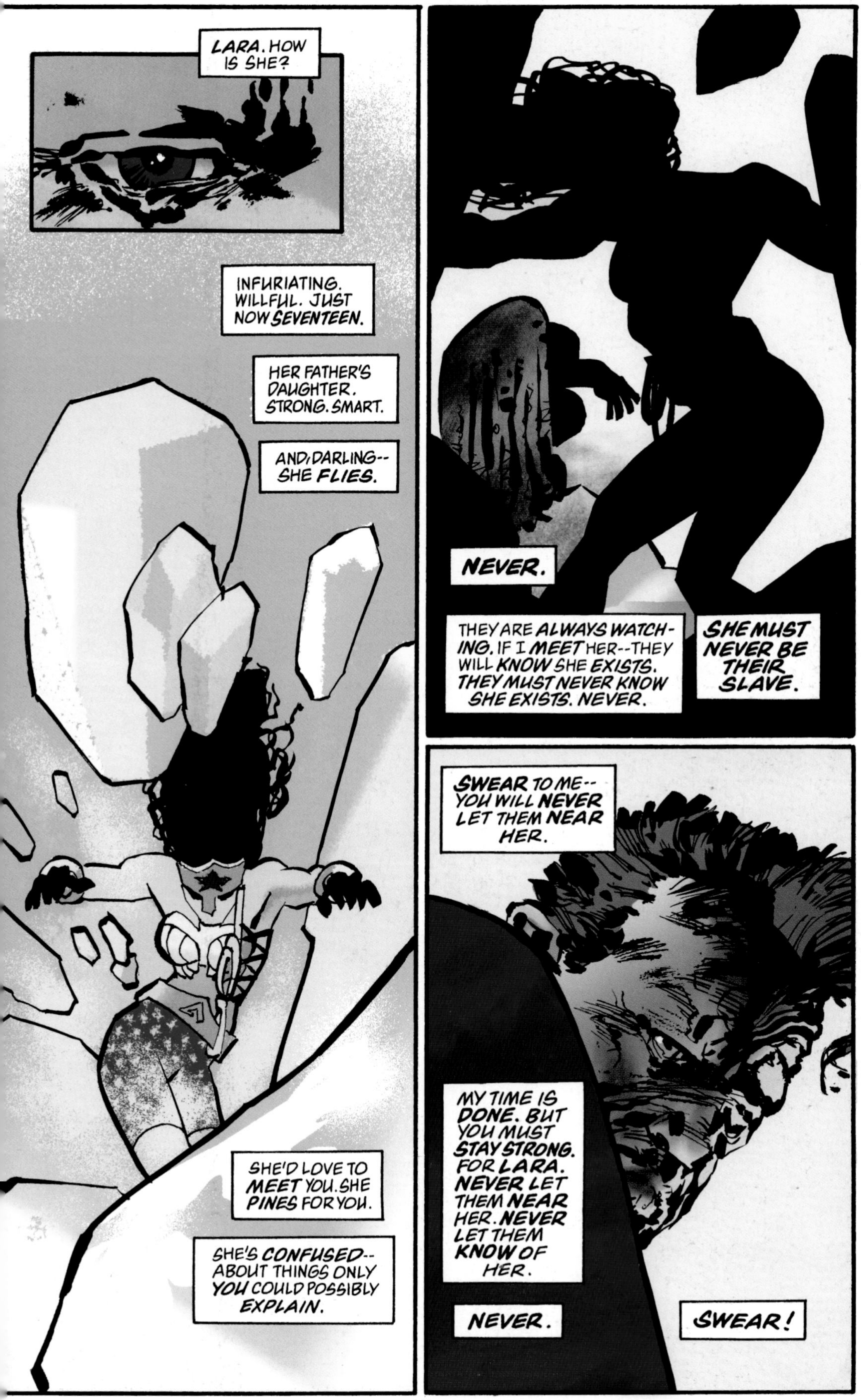

LARA. HOW IS SHE?
INFURIATING. WILLFUL. JUST NOW SEVENTEEN.
HER FATHER'S DAUGHTER. STRONG. SMART.
AND, DARLING-- SHE FLIES.
SHE'D LOVE TO MEET YOU. SHE PINES FOR YOU.
SHE'S CONFUSED-- ABOUT THINGS ONLY YOU COULD POSSIBLY EXPLAIN.
NEVER.
THEY ARE ALWAYS WATCHING. IF I MEET HER--THEY WILL KNOW SHE EXISTS. THEY MUST NEVER KNOW SHE EXISTS. NEVER.
SHE MUST NEVER BE THEIR SLAVE.
SWEAR TO ME-- YOU WILL NEVER LET THEM NEAR HER.
MY TIME IS DONE. BUT YOU MUST STAY STRONG. FOR LARA. NEVER LET THEM NEAR HER. NEVER LET THEM KNOW OF HER.
NEVER.
SWEAR!

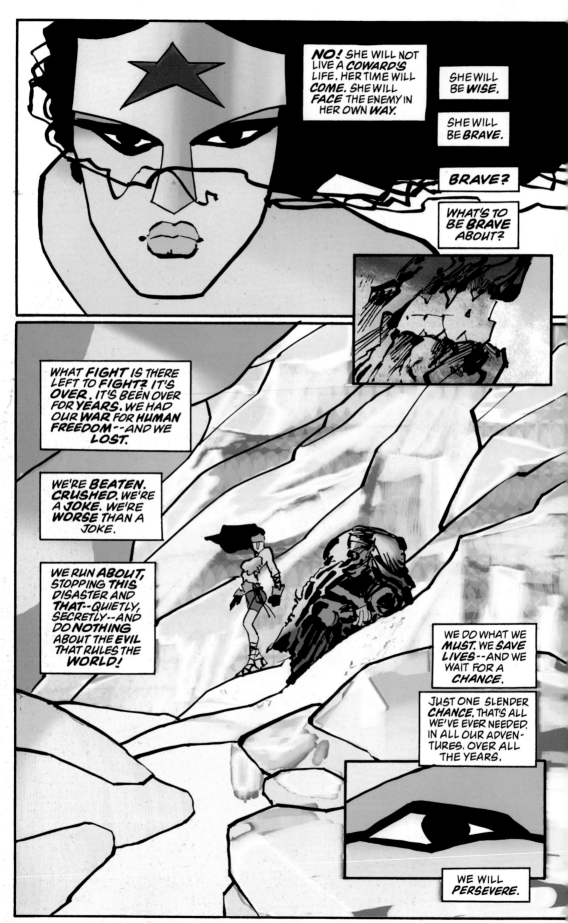

NO! SHE WILL NOT LIVE A COWARD'S LIFE. HER TIME WILL COME. SHE WILL FACE THE ENEMY IN HER OWN WAY.

SHE WILL BE WISE.

SHE WILL BE BRAVE.

BRAVE?

WHAT'S TO BE BRAVE ABOUT?

WHAT FIGHT IS THERE LEFT TO FIGHT? IT'S OVER. IT'S BEEN OVER FOR YEARS. WE HAD OUR WAR FOR HUMAN FREEDOM--AND WE LOST.

WE'RE BEATEN. CRUSHED. WE'RE A JOKE. WE'RE WORSE THAN A JOKE.

WE RUN ABOUT, STOPPING THIS DISASTER AND THAT--QUIETLY, SECRETLY--AND DO NOTHING ABOUT THE EVIL THAT RULES THE WORLD!

WE DO WHAT WE MUST. WE SAVE LIVES--AND WE WAIT FOR A CHANCE.

JUST ONE SLENDER CHANCE. THAT'S ALL WE'VE EVER NEEDED. IN ALL OUR ADVENTURES. OVER ALL THE YEARS.

WE WILL PERSEVERE.

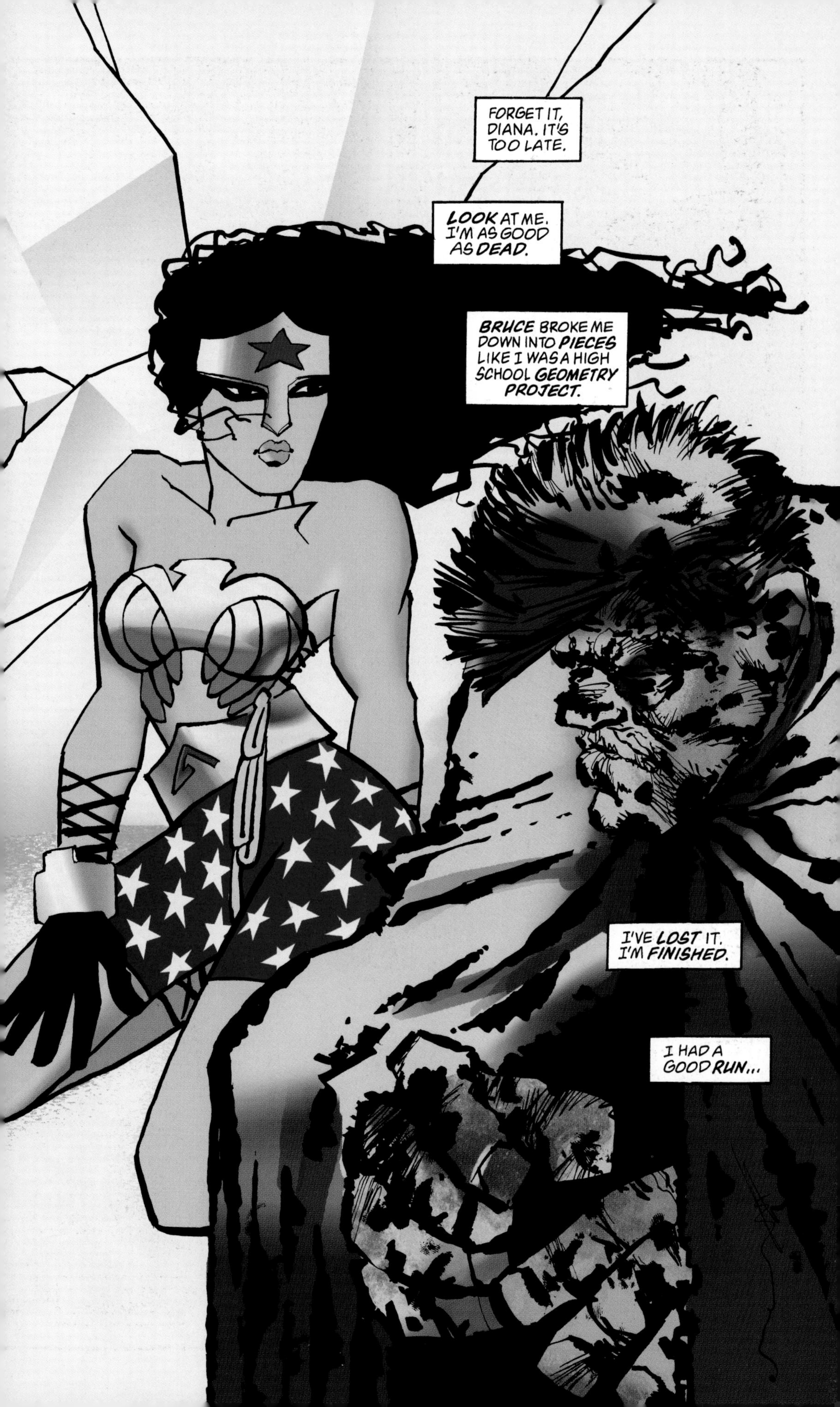
FORGET IT, DIANA. IT'S TOO LATE.
LOOK AT ME. I'M AS GOOD AS DEAD.
BRUCE BROKE ME DOWN INTO PIECES LIKE I WAS A HIGH SCHOOL GEOMETRY PROJECT.
I'VE LOST IT. I'M FINISHED.
I HAD A GOOD RUN...

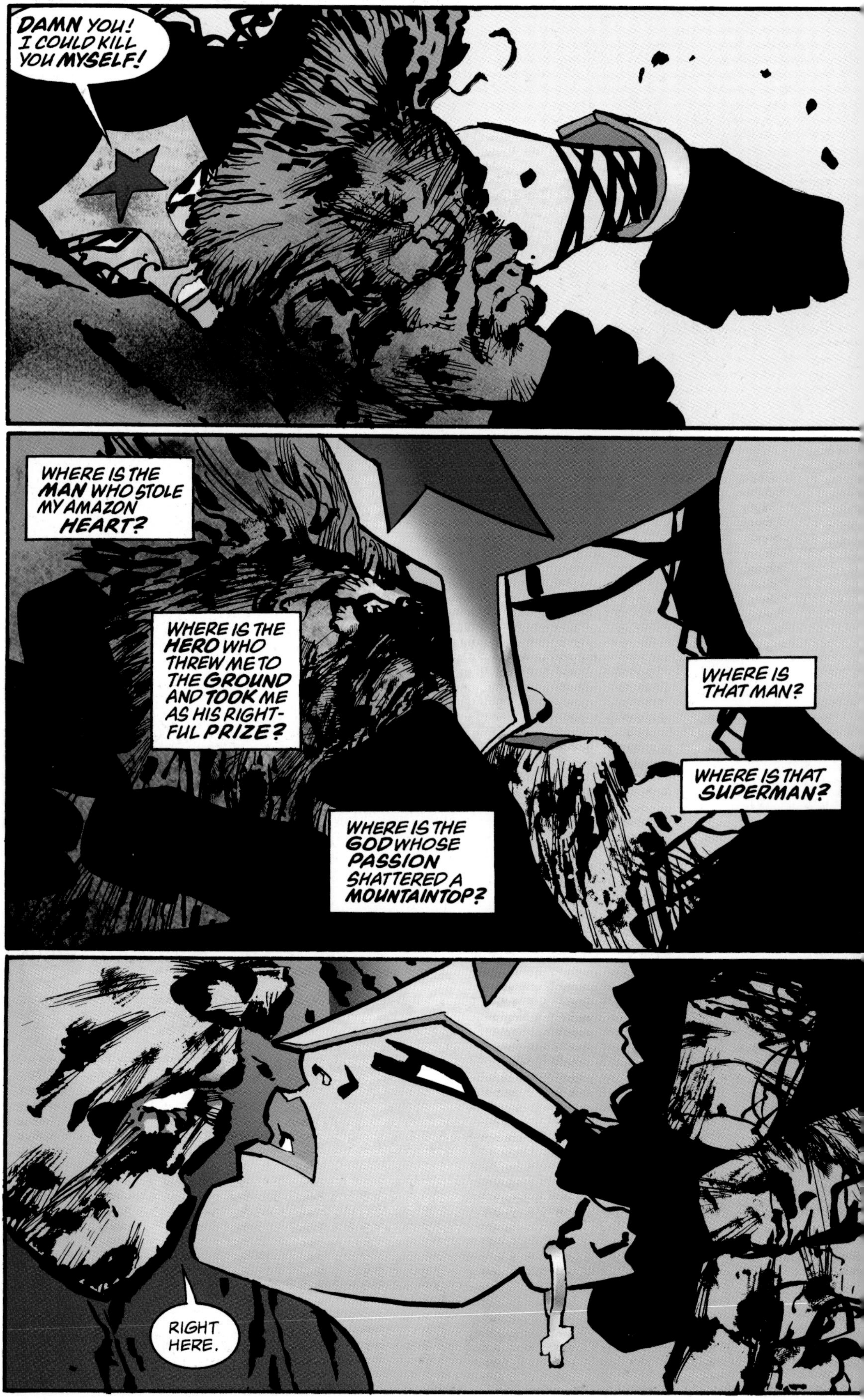

DAMN YOU! I COULD KILL YOU MYSELF!
WHERE IS THE MAN WHO STOLE MY AMAZON HEART?
WHERE IS THE HERO WHO THREW ME TO THE GROUND AND TOOK ME AS HIS RIGHT-FUL PRIZE?
WHERE IS THE GOD WHOSE PASSION SHATTERED A MOUNTAINTOP?
WHERE IS THAT MAN?
WHERE IS THAT SUPERMAN?
RIGHT HERE.

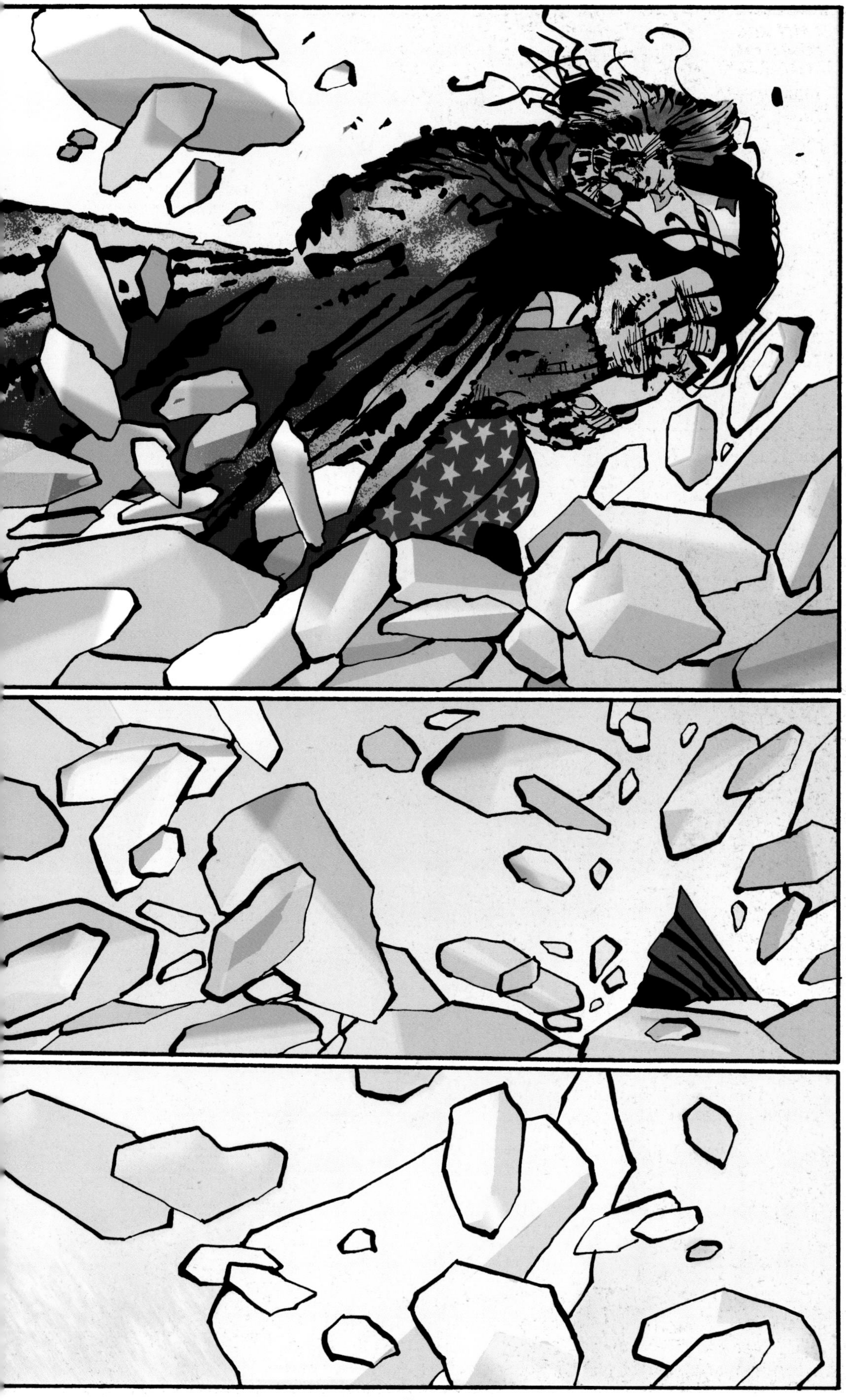

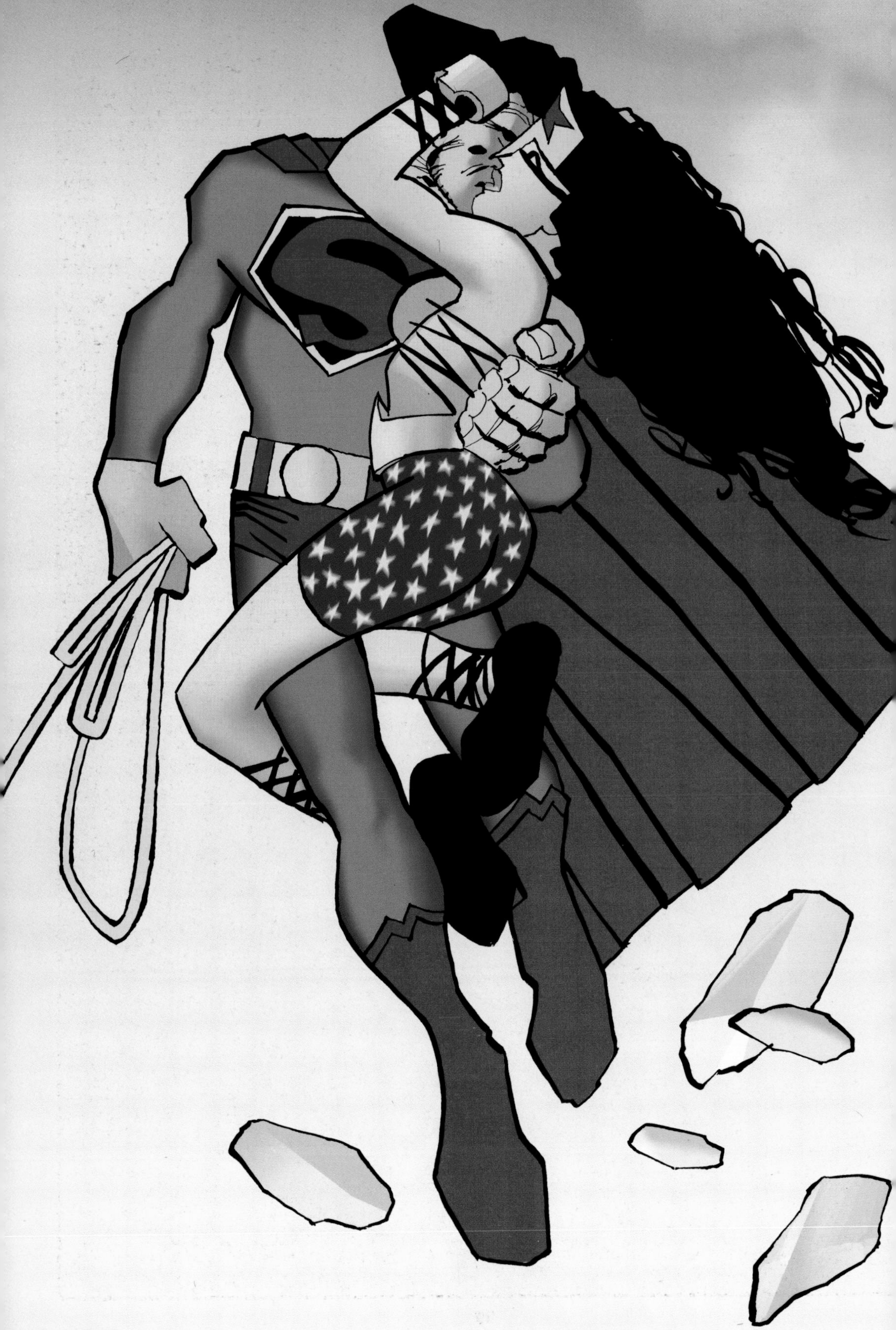

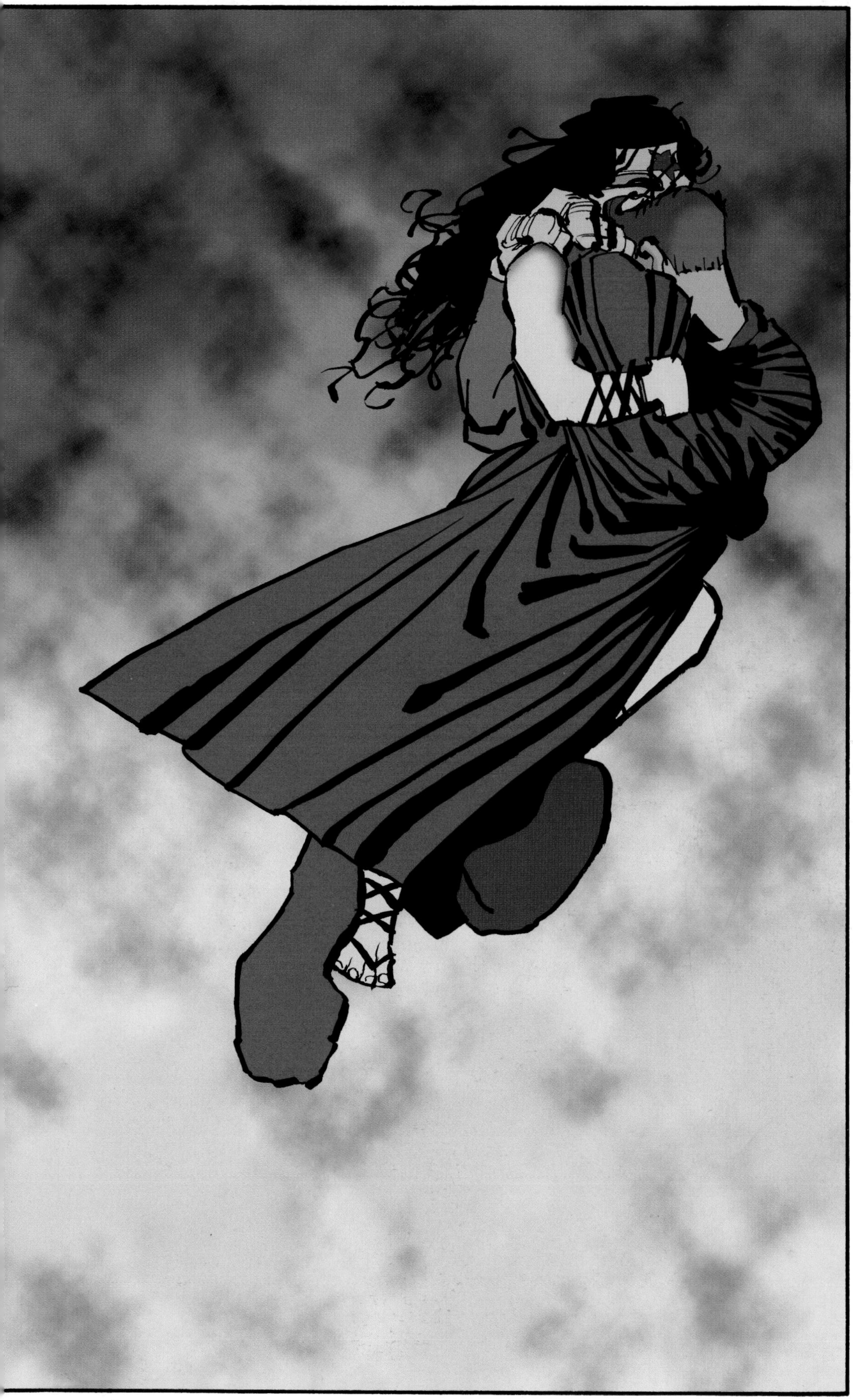

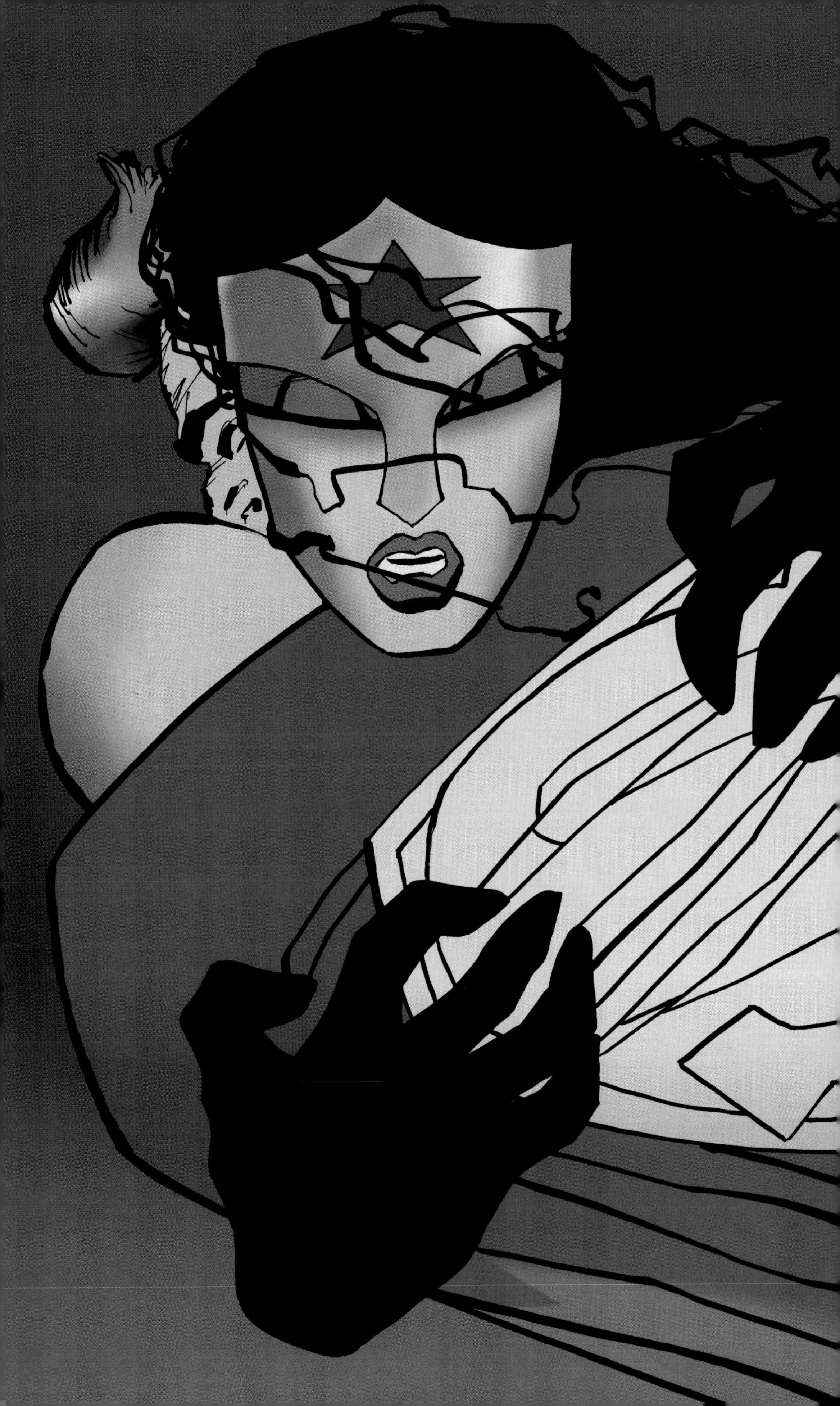

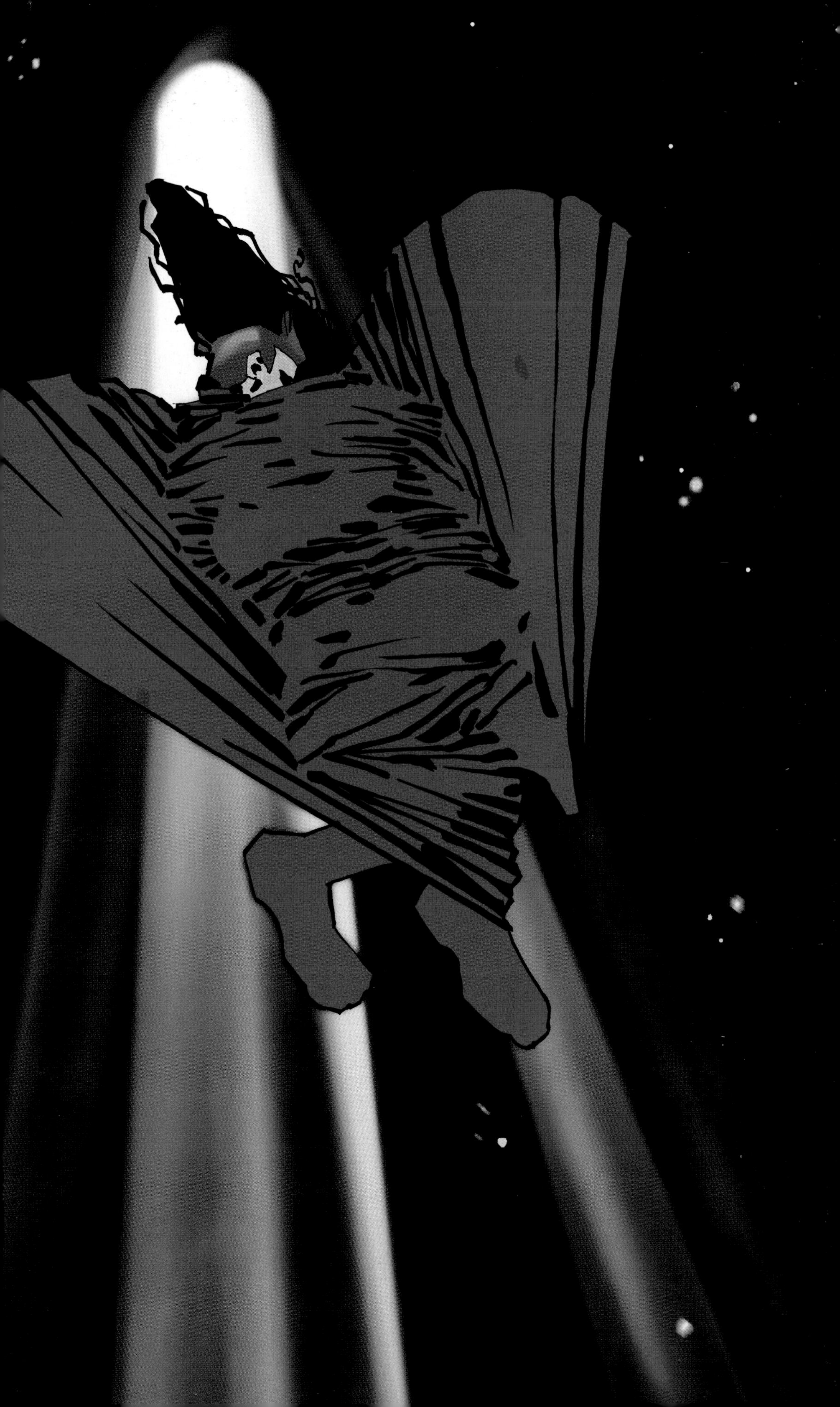

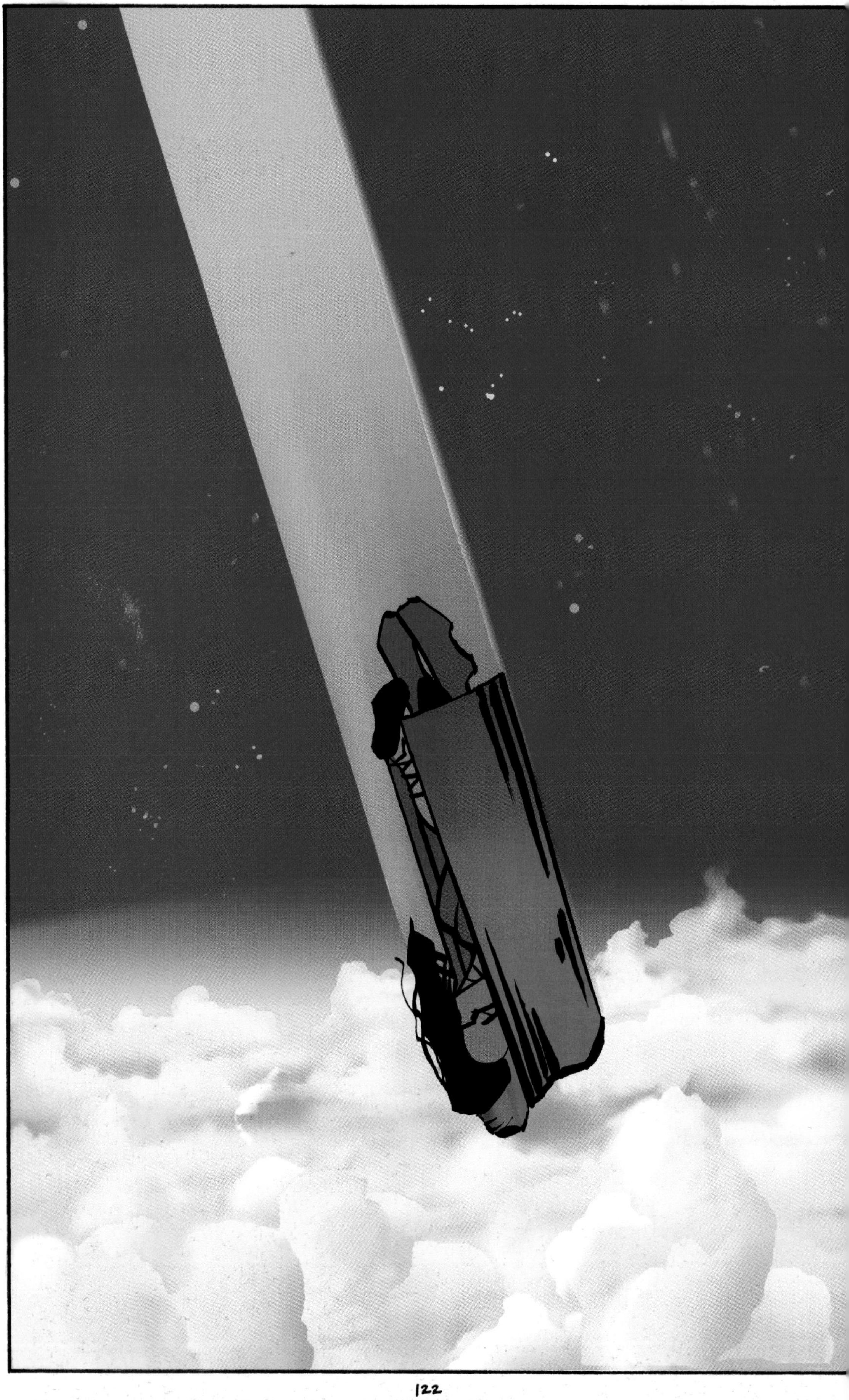

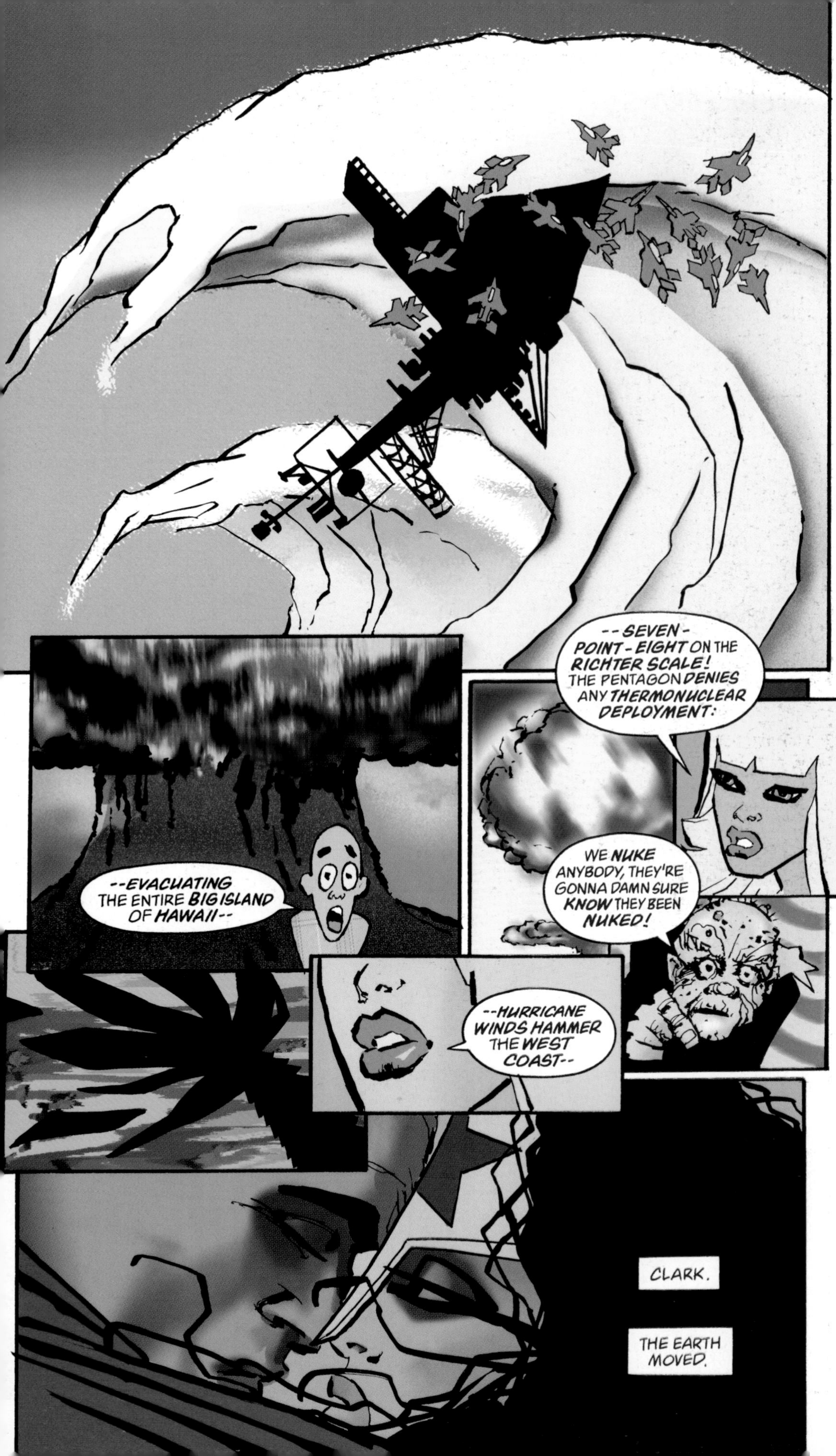
--SEVEN-POINT-EIGHT ON THE RICHTER SCALE! THE PENTAGON DENIES ANY THERMONUCLEAR DEPLOYMENT:
--EVACUATING THE ENTIRE BIG ISLAND OF HAWAII--
WE NUKE ANYBODY, THEY'RE GONNA DAMN SURE KNOW THEY BEEN NUKED!
--HURRICANE WINDS HAMMER THE WEST COAST--
CLARK.
THE EARTH MOVED.

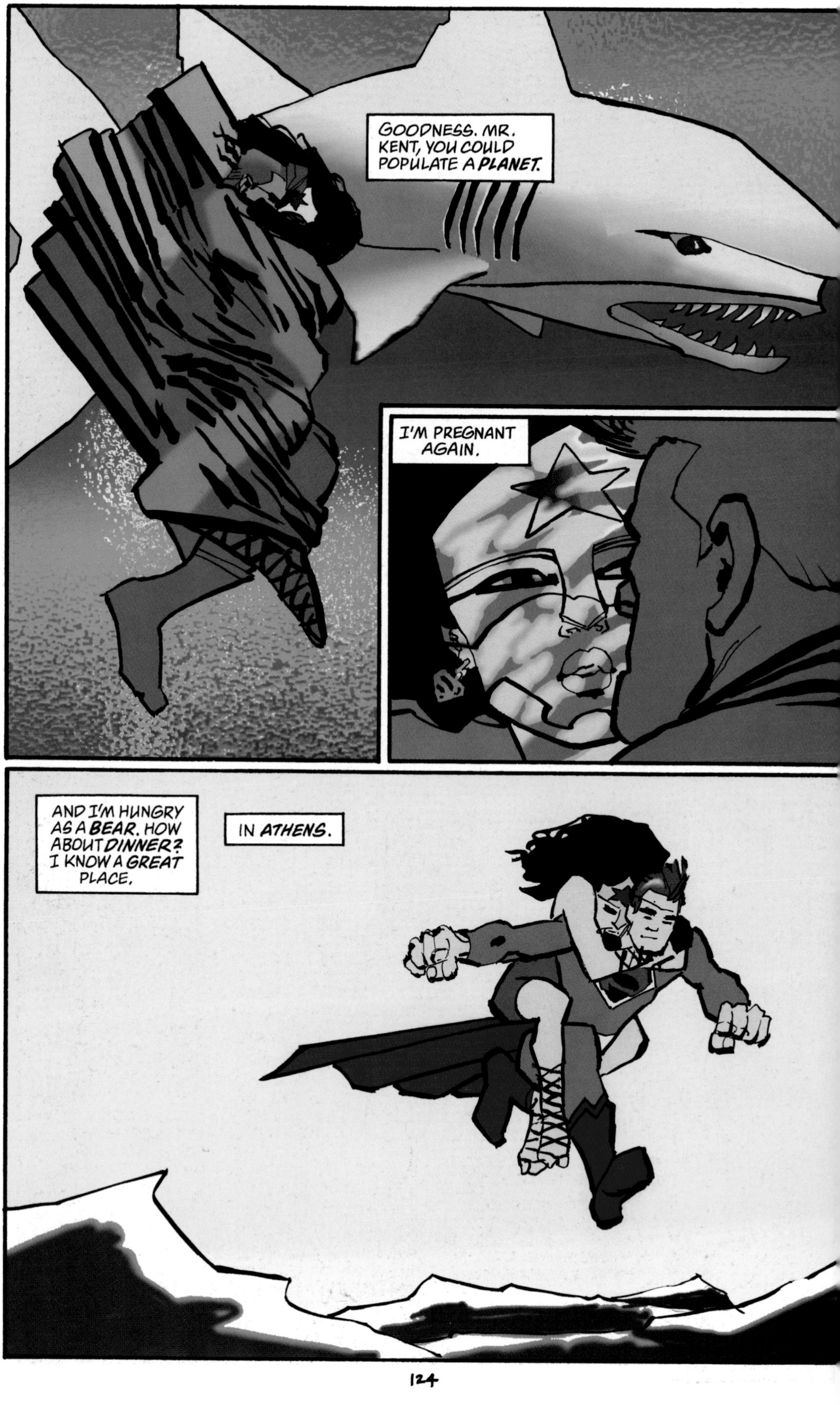
GOODNESS. MR. KENT, YOU COULD POPULATE A PLANET.
I'M PREGNANT AGAIN.
AND I'M HUNGRY AS A BEAR. HOW ABOUT DINNER? I KNOW A GREAT PLACE.
IN ATHENS.

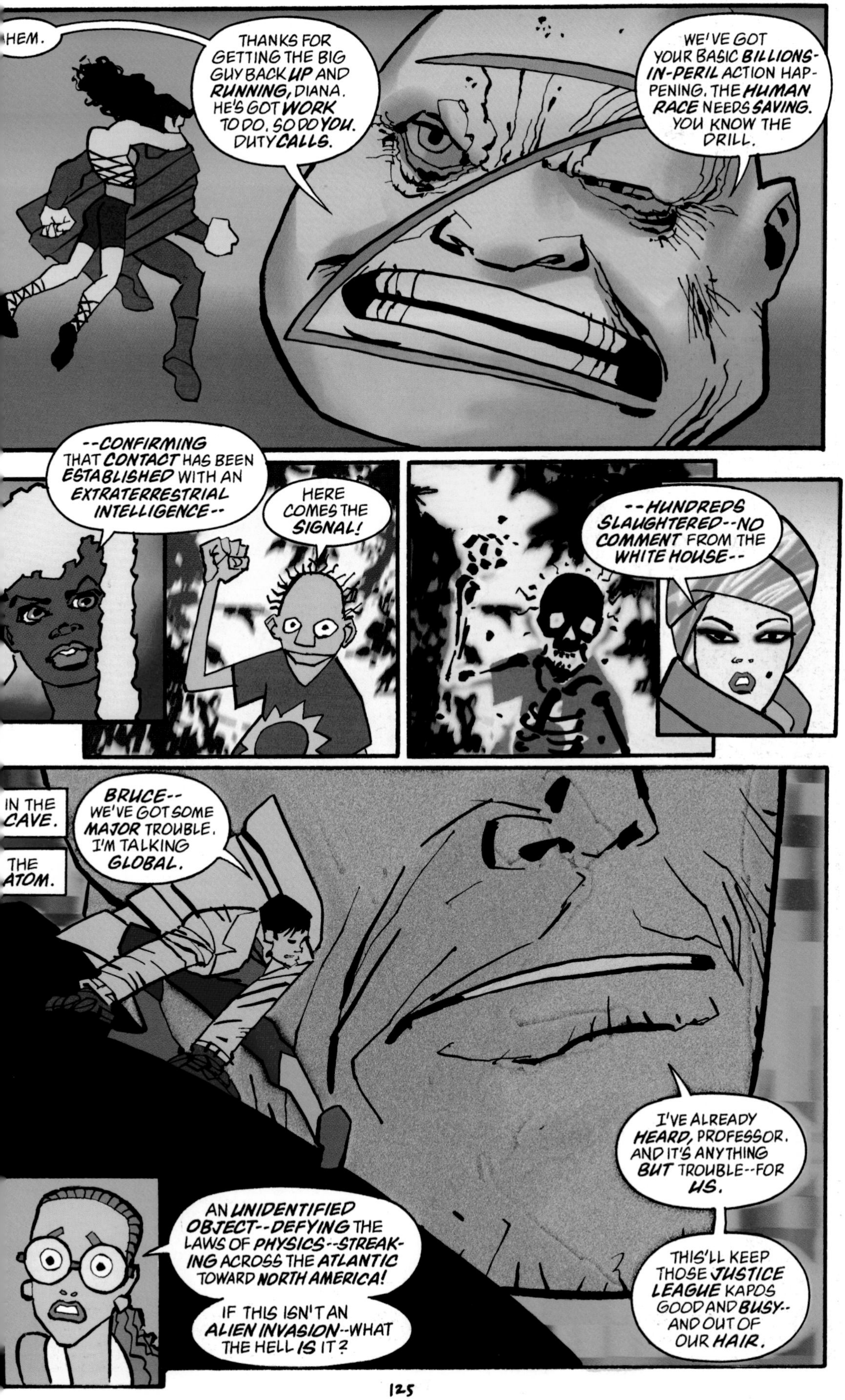

HEM.
THANKS FOR GETTING THE BIG GUY BACK UP AND RUNNING, DIANA. HE'S GOT WORK TO DO. SO DO YOU. DUTY CALLS.
WE'VE GOT YOUR BASIC BILLIONS-IN-PERIL ACTION HAPPENING. THE HUMAN RACE NEEDS SAVING. YOU KNOW THE DRILL.
--CONFIRMING THAT CONTACT HAS BEEN ESTABLISHED WITH AN EXTRATERRESTRIAL INTELLIGENCE--
HERE COMES THE SIGNAL!
--HUNDREDS SLAUGHTERED--NO COMMENT FROM THE WHITE HOUSE--
IN THE CAVE.
THE ATOM.
BRUCE-- WE'VE GOT SOME MAJOR TROUBLE. I'M TALKING GLOBAL.
I'VE ALREADY HEARD, PROFESSOR. AND IT'S ANYTHING BUT TROUBLE--FOR US.
AN UNIDENTIFIED OBJECT--DEFYING THE LAWS OF PHYSICS--STREAKING ACROSS THE ATLANTIC TOWARD NORTH AMERICA!
IF THIS ISN'T AN ALIEN INVASION--WHAT THE HELL IS IT?
THIS'LL KEEP THOSE JUSTICE LEAGUE KAPOS GOOD AND BUSY-- AND OUT OF OUR HAIR.

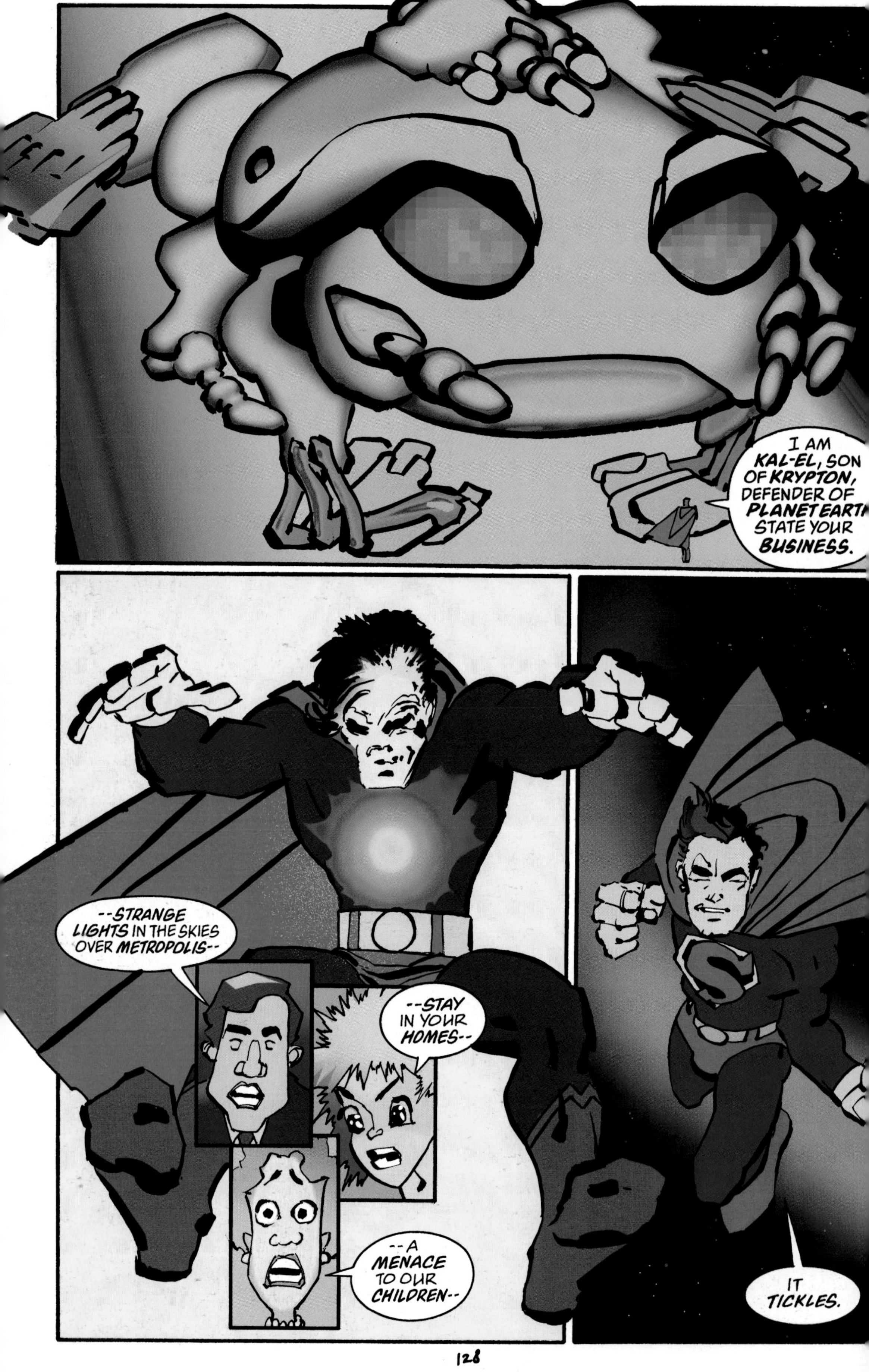
I AM KAL-EL, SON OF KRYPTON, DEFENDER OF PLANET EARTH STATE YOUR BUSINESS.
--STRANGE LIGHTS IN THE SKIES OVER METROPOLIS--
--STAY IN YOUR HOMES--
--A MENACE TO OUR CHILDREN--
IT TICKLES.

I KNOW BLACK CANARY'S SECRET IDENTITY.

WONDER CHICK GAVE ME THIS. SHE PEELED IT RIGHT OFF HER BUTT AND GAVE IT TO ME.

BATCHICK SENDS ME EMAILS.

HEY, I'D VIOLATE THOSE TRADEMARKS.

THE PRESIDENT'S LIKE, SMART AND EVERYTHING, BUT TOTALLY CLUELESS?

I'M LIKE, EXCUSE ME, BUT WE'RE LIKE, SERIOUSLY SERIOUS ARTISTS? WE'RE LIKE, TOTALLY EXPRESSING OURSELVES?

THEY'RE TOO SKINNY. IT'S NOT HEALTHY.

LOOK! UP IN THE SKY! IT'S--

--OH, SHIT--

YAAA--!

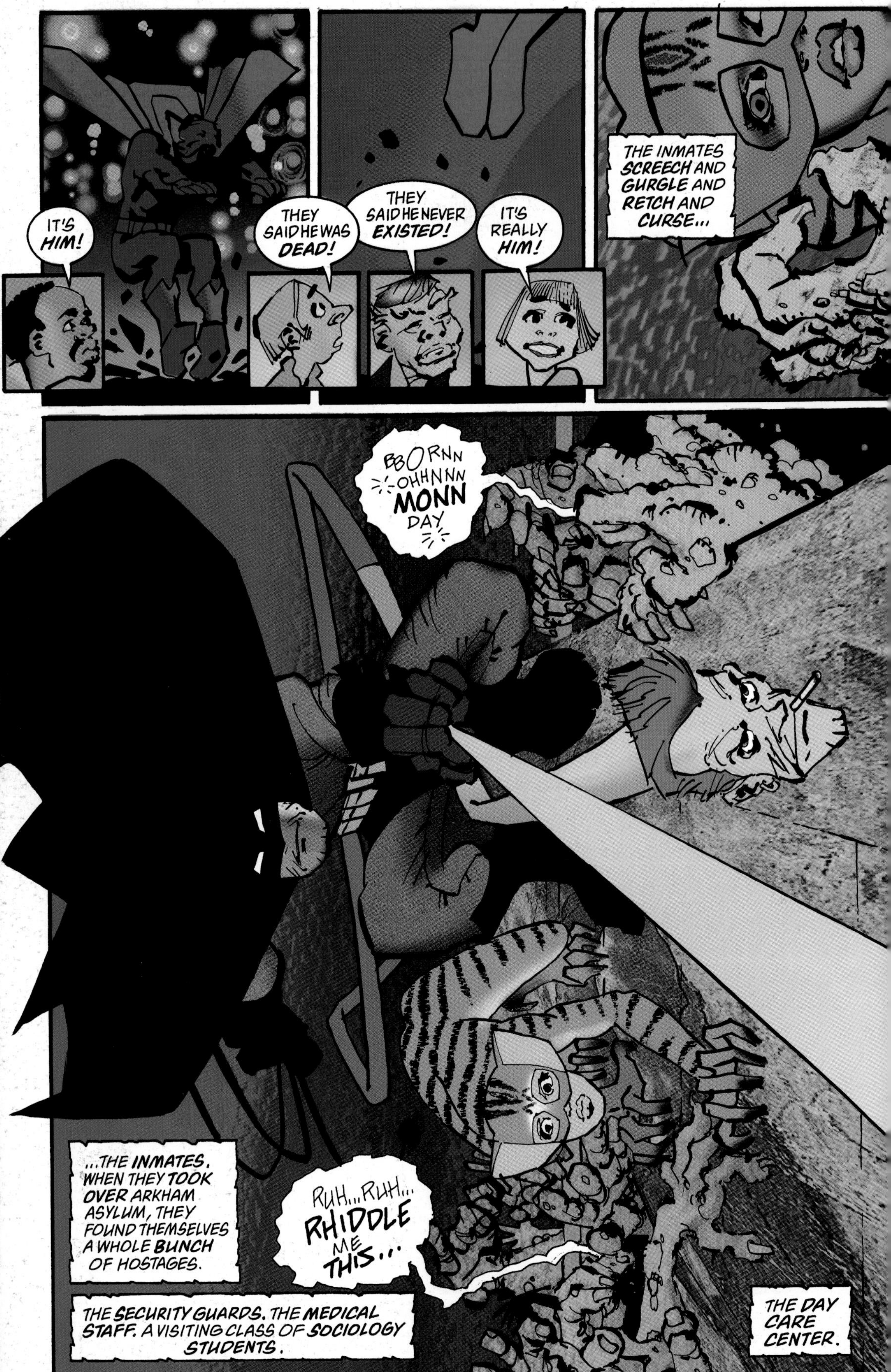

IT'S HIM!
THEY SAID HE WAS DEAD!
THEY SAID HE NEVER EXISTED!
IT'S REALLY HIM!
THE INMATES SCREECH AND GURGLE AND RETCH AND CURSE...
BBORNN OHHNNNN MONN DAY
...THE INMATES. WHEN THEY TOOK OVER ARKHAM ASYLUM, THEY FOUND THEMSELVES A WHOLE BUNCH OF HOSTAGES.
RUH...RUH... RHIDDLE ME THIS...
THE SECURITY GUARDS. THE MEDICAL STAFF. A VISITING CLASS OF SOCIOLOGY STUDENTS.
THE DAY CARE CENTER.

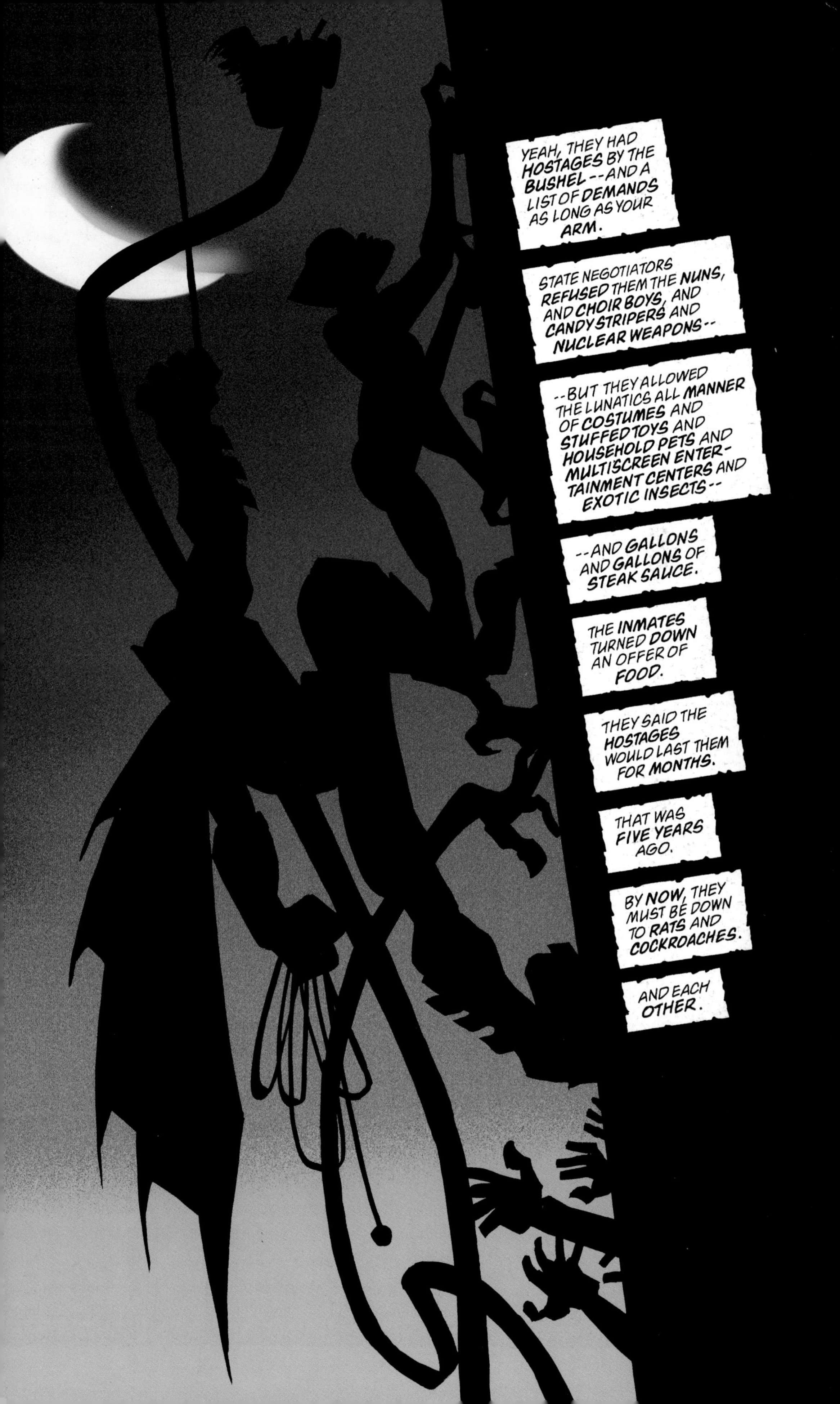
YEAH, THEY HAD HOSTAGES BY THE BUSHEL--AND A LIST OF DEMANDS AS LONG AS YOUR ARM.
STATE NEGOTIATORS REFUSED THEM THE NUNS, AND CHOIR BOYS, AND CANDY STRIPERS AND NUCLEAR WEAPONS--
--BUT THEY ALLOWED THE LUNATICS ALL MANNER OF COSTUMES AND STUFFED TOYS AND HOUSEHOLD PETS AND MULTISCREEN ENTER-TAINMENT CENTERS AND EXOTIC INSECTS--
--AND GALLONS AND GALLONS OF STEAK SAUCE.
THE INMATES TURNED DOWN AN OFFER OF FOOD.
THEY SAID THE HOSTAGES WOULD LAST THEM FOR MONTHS.
THAT WAS FIVE YEARS AGO.
BY NOW, THEY MUST BE DOWN TO RATS AND COCKROACHES.
AND EACH OTHER.

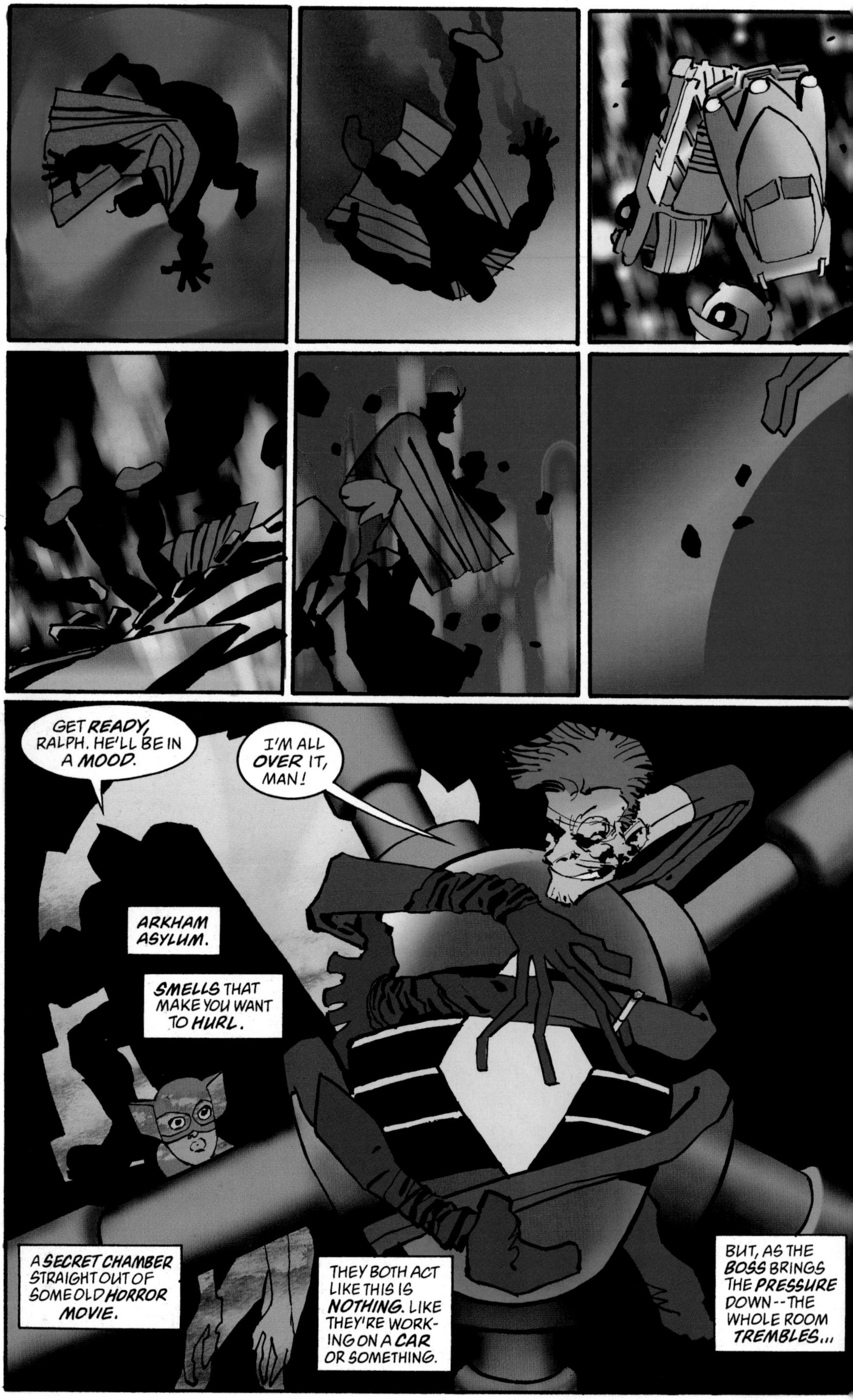
GET READY, RALPH. HE'LL BE IN A MOOD.
I'M ALL OVER IT, MAN!
ARKHAM ASYLUM.
SMELLS THAT MAKE YOU WANT TO HURL.
A SECRET CHAMBER STRAIGHT OUT OF SOME OLD HORROR MOVIE.
THEY BOTH ACT LIKE THIS IS NOTHING. LIKE THEY'RE WORKING ON A CAR OR SOMETHING.
BUT, AS THE BOSS BRINGS THE PRESSURE DOWN--THE WHOLE ROOM TREMBLES...

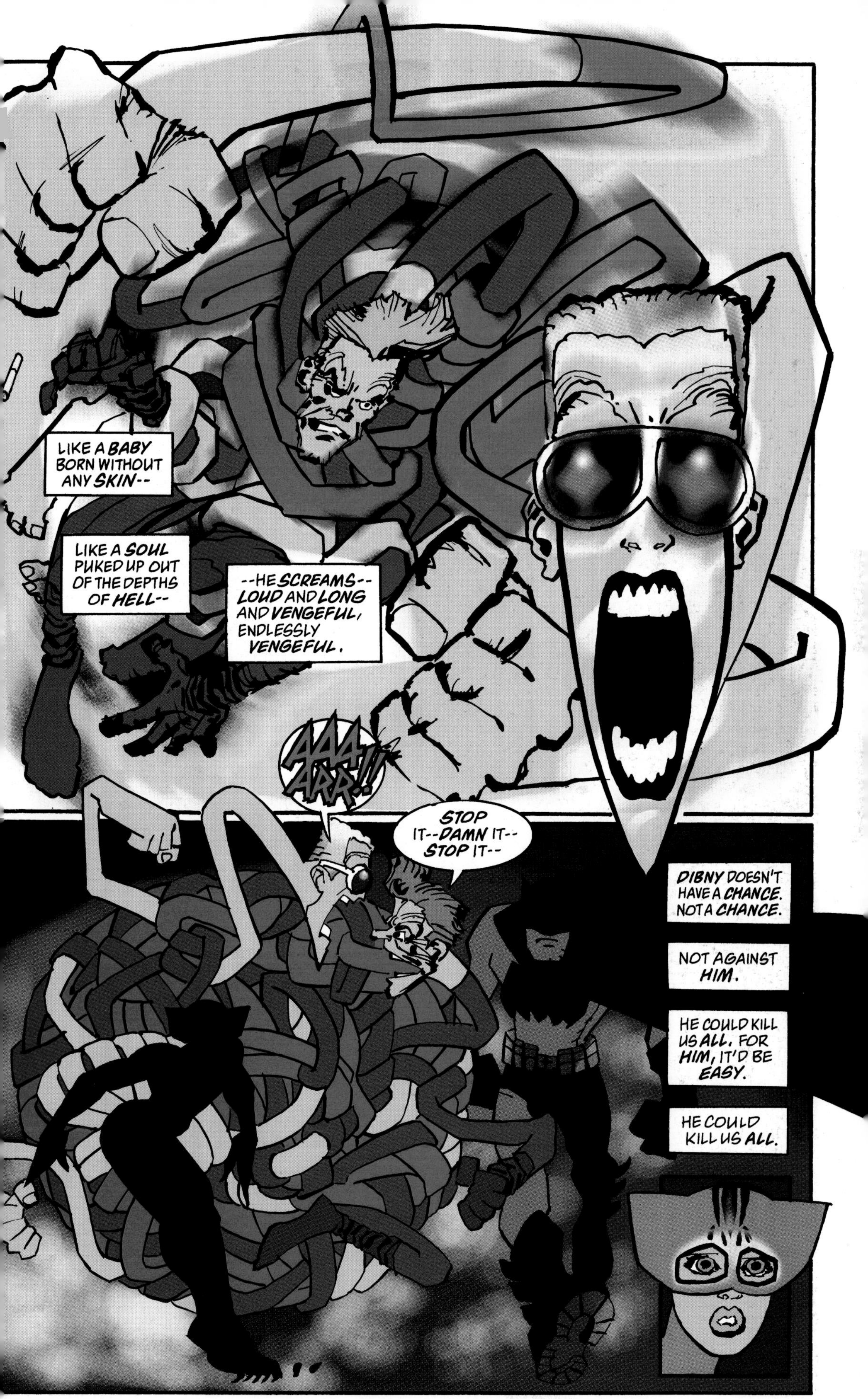

LIKE A BABY BORN WITHOUT ANY SKIN--
LIKE A SOUL PUKED UP OUT OF THE DEPTHS OF HELL--
--HE SCREAMS--LOUD AND LONG AND VENGEFUL, ENDLESSLY VENGEFUL.
AAAARRR!!
STOP IT--DAMN IT--STOP IT--
DIBNY DOESN'T HAVE A CHANCE. NOT A CHANCE.
NOT AGAINST HIM.
HE COULD KILL US ALL. FOR HIM, IT'D BE EASY.
HE COULD KILL US ALL.

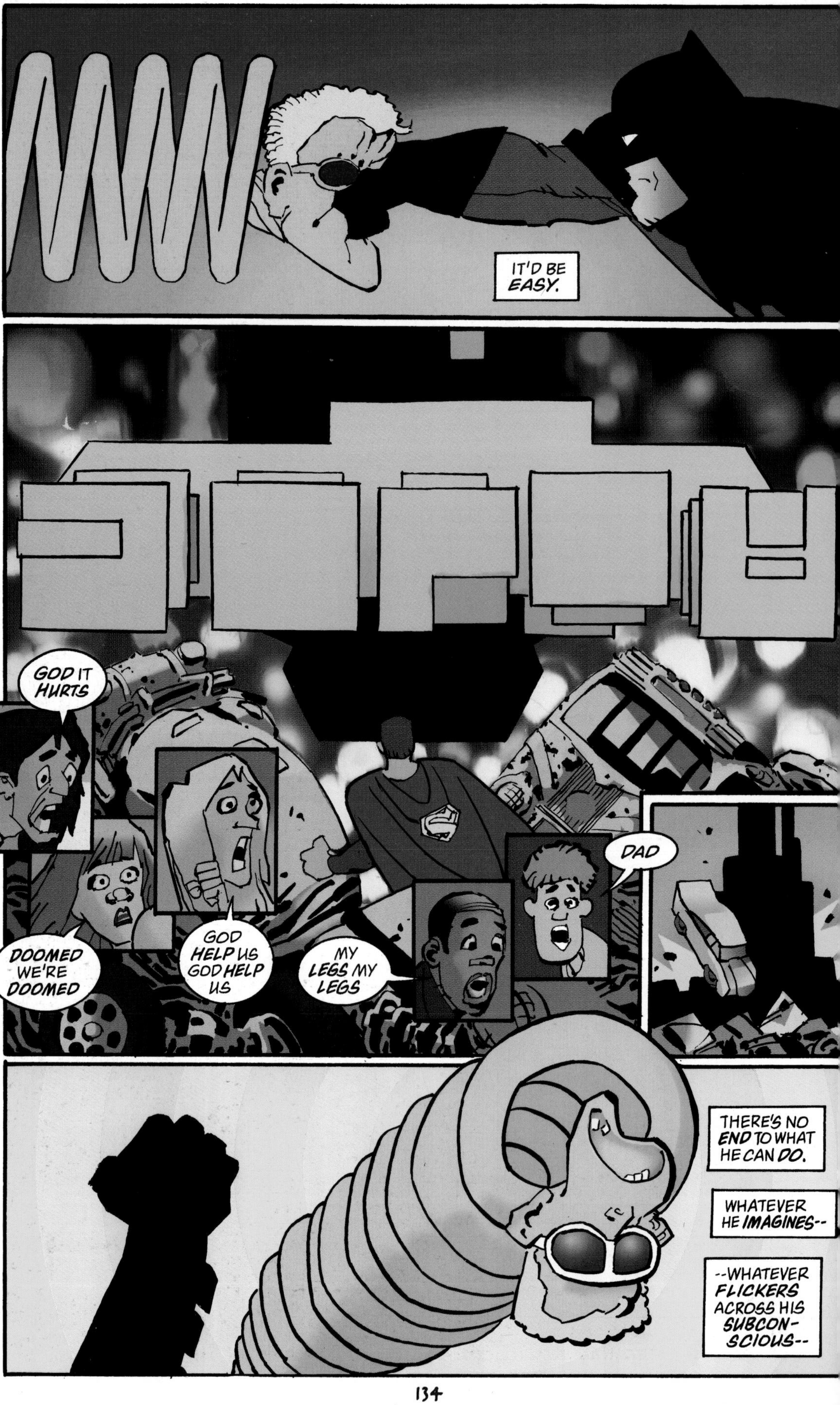
IT'D BE EASY.
GOD IT HURTS
DOOMED WE'RE DOOMED
GOD HELP US GOD HELP US
MY LEGS MY LEGS
DAD
THERE'S NO END TO WHAT HE CAN DO.
WHATEVER HE IMAGINES--
--WHATEVER FLICKERS ACROSS HIS SUBCON-SCIOUS--

--HE *BECOMES.*

HEY!

THANKS, BATS. YOU'VE ALWAYS KNOWN HOW TO SLAP A LITTLE *SENSE* INTO ME. I'M *READY* AND *RARIN'* TO GO!

SAY--WHAT *YEAR* IS IT, ANYWAY?

THE YEAR WE *FIX* THINGS. THE YEAR WE *SET THINGS STRAIGHT.*

WITH YA, DUDE.

YOU KNOW, I REALLY HOPE THIS IS ACTUALLY HAPPENING. THAT I'M NOT STILL IN THAT *EGG* HAVING ONE OF THOSE DREAMS. I MEAN, THAT'D BE *OKAY,* BUT IT'D BE COOL IF THIS WAS REAL.

...IT'S *GOTTA* BE REAL. I NEVER COULDA DREAMED UP ANYBODY AS *BORING* AS *YOU.*

LOOK AT YOU. YOU'RE *PATHETIC.* ALL YOU DO IS *STRETCH.* YOU DON'T EVEN *TURN* INTO STUFF.

WAIT A MINUTE...

I DON'T GET ANY *COMPLAINTS* FROM THE *BABES,* SILLY PUTTY BOY!

BABES? HEY. I DO BABES.

LET'S GET ROLLING, GUYS.

EEL O'BRIEN.

PLASTIC MAN.

IMMEASURABLY *POWERFUL.*

ABSOLUTELY *NUTS.*

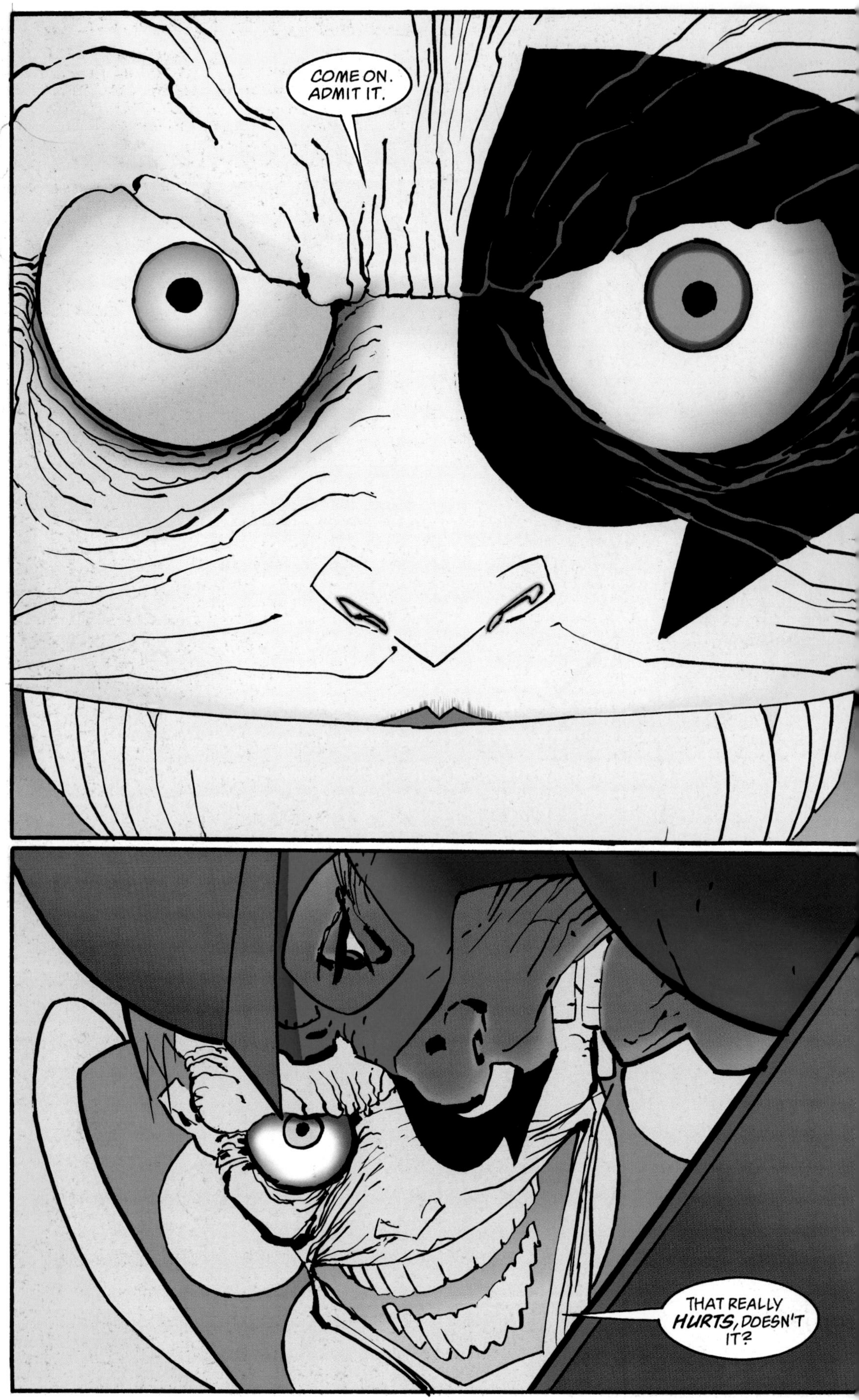
COME ON. ADMIT IT.
THAT REALLY HURTS, DOESN'T IT?

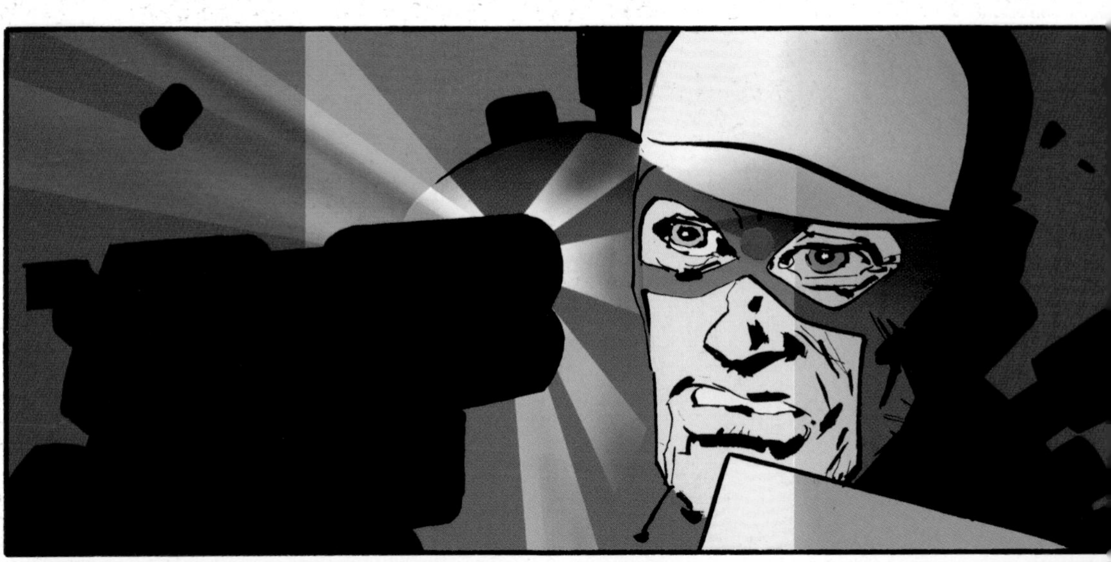

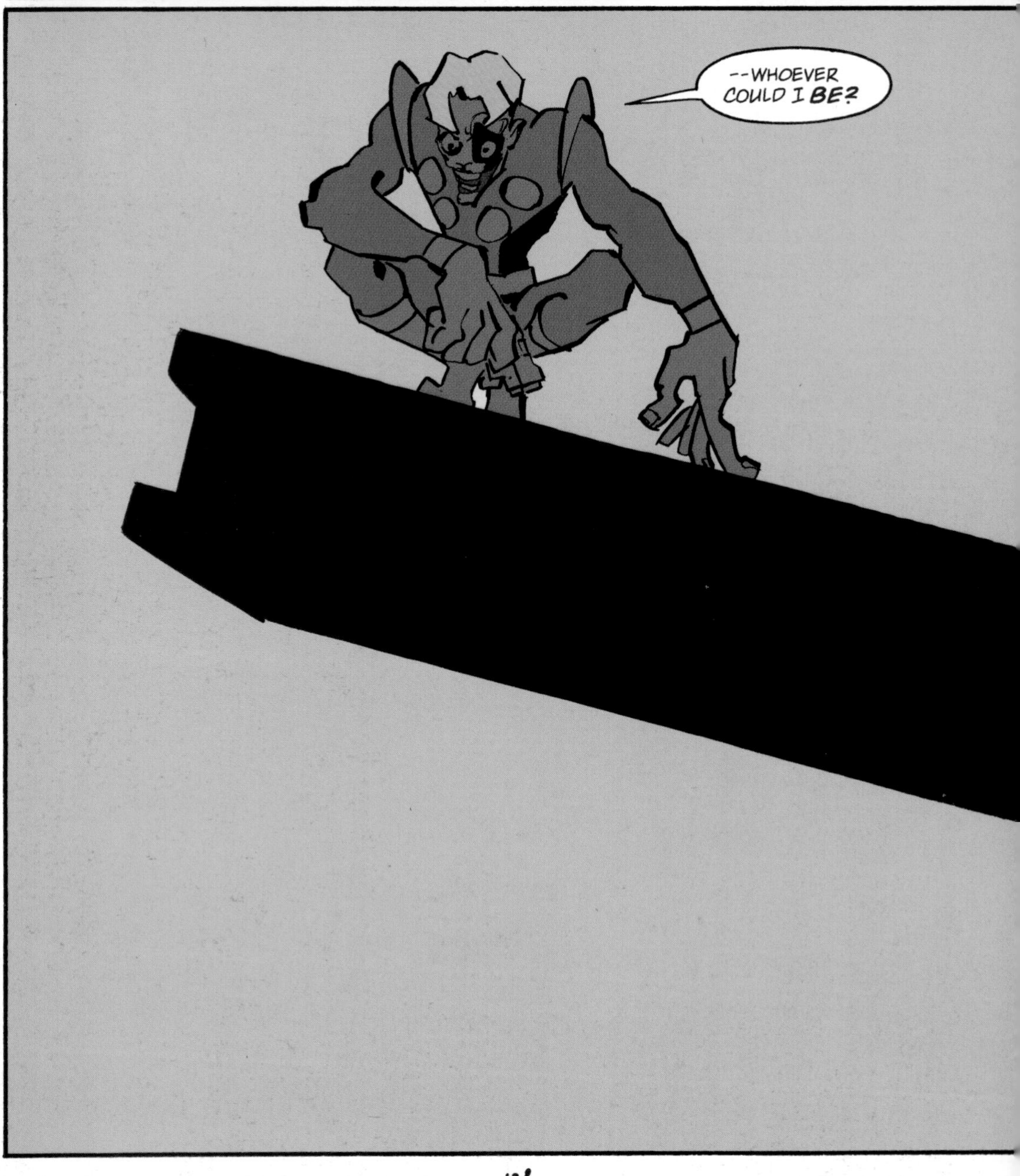
--WHOEVER COULD I BE?

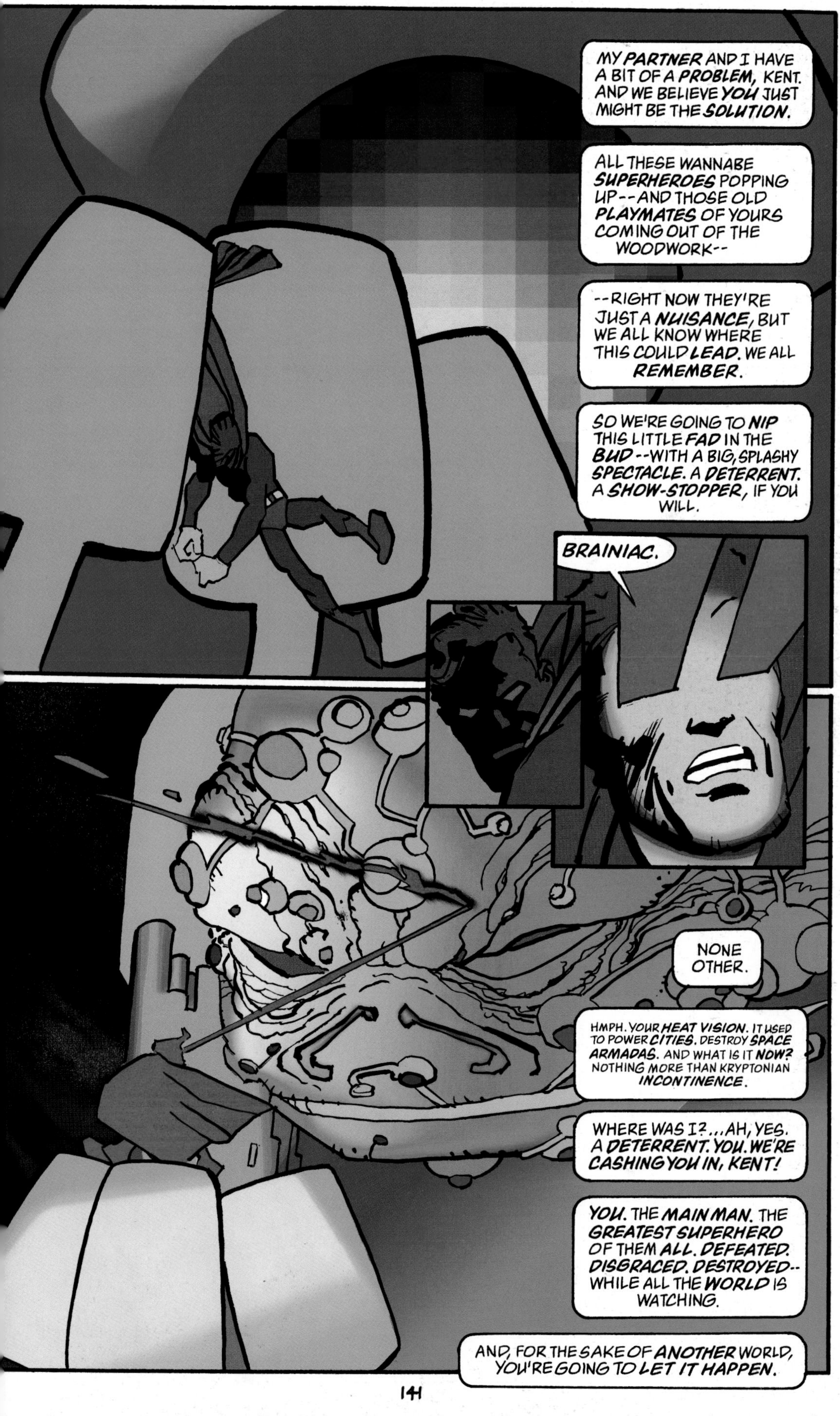
MY PARTNER AND I HAVE A BIT OF A PROBLEM, KENT. AND WE BELIEVE YOU JUST MIGHT BE THE SOLUTION.
ALL THESE WANNABE SUPERHEROES POPPING UP--AND THOSE OLD PLAYMATES OF YOURS COMING OUT OF THE WOODWORK--
--RIGHT NOW THEY'RE JUST A NUISANCE, BUT WE ALL KNOW WHERE THIS COULD LEAD. WE ALL REMEMBER.
SO WE'RE GOING TO NIP THIS LITTLE FAD IN THE BUD--WITH A BIG, SPLASHY SPECTACLE. A DETERRENT. A SHOW-STOPPER, IF YOU WILL.
BRAINIAC.
NONE OTHER.
HMPH. YOUR HEAT VISION. IT USED TO POWER CITIES. DESTROY SPACE ARMADAS. AND WHAT IS IT NOW? NOTHING MORE THAN KRYPTONIAN INCONTINENCE.
WHERE WAS I?...AH, YES. A DETERRENT. YOU. WE'RE CASHING YOU IN, KENT!
YOU. THE MAIN MAN. THE GREATEST SUPERHERO OF THEM ALL. DEFEATED. DISGRACED. DESTROYED--WHILE ALL THE WORLD IS WATCHING.
AND, FOR THE SAKE OF ANOTHER WORLD, YOU'RE GOING TO LET IT HAPPEN.

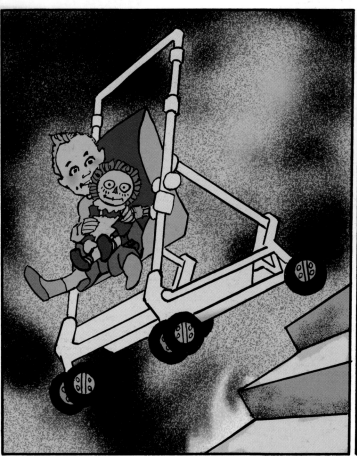

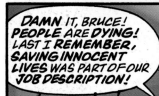

DAMN IT, BRUCE! PEOPLE ARE DYING! LAST I REMEMBER, SAVING INNOCENT LIVES WAS PART OF OUR JOB DESCRIPTION!

MAN, YOU'RE AS THICK AS CLARK IS! THAT ROBOT IS A TRICK--TO FLUSH US OUT--SO THEY CAN KILL US!

THIS IS MY SHOW! MY WAR! WE FOLLOW MY STRATEGY!

IN THE CAVE.

BARRY ALLEN. THE FLASH.

HE'S GETTING A LITTLE WEAK IN THE KNEES.

YOUR "WAR"--IT'S ALWAYS BEEN A WAR TO YOU, HASN'T IT?

IT SURE AS HELL HAS! AND IF ALL YOU DEPUTIZED LITTLE PUBLIC SERVANTS HAD SEEN IT FOR WHAT IT IS, WE WOULDN'T BE LIVING IN A DAMN SLAVE STATE!

GENTLEMEN--I'M GETTING SOME MAJOR READINGS FROM THE PENTAGON. SOMETHING'S GOING DOWN LARGE.

GUYS?

145

The place STINKS of SMOKE and URINE and VOMIT. Its every SURFACE is TACKY with carcinogenic TAR.

They call it a "WATERING HOLE." That is a LIE. WATER brings LIFE. LIQUOR brings FALSE CONFIDENCE and DULL WITS and BROKEN LIVES and SLOW DEATH.

Someone COUGHS incessantly.

GUY WAITING FOR YOU, TABLE IN BACK. HE'S GOT NO FACE.

HEARD ABOUT SUPERMAN? FIGHT'S GONE OUTTA HIM.

IT HAPPENS.

SAGE. BEEN A WHILE.

SO WHEN'D YOU TAKE UP DRINKING, BUD? NEVER THOUGHT I'D SEE THE DAY.

YOU STILL HAVEN'T.

I WISHED TO SIT HERE. I PAID FAIR RENTAL FOR THIS CHAIR AND TABLE.

CUSTOM DICTATED I BE GIVEN THIS GLASS OF POISON.

I AM NOT, HOWEVER, UNDER ANY OBLIGATION TO CONSUME IT.

YEAH, I FIGURED IT WAS SOMETHING LIKE THAT. JUST TRYING TO GET YOUR GOAT.

YOU SHOULDN'T OUGHTA HAVE COME LOOKING ME UP, VIC. YOU'RE WASTING YOUR TIME.

I KNOW WHY YOU'RE HERE-- AND I'M USE-LESS TO YOU.

JOHN JONES.

MANHUNTER from MARS.

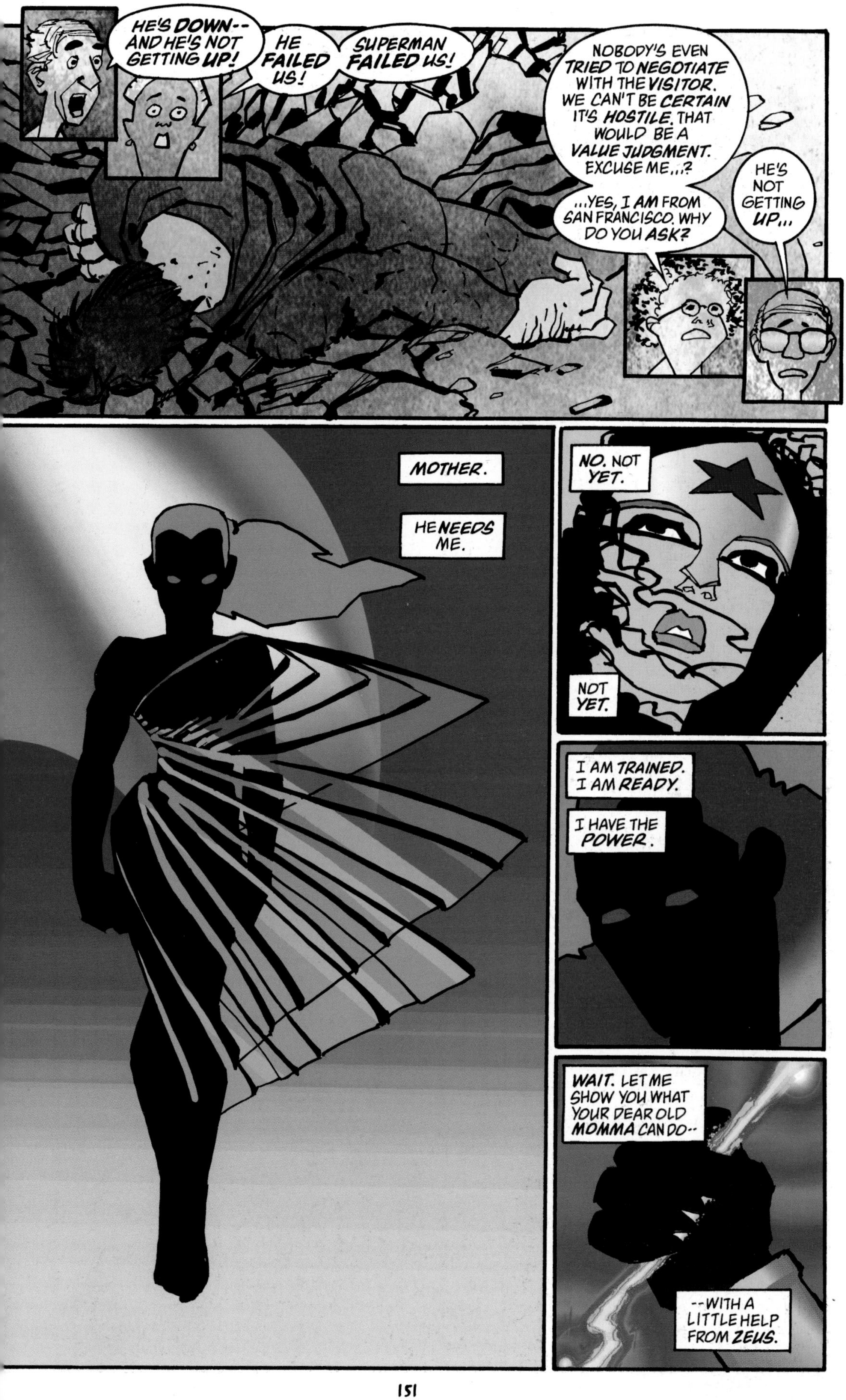
HE'S DOWN-- AND HE'S NOT GETTING UP!
HE FAILED US!
SUPERMAN FAILED US!
NOBODY'S EVEN TRIED TO NEGOTIATE WITH THE VISITOR. WE CAN'T BE CERTAIN IT'S HOSTILE. THAT WOULD BE A VALUE JUDGMENT. EXCUSE ME...?
...YES, I AM FROM SAN FRANCISCO. WHY DO YOU ASK?
HE'S NOT GETTING UP...
MOTHER.
HE NEEDS ME.
NO. NOT YET.
NOT YET.
I AM TRAINED. I AM READY.
I HAVE THE POWER.
WAIT. LET ME SHOW YOU WHAT YOUR DEAR OLD MOMMA CAN DO--
--WITH A LITTLE HELP FROM ZEUS.

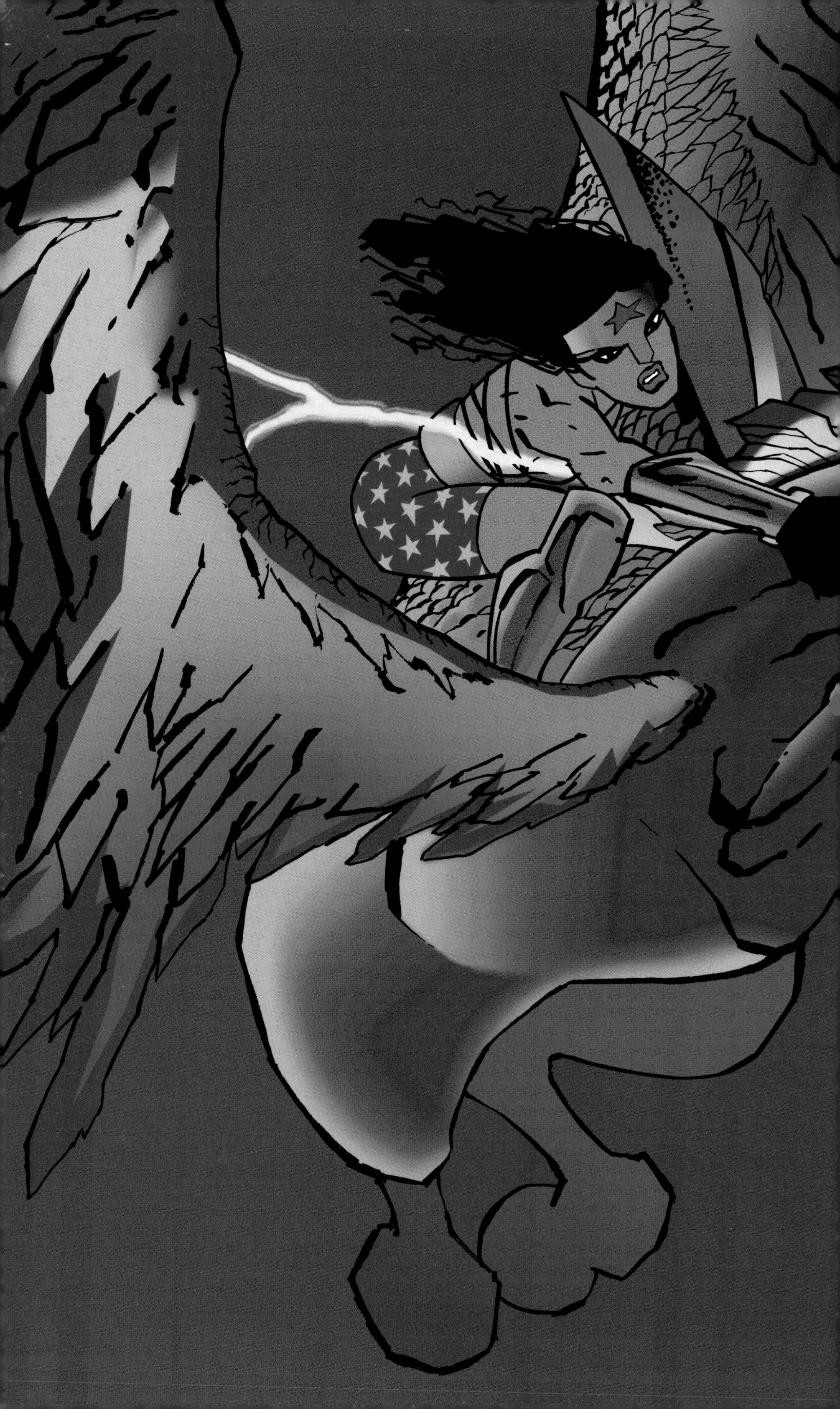

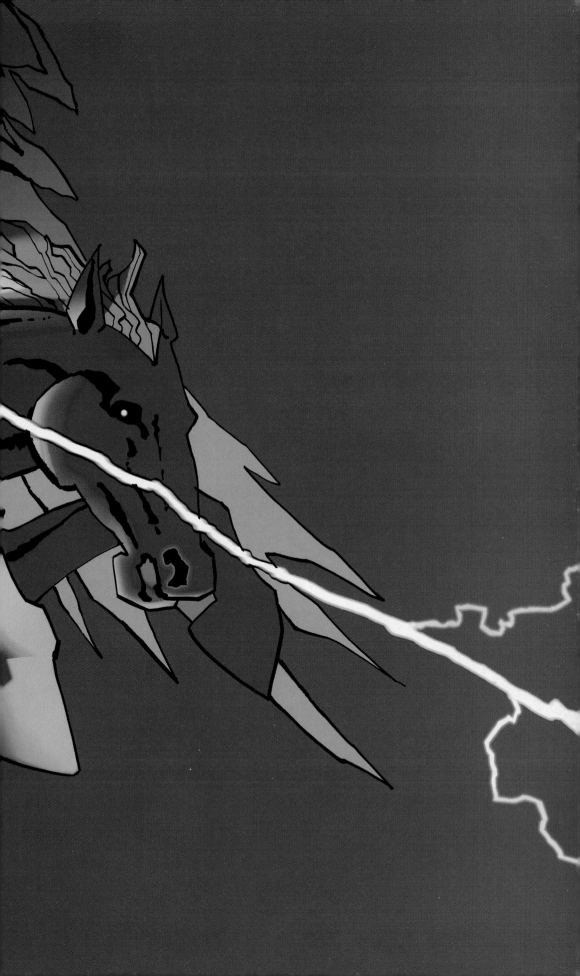

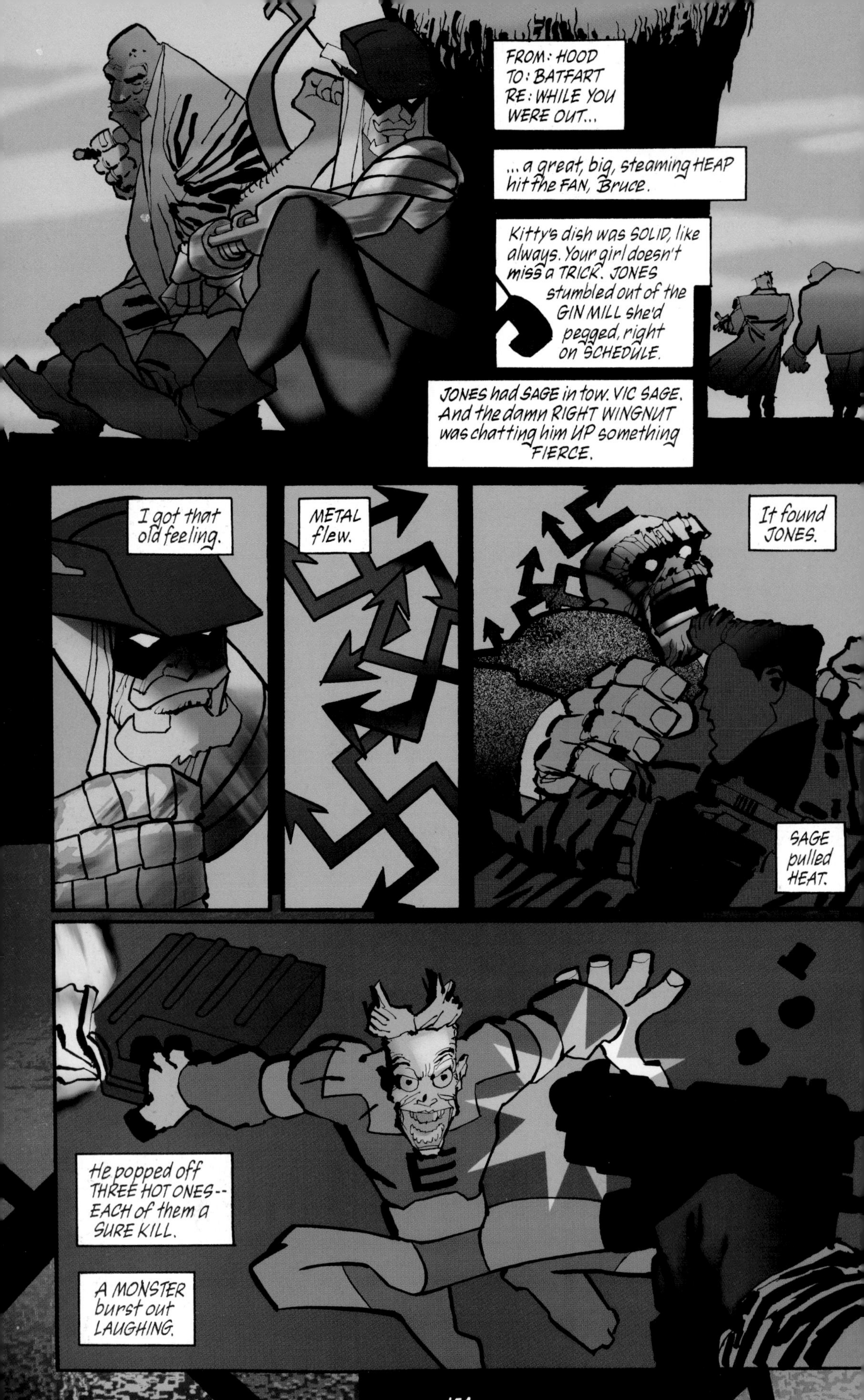
FROM: HOOD
TO: BATFART
RE: WHILE YOU WERE OUT...
... a great, big, steaming HEAP hit the FAN, Bruce.
Kitty's dish was SOLID, like always. Your girl doesn't miss a TRICK. JONES stumbled out of the GIN MILL she'd pegged, right on SCHEDULE.
JONES had SAGE in tow. VIC SAGE. And the damn RIGHT WINGNUT was chatting him UP something FIERCE.
I got that old feeling.
METAL flew.
It found JONES.
SAGE pulled HEAT.
He popped off THREE HOT ONES-- EACH of them a SURE KILL.
A MONSTER burst out LAUGHING.

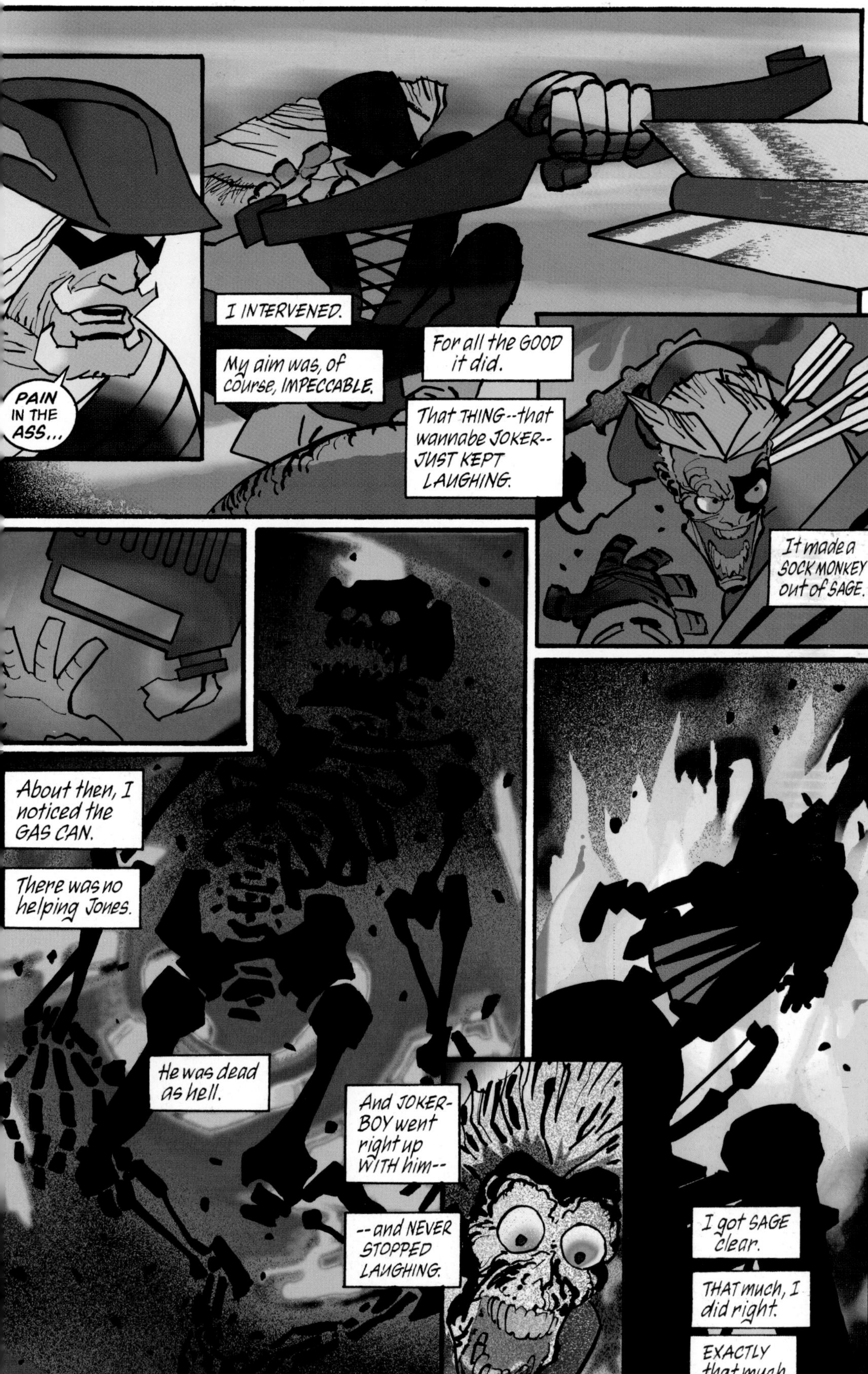
I INTERVENED.
My aim was, of course, IMPECCABLE.
PAIN IN THE ASS...
For all the GOOD it did.
That THING--that wannabe JOKER--JUST KEPT LAUGHING.
It made a SOCK MONKEY out of SAGE.
About then, I noticed the GAS CAN.
There was no helping Jones.
He was dead as hell.
And JOKER-BOY went right up WITH him--
--and NEVER STOPPED LAUGHING.
I got SAGE clear.
THAT much, I did right.
EXACTLY that much.

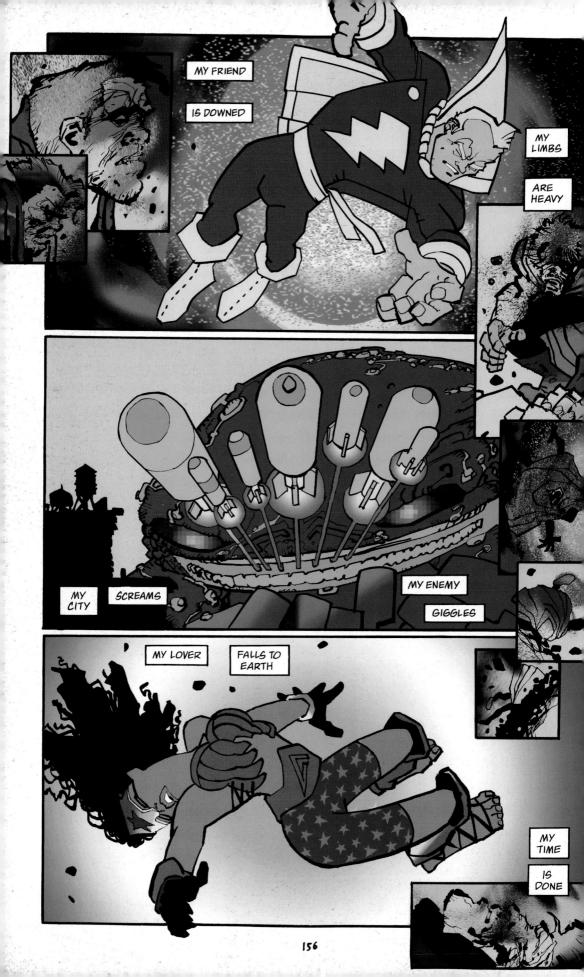

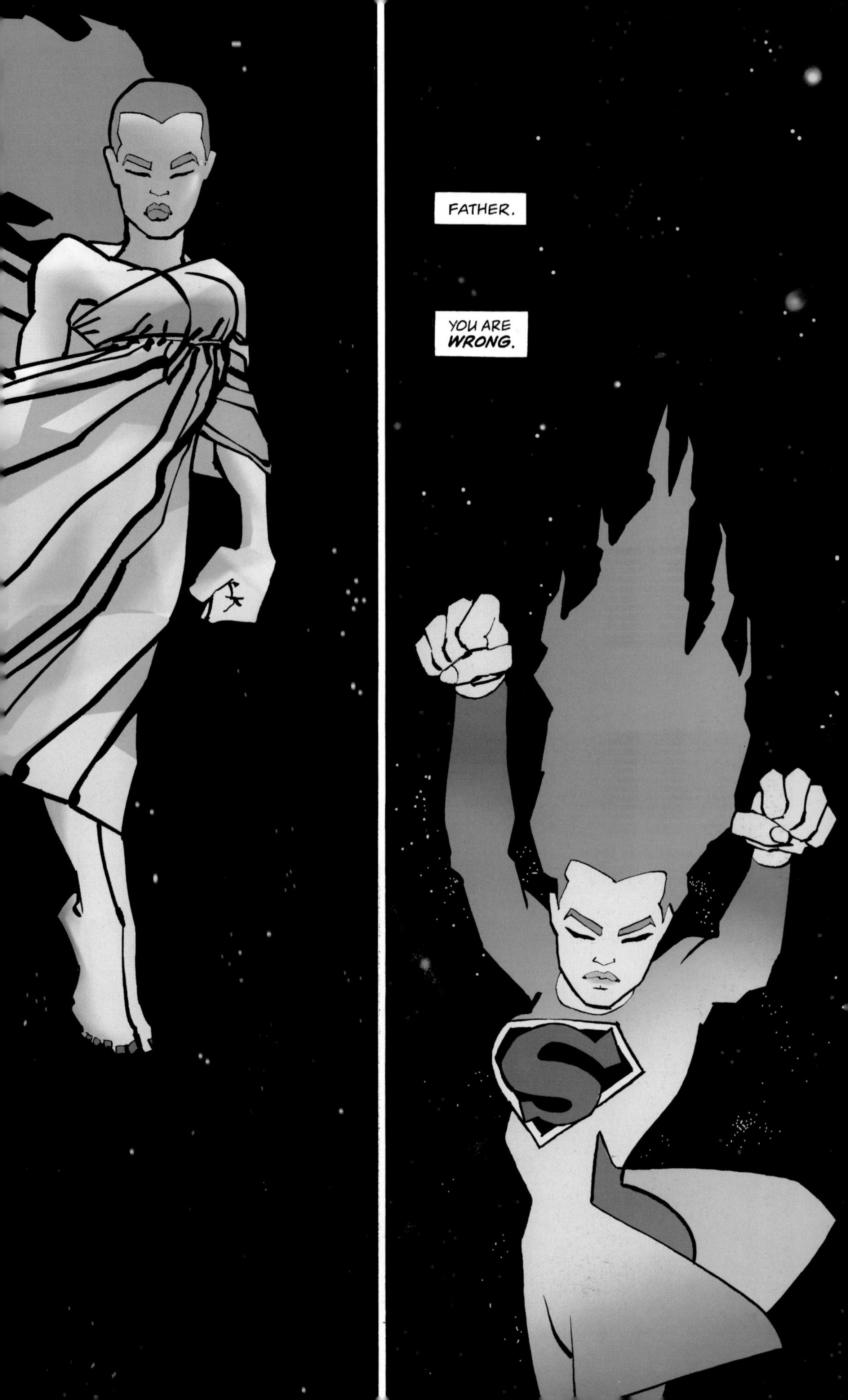
FATHER.
YOU ARE WRONG.

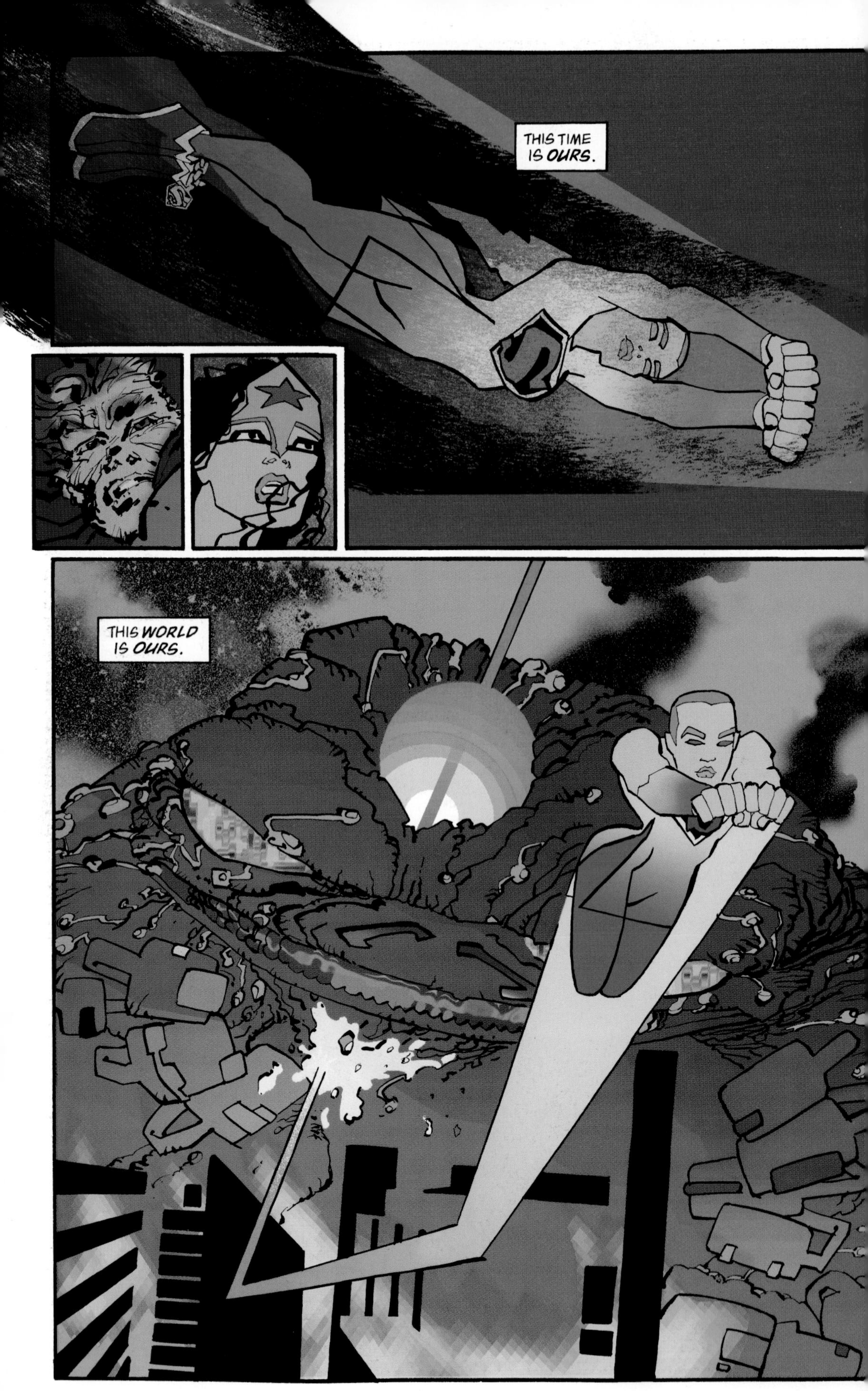
THIS TIME
IS OURS.
THIS WORLD
IS OURS.

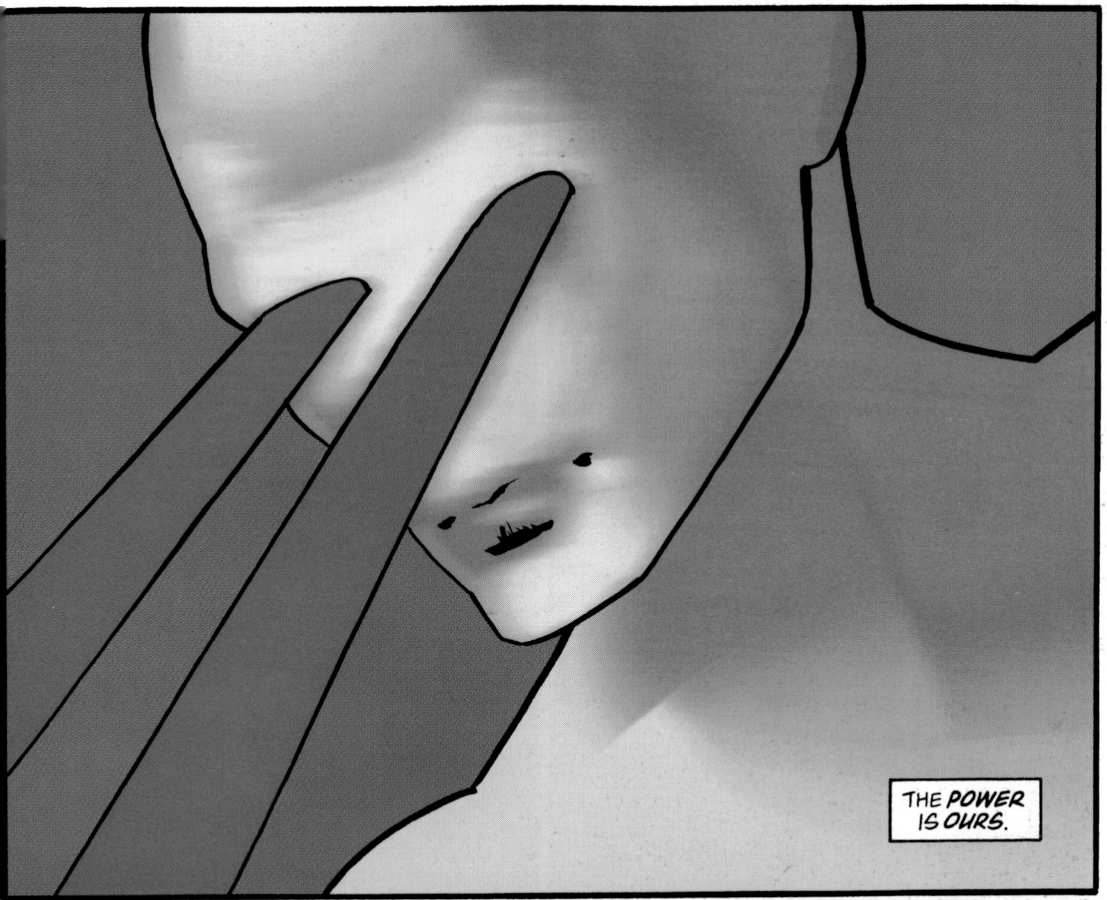
THE POWER
IS OURS.

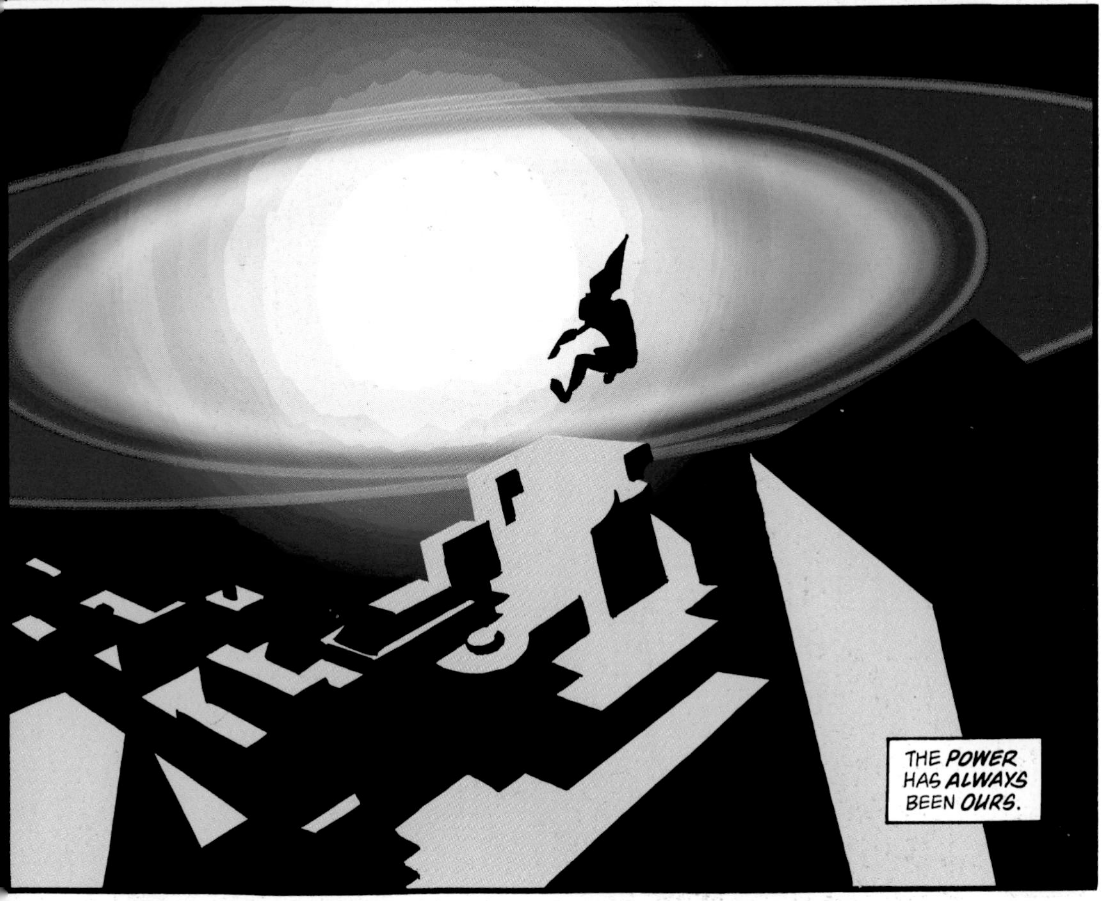
THE POWER
HAS ALWAYS
BEEN OURS.

YOUR *WORLD* TURNED AGAINST ITS *HEROES*.

MOTHER AND *FATHER* TRIED TO TAKE US *AWAY* FROM YOUR PLANET-- TO *RETURN* TO OUR HOMEWORLD *THANAGAR*.

WE WERE *BLASTED* FROM THE *SKY*.

WE CRASHED *HERE*. IN THIS *FOREST*.

THOUGH IN *EXILE*, WE *THRIVED*.

FATHER BUILT OUR *HOME*.

MOTHER USED THANAGARIAN *SCIENCE* AND HER OWN FERTILE *WITS* TO BRING ANCIENT *SPECIES* BACK TO LIFE.

MY *SISTER* AND I EARNED OUR *WINGS*.

THIS WAS A *HAPPY* PLACE.

THEN CAME THE *FIRE*.

FROM THE *SKY*.

MOTHER ORDERED US *HERE*. INTO THIS *CAVE*.

AND SHE *FLEW*.

160

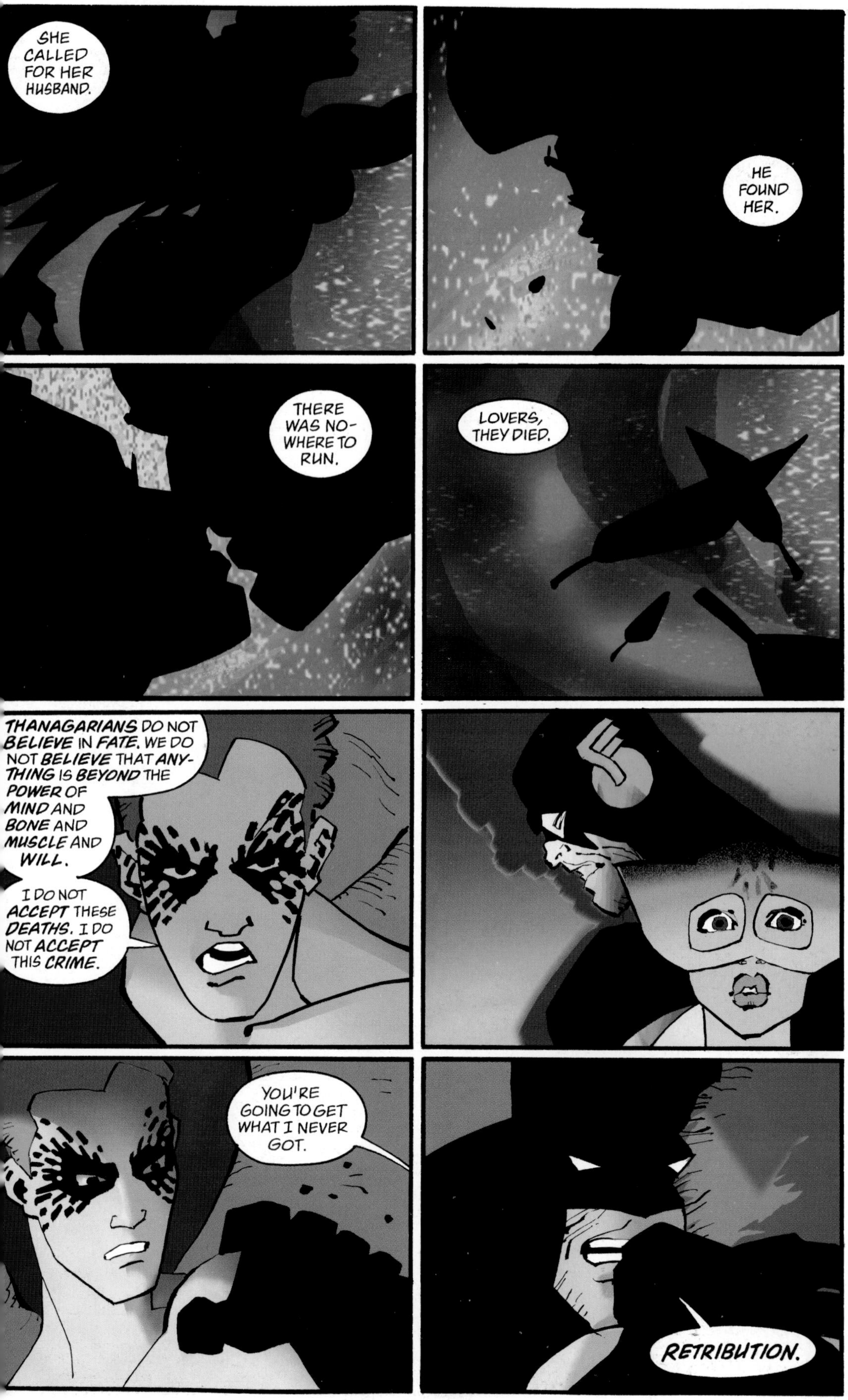
SHE CALLED FOR HER HUSBAND.
HE FOUND HER.
THERE WAS NO-WHERE TO RUN.
LOVERS, THEY DIED.
THANAGARIANS DO NOT BELIEVE IN FATE. WE DO NOT BELIEVE THAT ANYTHING IS BEYOND THE POWER OF MIND AND BONE AND MUSCLE AND WILL.
I DO NOT ACCEPT THESE DEATHS. I DO NOT ACCEPT THIS CRIME.
YOU'RE GOING TO GET WHAT I NEVER GOT.
RETRIBUTION.

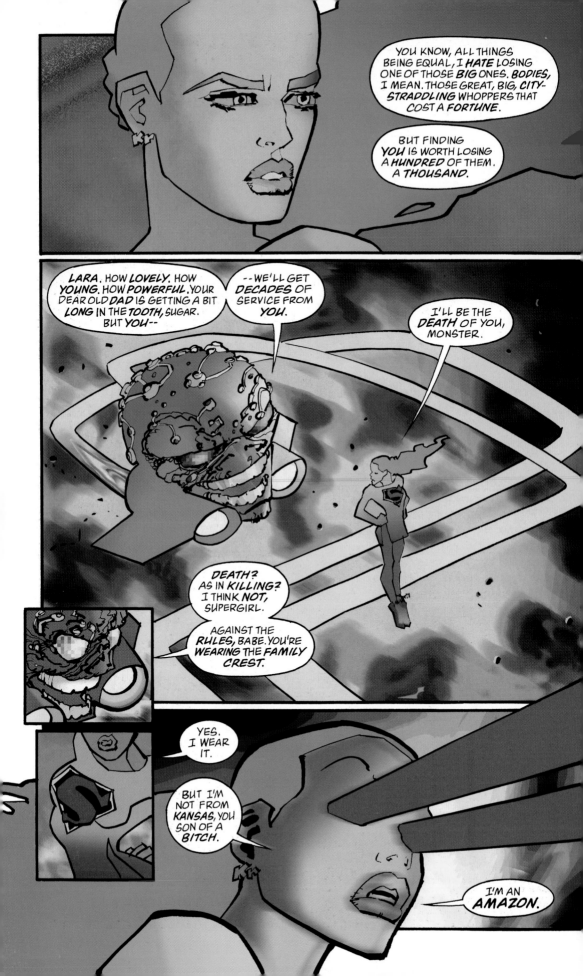

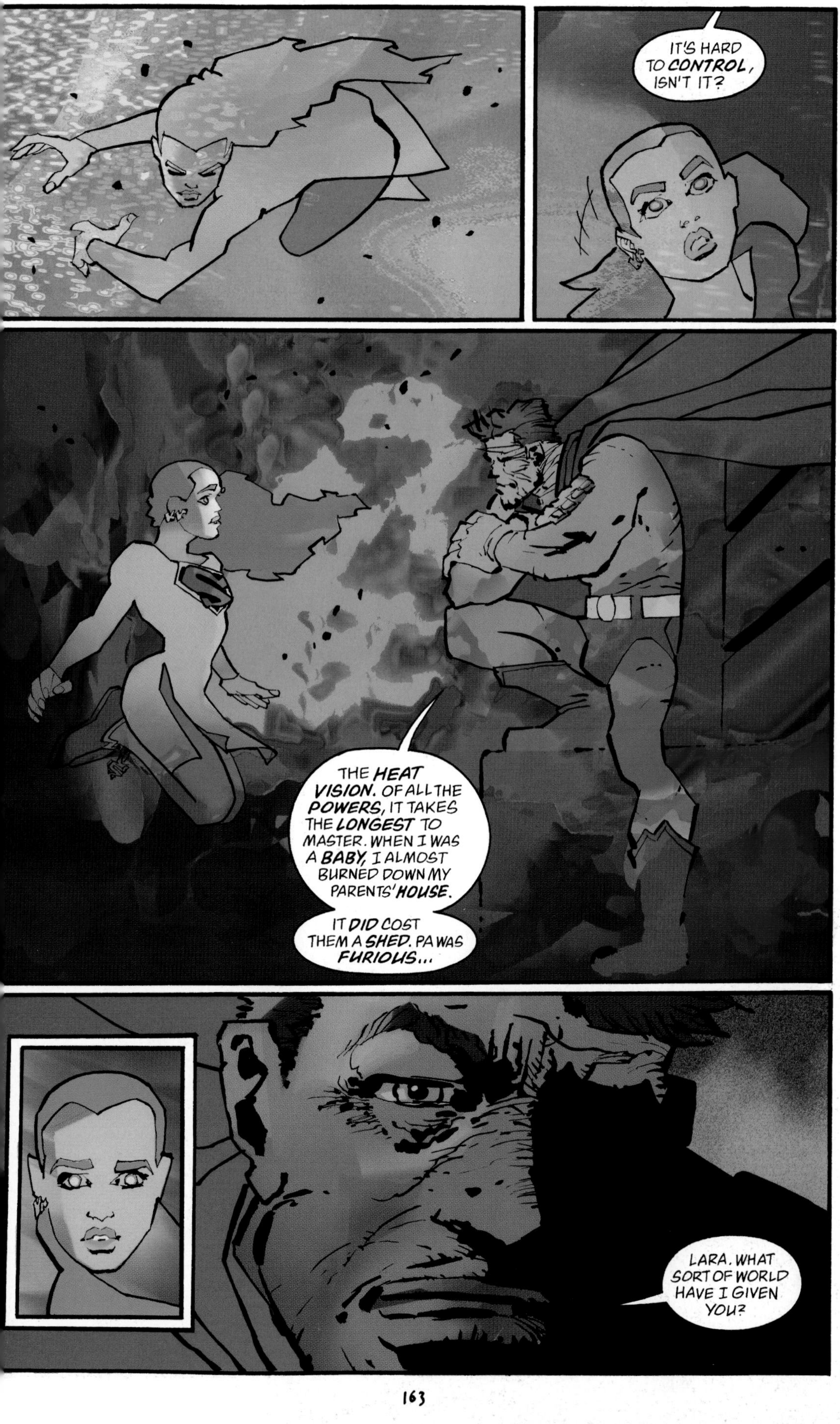
IT'S HARD TO CONTROL, ISN'T IT?
THE HEAT VISION. OF ALL THE POWERS, IT TAKES THE LONGEST TO MASTER. WHEN I WAS A BABY, I ALMOST BURNED DOWN MY PARENTS' HOUSE.
IT DID COST THEM A SHED. PA WAS FURIOUS...
LARA. WHAT SORT OF WORLD HAVE I GIVEN YOU?

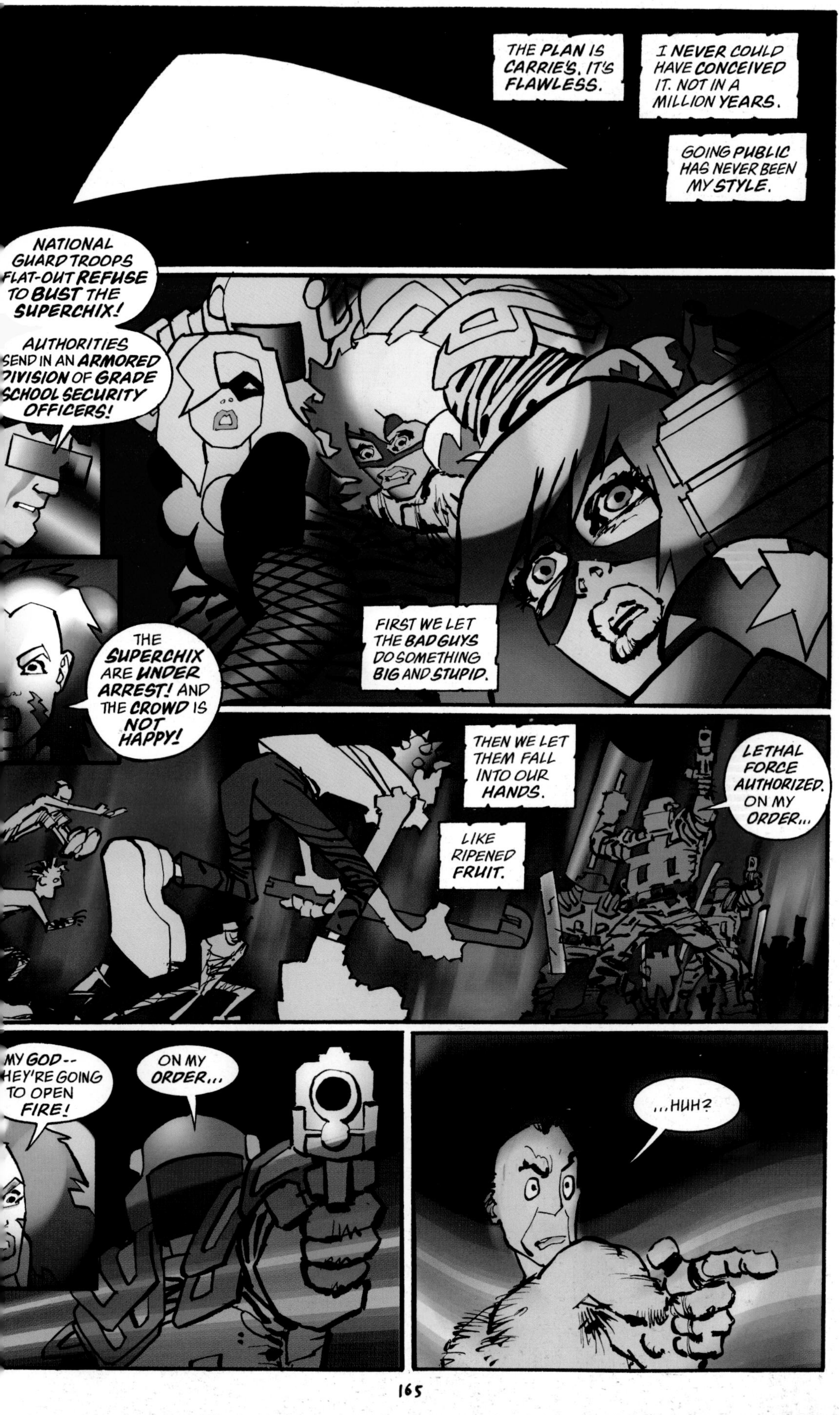
THE PLAN IS CARRIE'S. IT'S FLAWLESS.
I NEVER COULD HAVE CONCEIVED IT. NOT IN A MILLION YEARS.
GOING PUBLIC HAS NEVER BEEN MY STYLE.
NATIONAL GUARD TROOPS FLAT-OUT REFUSE TO BUST THE SUPERCHIX!
AUTHORITIES SEND IN AN ARMORED DIVISION OF GRADE SCHOOL SECURITY OFFICERS!
FIRST WE LET THE BAD GUYS DO SOMETHING BIG AND STUPID.
THE SUPERCHIX ARE UNDER ARREST! AND THE CROWD IS NOT HAPPY!
THEN WE LET THEM FALL INTO OUR HANDS.
LIKE RIPENED FRUIT.
LETHAL FORCE AUTHORIZED. ON MY ORDER...
MY GOD-- HEY'RE GOING TO OPEN FIRE!
ON MY ORDER...
...HUH?

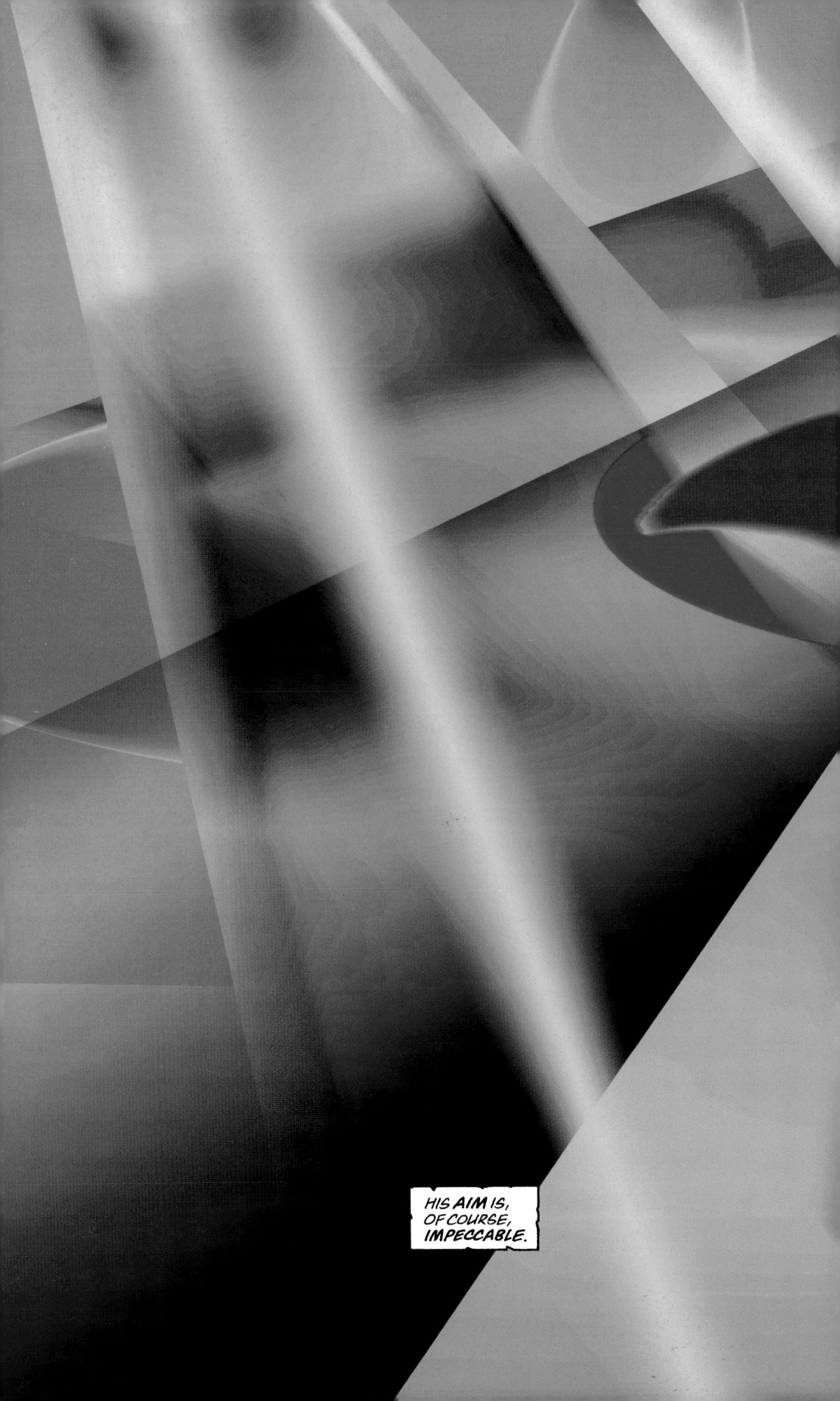
HIS AIM IS, OF COURSE, IMPECCABLE.

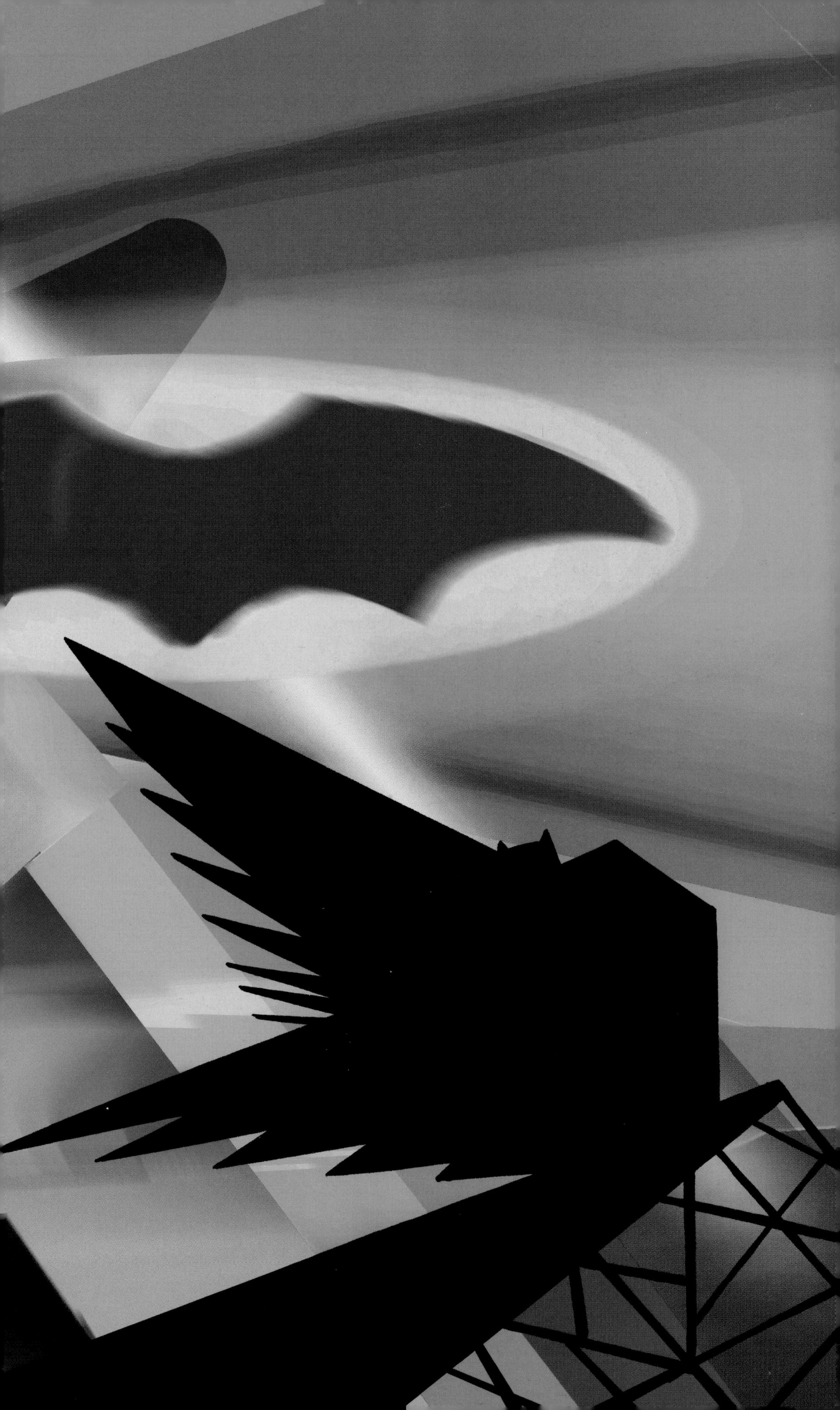

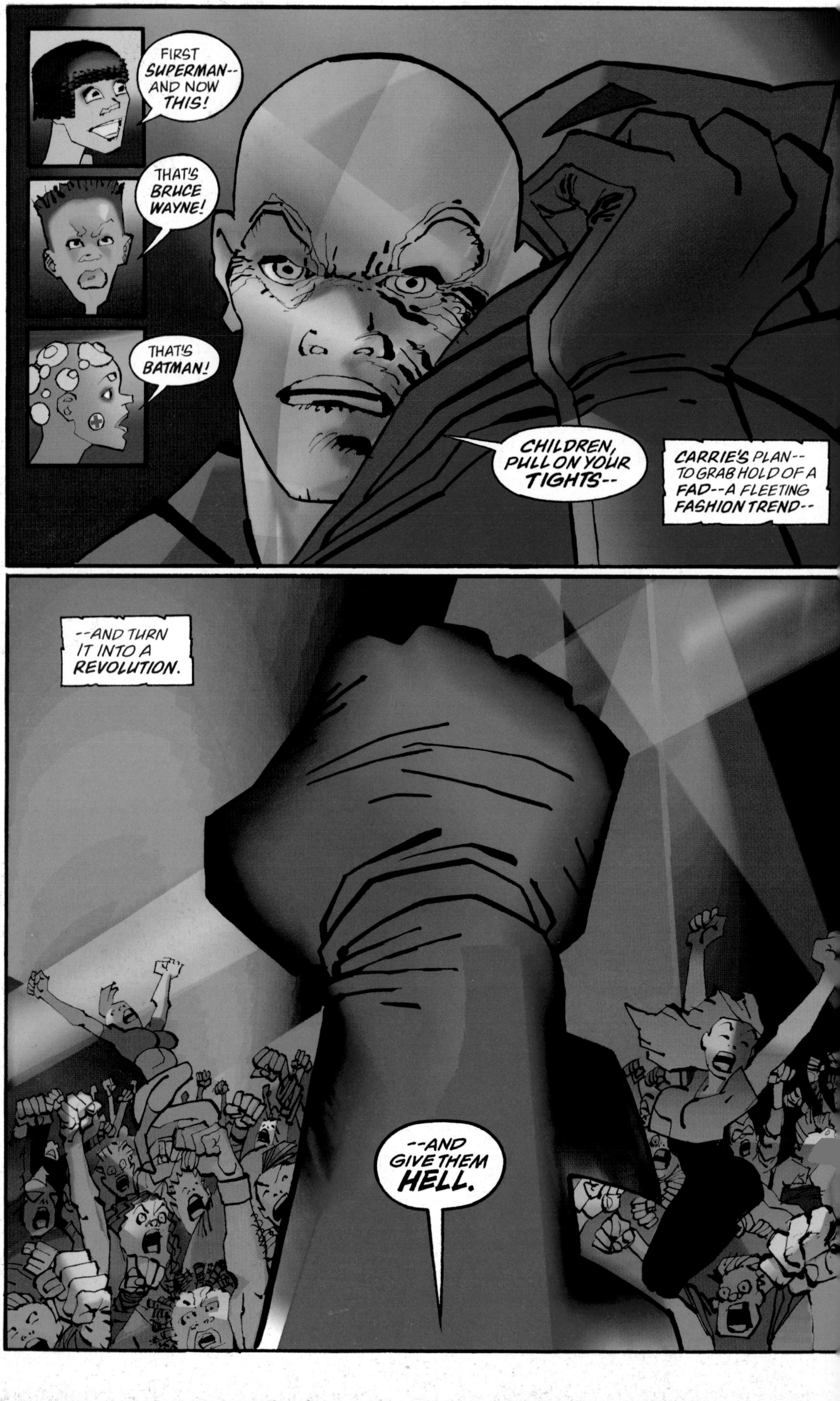

FIRST SUPERMAN-- AND NOW THIS!
THAT'S BRUCE WAYNE!
THAT'S BATMAN!
CHILDREN, PULL ON YOUR TIGHTS--
CARRIE'S PLAN-- TO GRAB HOLD OF A FAD--A FLEETING FASHION TREND--
--AND TURN IT INTO A REVOLUTION.
--AND GIVE THEM HELL.

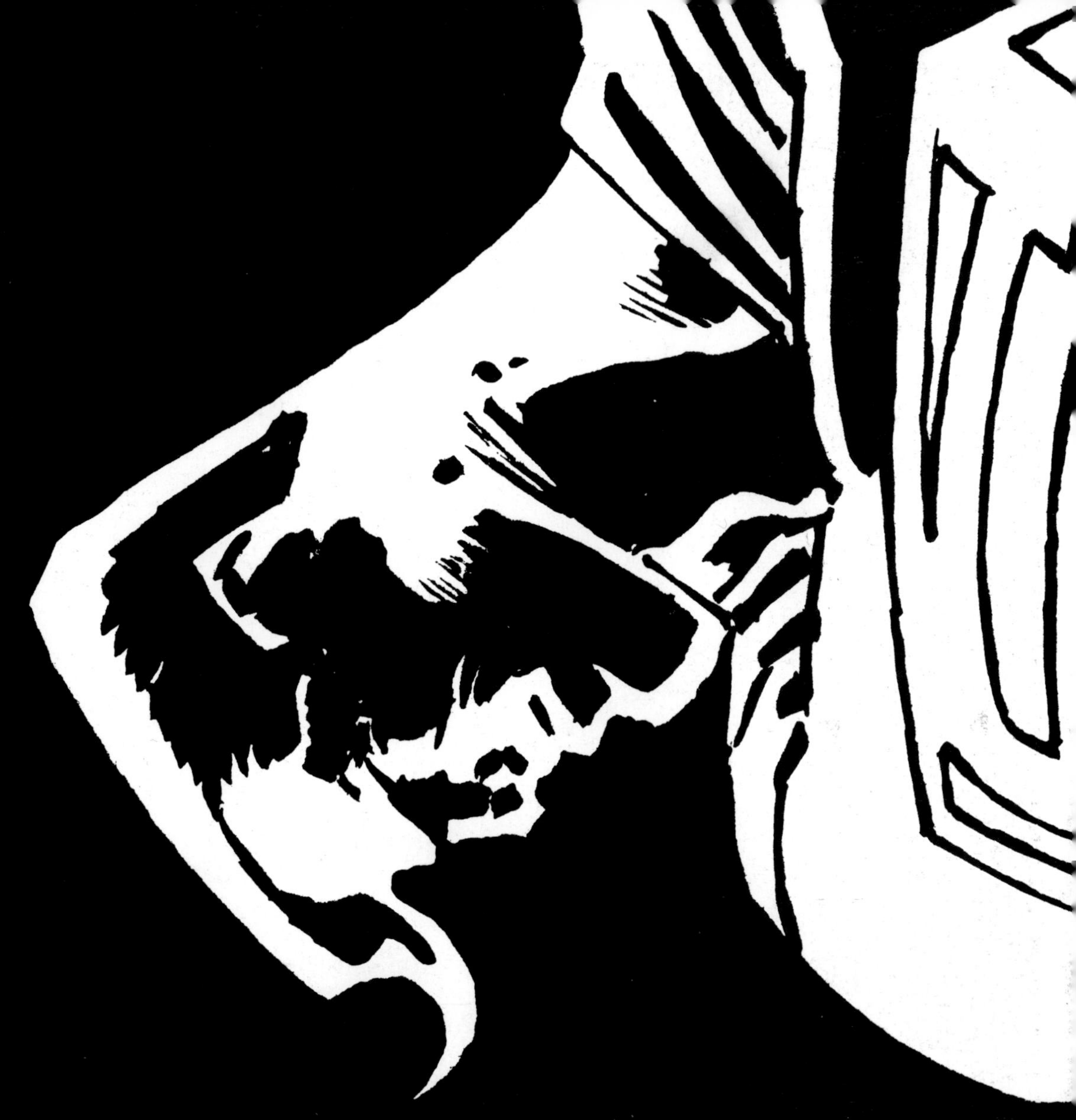

BOOK THREE.

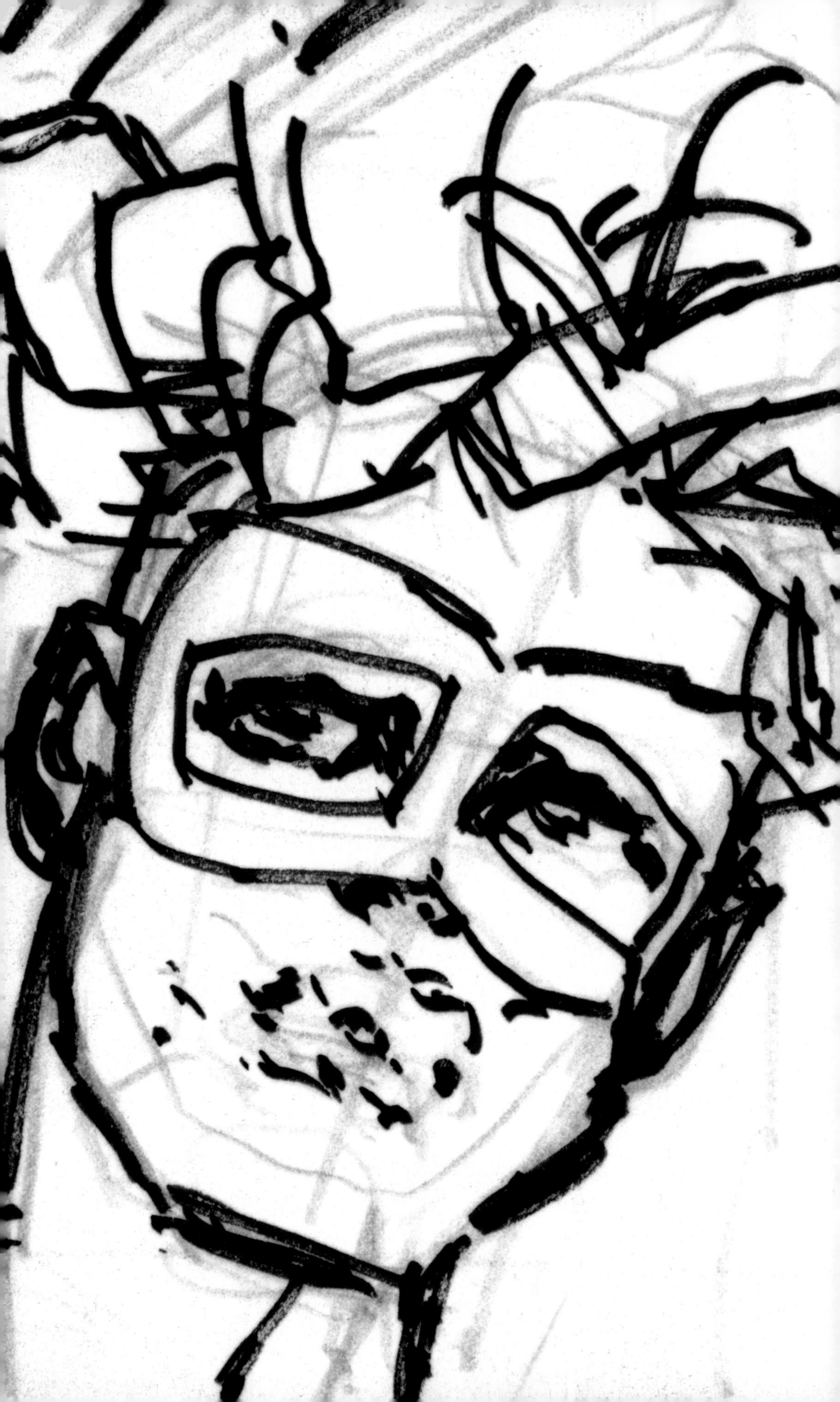

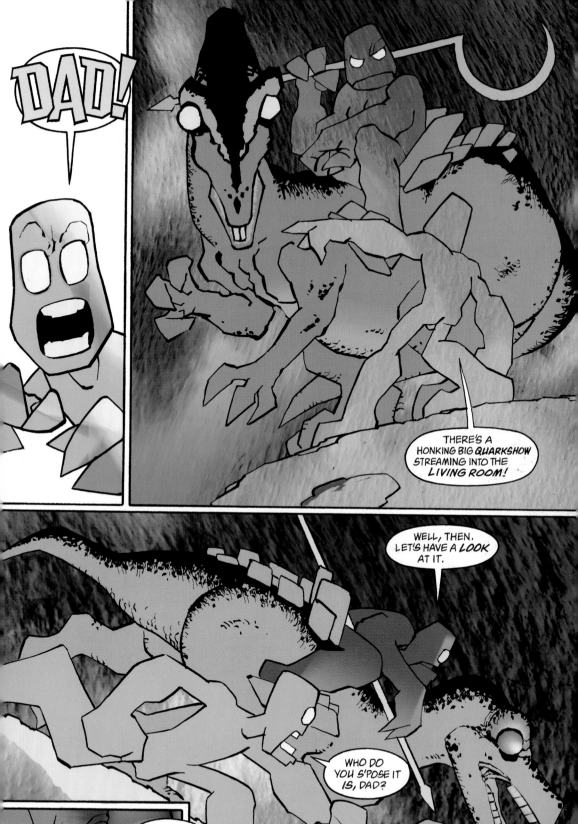

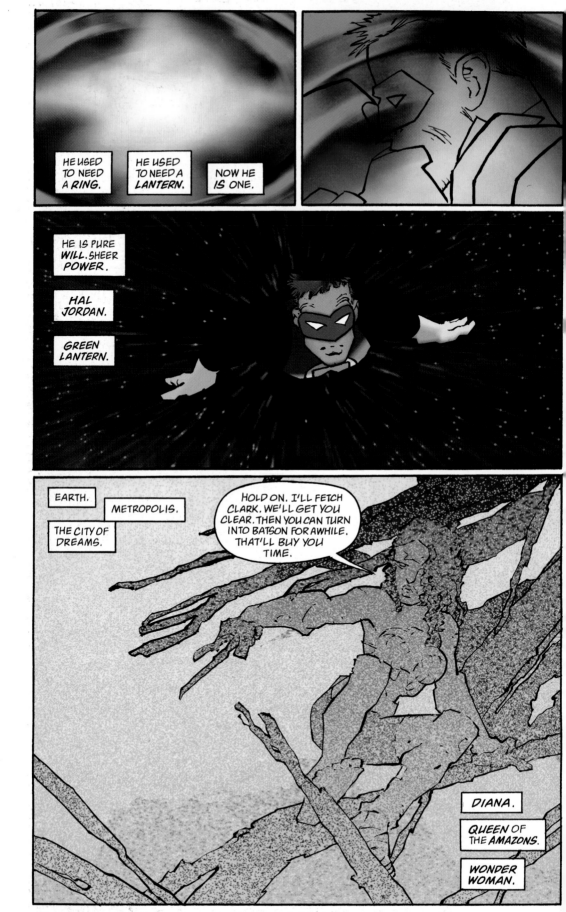

HE USED TO NEED A *RING*.

HE USED TO NEED A *LANTERN*.

NOW HE IS ONE.

HE IS PURE *WILL*. SHEER POWER.

HAL JORDAN.

GREEN LANTERN.

EARTH.

METROPOLIS.

THE CITY OF DREAMS.

HOLD ON. I'LL FETCH CLARK. WE'LL GET YOU CLEAR. THEN YOU CAN TURN INTO BATSON FOR AWHILE. THAT'LL BUY YOU TIME.

DIANA.

QUEEN OF THE *AMAZONS*.

WONDER WOMAN.

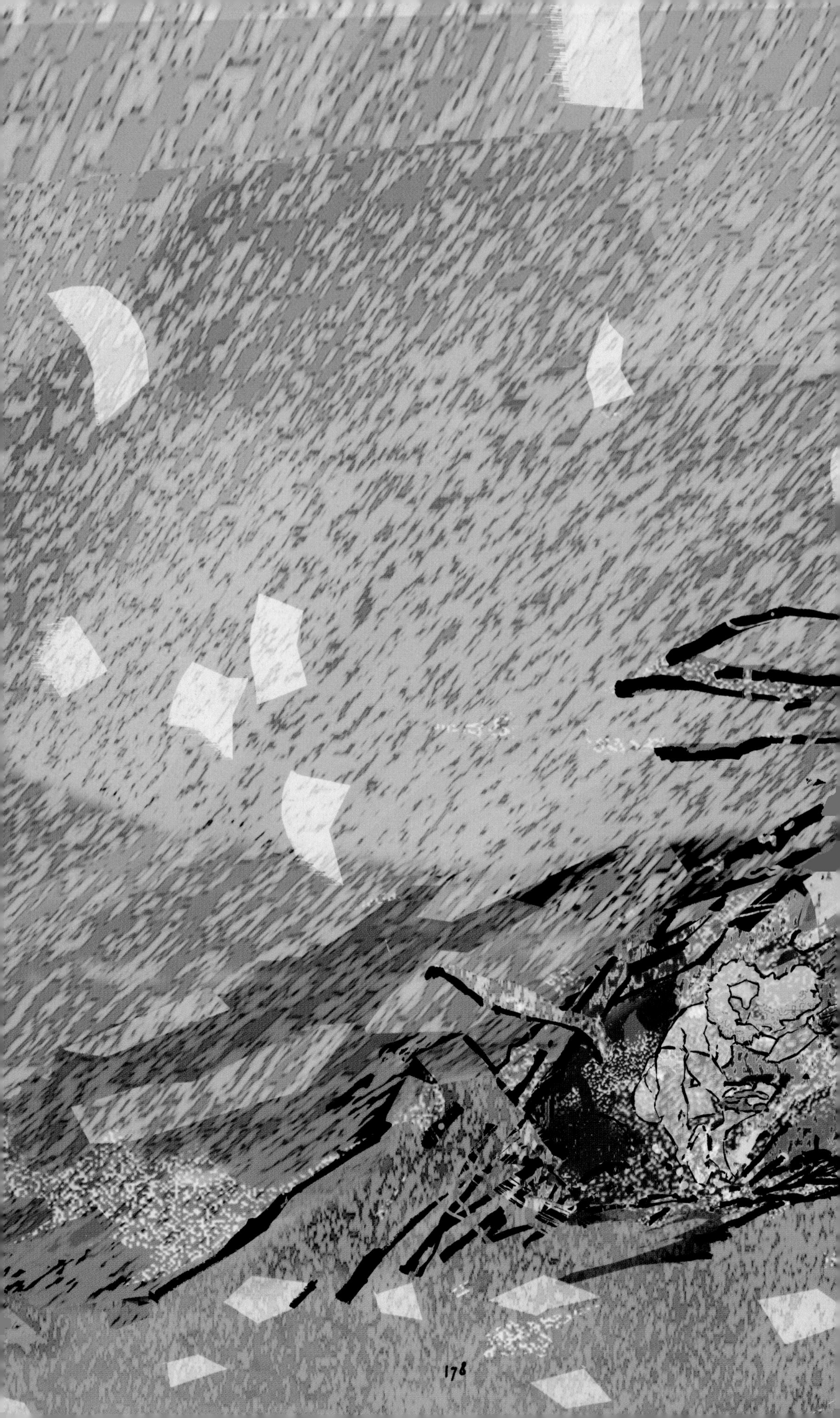

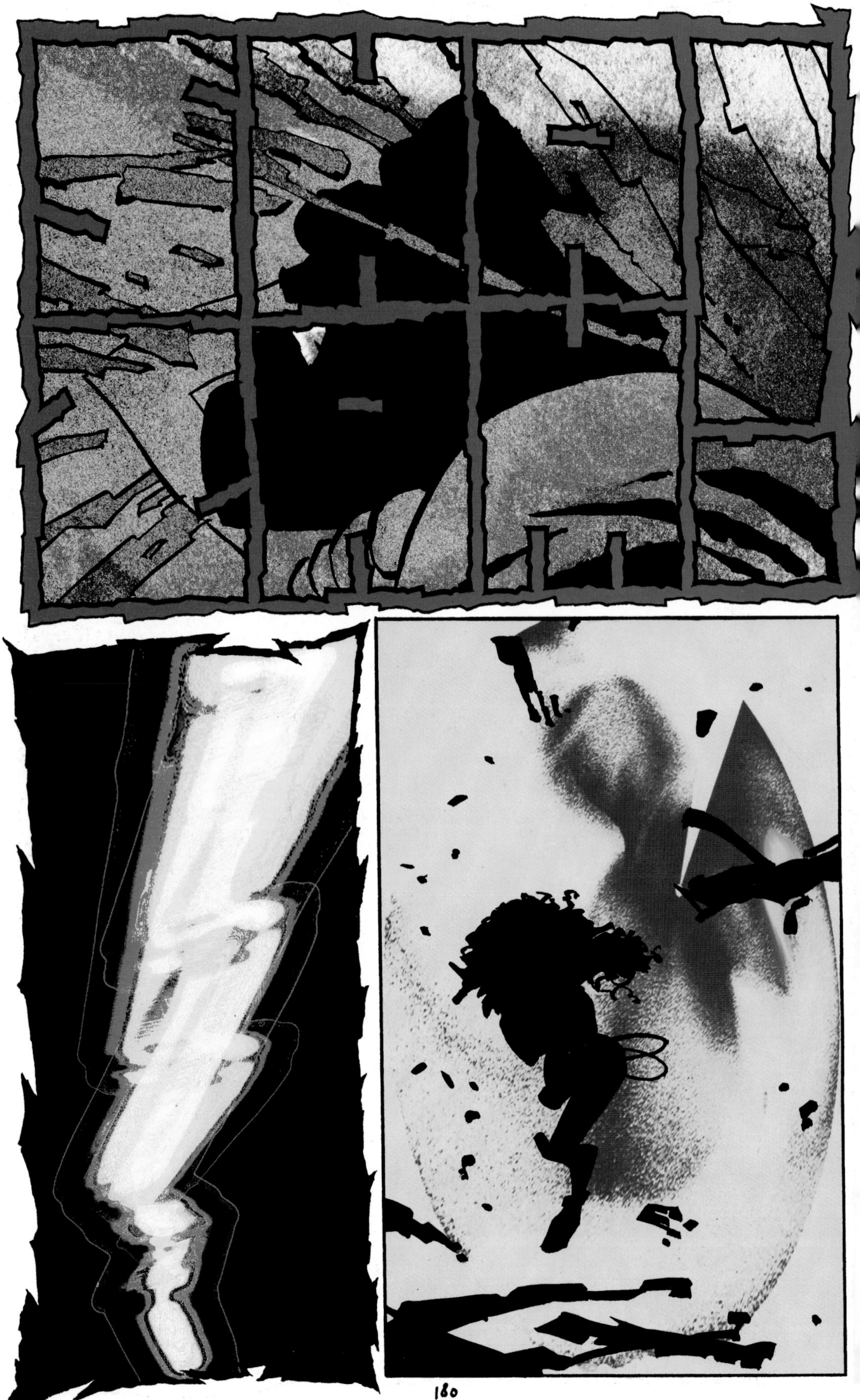

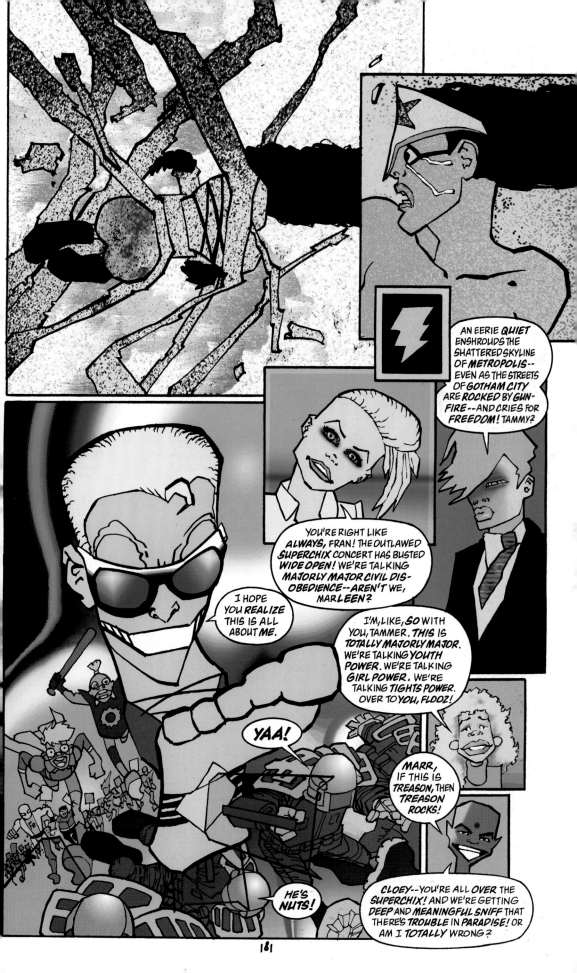

WE JUST WANT TO *THANK* ALL OUR *FANS* FOR LEAVING US SO *DEEPLY* GRATIFIED.

SO VERY DEEPLY.

I'D *HOPE* WE'VE GOT MORE TO SAY THAN *THAT*. WE'RE LOOKING AT A *SEISMIC CULTURAL SHIFT*, HERE, WITH *PROFOUND POLITICAL CONSEQUENCES*.

THAT'S WHY EVERYBODY'S WEARING THE *TIGHTS* ALL OF A SUDDEN. IT'S IN THE *ZEITGEIST*.

WRONG YOU *AREN'T*, FLOOZ! CHECK *THIS* OUT:

WHAT'S A *ZEITGEIST*? IT SOUNDS LIKE A *DISEASE*?

GOD, YOU ARE *SO* IGNORANT.

AND YOU ARE SO *TOTALLY* A TOTAL *BITCH*?

AND I'M, LIKE, SO *TOTALLY OUT OF THIS GROUP*?

OHMYGOD!!! A *SUPERCHIX* MELT-*DOWN!!!* IT'S A *TOTAL TRAGEDY!!!* BUT YOU COULDN'T EVEN *HEAR* ABOUT IT WITH ALL THE *NOISE* AND *SHOOTING* AND STUFF!!! AND BESIDES WHICH, THERE WAS ONLY *ONE GUY* ANYBODY WANTED TO HEAR FROM!!!

BATMAN!!! BRUCE WAYNE!!! THE ACTUALLY LITERALLY SERIOUSLY REAL *BATMAN!!!*

AND DID HE *EVER* KNOW JUST WHAT TO *SAY!!!*

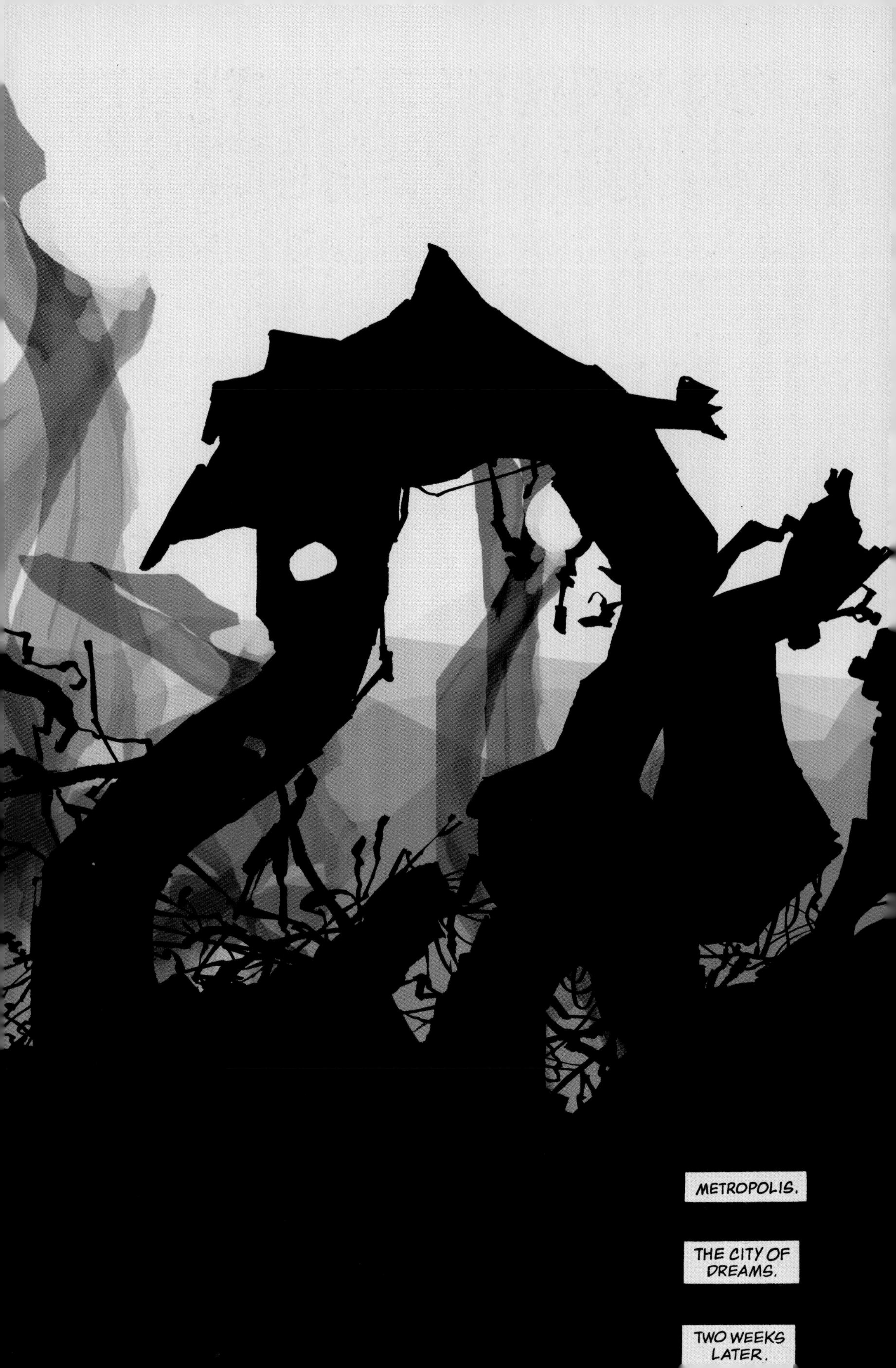
METROPOLIS.
THE CITY OF DREAMS.
TWO WEEKS LATER.

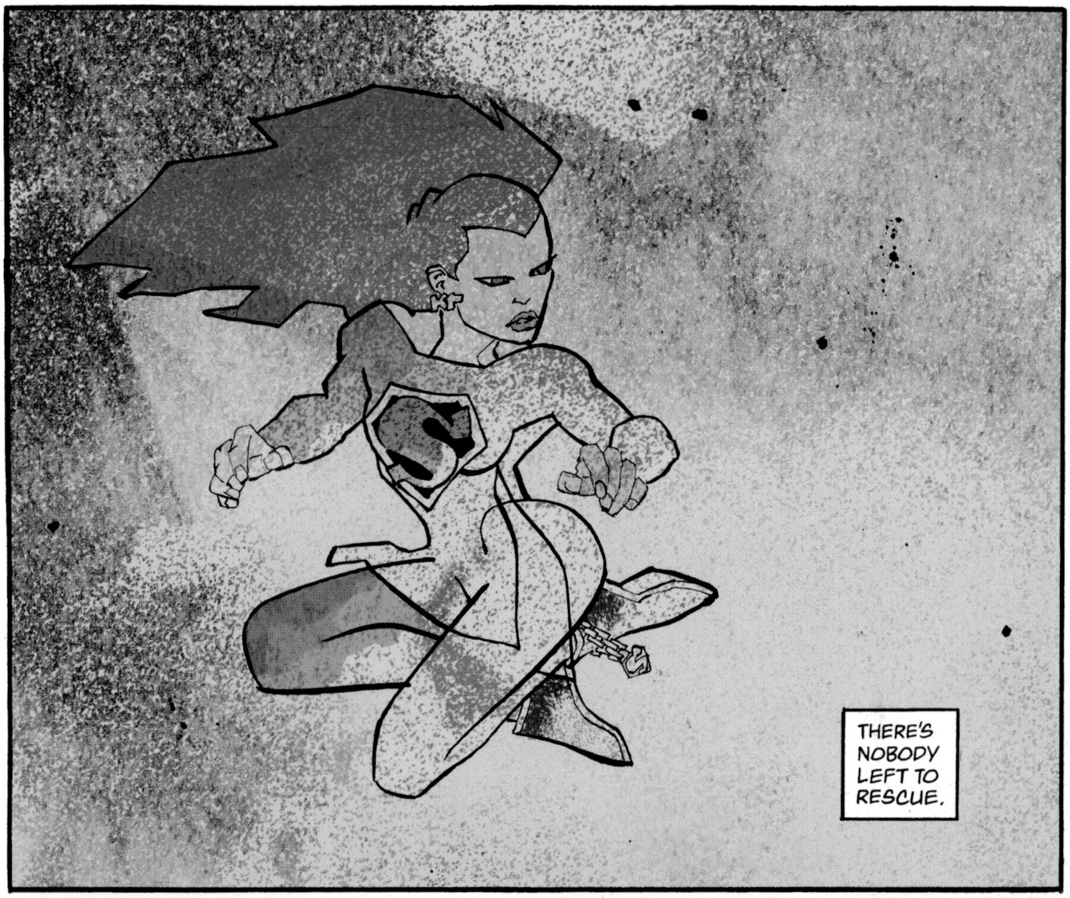
THERE'S NOBODY LEFT TO RESCUE.

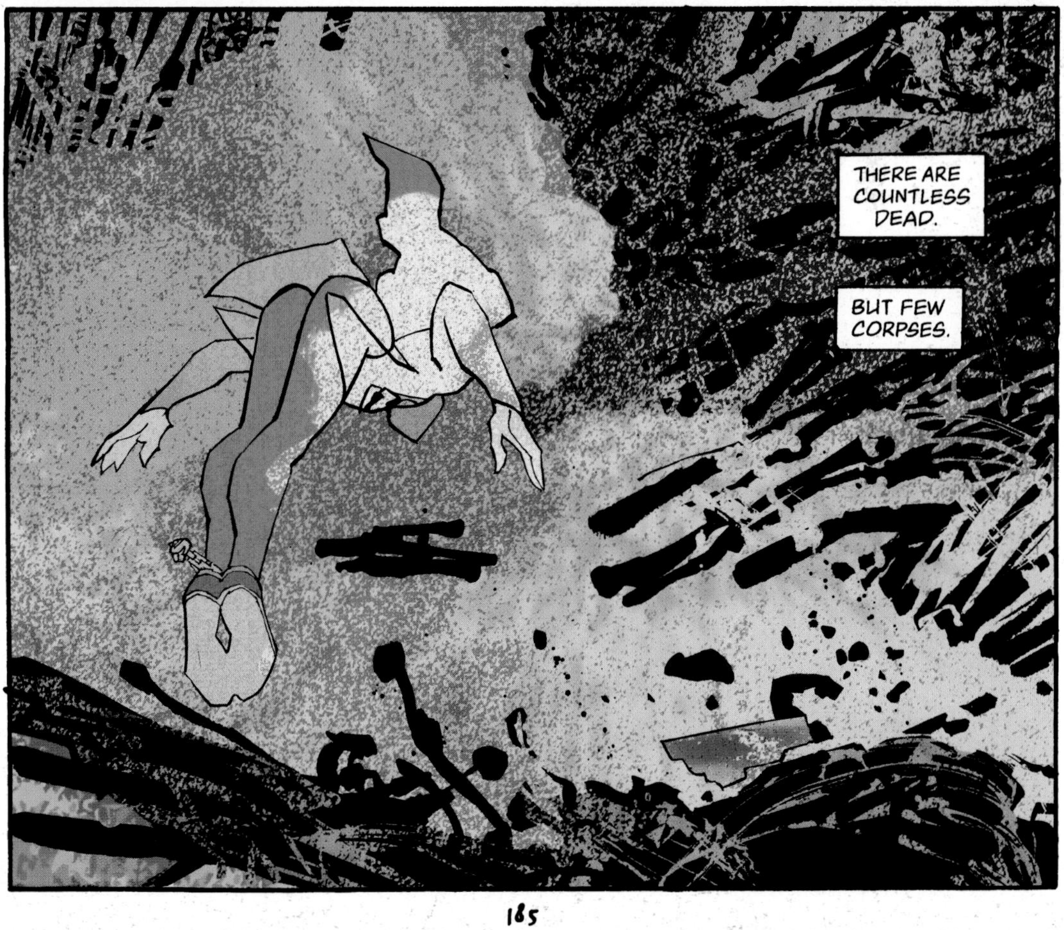
THERE ARE COUNTLESS DEAD.
BUT FEW CORPSES.

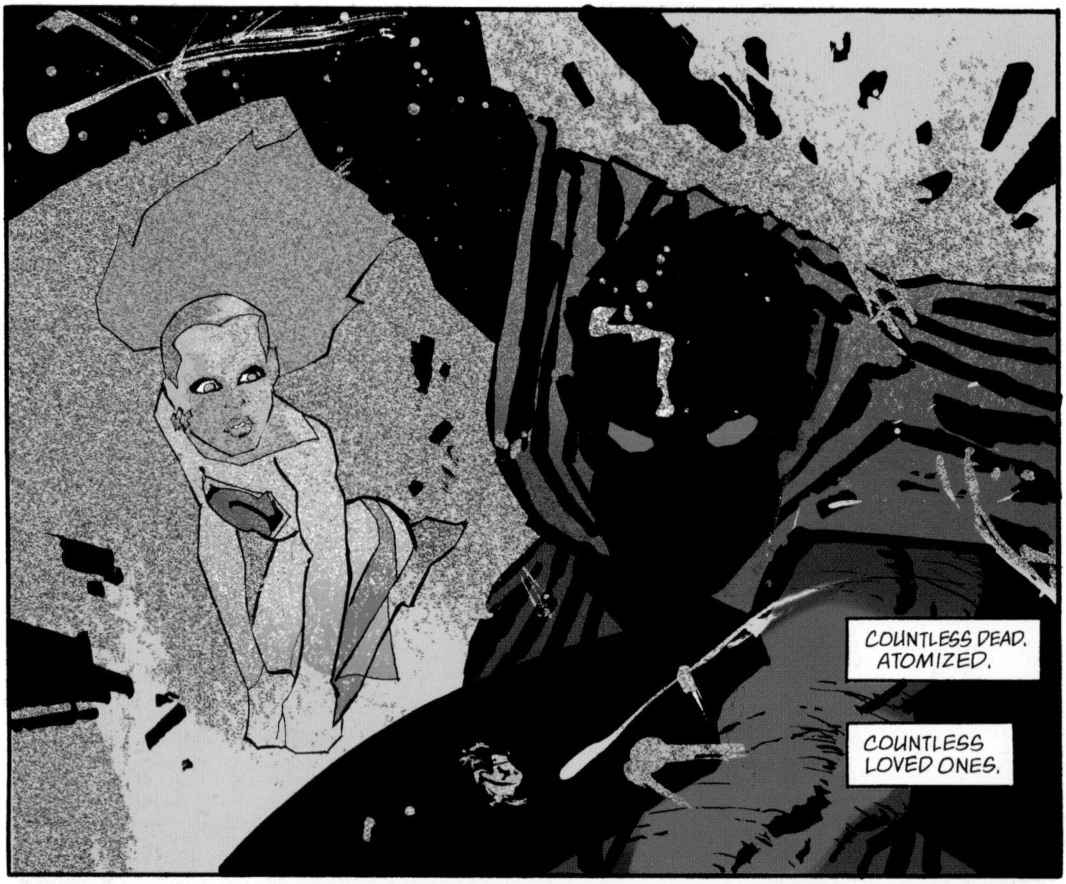
COUNTLESS DEAD. ATOMIZED.
COUNTLESS LOVED ONES.

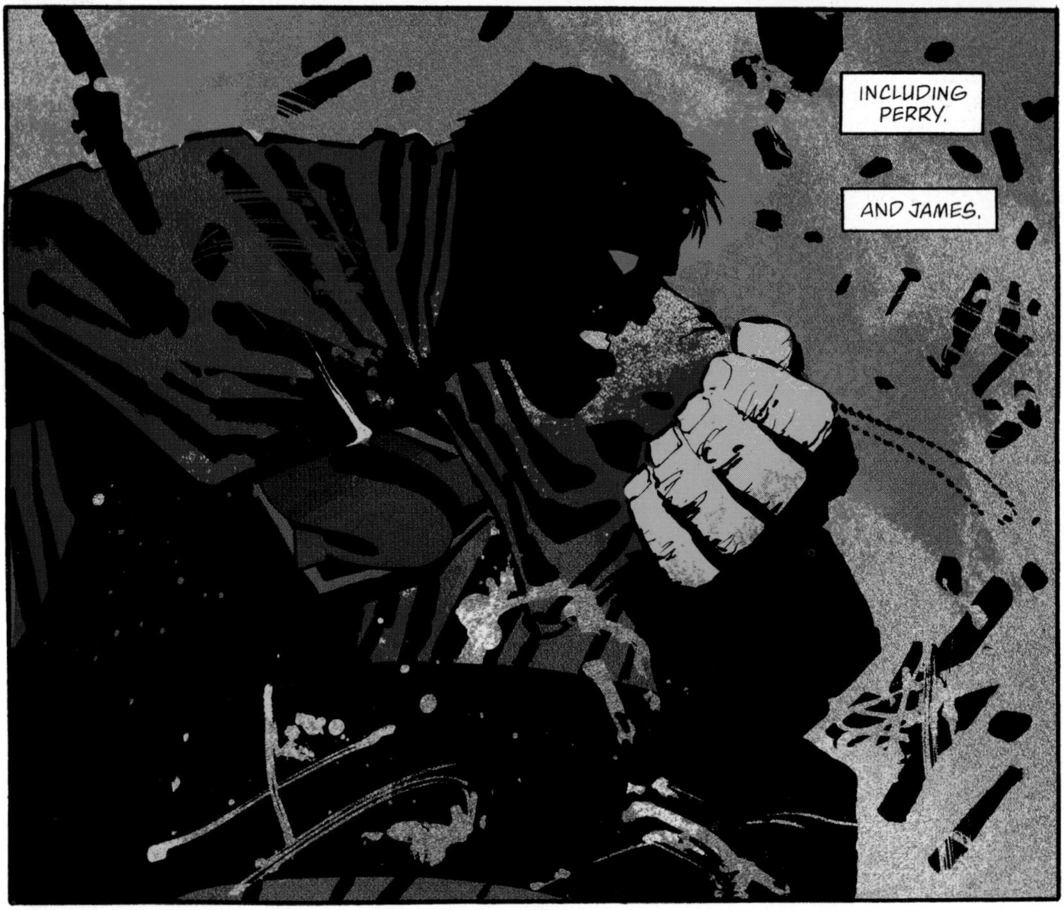
INCLUDING PERRY.
AND JAMES.

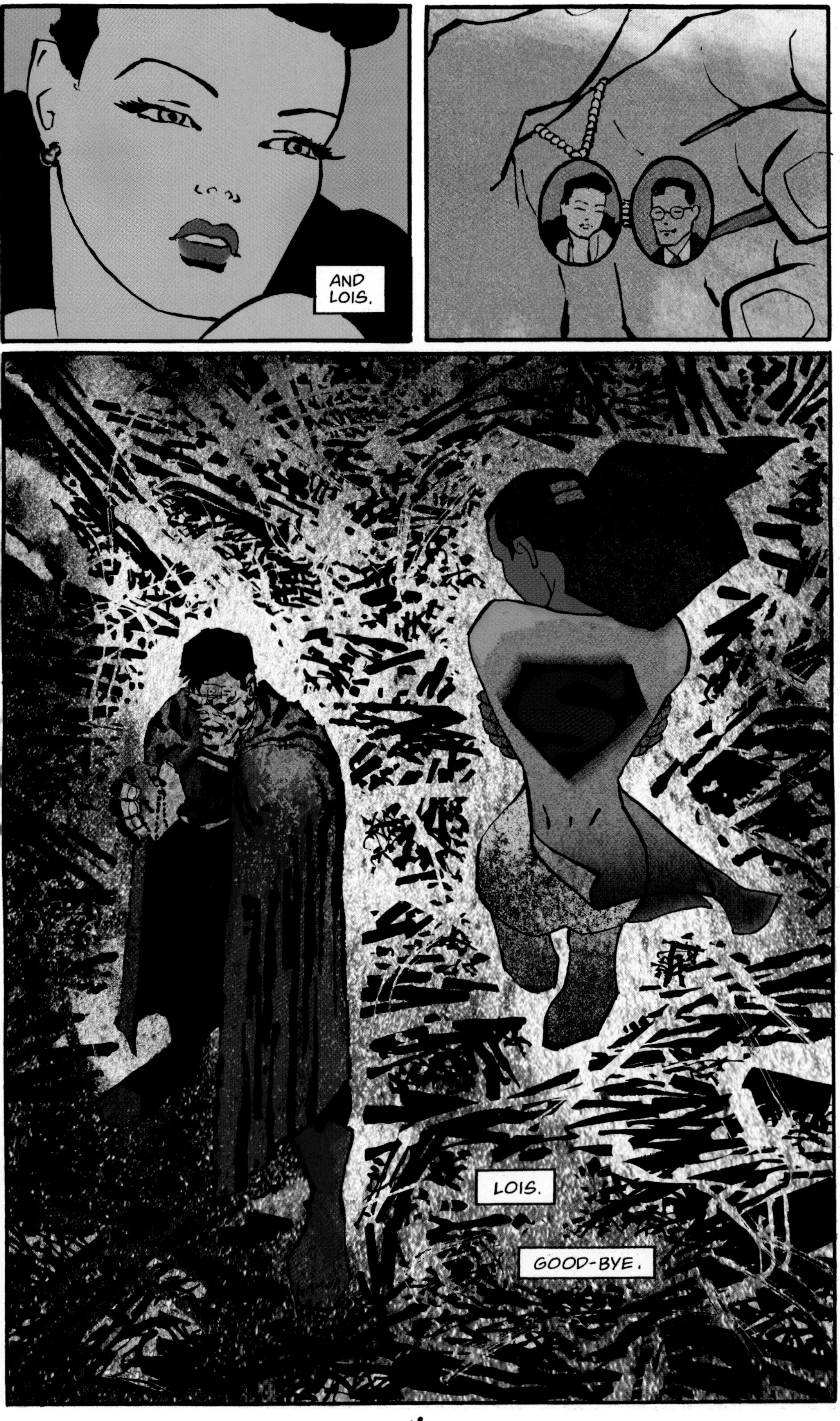
AND LOIS.
LOIS.
GOOD-BYE.

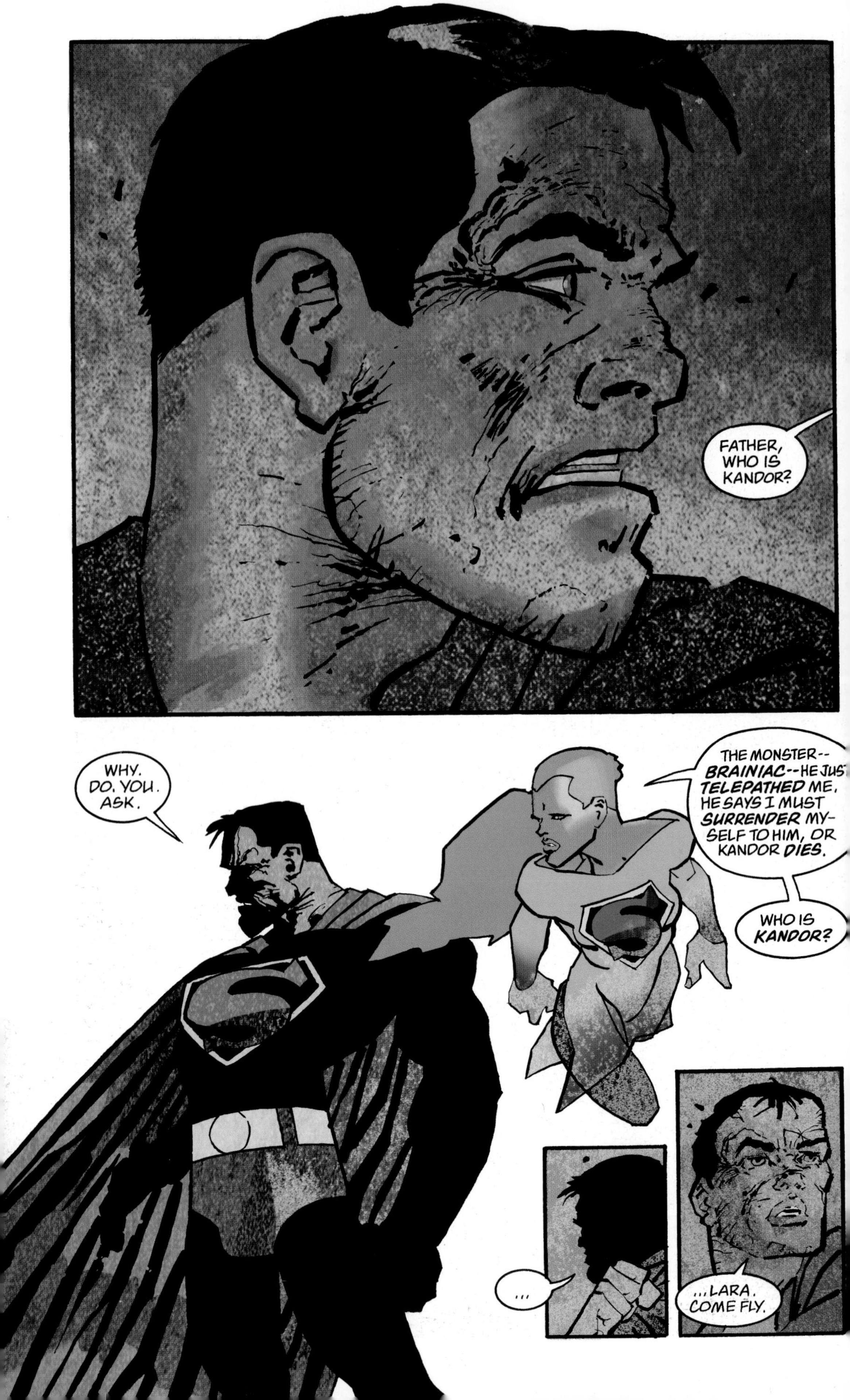
FATHER, WHO IS KANDOR?
WHY. DO. YOU. ASK.
THE MONSTER-- BRAINIAC--HE JUST TELEPATHED ME. HE SAYS I MUST SURRENDER MY-SELF TO HIM, OR KANDOR DIES.
WHO IS KANDOR?
...
...LARA. COME FLY.

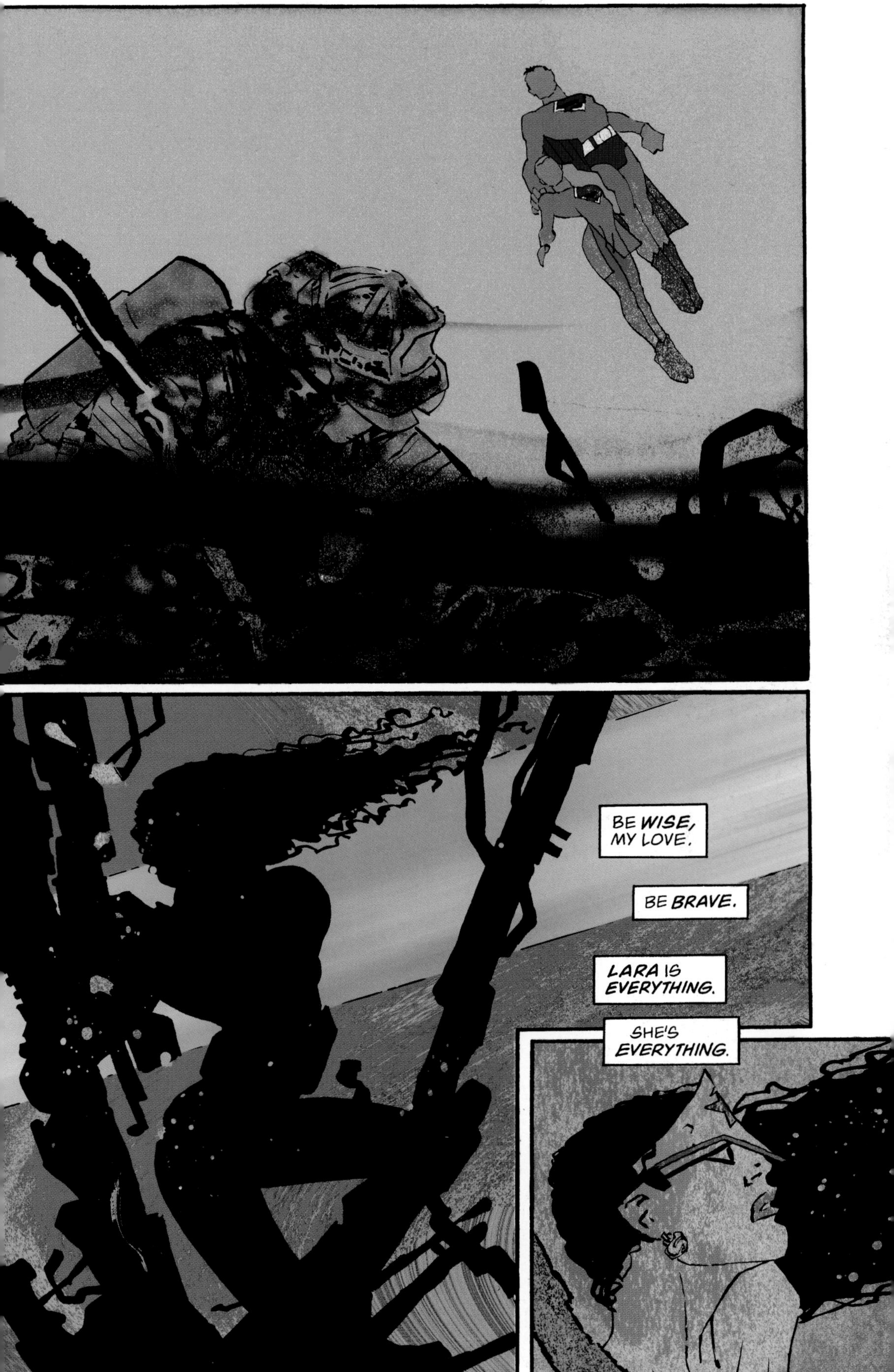
BE WISE, MY LOVE.
BE BRAVE.
LARA IS EVERYTHING.
SHE'S EVERYTHING.

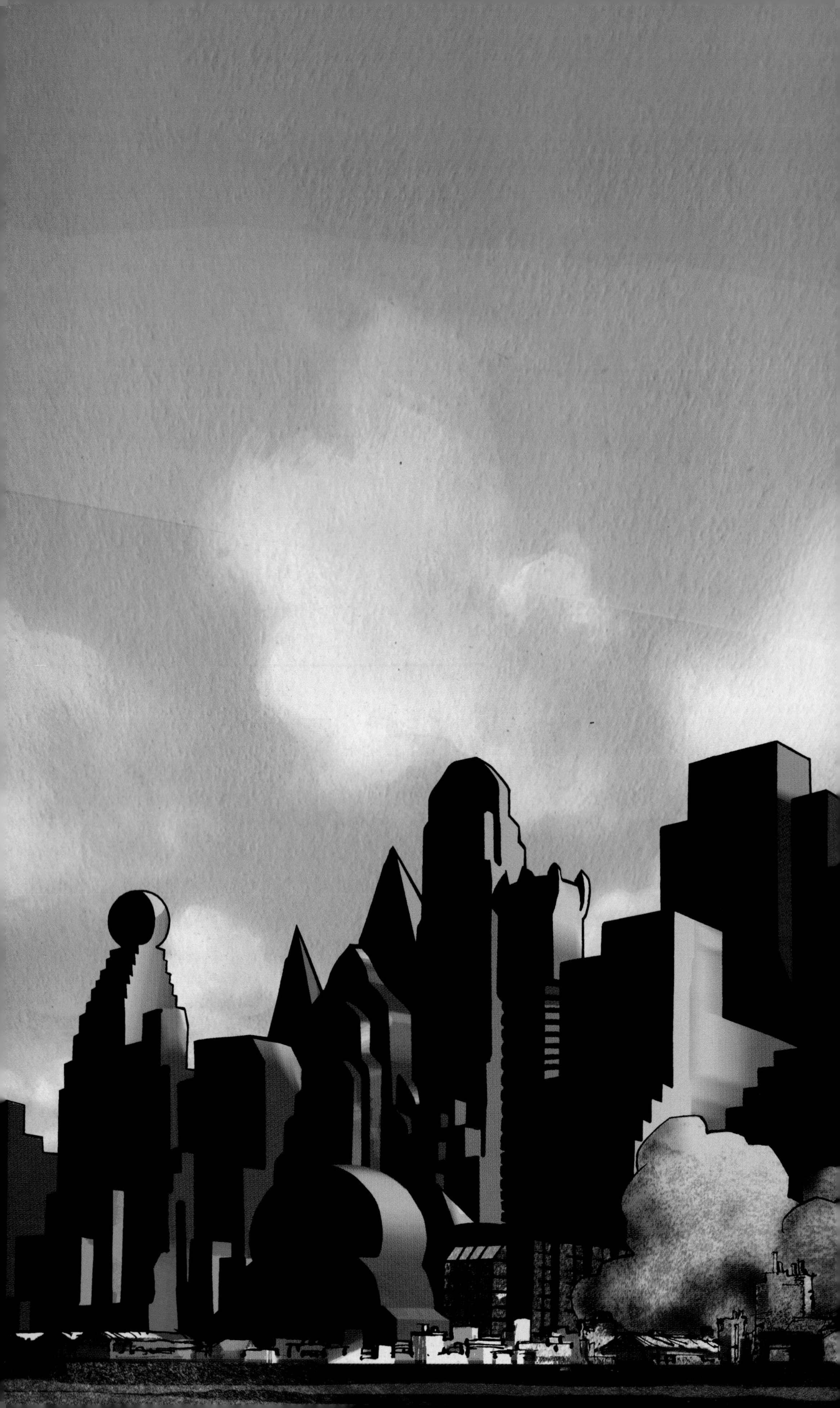

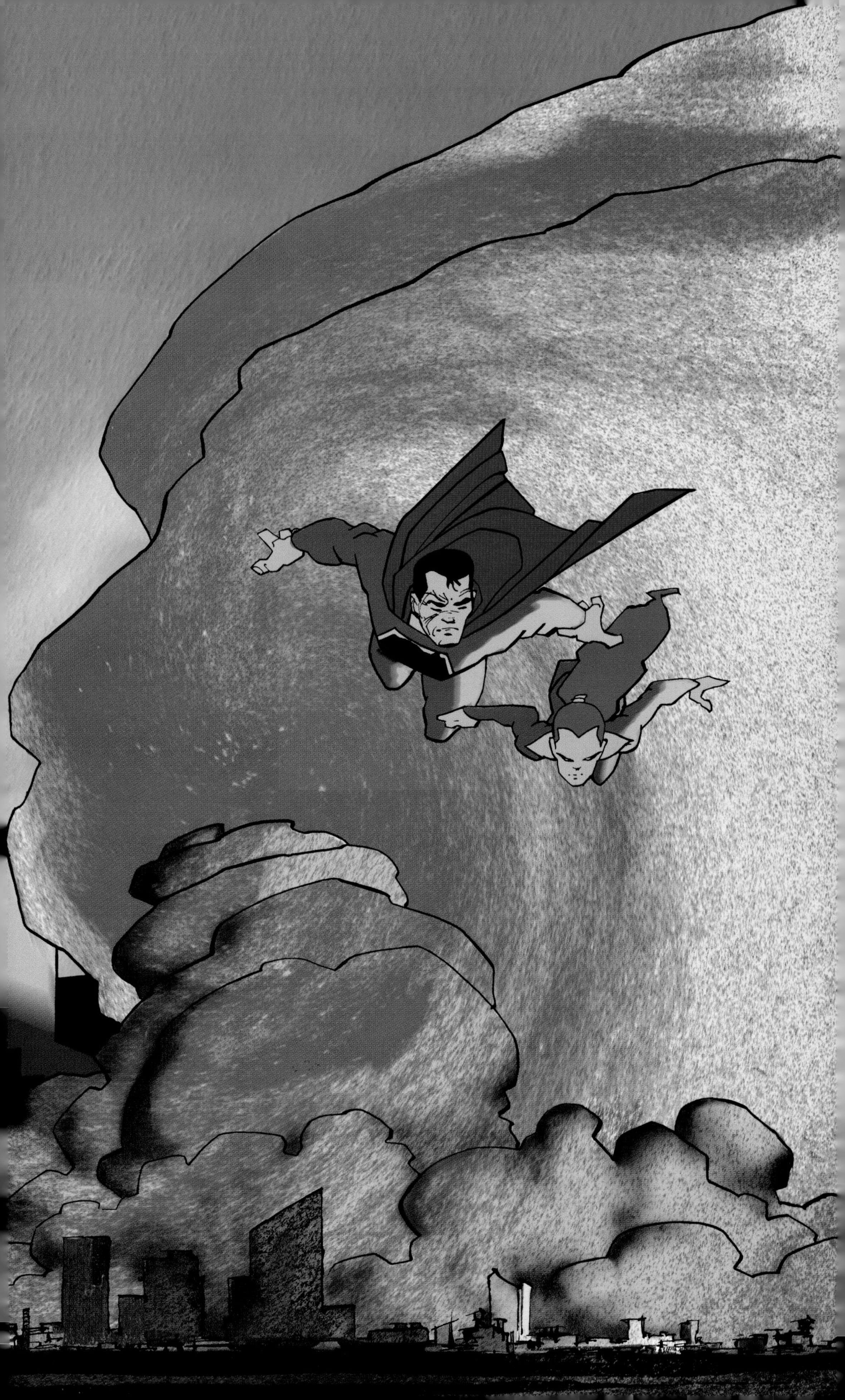

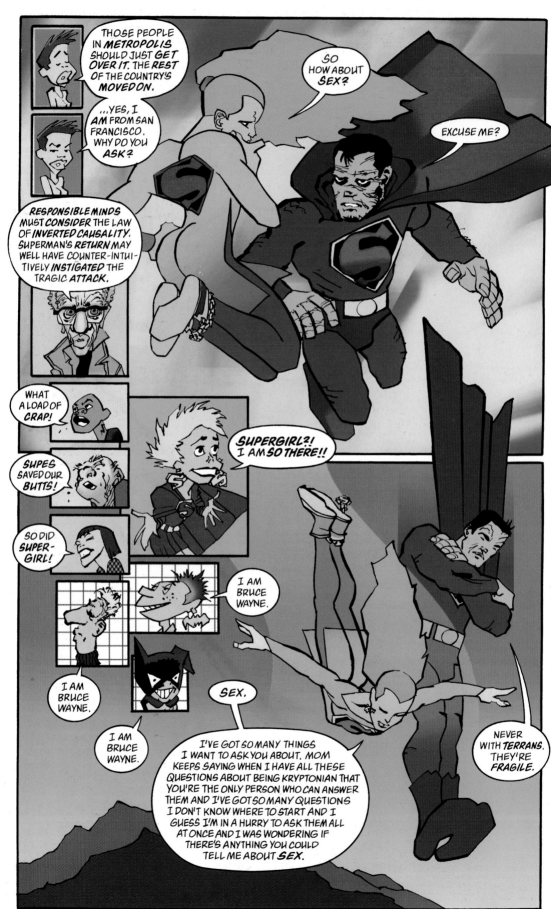

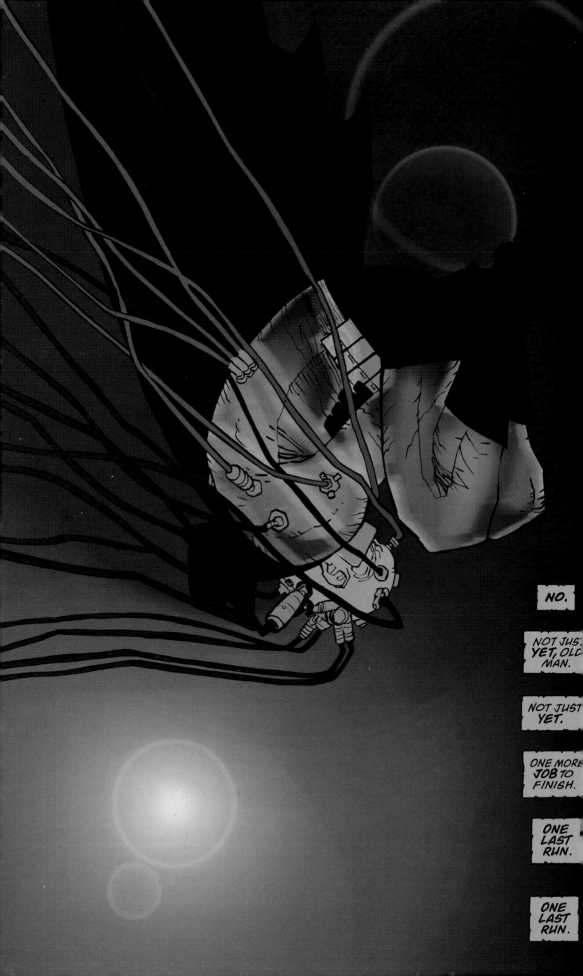

THIS IS *IT*, YOU RUNNING-DOG *LACKEYS!* THE *PEOPLE* ARE FINDING THEIR *VOICE*, YOU MULTINATIONAL-CONGLOMERATE SONS OF *BITCHES!*

YOU CAN'T FIGHT *COLLECTIVISM* WITH *COL-LECTIVISM*, YOU MARXIST *TWIT!*

OH, *YEAH?* HOW'S ABOUT WE TAKE THIS LITTLE DISCUSSION OUT *BACK*, MR. LET'S-PRIVATIZE-THE-FIRE-DEPARTMENT?

--FIRST IN THE *DOZENS*, THEN BY THE *HUNDREDS*, THEY *FLED* THE *ORPHANAGE*--THESE SAD, *MISSHAPEN* THINGS, THESE *CREATURES* WE COULD SCARCELY CALL *CHILDREN*--

WHAT THE *HECK* WAS GOING *ON* IN THAT PLACE?

THEY *POKES NEEDLES* IN US! AND THEY *STUCKS WIRES* IN OUR *HEADS!* ALLA TIME!

MIDVALE DIRECTOR *DICK WILSON* FLATLY *DENIED* RUMORS OF *GENETIC MANIPULA-TION...*

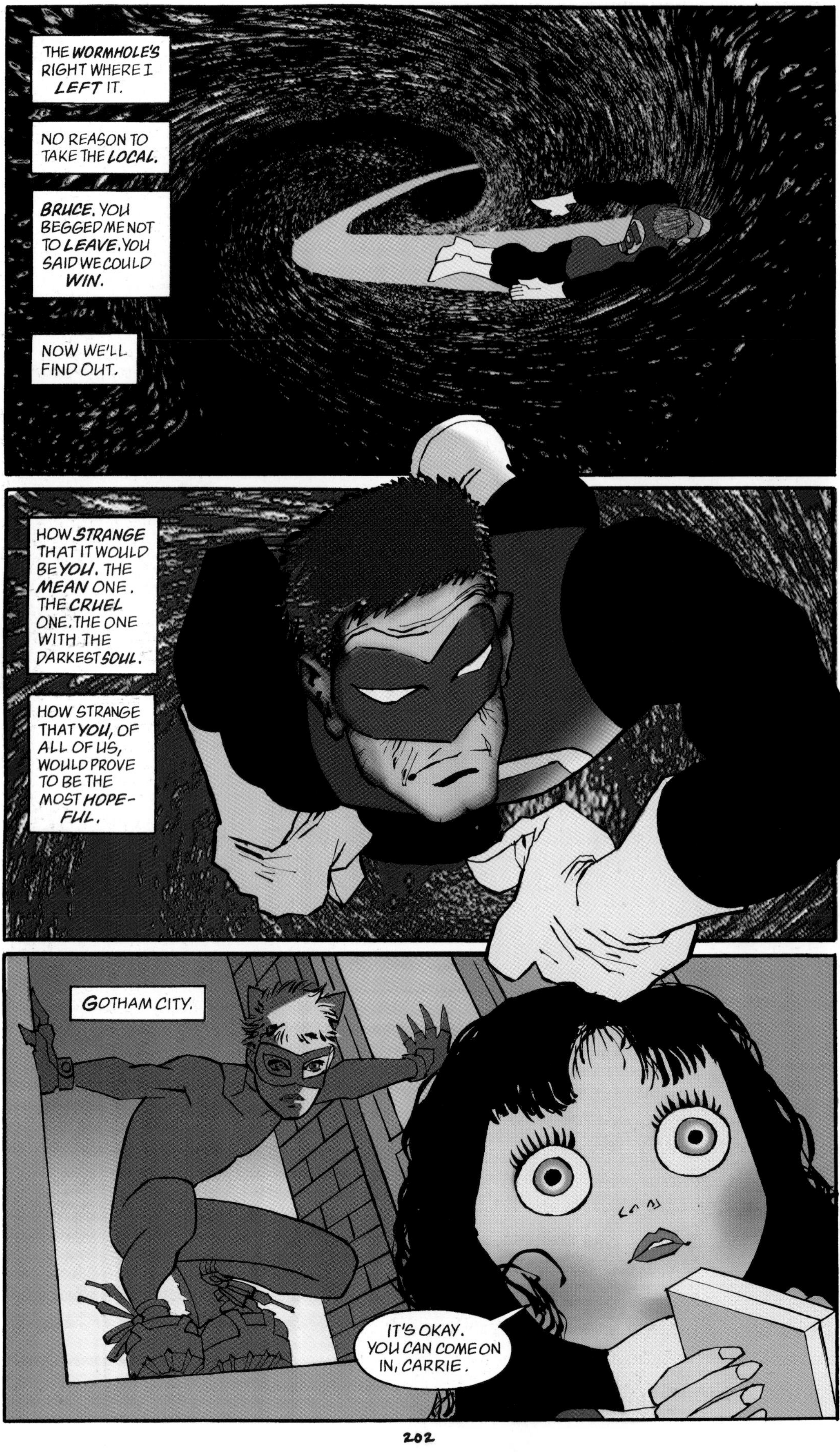
THE WORMHOLE'S RIGHT WHERE I LEFT IT.
NO REASON TO TAKE THE LOCAL.
BRUCE. YOU BEGGED ME NOT TO LEAVE. YOU SAID WE COULD WIN.
NOW WE'LL FIND OUT.
HOW STRANGE THAT IT WOULD BE YOU. THE MEAN ONE. THE CRUEL ONE. THE ONE WITH THE DARKEST SOUL.
HOW STRANGE THAT YOU, OF ALL OF US, WOULD PROVE TO BE THE MOST HOPE-FUL.
GOTHAM CITY.
IT'S OKAY. YOU CAN COME ON IN, CARRIE.

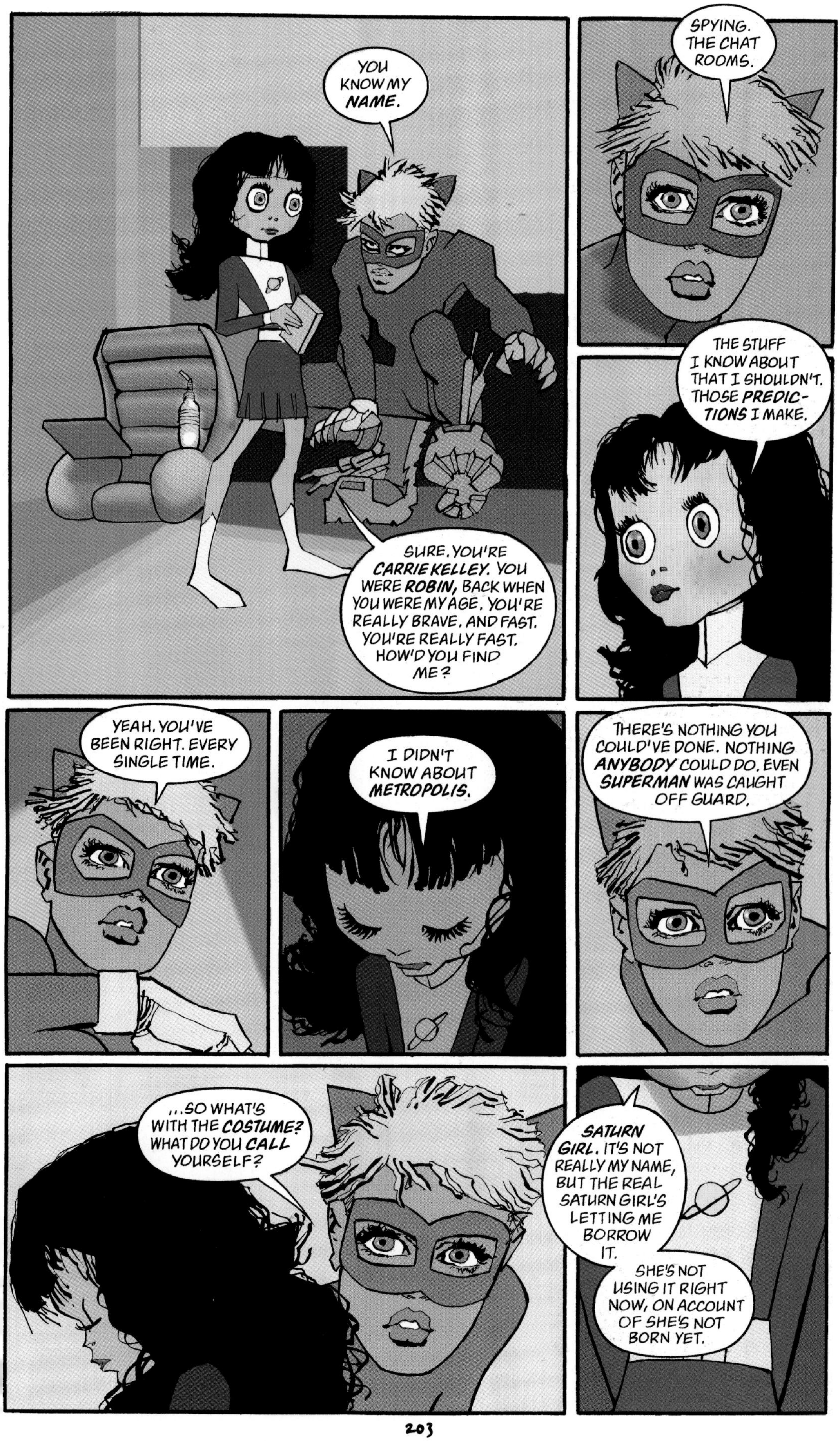
YOU KNOW MY NAME.
SURE. YOU'RE CARRIE KELLEY. YOU WERE ROBIN, BACK WHEN YOU WERE MY AGE. YOU'RE REALLY BRAVE. AND FAST. YOU'RE REALLY FAST. HOW'D YOU FIND ME?
SPYING. THE CHAT ROOMS.
THE STUFF I KNOW ABOUT THAT I SHOULDN'T. THOSE PREDICTIONS I MAKE.
YEAH. YOU'VE BEEN RIGHT. EVERY SINGLE TIME.
I DIDN'T KNOW ABOUT METROPOLIS.
THERE'S NOTHING YOU COULD'VE DONE. NOTHING ANYBODY COULD DO. EVEN SUPERMAN WAS CAUGHT OFF GUARD.
...SO WHAT'S WITH THE COSTUME? WHAT DO YOU CALL YOURSELF?
SATURN GIRL. IT'S NOT REALLY MY NAME, BUT THE REAL SATURN GIRL'S LETTING ME BORROW IT.
SHE'S NOT USING IT RIGHT NOW, ON ACCOUNT OF SHE'S NOT BORN YET.

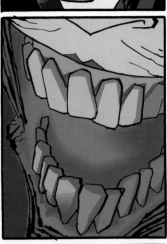

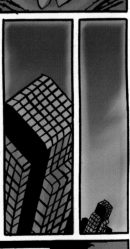

SO I KILLED HIM.

OLIVER SAID HE'D DONE THE MONSTER IN WITH AN INCENDIARY.

AND OLIVER DOESN'T MISS. NOT EVER.

SO IF THIS THING WASN'T DEAD-- HE WAS TOUGH.

SO I KILLED HIM.

I TOOK HIM APART.

PIECE BY PIECE.

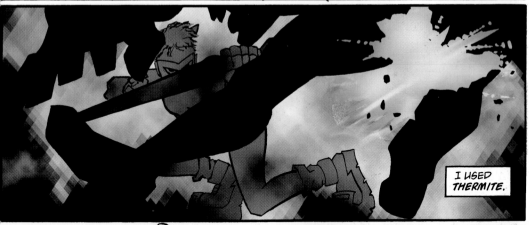

I USED THERMITE.

I USED ACID.

I USED C4.

I TOOK HIM APART.

PIECE BY PIECE.

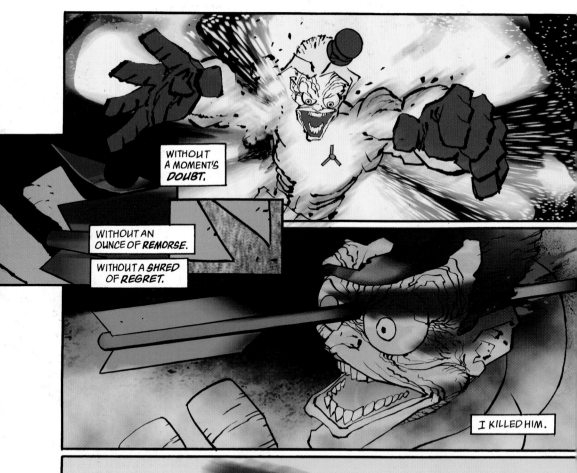

WITHOUT A MOMENT'S **DOUBT.**

WITHOUT AN OUNCE OF **REMORSE.**

WITHOUT A **SHRED** OF **REGRET.**

I KILLED HIM.

I KILLED HIM.

HE'S DEAD.

HE'S GOT TO BE DEAD.

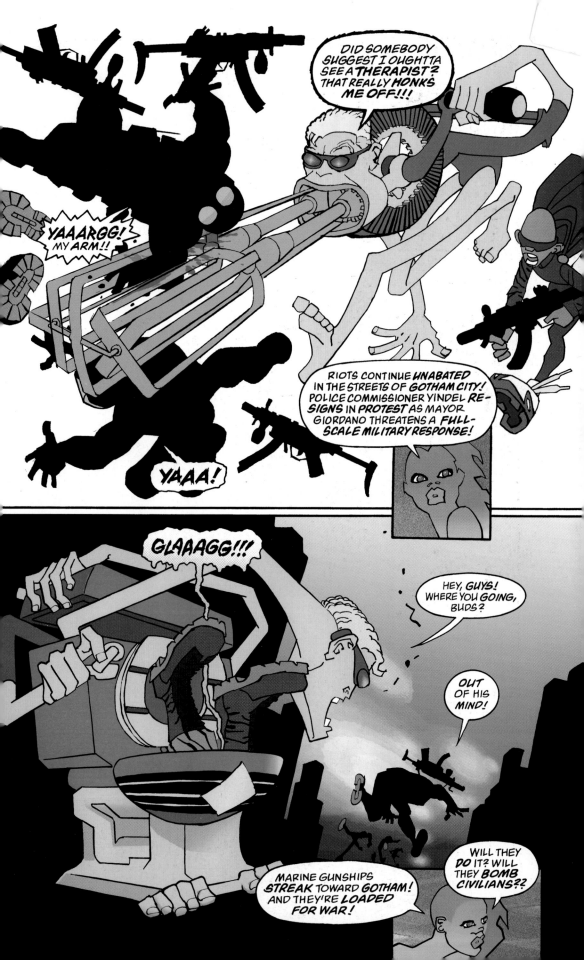

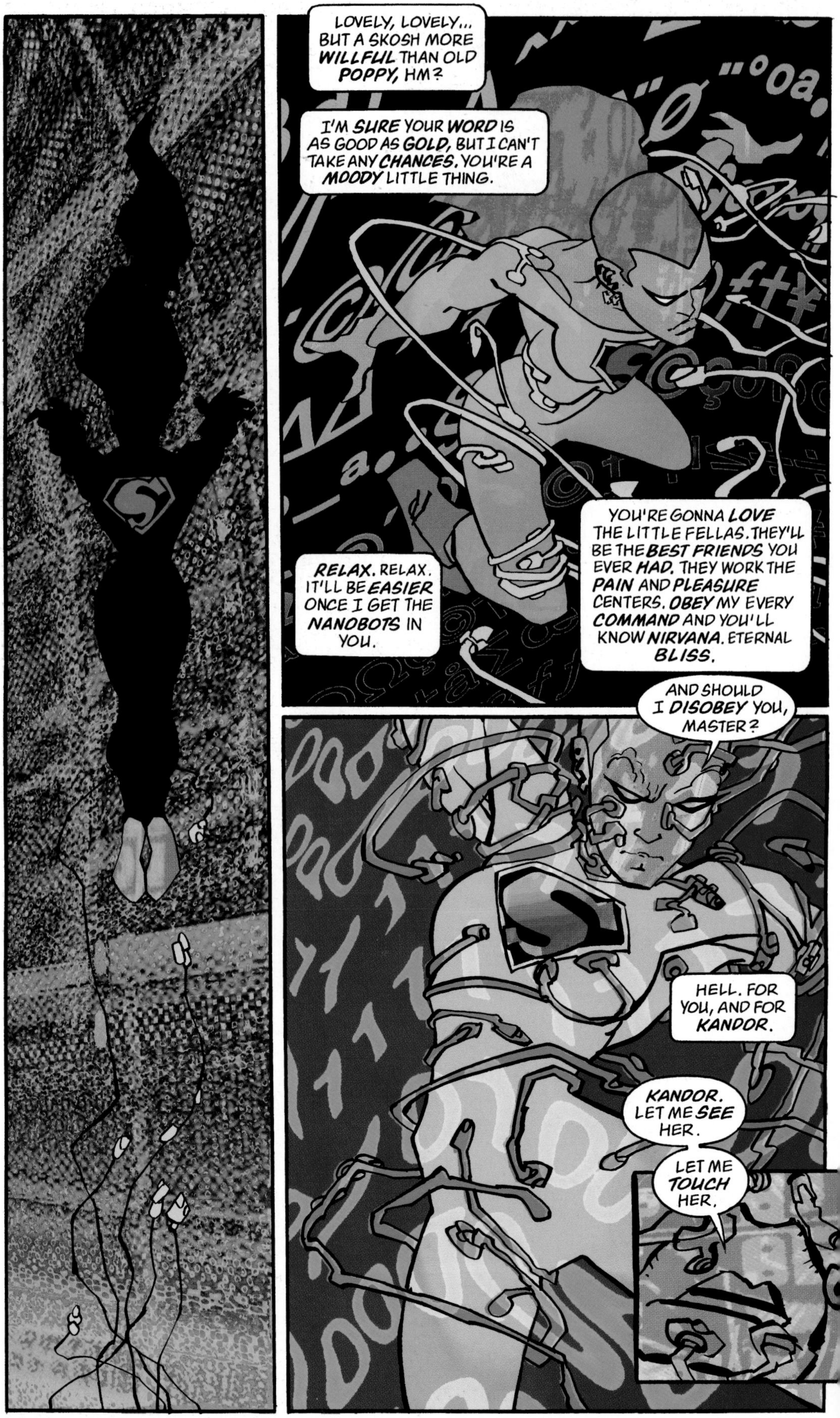

LOVELY, LOVELY... BUT A SKOSH MORE WILLFUL THAN OLD POPPY, HM?
I'M SURE YOUR WORD IS AS GOOD AS GOLD, BUT I CAN'T TAKE ANY CHANCES. YOU'RE A MOODY LITTLE THING.
RELAX. RELAX. IT'LL BE EASIER ONCE I GET THE NANOBOTS IN YOU.
YOU'RE GONNA LOVE THE LITTLE FELLAS. THEY'LL BE THE BEST FRIENDS YOU EVER HAD. THEY WORK THE PAIN AND PLEASURE CENTERS. OBEY MY EVERY COMMAND AND YOU'LL KNOW NIRVANA. ETERNAL BLISS.
AND SHOULD I DISOBEY YOU, MASTER?
HELL. FOR YOU, AND FOR KANDOR.
KANDOR. LET ME SEE HER.
LET ME TOUCH HER.

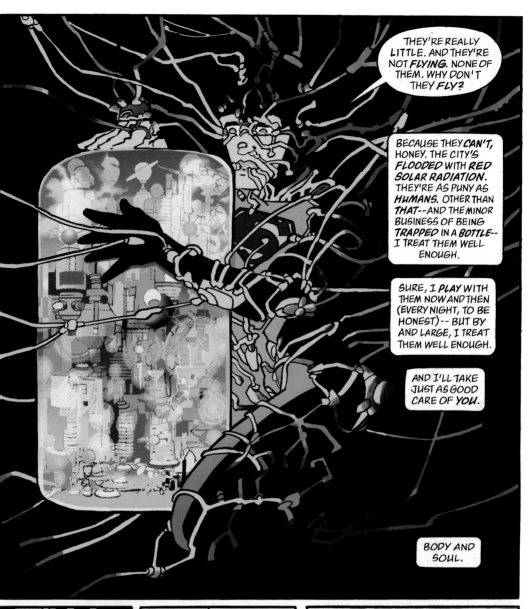

THEY'RE REALLY LITTLE. AND THEY'RE NOT *FLYING.* NONE OF THEM. WHY DON'T THEY *FLY?*

BECAUSE THEY *CAN'T,* HONEY. THE CITY'S *FLOODED* WITH *RED SOLAR RADIATION.* THEY'RE AS PUNY AS *HUMANS.* OTHER THAN *THAT*-- AND THE MINOR BUSINESS OF BEING *TRAPPED* IN A *BOTTLE*-- I TREAT THEM WELL ENOUGH.

SURE, I *PLAY* WITH THEM NOW AND THEN (EVERY NIGHT, TO BE HONEST)-- BUT BY AND LARGE, I TREAT THEM WELL ENOUGH.

AND I'LL TAKE JUST AS GOOD CARE OF *YOU.*

BODY AND SOUL.

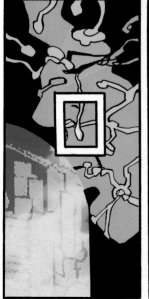

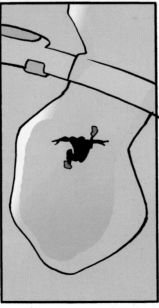

213

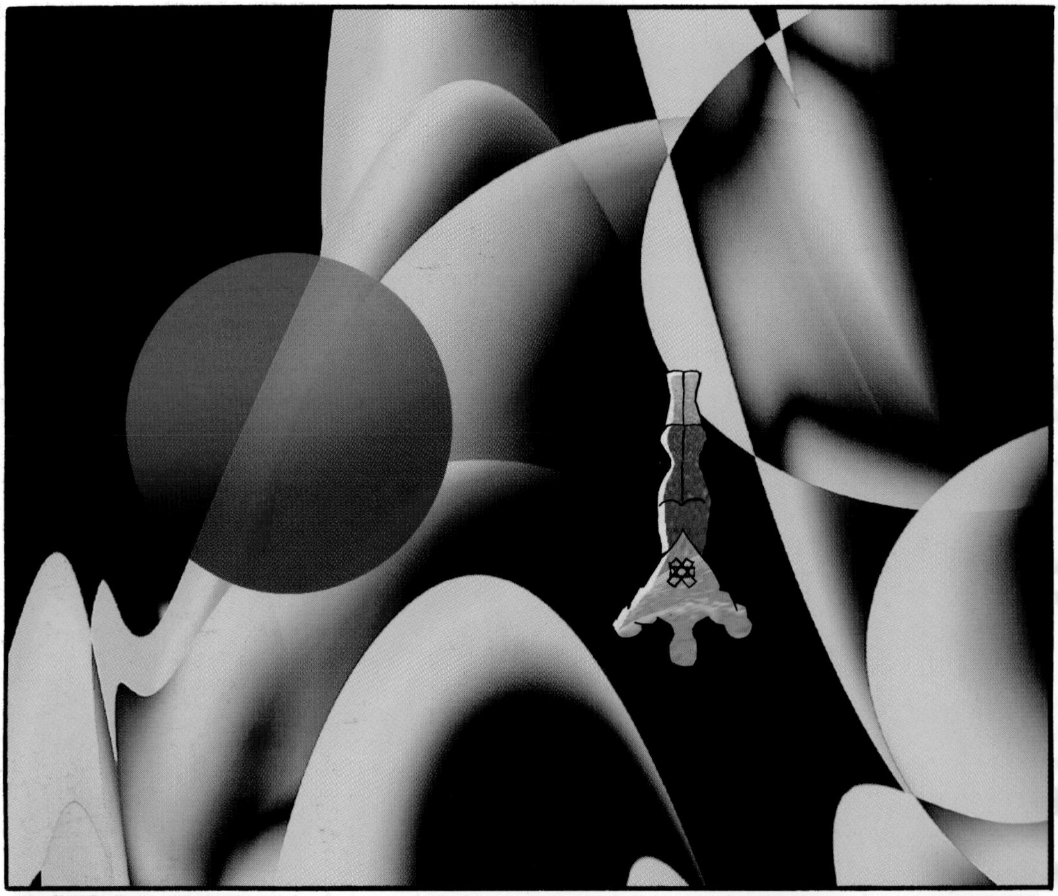

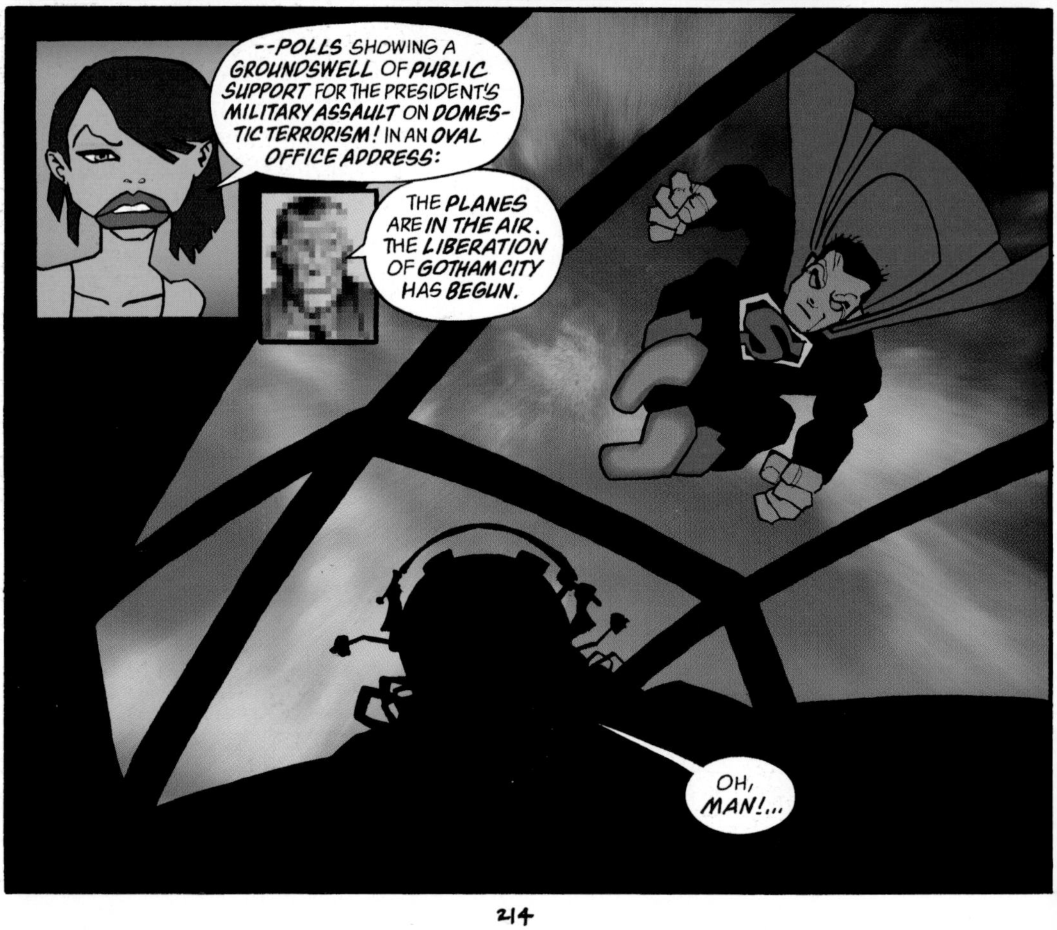

--POLLS SHOWING A GROUNDSWELL OF PUBLIC SUPPORT FOR THE PRESIDENT'S MILITARY ASSAULT ON DOMESTIC TERRORISM! IN AN OVAL OFFICE ADDRESS:
THE PLANES ARE IN THE AIR. THE LIBERATION OF GOTHAM CITY HAS BEGUN.
OH, MAN!...

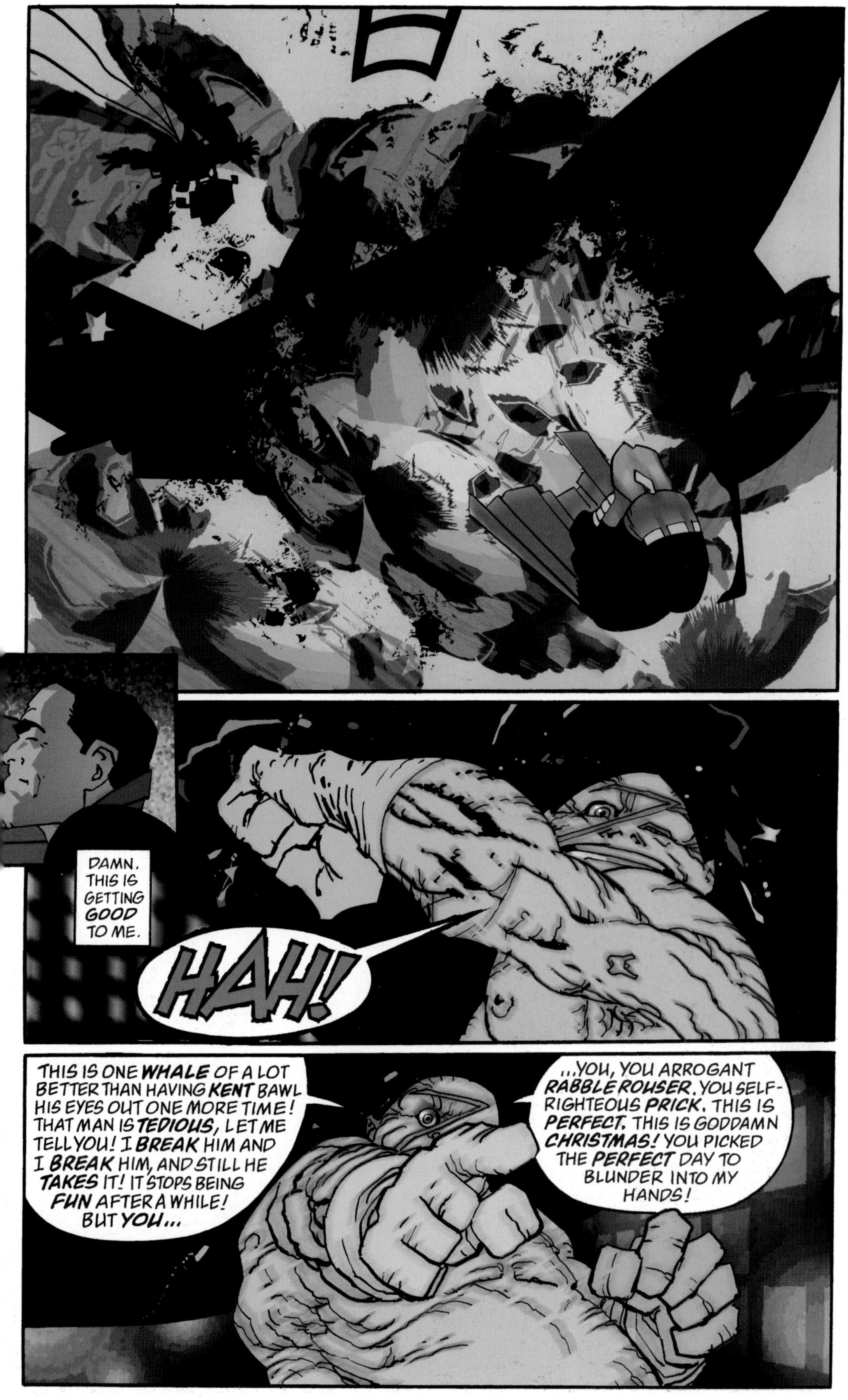
DAMN. THIS IS GETTING GOOD TO ME.
HAH!
THIS IS ONE WHALE OF A LOT BETTER THAN HAVING KENT BAWL HIS EYES OUT ONE MORE TIME! THAT MAN IS TEDIOUS, LET ME TELL YOU! I BREAK HIM AND I BREAK HIM, AND STILL HE TAKES IT! IT STOPS BEING FUN AFTER A WHILE! BUT YOU...
...YOU, YOU ARROGANT RABBLE ROUSER. YOU SELF-RIGHTEOUS PRICK. THIS IS PERFECT. THIS IS GODDAMN CHRISTMAS! YOU PICKED THE PERFECT DAY TO BLUNDER INTO MY HANDS!

LOOK THERE! ANOTHER FIRE! ANOTHER PACK OF YOUR MILITANTS, NO DOUBT. LOOKS LIKE THE OLD 38th STREET ARMORY GOING UP. HAH! THEY WANT FIRE? I'LL SHOW THEM FIRE! RIGHT SOON, I'LL SHOW THEM FIRE!

THIS CITY HAS SERVED ME WELL. I'LL MISS IT.

IT WON'T MISS YOU--

≥KHAAFF≥

LEX LUTHOR. EVIL GENIUS. ARCHFIEND. HEADED FOR A FALL.

THAT'S UNLESS I'M AS CRAZY AS EVERYBODY THINKS I AM.

HELL. MAYBE I AM NUTS. MAYBE I'M STILL LYING ON THE CAVE FLOOR, CLUTCHING MY CHEST...

HAH! LOOK AT IT. LOOK AT DEAR METROPOLIS. BUILT WITH THE SWEAT AND BLOOD OF GENERA-TIONS. FIRST IN WOOD AND BRICK. THEN IN GRANITE AND CONCRETE AND GLASS. THEN IN STEEL AND PYREX. THEN IN HARD PLASTIC AND TRANSPARENT POLYMERS.

METROPOLIS. THE CITY OF DREAMS. REACHING FOR THE SKY.

AND IN THE BLINK OF AN EYE, METROPOLIS WILL CEASE TO EXIST.

TEN MINUTES FROM NOW. IT'S GONNA BE GORGEOUS.

SURE OF THAT, ARE YOU?

OUR SPACE CANNONS HAVE BEEN TESTED AND RETESTED. THEY WORK.

THEY WORK DAMNABLY WELL. WITH UNCANNY PRECISION.

THEY VAPOR-IZED OLD KENT'S ARCTIC FORTRESS.

THEY ERASED THE RAIN FOREST REFUGE OF YOUR BUDDIES FROM PLANET THANAGAR.

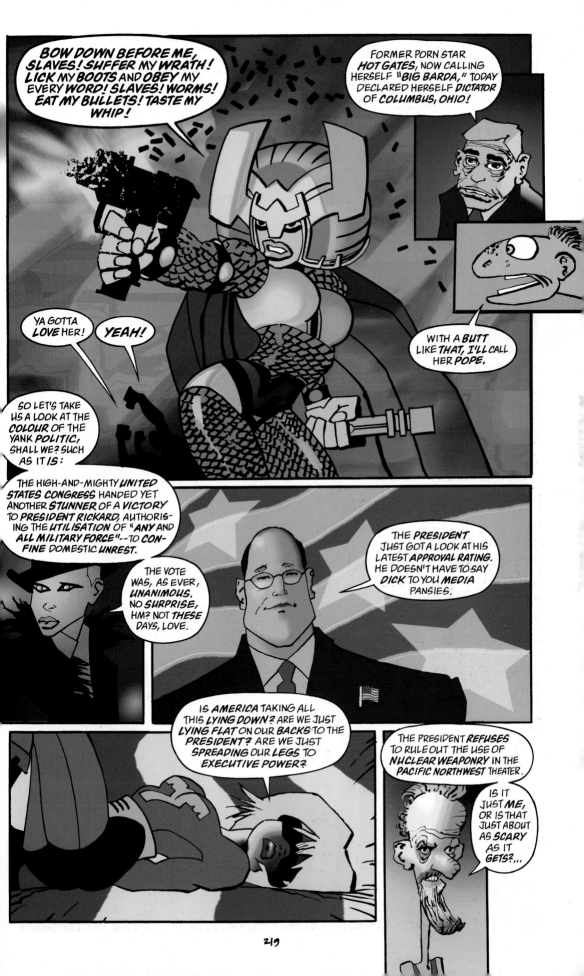

219

MA. PA.
YOU WERE WRONG.
I WILL ALWAYS CHERISH YOUR MEMORY-- BUT YOU WERE WRONG.
I WILL ALWAYS CHERISH THIS PLANET AND ITS CREATURES-- BUT YOU WERE WRONG.
I AM NOT ONE OF THEM.
OH, MAN!...
I AM NOT HUMAN.

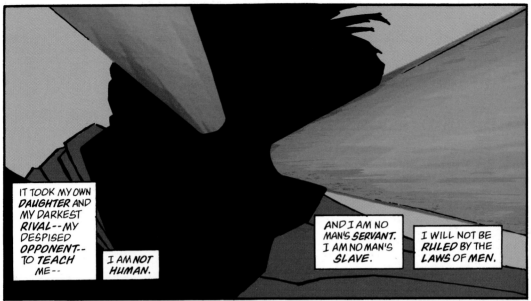

IT TOOK MY OWN *DAUGHTER* AND MY DARKEST *RIVAL*--MY DESPISED *OPPONENT*--TO *TEACH* ME--

I AM *NOT HUMAN.*

AND I AM NO MAN'S *SERVANT.* I AM NO MAN'S *SLAVE.*

I WILL NOT BE *RULED* BY THE *LAWS* OF MEN.

JESUS! WHAT'S GOTTEN INTO *HIM?*

I AM *NO MAN.*

I AM *SUPERMAN.*

MANHATTAN.

JUST OFF *CHRISTOPHER STREET.*

WE CAN STILL SQUEEZE INTO THE *TIGHTS.* WHAT DO YOU *SAY,* PARTNER? READY FOR *ACTION?* IT'S ALL THE *RAGE.*

BUT, *HAANK!* BACK THEN, ALL WE DID WAS *ARGUE!*

THE *HAWK* AND THE *DOVE.*

DON'T ASK.

AT LAST.

EARTH.

ONE OF THE GALAXY'S *CROWN JEWELS.*

BUT IT'S A JEWEL NOT TO BE *TOUCHED.*

NO. SPACE TRAVELERS STEER CLEAR OF EARTH, FOR ALL ITS RESOURCES, ALL ITS BEAUTY.

IT'S ONLY *SENSIBLE* TO AVOID *CONTACT* WITH A *SPECIES* THAT POINTS *WEAPONS* AT ITS OWN *TERRITORY.*

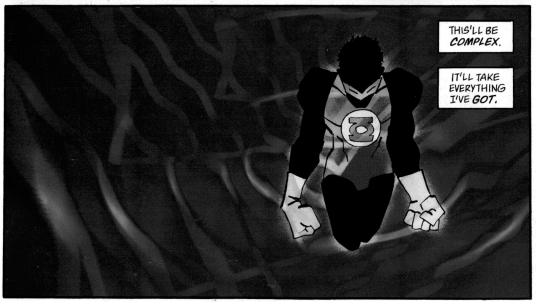

THIS'LL BE *COMPLEX.*

IT'LL TAKE EVERYTHING I'VE *GOT.*

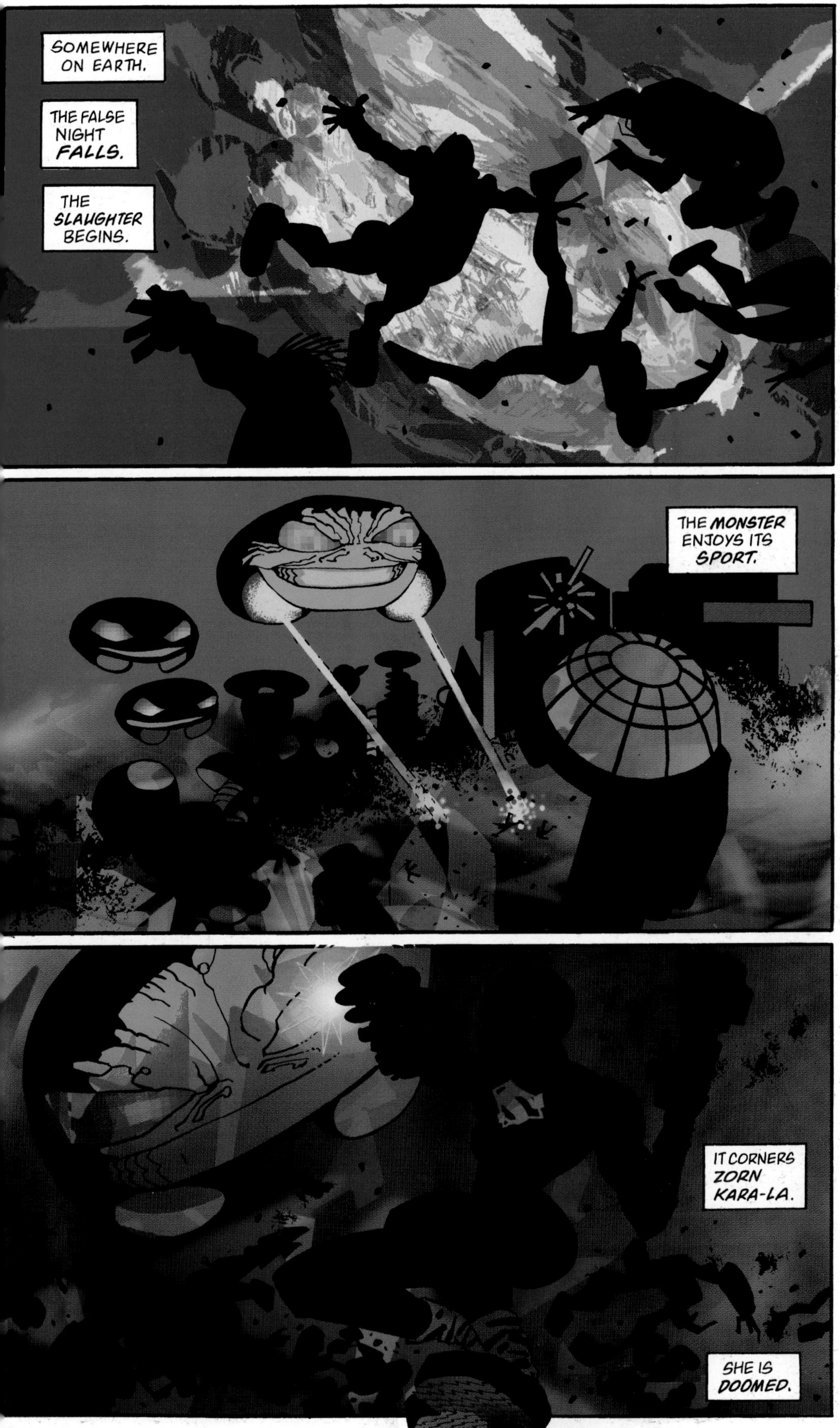
SOMEWHERE ON EARTH.
THE FALSE NIGHT FALLS.
THE SLAUGHTER BEGINS.
THE MONSTER ENJOYS ITS SPORT.
IT CORNERS ZORN KARA-LA.
SHE IS DOOMED.

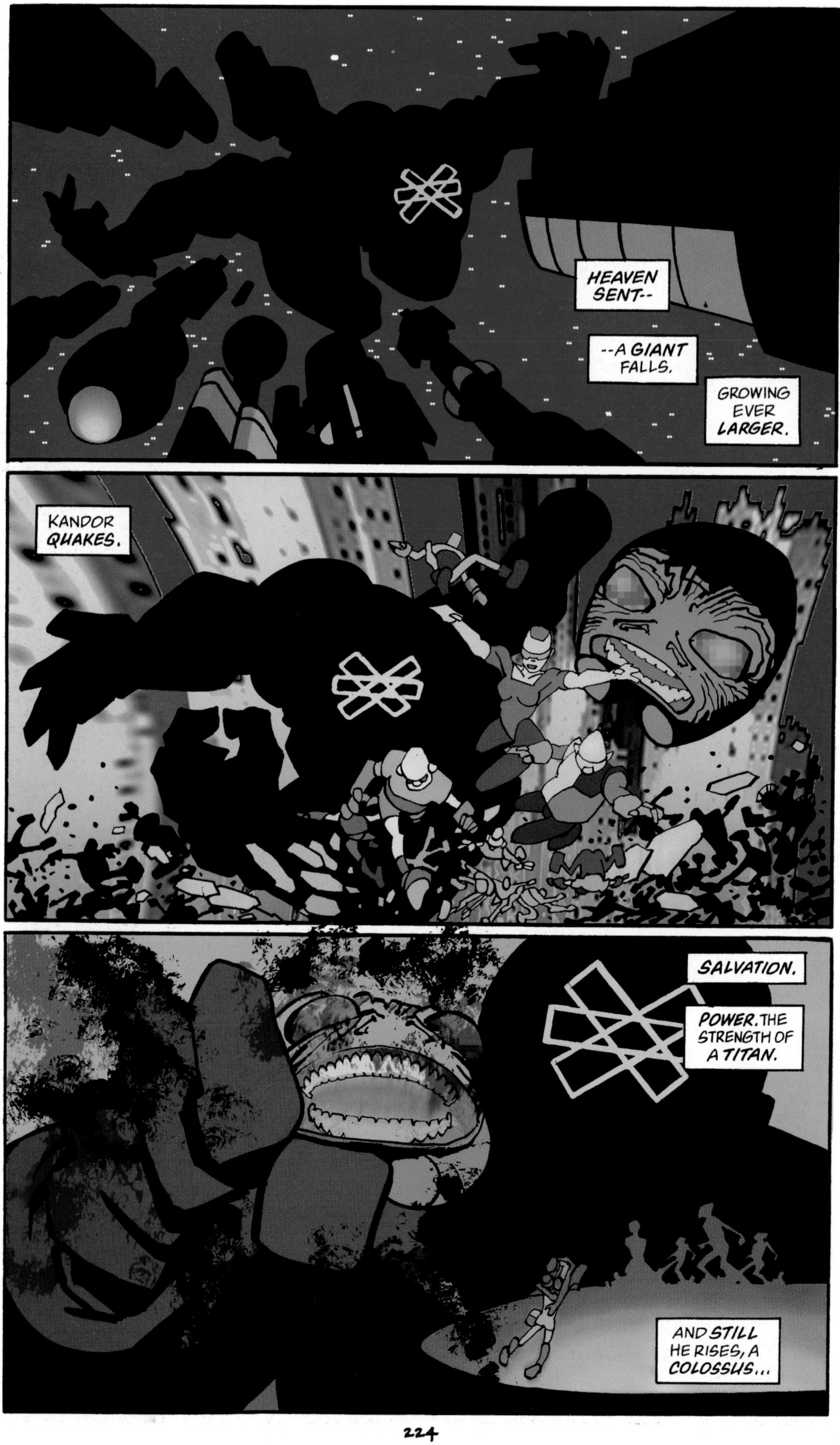
HEAVEN SENT--
--A GIANT FALLS.
GROWING EVER LARGER.
KANDOR QUAKES.
SALVATION.
POWER. THE STRENGTH OF A TITAN.
AND STILL HE RISES, A COLOSSUS...

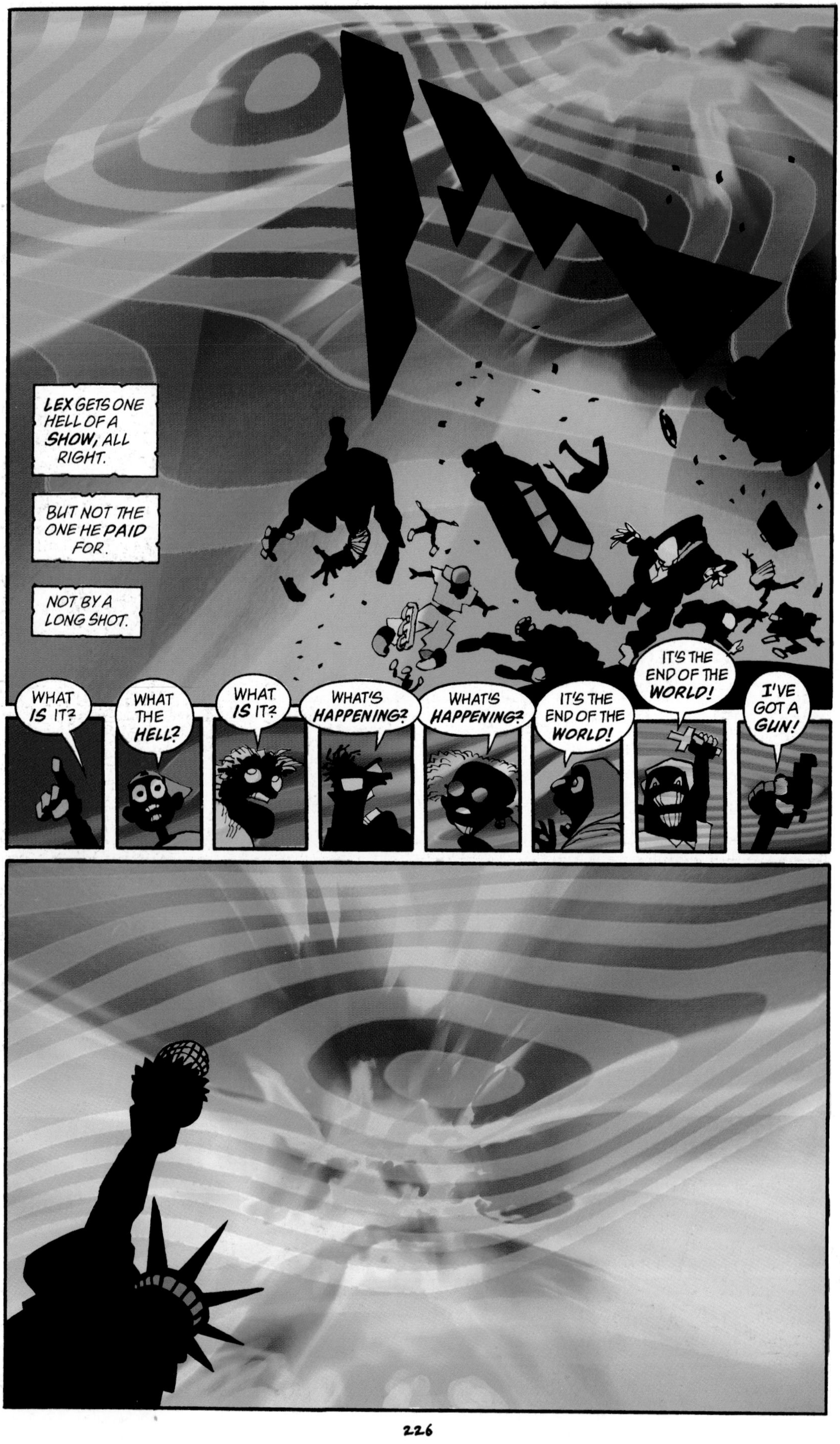
LEX GETS ONE HELL OF A SHOW, ALL RIGHT.
BUT NOT THE ONE HE PAID FOR.
NOT BY A LONG SHOT.
WHAT IS IT?
WHAT THE HELL?
WHAT IS IT?
WHAT'S HAPPENING?
WHAT'S HAPPENING?
IT'S THE END OF THE WORLD!
IT'S THE END OF THE WORLD!
I'VE GOT A GUN!

LAWD, LAWD, LAWD IT'S A **WRATHA GOD**, LAWD, LAWD, IT'S A HUNKA HUNKA **WRATHA GOD**, LAWD, LAWD,...GIT ON BOARD THUH **GLORY BOAT**...

VISA AND MASTERCARD **ACCEPTED**, LAWD, LAWD...

THE KING IS HERE!

I NO **SAY** IT A RAPTURE, IT NO **BE** IT A RAPTURE!

JIHAD!

AAAAHH, **SHADDUP**...

UH, **HOUSTON**? WE'VE LOST, LIKE,... **EARTH**?

IT'S EVERY-WHERE!

RUN!

RUN **WHERE**? IT'S **EVERY-WHERE**!

IT'S **SOURCE** AND **NATURE** REMAIN **MYSTERIES**. YET THE SHEER **SCALE** AND **COMPLEXITY** OF THE PHENOMENON SUGGEST **INTELLIGENT DESIGN**. IT WOULD SEEM TO BE OF **EXTRATERRESTRIAL ORIGIN**--

-- AND IT WOULD SEEM TO KNOW **EXACTLY** WHAT IT'S DOING.

A PROMINENT **SCIENTIST**

AND IT CAN **DO** WHAT-EVER IT **WANTS** TO US. WE'RE **HELPLESS**. AN **ENERGY MATRIX** HAS SUCKED BACK **PLANET EARTH** LIKE IT WAS AN **OYSTER**.

THE **GULF STREAM** HAS REVERSED **COURSE**. THE **ELECTRO-MAGNETIC FIELD** HAS GONE ALL **SPASTIC**. OUR **SATELLITES** ARE ACTING LIKE THEY'RE ON **DRUGS**. IT'S **EVERYWHERE**-- AND IT CAN DO **ANYTHING**!

ANOTHER PROMINENT SCIENTIST

WOW! AND THAT'S A *WAY SERIOUSLY REAL SCIENTIST* TALKING! THIS STORY IS *TOTALLY RUTHLESS*--AND THAT *ENERGY FIELD* THING IS *TOTALLY RUTHLESSLY SERIOUSLY GLOBAL!*

WHAT'S THE *SNIFF* OVER THERE AT THE *PENTAGON,* JOLAYNE?

I COULD *PEE,* BER*NAYZE!* YOU KNOW THAT *GENERAL* GUY? THE REALLY *OLD* ONE WITH ALL THOSE *MEDALS* ALL OVER HIM WHO TELLS THE *PRESIDENT* WHO TO *BOMB?* HE'S, LIKE, LOOKING STRAIGHT *AT* US AND HE'S, LIKE, TOTALLY "*I DON'T KNOW*"?

IS THAT AN *ICE-DOUCHE,* OR *WHAT,* CONUNDRA?

YOU ARE *SO SPOT ON,* JOLAYNE! THIS WHOLE *PHENOM* THING IS DEEPLY *RUTHLESSLY RUTHLESS!* I AM SO ALL OVER THIS!

HERE'S *CLYTEMNESTRA* WITH THE DISH FROM *GOTHAM!* CLYT?

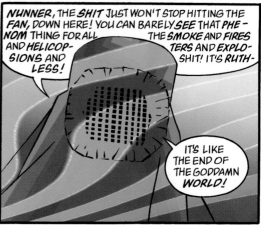

NUNNER, THE *SHIT* JUST WON'T STOP HITTING THE FAN, DOWN HERE! YOU CAN BARELY *SEE* THAT *PHE-NOM* THING FOR ALL AND *HELICOP-SIONS* AND LESS! THE *SMOKE* AND *FIRES* TERS AND *EXPLO-SHIT!* IT'S *RUTH-*

IT'S LIKE THE END OF THE GODDAMN *WORLD!*

YES, HOUSTON. WE'RE *FINE.* WE'RE ALL *JUST FINE.* BUT THOSE *SPACE CAN-NONS* OF OURS?

NOT EVEN *TOAST,* THEY'RE *GONE.*

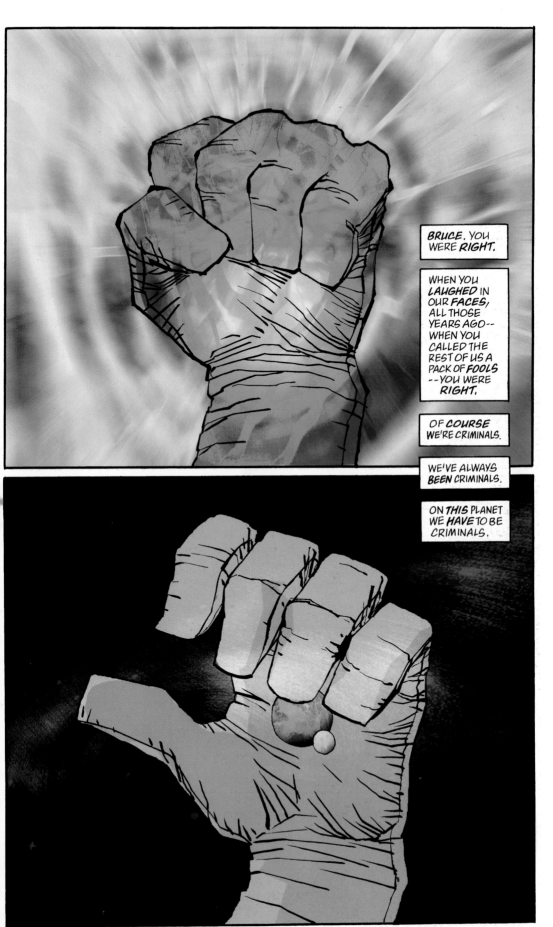

BRUCE, YOU WERE *RIGHT*.

WHEN YOU *LAUGHED* IN OUR *FACES*, ALL THOSE YEARS AGO-- WHEN YOU CALLED THE REST OF US A PACK OF *FOOLS* --YOU WERE *RIGHT*.

OF *COURSE* WE'RE CRIMINALS.

WE'VE ALWAYS *BEEN* CRIMINALS.

ON *THIS* PLANET WE *HAVE* TO BE CRIMINALS.

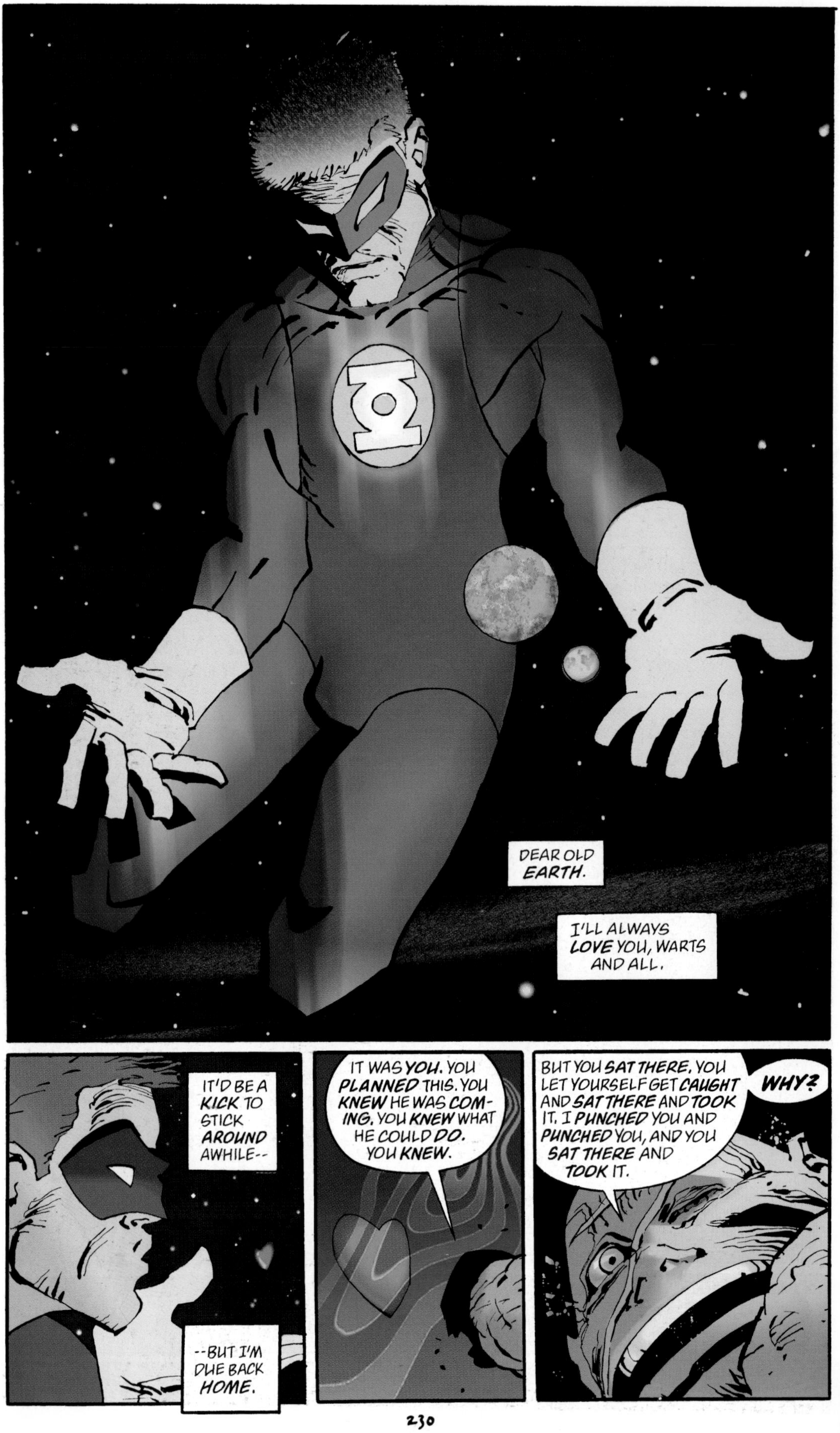
DEAR OLD EARTH.
I'LL ALWAYS LOVE YOU, WARTS AND ALL.
IT'D BE A KICK TO STICK AROUND AWHILE--
--BUT I'M DUE BACK HOME.
IT WAS YOU. YOU PLANNED THIS. YOU KNEW HE WAS COMING. YOU KNEW WHAT HE COULD DO. YOU KNEW.
BUT YOU SAT THERE. YOU LET YOURSELF GET CAUGHT AND SAT THERE AND TOOK IT. I PUNCHED YOU AND PUNCHED YOU, AND YOU SAT THERE AND TOOK IT.
WHY?

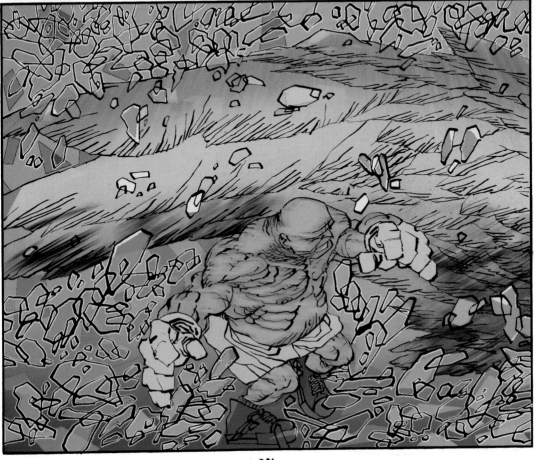

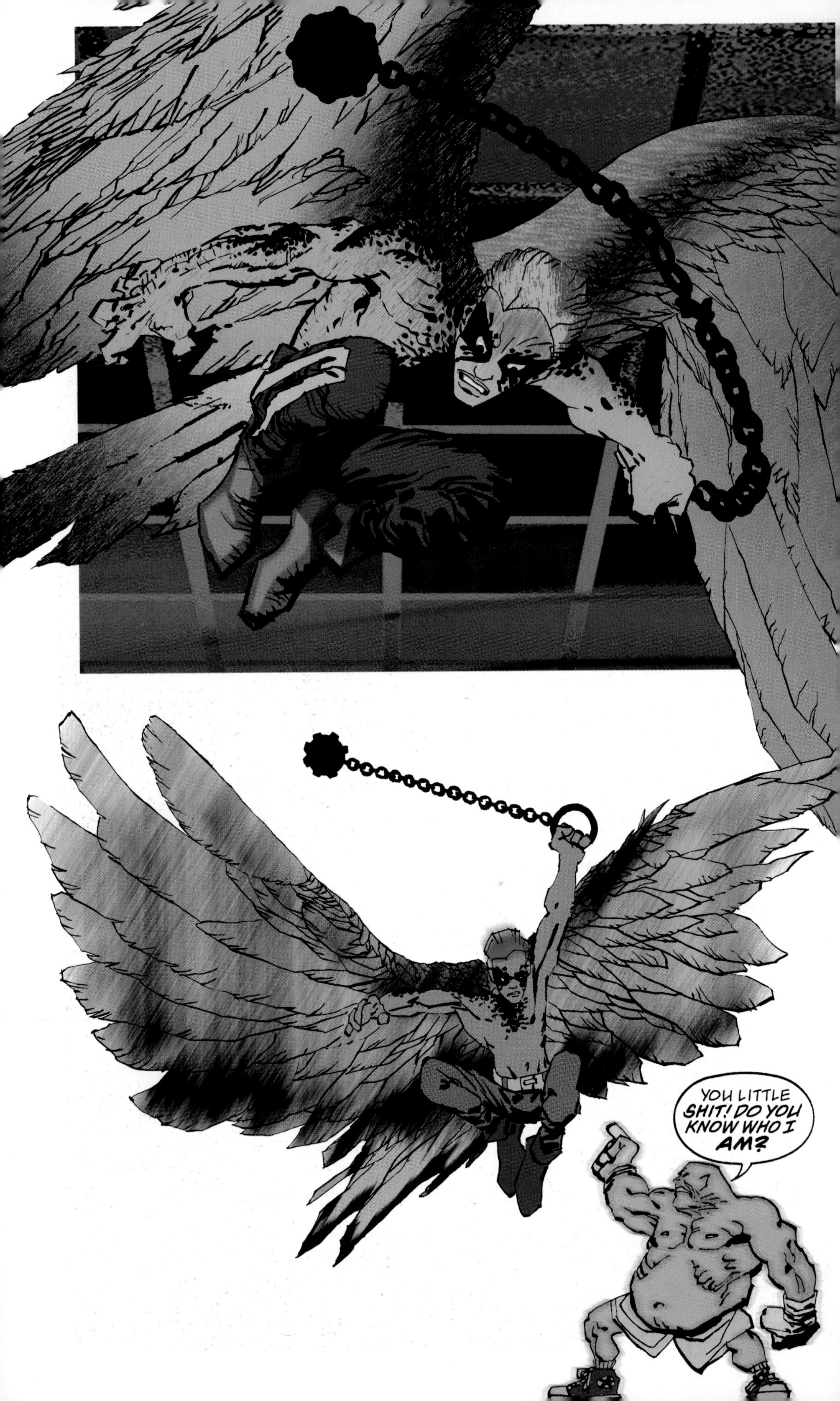
YOU LITTLE SHIT! DO YOU KNOW WHO I AM?

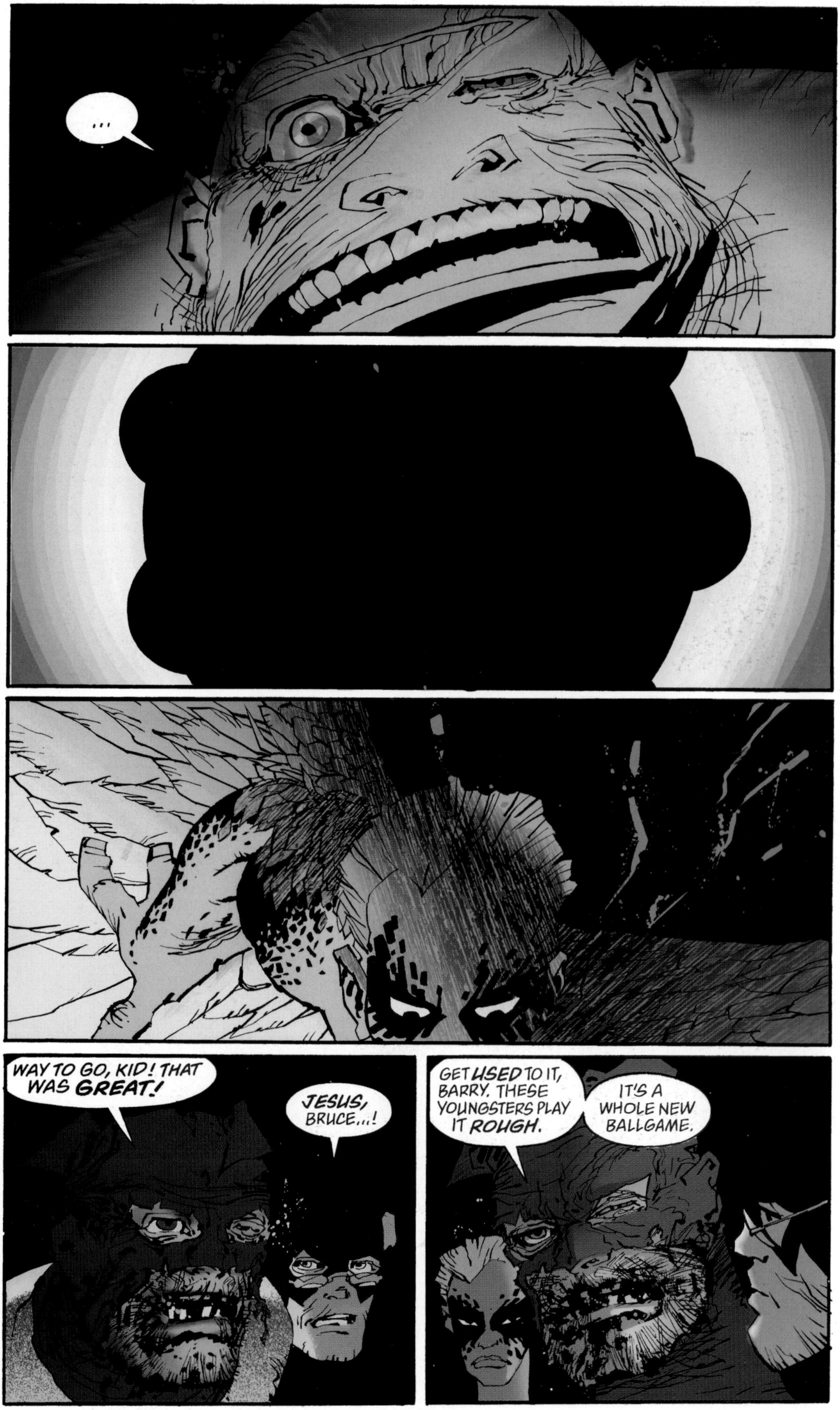
...
WAY TO GO, KID! THAT WAS GREAT!
JESUS, BRUCE...!
GET USED TO IT, BARRY. THESE YOUNGSTERS PLAY IT ROUGH.
IT'S A WHOLE NEW BALLGAME.

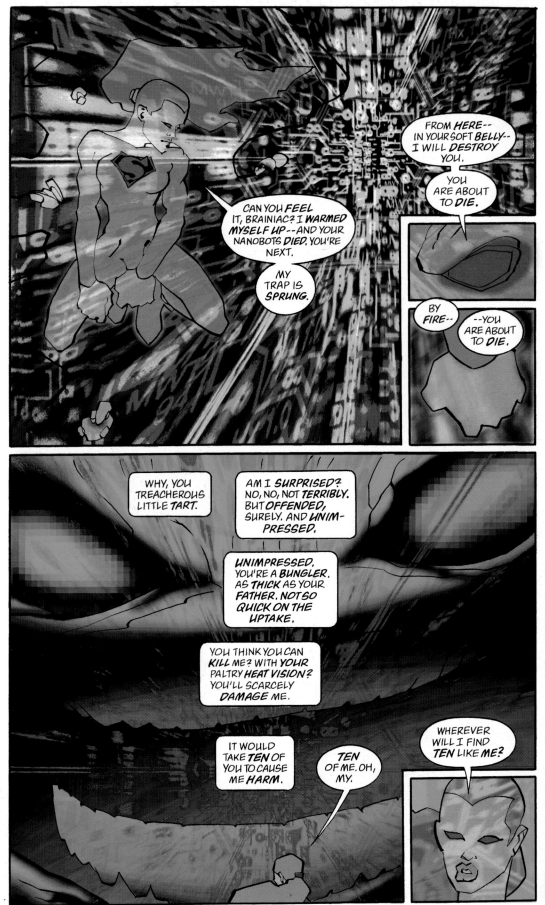

FREEDOM. OUR BONDS ARE **SHATTERED**.

OUR SPIRITS **SOAR**.

SO DO **WE**.

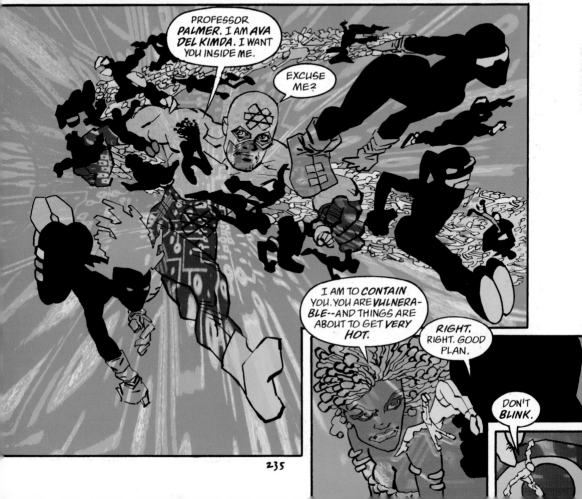

PROFESSOR **PALMER**. I AM **AVA DEL KIMDA**. I WANT YOU INSIDE ME.

EXCUSE ME?

I AM TO **CONTAIN** YOU. YOU ARE **VULNERABLE**--AND THINGS ARE ABOUT TO GET **VERY HOT**.

RIGHT. RIGHT. GOOD PLAN.

DON'T **BLINK**.

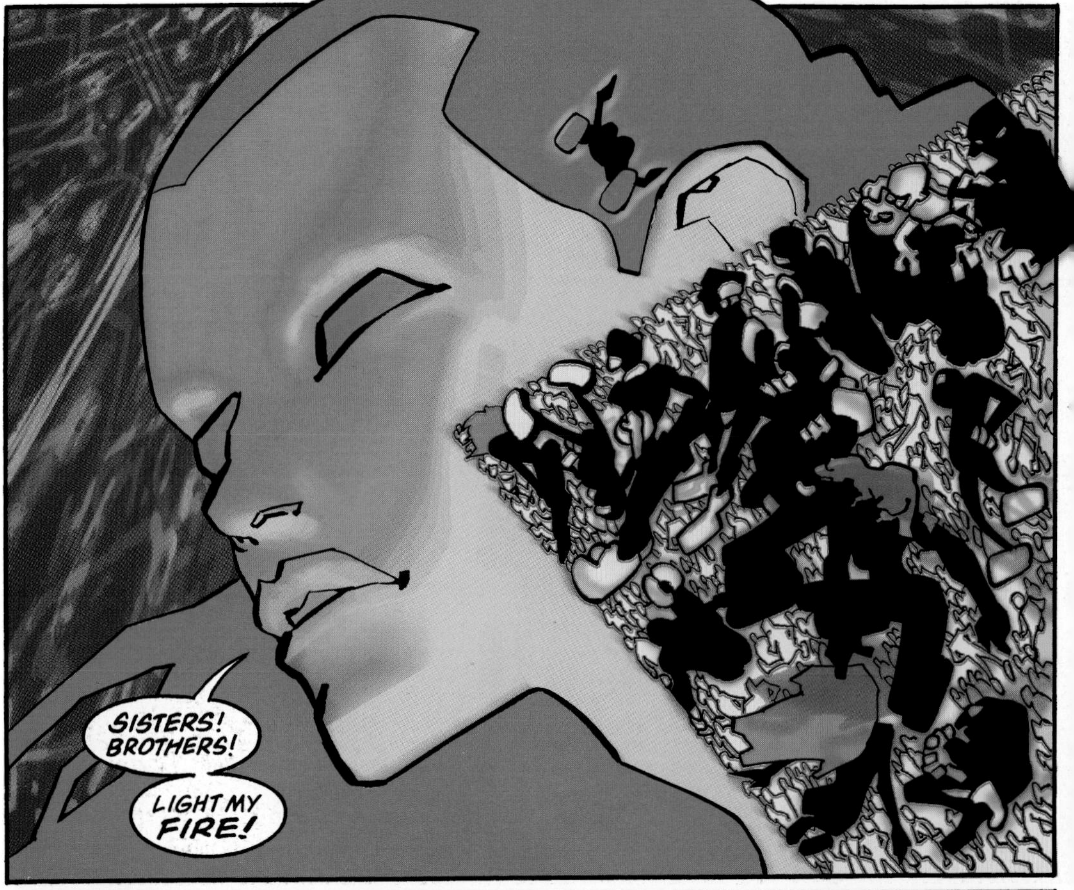
SISTERS! BROTHERS!
LIGHT MY FIRE!

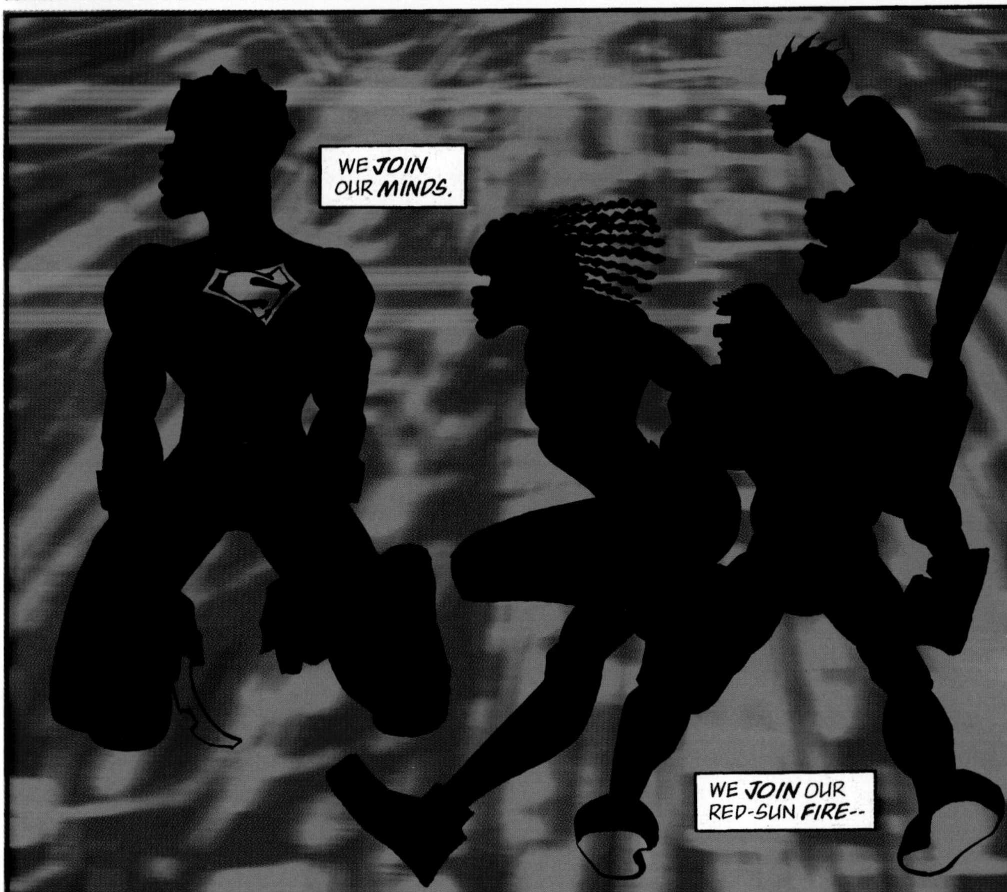
WE JOIN OUR MINDS.
WE JOIN OUR RED-SUN FIRE--

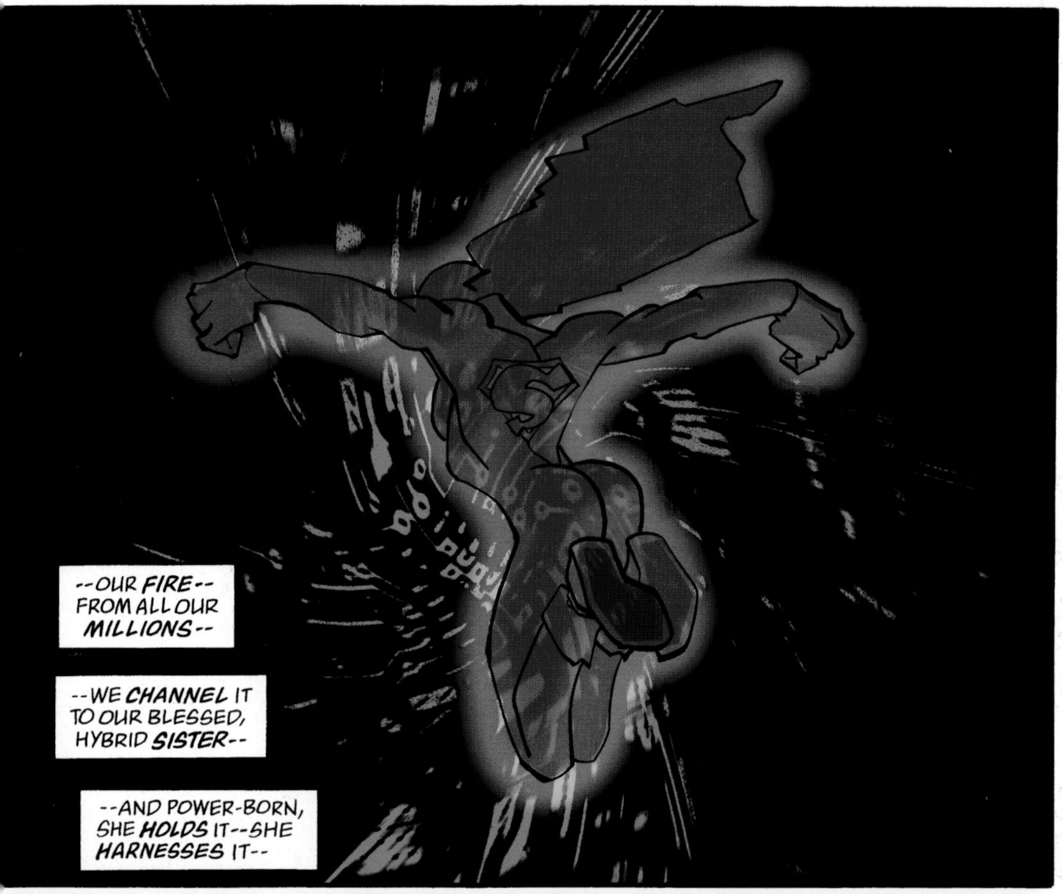
--OUR FIRE--
FROM ALL OUR
MILLIONS--
--WE CHANNEL IT
TO OUR BLESSED,
HYBRID SISTER--
--AND POWER-BORN,
SHE HOLDS IT--SHE
HARNESSES IT--

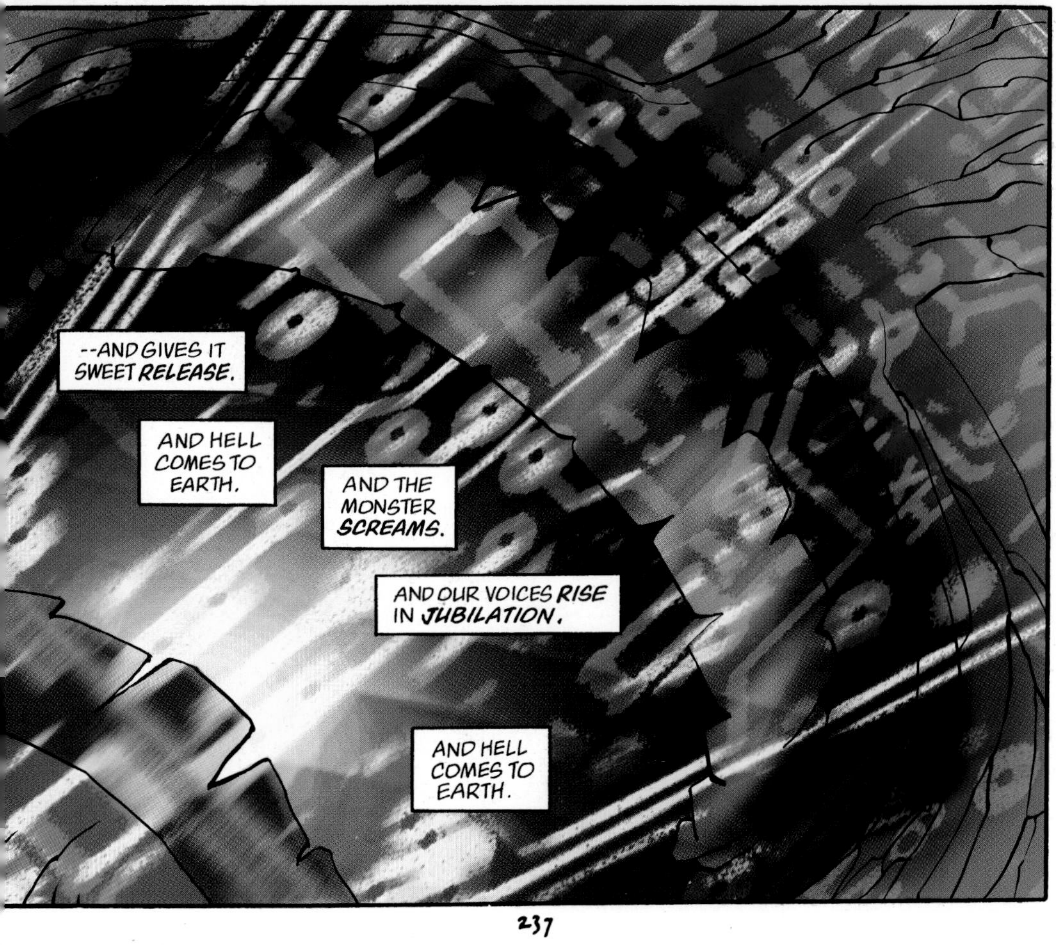
--AND GIVES IT
SWEET RELEASE.
AND HELL
COMES TO
EARTH.
AND THE
MONSTER
SCREAMS.
AND OUR VOICES RISE
IN JUBILATION.
AND HELL
COMES TO
EARTH.

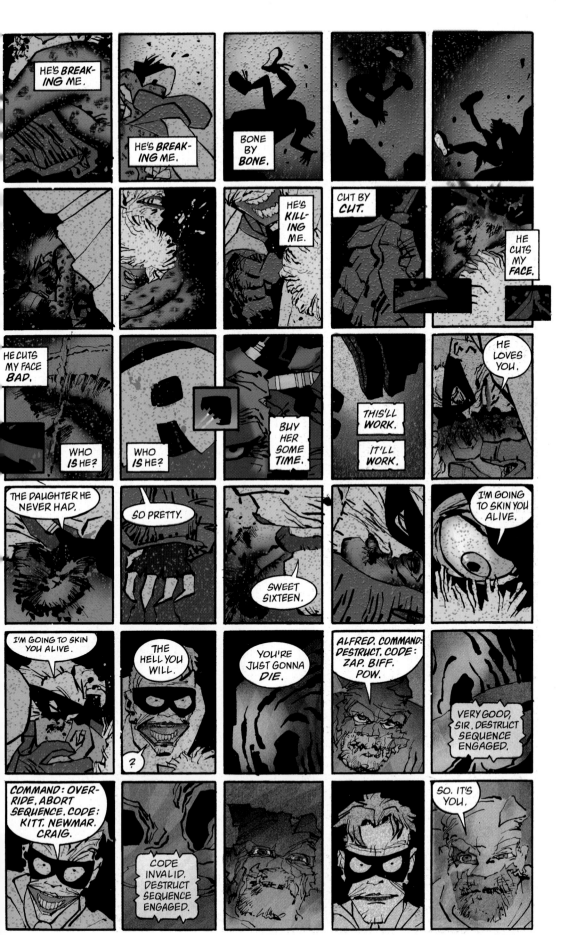

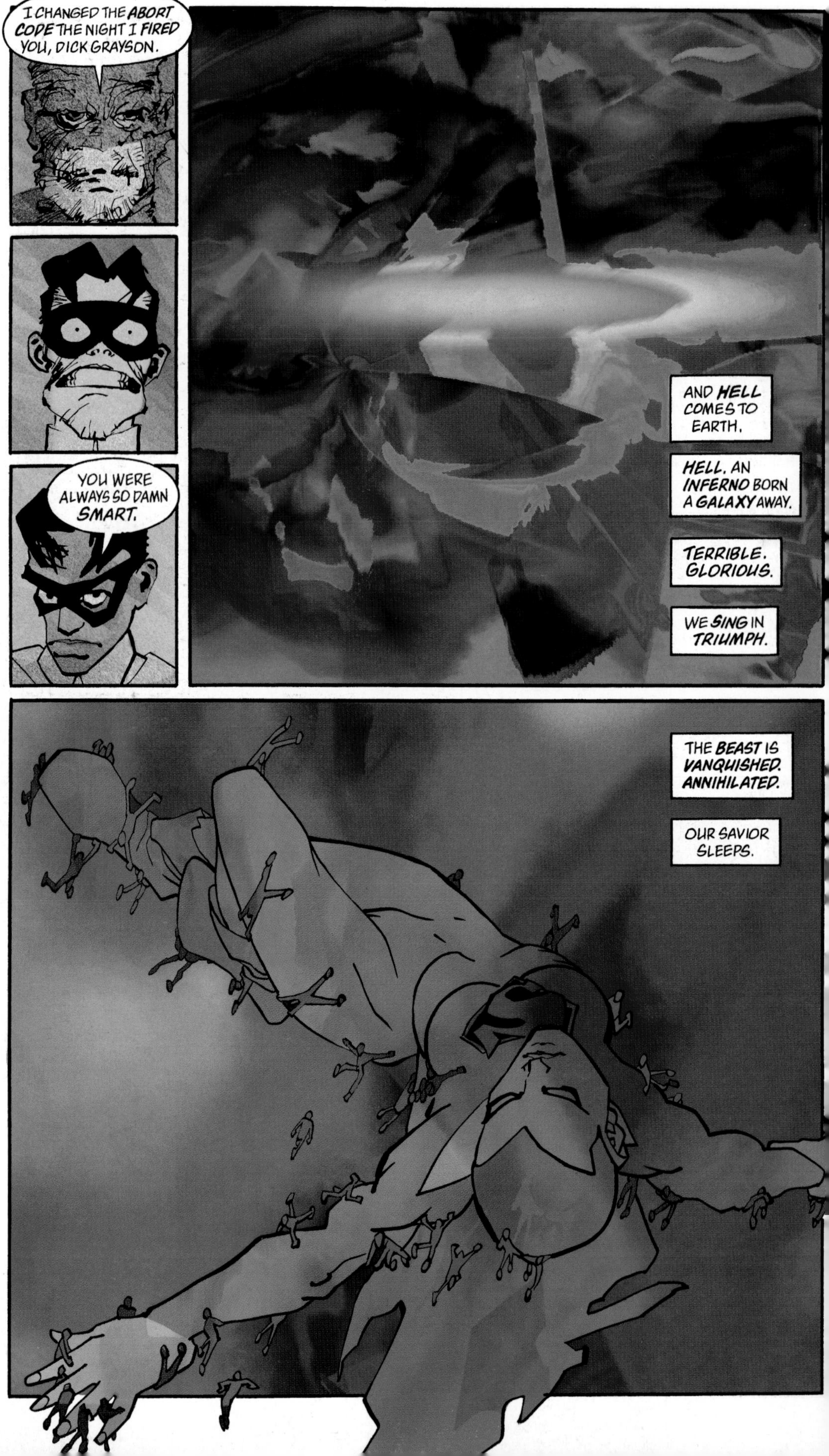

I CHANGED THE ABORT CODE THE NIGHT I FIRED YOU, DICK GRAYSON.
YOU WERE ALWAYS SO DAMN SMART.
AND HELL COMES TO EARTH.
HELL. AN INFERNO BORN A GALAXY AWAY.
TERRIBLE. GLORIOUS.
WE SING IN TRIUMPH.
THE BEAST IS VANQUISHED. ANNIHILATED.
OUR SAVIOR SLEEPS.

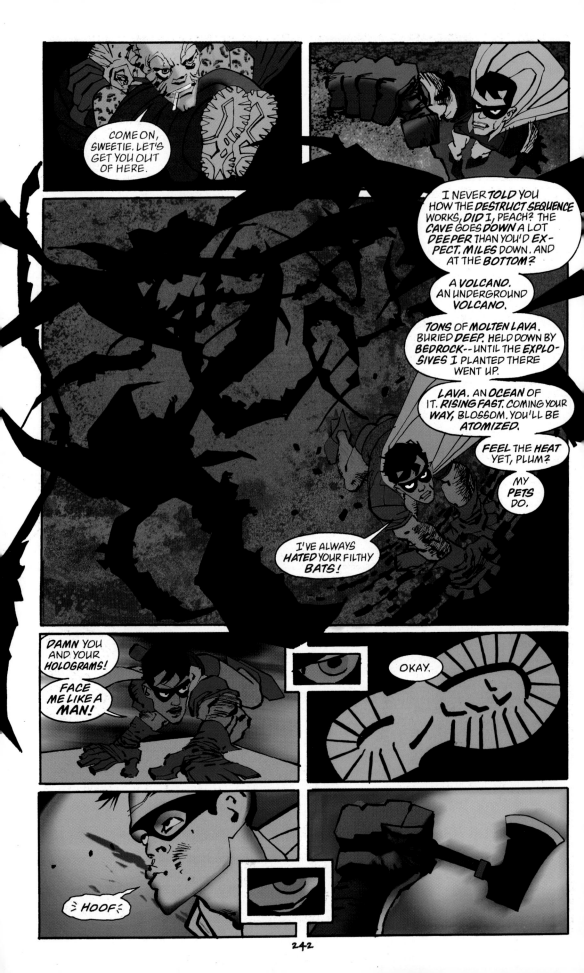

I'M NO **THANA-GARIAN**, BUT IT'S A GOOD, CLEAN **CUT**.

IT DOES THE **JOB**.

DAMN YOU!

DAMN YOU! I **LOVED** YOU!

SO **WHAT?** YOU WERE **USELESS**. YOU DIDN'T HAVE THE **CHOPS**. YOU COULDN'T **CUT THE MUSTARD**.

AW, **HELL**.

HE **CAUGHT** THE **HEAD**.

I **LOVED** YOU! I WOULD'VE DONE **ANYTHING** FOR YOU!

YOU'RE BREAKING MY **HEART**.

LET'S DIE.

THIS...

...WOULD BE A **GRAND DEATH**...

...COULDN'T ASK FOR **BETTER**.

WHERE AM I?

YOU'RE IN THE **BAT-MOBILE**, KITTEN. YOU'RE GOING TO **MAKE IT**.

THE **BOSS**. WHERE IS HE?

HE'S STILL IN THE **CAVE**. HE DIDN'T LEAVE HIMSELF A WAY OUT. I'M SORRY.

NO. YOU'RE **WRONG**. HE'S **GOT** TO FIND A **WAY**. HE **ALWAYS** FINDS A **WAY**.

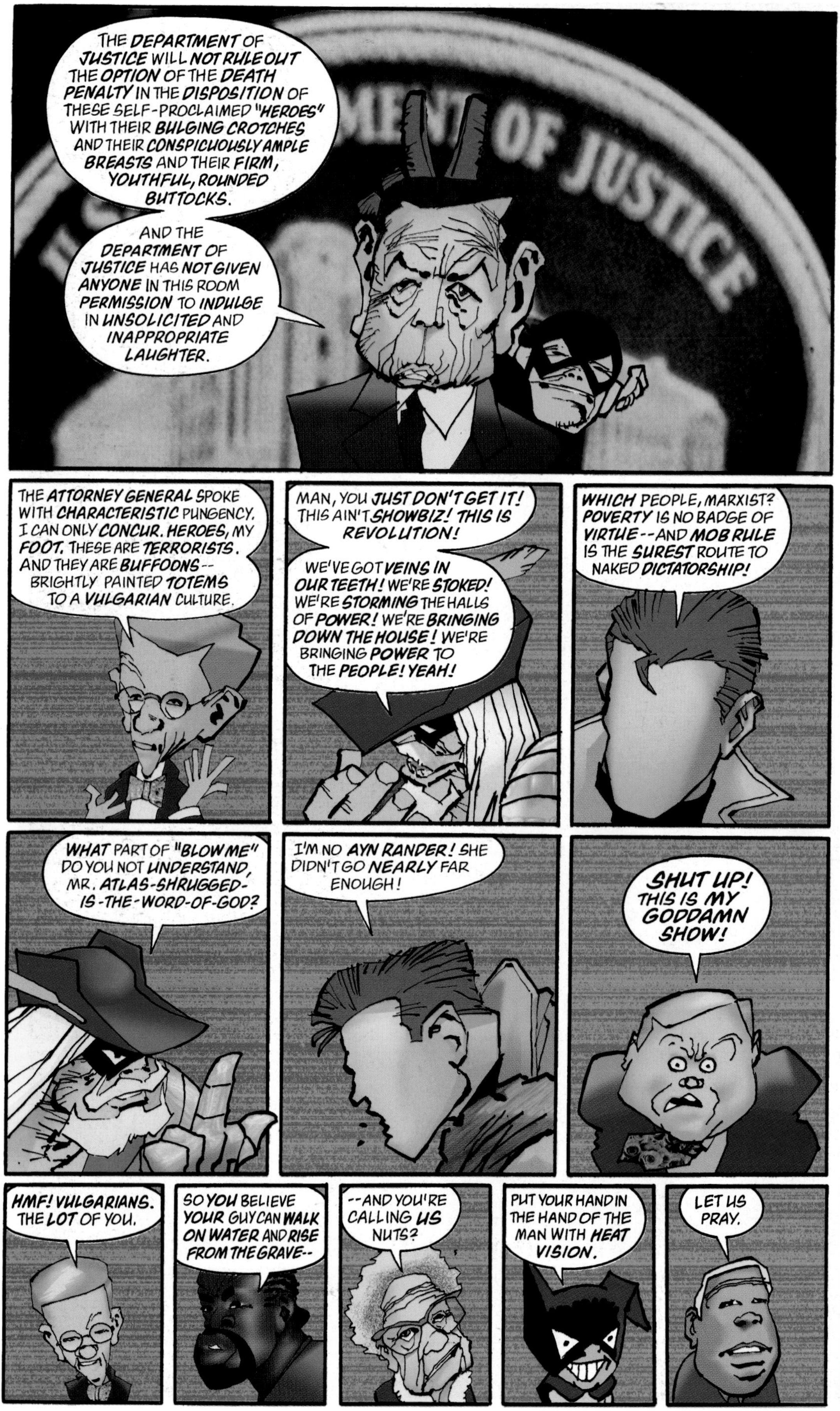
THE DEPARTMENT OF JUSTICE WILL NOT RULE OUT THE OPTION OF THE DEATH PENALTY IN THE DISPOSITION OF THESE SELF-PROCLAIMED "HEROES" WITH THEIR BULGING CROTCHES AND THEIR CONSPICUOUSLY AMPLE BREASTS AND THEIR FIRM, YOUTHFUL, ROUNDED BUTTOCKS.
AND THE DEPARTMENT OF JUSTICE HAS NOT GIVEN ANYONE IN THIS ROOM PERMISSION TO INDULGE IN UNSOLICITED AND INAPPROPRIATE LAUGHTER.
THE ATTORNEY GENERAL SPOKE WITH CHARACTERISTIC PUNGENCY. I CAN ONLY CONCUR. HEROES, MY FOOT. THESE ARE TERRORISTS. AND THEY ARE BUFFOONS-- BRIGHTLY PAINTED TOTEMS TO A VULGARIAN CULTURE.
MAN, YOU JUST DON'T GET IT! THIS AIN'T SHOWBIZ! THIS IS REVOLUTION!
WE'VE GOT VEINS IN OUR TEETH! WE'RE STOKED! WE'RE STORMING THE HALLS OF POWER! WE'RE BRINGING DOWN THE HOUSE! WE'RE BRINGING POWER TO THE PEOPLE! YEAH!
WHICH PEOPLE, MARXIST? POVERTY IS NO BADGE OF VIRTUE--AND MOB RULE IS THE SUREST ROUTE TO NAKED DICTATORSHIP!
WHAT PART OF "BLOW ME" DO YOU NOT UNDERSTAND, MR. ATLAS-SHRUGGED-IS-THE-WORD-OF-GOD?
I'M NO AYN RANDER! SHE DIDN'T GO NEARLY FAR ENOUGH!
SHUT UP! THIS IS MY GODDAMN SHOW!
HMF! VULGARIANS. THE LOT OF YOU.
SO YOU BELIEVE YOUR GUY CAN WALK ON WATER AND RISE FROM THE GRAVE--
--AND YOU'RE CALLING US NUTS?
PUT YOUR HAND IN THE HAND OF THE MAN WITH HEAT VISION.
LET US PRAY.

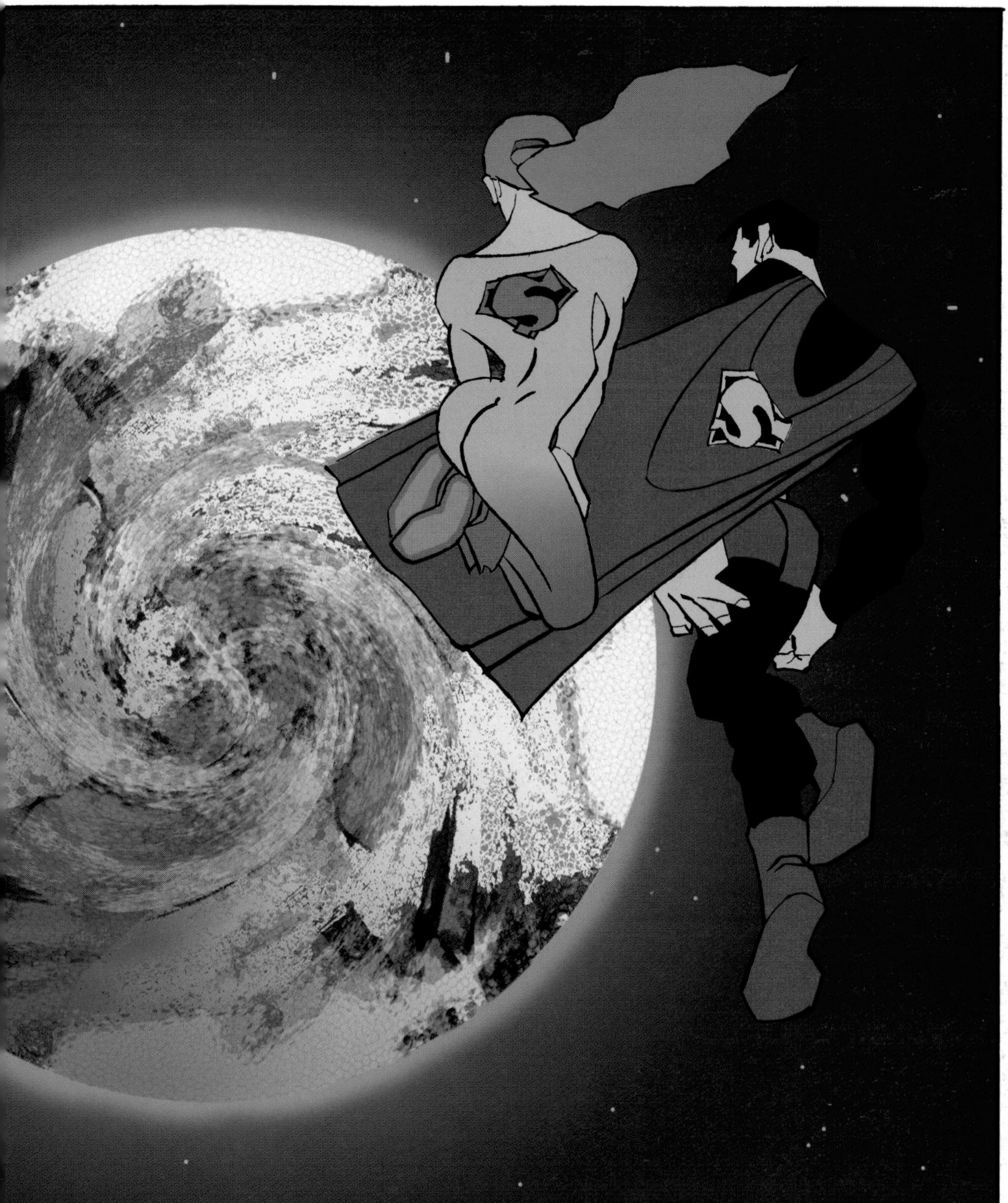

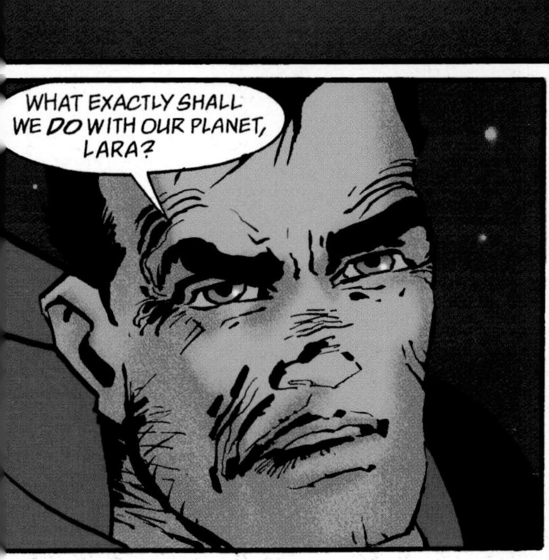
WHAT EXACTLY SHALL WE DO WITH OUR PLANET, LARA?

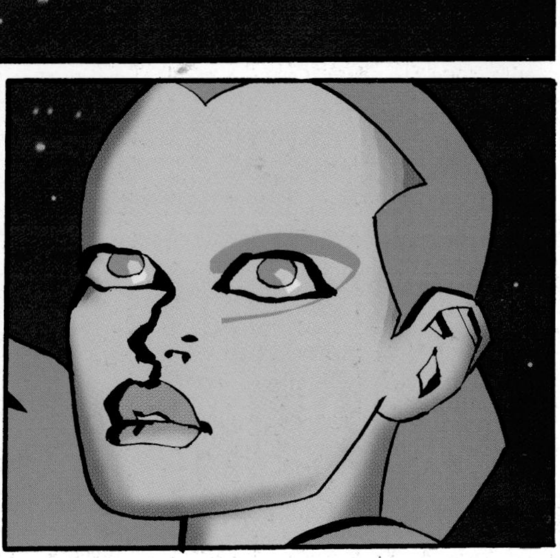

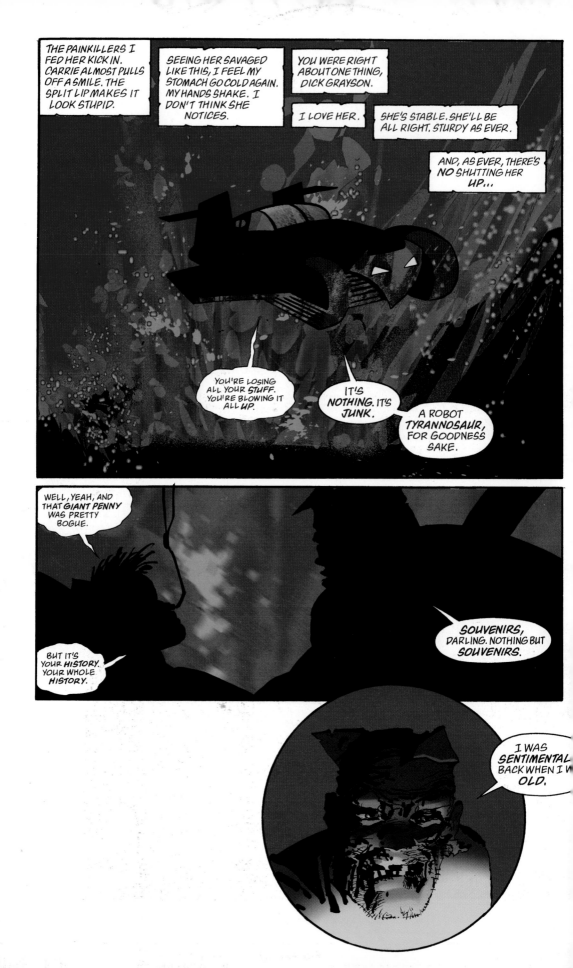

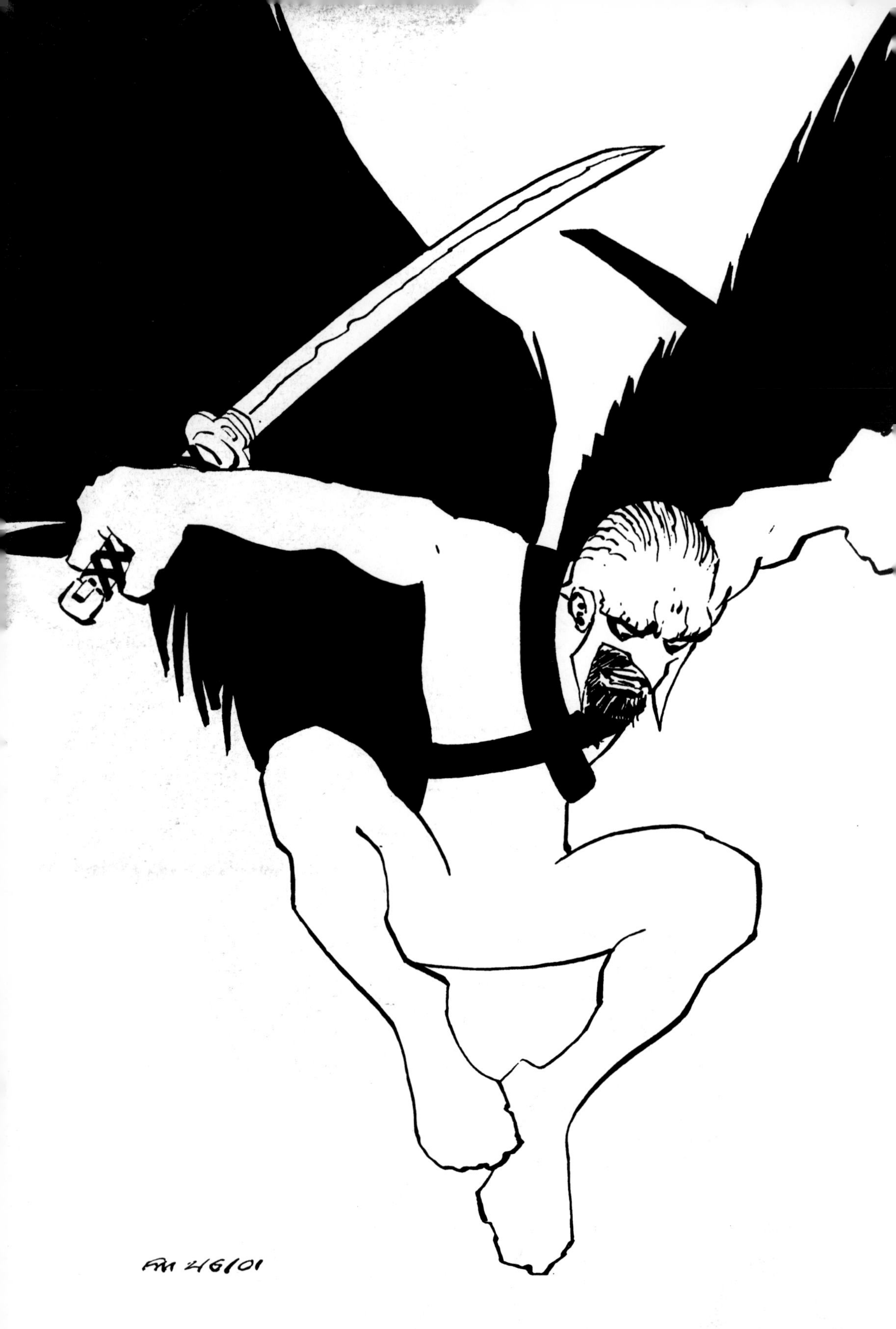

SKETCHBOOK.

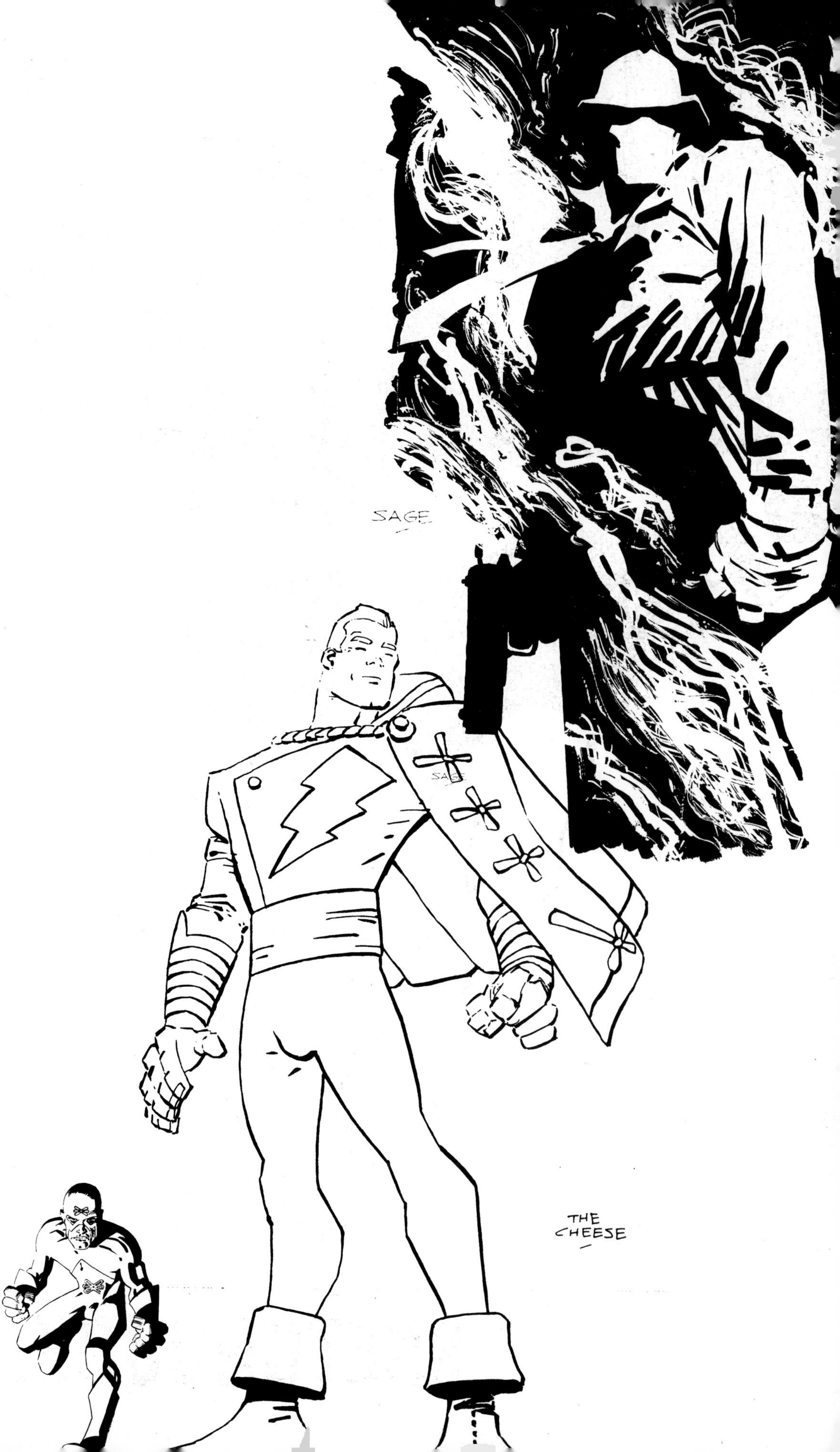
SAGE
SAGE
THE CHEESE

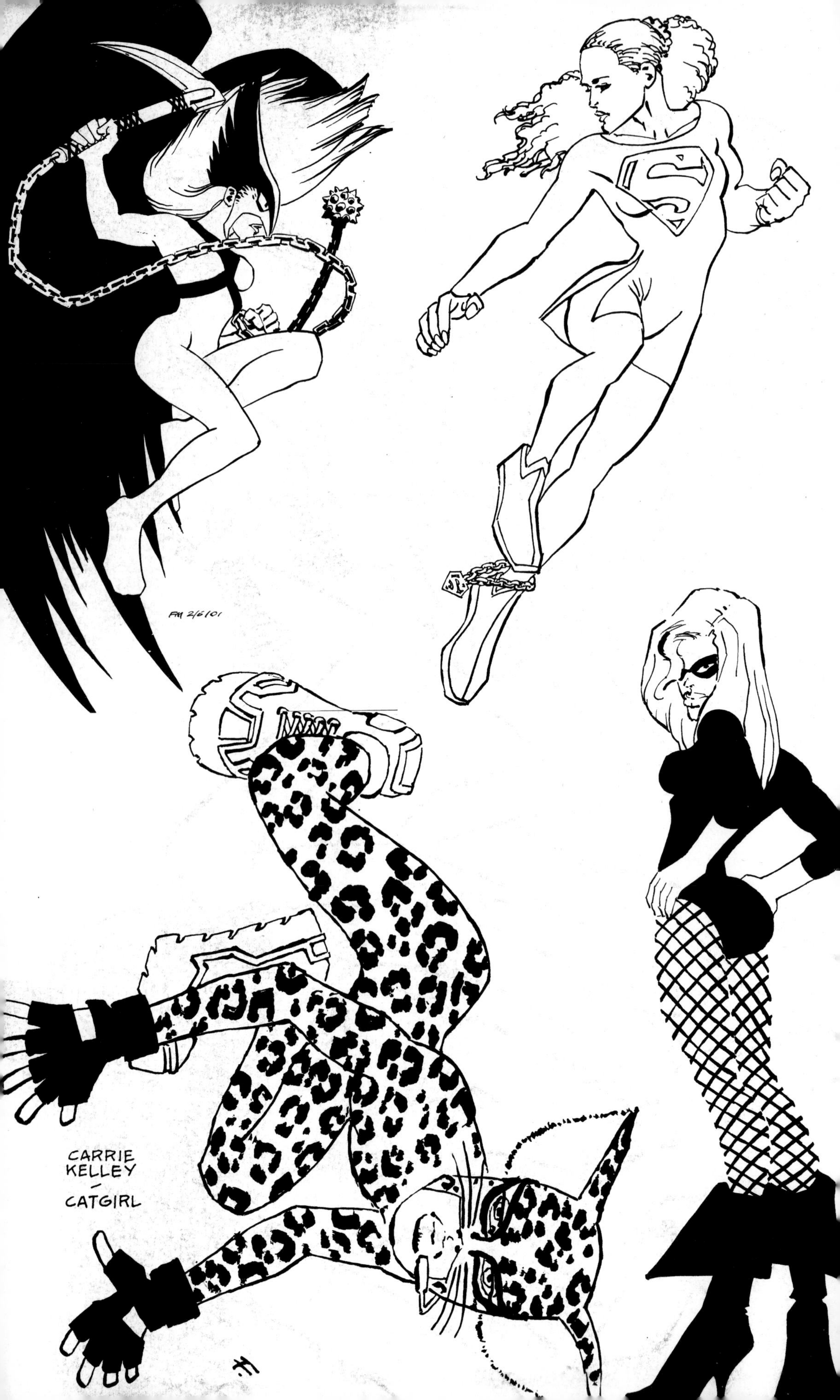
FM 2/6/01
CARRIE
KELLEY
-
CATGIRL
F.

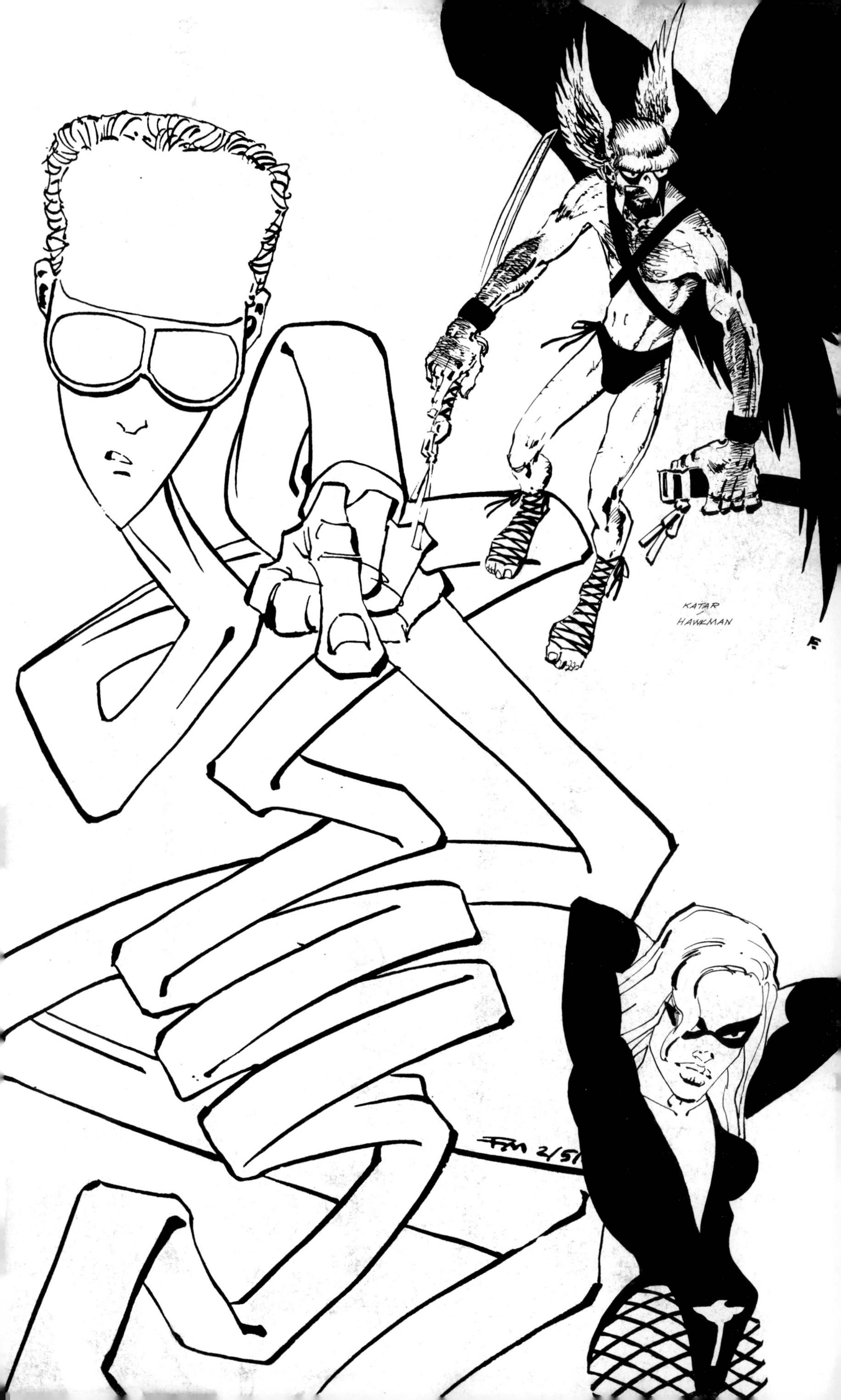
KATAR
/
HAWKMAN

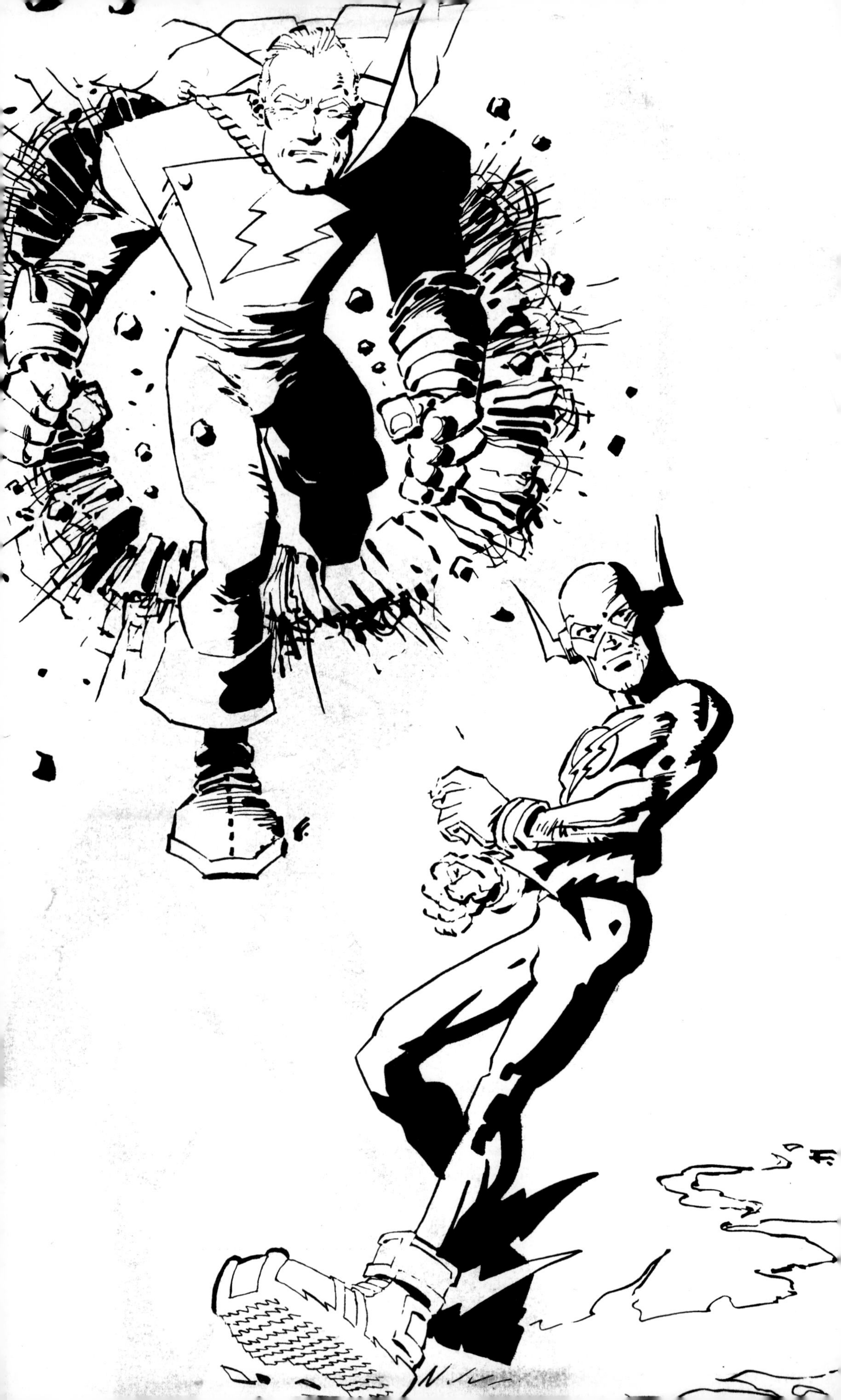

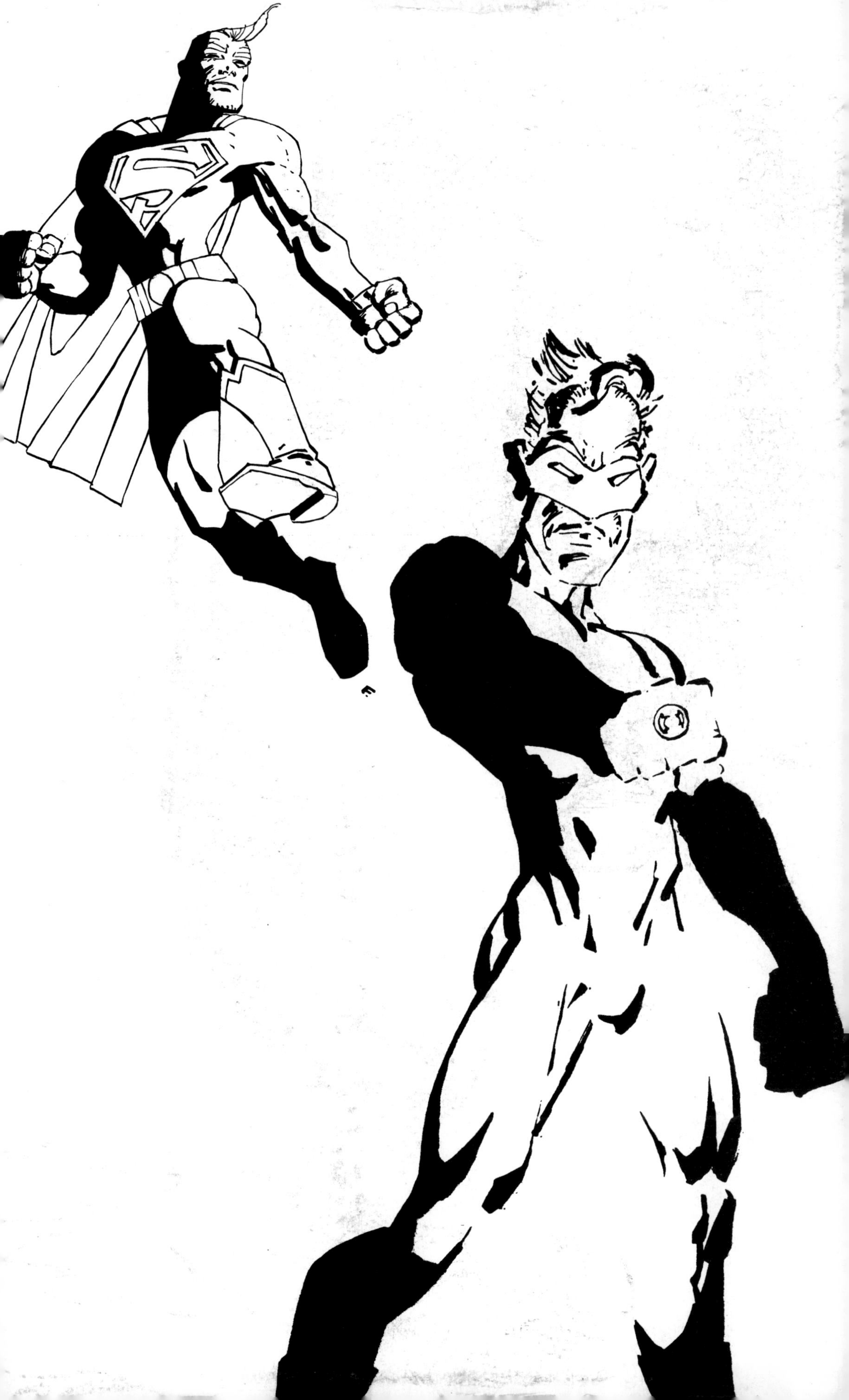